Studies in Diversity Linguistics

Chief Editor: Martin Haspelmath

In this series:

ISSN: 2363-5568

The languages of Malta

Edited by

Patrizia Paggio

Albert Gatt

language
science
press

Patrizia Paggio & Albert Gatt (eds.). 2018. *The languages of Malta* (Studies in Diversity Linguistics 17). Berlin: Language Science Press.

This title can be downloaded at:
http://langsci-press.org/catalog/book/182
© 2018, the authors
Published under the Creative Commons Attribution 4.0 Licence (CC BY 4.0):
http://creativecommons.org/licenses/by/4.0/
ISBN: 978-3-96110-070-5 (Digital)
        978-3-96110-071-2 (Hardcover)

ISSN: 2363-5568
DOI:10.5281/zenodo.1181783
Source code available from www.github.com/langsci/182
Collaborative reading: paperhive.org/documents/remote?type=langsci&id=182

Cover and concept of design: Ulrike Harbort
Typesetting: Albert Gatt, Felix Kopecky, Sebastian Nordhoff, Patrizia Paggio
Proofreading: Aaron Huey Sonnenschein, Alexandr Rosen, Annie Zaenen, Brett Reynolds, Daniil Bondarenko, Gracious Temsen, Jeroen van der Weijer, Kate Bellamy, Lea Schäfer, Melanie Röthlisberger, Mykel Brinkerhoff, Paulson Skerrit, Steven Kaye, Vadim Kimmelman
Fonts: Linux Libertine, Arimo, DejaVu Sans Mono
Typesetting software: XƎLATEX

Language Science Press
Unter den Linden 6
10099 Berlin, Germany
langsci-press.org

Storage and cataloguing done by FU Berlin

Freie Universität Berlin

Contents

Contents

Acknowledgments

The help and support of Martin Haspelmath and Sebastian Nordhoff in the preparation of this volume is gratefully acknowledged.

We would also like to thank the authors of the chapters in this volume for their cooperation during the editing process and especially for their input to the reviewing of chapters by their peers.

We especially thank the following additional external reviewers, who contributed their time and expertise to provide independent peer review for the papers in this collection: Lisa Bonnici, Jason Brown, Elisabet Engdahl, Marieke Hoetjes, Beth Hume, Anne O'Keefe, Adam Schembri, Thomas Stolz, Andy Wedel and Shuly Wintner.

Chapter 1

Introduction

Patrizia Paggio

Institute of Linguistics and Language Technology, University of Malta; CST, University of Copenhagen

Albert Gatt

Institute of Linguistics and Language Technology, University of Malta

The purpose of this publication is to present a snapshot of the state of the art of research on the languages of the Maltese islands, which include standard Maltese, Maltese English and Maltese Sign Language.

Malta is a tiny but densely populated country, with over 422,000 inhabitants spread over only 316 square kilometers. It is a bilingual country, with Maltese and English as official languages. Maltese is a descendant of Arabic, but due to the history of the island, it has borrowed extensively from Sicilian, Italian and English. Furthermore, local dialects still coexist alongside the official standard variety. The status of English as a second language dates back to British colonial rule, and just as in other former British colonies, a characteristic Maltese variety of English has developed. To these languages must be added Maltese Sign Language (*Lingwa tas-Sinjali Maltija*; LSM), which is the language of the Maltese Deaf community. LSM was recently recognised as Malta's third official language by an Act of Parliament in 2016.

While a volume such as the present one can hardly do justice to all aspects of a diverse and complex linguistic situation, even in a small community like that of Malta, our aim in editing this book was to shed light on the main strands of research being undertaken in the Maltese linguistic context.

Patrizia Paggio & Albert Gatt. Introduction. In Patrizia Paggio & Albert Gatt (eds.), *The languages of Malta*, 1–6. Berlin: Language Science Press.
DOI:10.5281/zenodo.1181785

Patrizia Paggio & Albert Gatt

1 Overview of the volume

Of the three languages (or, in the case of Maltese English, varieties) represented in this collection, Maltese is perhaps the best-studied, with a rich tradition of descriptive and theoretical work and, more recently, experimental and computational studies. Maltese is the focus of six of the contributions in this book.

Puech's paper on "Loss of emphatic and guttural consonants" traces the development of emphatic obstruents and gutturals that Maltese inherited from Arabic, but which underwent substantial change in the transition from Medieval to Contemporary Maltese. Puech's argument centres on evidence from documentary and other sources in the history of Maltese which, while written, nevertheless contain valuable insights and observations into ongoing changes in the Maltese sound system, enabling the contemporary linguist to map such changes over the long term.

By contrast, Galea and Ussishkin's paper on "Onset clusters, syllable structure and syllabification in Maltese" contributes to an already sizeable body of work on the description of Maltese phonotactic constraints and syllable structure, here couched within an Onset-Rhyme model and stressing the role of sonority in determining possible onset clusters in Maltese syllables, yielding an exhaustive and fine-grained description of possible clusters that will provide solid grounds for future work on Maltese syllabification strategies and phonotactics.

The contribution by Paggio, Galea and Vella, entitled "Prosodic and gestural marking of complement fronting in Maltese", is also concerned with phonological processes, but focusses on their interaction with gesture in spoken Maltese, a topic which has received comparatively little attention. The authors rely on a sample of annotated, spontaneous conversations in Maltese, identifying a subset of utterances that evince complement fronting, which is further broken down into subtypes (topicalisation, focus movement and left dislocation). These instances are further analysed according to gestural and prosodic characteristics, showing that fronted complements have a strong tendency to be accompanied by gestures and a falling pitch accent. At the same time, the phonological complexity and the tendency to co-occur with gestures is also dependent on the type of complement fronting in question. To date, this study is one of only a handful of studies on gesture and its interaction with other levels of linguistic analysis in Maltese.

Of the remaining three contributions on Maltese, two papers, one by Lucas and Spagnol and another by Gatt and Fabri, focus on morphology. Like the work of Paggio et al, both have a strong empirical orientation.

Lucas and Spagnol's paper "Conditions on /t/-insertion in Maltese numeral phrases: A reassessment" investigates the factors which determine the insertion of a /t/ in cardinal numerals preceding a plural noun. The main puzzle here is the apparent optionality of /t/-insertion. This motivates the question whether the distribution of /t/-insertion is due to phonological and/or morphological constraints. Lucas and Spagnol present an exhaustive analysis of data collected from a production experiment in which numeral phrases were elicited orally, using nouns with complex word-initial clusters consisting of two consonants. Their conclusion is that the primary influence on /t/-insertion is a morphological pattern, though this also interacts with phonological properties. According to these new findings, certain morphological patterns determining the arrangement of root consonants and vowels in plural nouns are strongly resistant to /t/-insertion. At the same time, the findings do not support a strict separation along the lines drawn in previous descriptive work, for example, between whole and broken plurals (the former do allow /t/-insertion, albeit less frequently). Finally, the authors also shed light on potential sociolinguistic variables, especially gender, that could influence the inter-speaker variation in /t/-insertion.

The paper "Borrowed affixes and morphological productivity: A case study of two Maltese nominalisations" by Gatt and Fabri deals with derivational processes in Maltese. In particular, it focusses on two non-Semitic derivational suffixes, *-Vr* and *-(z)zjoni*, and asks the question how productive they are. The paper gives an outline of morphological derivation in Maltese, and explains both Semitic and Romance derivational processes before describing the two nominalisations of interest. It then presents a careful and detailed corpus analysis based on data from the *Korpus Malti*, an online corpus of Maltese. Several different measures of productivity are estimated, with tests of the degree to which the two affixes can be considered indirectly borrowed, that is first borrowed from another language and then gradually becoming likely to form novel derivations in combination with native stems. The various statistical measures nicely converge towards a view of *-Vr* as the more productive of the two deverbal suffixes, and the more likely to be used with both Semitic and Romance stems, in spite of *-(z)zjoni* being the most frequently used.

The final paper on Maltese is Camilleri's contribution "On raising and copy raising in Maltese". Here, Camilleri seeks to give, first, a descriptive account and a typology of types of raising phenomena in Maltese; and second, a formalisation couched within the framework of Lexical-Functional Grammar (LFG). Consistent with this lexicalist orientation, Camilleri first seeks to identify the properties of raising predicates and gives a precise characterisation of their lexical entries, before proposing a twofold account of raising, whereby some raising phenomena are accounted for in terms of structure-sharing, determined via constraints stipulated at the level of *f(unctional)*-structure, while others are better explained in terms of anaphoric binding. Camilleri's work, while an important contribution to LFG in its own right, is also strongly empirical in flavour, with conclusions based on naturally-occurring examples obtained from corpora, among other sources.

The study of Maltese English, especially with the purpose of establishing the defining characteristics of this variety of English, is a relatively new area of research. Three of the contributions included in this volume deal with Maltese English, which is explored from the different perspectives of rhythm, the syntax of nominal phrases and lexical choice.

The paper by Grech and Vella, "Rhythm in Maltese English", studies variability in vowel duration in six Maltese English speakers. An average durational variability measure is calculated for each speaker in terms of a normalised Pairwise Variability Index (nPVI), which is based on the differences in duration between all successive vowel pairs. The six speakers were rated in a previous study for the degree to which they could be identified as speakers of Maltese English. In the present paper, the authors find a negative correlation between the speakers' nPVI and their degree of identifiability as Maltese English speakers. In other words, the less variability in vowel duration they display, the more they are perceived as speaking Maltese English. This correlation indicates that rhythm, measured in terms of vowel duration, is a significant feature in listeners' perception of a specific Maltese variety of English.

The paper by Schembri "On the characterisation of Maltese English" applies error analysis to identify fossilised transfer errors that have acquired status as stable features of Maltese English. A theoretical distinction is made between developmental errors on the one hand, which are due to simplification of target language structures, and transfer errors on the other. The latter are caused by native language interference. When transfer errors still appear at advanced learner level, and occur systematically in a community of speakers in a bilingual context, they can be said to mark a regional variant of the language. The empirical data studied in the paper consist of a corpus of 7,500 noun phrases extracted from English examination scripts by Maltese university students. Schembri discusses errors in the use of prepositions, nominal affixation and compounding, and concludes that the feature most likely to become a stable marker of Maltese English is the overuse of the preposition *of*.

The third paper on Maltese English, "Language change in Maltese English: The influence of age and parental languages" by Krug and Sönning, deals with lexical choice in Maltese English between British and American variants. The paper presents data from a questionnaire in which 424 Maltese informants were asked about their preferences concerning lexical variants. The results are described, and specific words are discussed in detail. A mixed-effects model of the data is then run with age and the parents' native language as factors, and it is found that age has the strongest effect on the informants' preferences. Interestingly, the pattern created by age shows an increasingly stronger trend towards less British usage in the youngest generations. The authors take this as evidence of an ongoing change, probably due to globalisation. The model also shows that the mother's language has a stronger influence on informants' choices than the father's, probably due to the different roles of the two parents in Maltese families.

The last contribution to this volume, "Maltese Sign Language: Parallel interwoven journeys of the Deaf community and the researchers" by Marie Azzopardi-Alexander, discusses the way in which LSM has evolved in parallel with the development of LSM research. The author explains how sign languages emerge naturally when communities of profound deaf people are formed. The origins of LSM can probably be traced back to the 70's, when young Maltese signers started to develop the first signs distinct from British Sign Language, and which reflected specific traits of Maltese society. Initial iconic gestures used for every day purposes changed gradually into conventionalised signs, and the vocabulary of LSM grew rapidly to include the abstract signs necessary to cover the vocabulary of school subjects for which a sign interpreting service had become available. The author argues that LSM research has played a crucial role in empowering deaf signers and directly contributed to the LSM vocabulary growth by involving Deaf users in the Maltese Sign Language Research Project at the University of Malta Institute of Linguistics. The material made available through the project also stimulated important studies on several aspects of LSM, which are briefly summarised in the paper.

2 Summary

In summary, we believe the present volume has the potential to present a unique snapshot of a complex linguistic situation in a geographically restricted area. Given the nature and range of topics proposed, the volume will likely be of interest to researchers in both theoretical and comparative linguistics, as well as those working with experimental and corpus-based methodologies. Our hope is that the studies presented here will also serve to pave the way for further research on the languages of Malta, encouraging researchers to also take new directions, including the exploration of variation and sociolinguistic factors which, while often raised as explanatory constructs in the papers presented here, remain under-researched.

Chapter 2

Loss of emphatic and guttural consonants: From medieval to contemporary Maltese

Gilbert Puech

Medieval Maltese inherited a set of three contrastive 'emphatic' obstruents from Arabic: ṭ, ḍ, ṣ, completed by sonorant ṛ. It also inherited a set of 'gutturals': plosive q, fricatives χ and ħ, sonorants ɣ and ʕ, and laryngeal h. In late medieval Maltese, the contrast between emphatic and plain consonants was lost, while stem vowels took over relevant lexical contrasts. In the eighteenth century, Maltese grammarians took note of ongoing changes in gutturals: weakness of h, loss of χ merged with ħ, and of ɣ merged with ʕ. In the nineteenth century, the set of distinctive gutturals was reduced to three consonants in most dialects: voiceless stop q, or its modern reflex ʔ, voiceless fricative ħ, and sonorant ʕ. The latter triggered complex processes of vowel diphthongization and pharyngealization. In modern Maltese, ʕ and vowel pharyngealization were lost. In contemporary Maltese, the allophonic realization [h], without pharyngeal constriction, gains ground over [ħ]. In Element Theory (ET), consonants share melodic elements {I}, {U} and {A} with vowels. Element{A}, which characterized the whole set of medieval emphatic and guttural consonants, is only involved in contemporary Maltese for /ʔ/ and /h/, corresponding to orthographic q and ħ respectively. I also propose a version of ET in which the element {C} characterizes surfacing consonants; the position is left empty if the consonant is lost. Empty positions are part of the phonological word structure and contribute to determining syllabic structure and stress assignment.

1 Introduction

The earliest attestation of written Maltese is a poem which came down to us through a copy unexpectedly found among notarial documents dating back from 1585, but composed in the mid-fifteenth century. The text, in Latin script, has

Gilbert Puech. Loss of emphatic and guttural consonants: From medieval to contemporary Maltese. In Patrizia Paggio & Albert Gatt (eds.), *The languages of Malta*, 7–53. Berlin: Language Science Press. DOI:10.5281/zenodo.1181787

been established by the poem's discoverers in a seminal publication: *Peter Caxaro's Cantilena, a Poem in Medieval Maltese* (Wettinger & Fsadni 1968). Philological variants have been proposed by these authors in 1983. Cohen & Vanhove (1991) undertook a linguistic analysis of the Cantilena and suggested alternative philological variants.

Furthermore, in his book on *The Jews of Malta in the Late Middle Ages*, Wettinger (1985) published notarial dócuments written in Hebrew script. According to the author, these texts deserve to be called "Judaeo-Maltese". They attest the use of three Hebrew letters for emphatic consonants not only in Arabic words but also in words of Romance origin:

Table 1: Hebrew letters for emphatic consonants

Hebrew	Arabic	Transcription	Examples	Modern Maltese	Gloss
ט	ط	ṭ	qunṭinṭ	*kuntent*	satisfied
			nṭr	*nutar*	notary
			juḡṭi	*jagħti*	he gives
צ	ص	ṣ	nṣf	*nofs*	half
			ṣḥḥ	*saħħa*	strength
צ̇	ض	ḍ	ajḍa	= *ukoll*	also
			ḫḍrh	*ħadra*	green

Even before such *prima facie* evidence was published, Cowan (1966), among others, had postulated the emphatic consonants mentioned in Table 1, and *ṛ*, for medieval Maltese by internal reconstruction. After the sixteenth century no Maltese spelling system used special symbols to represent emphatic consonants.[1]

Maltese also inherited from Arabic a set of consonants produced with primary constriction in the posterior region of the vocal tract. For Hayward & Hayward (1989: 179):

> One class of sounds which has been given recognition in traditional descriptions of Semitic languages is that of 'gutturals' or 'laryngeals'. This class includes the laryngeals proper (IPA [h], [ʔ]), the pharyngeals (IPA [ħ], [ʕ]) and, though somewhat less frequently, the uvulars (IPA [q], [χ], [ʁ]), though

---

[1]Notice, however, that Saada (1986) transcribes consonants coarticulated with back vowels as emphatic in her study of Maltese in Tunisia. This choice of transcription may have been influenced by Tunisian Arabic; cf. Ghazeli (1977).

the exact composition of the class will vary from language to language. It is typically associated with low vowels and/or phonological processes involving vowel lowering. We wish to argue that 'guttural' needs recognition as a natural class in generative phonology as well.

According to McCarthy (1994: 191) "Standard Arabic and most modern Arabic dialects have retained the full set of gutturals usually reconstructed for Proto-Semitic: laryngeals ʔ and h; pharyngeals ħ and ʕ; and uvulars χ and ʁ".

This applies to pre-modern Maltese. However, it should be carefully noted that the modern Maltese glottal stop is the reflex of the voiceless uvular stop q, not the reflex of Arabic 'hamza'.

By the end of the Middle Ages, emphatic consonants had been subtracted from the sound pattern with compensatory phonologization of back stem vowels; cf. Comrie (1991: 237). In (pre)modern times, Agius de Soldanis (1750) and Vassalli (1796) took note of ongoing changes in gutturals: persistent weakness of h, loss of χ merged with ħ, and of ɣ merged with ʕ. In the nineteenth century, complex processes of diphthongization and pharyngealization triggered by the pharyngeal sonorant on adjacent vowels are attested. During the twentieth century, ʕ was lost in almost all dialects, and vowel pharyngealization ceased being discriminant, except residually. As already observed, the uvular stop q has been progressively replaced by laryngeal ʔ in mainstream Maltese, a change which also took place in many modern Arabic dialects.

After this introduction, I review different approaches to the phonological representation of emphatic and guttural consonants in medieval Maltese. Then I analyze data in pre-modern Maltese, modern Maltese, and contemporary Maltese (sections 3 to 5). §6 is devoted to what kinds of abstractness should be allowed in phonology. Sections 7 and 8 are devoted to the representation of sounds involving orthographic h or għ. §9 introduces the table of contemporary consonants in Element Theory, to be compared to that given in section 2 for medieval Maltese. I conclude on the metamorphosis of 'gutturals' during the last millenium. Diachronic steps are recapitulated in the appendix.

2 Phonological features for "back" consonants

2.1 SPE features, Feature Geometry, and Elements

In his synchronic analysis of modern Maltese, Brame (1972) divides consonants into major classes with two SPE binary features: [±consonant] and [±sonorant].

Consonants and vowels share features [±low] and [±back]. There is an interaction between guttural consonants, which are [+low] and [+back], and vowels through a rule of 'Guttural Assimilation': "the vowel *i* assimilates to *ħ* and *ʔ* in lowness and backness":

(1) Guttural Assimilation: i → a / ___ $\begin{bmatrix} +\text{CONS} \\ +\text{LOW} \\ +\text{BACK} \end{bmatrix}$ (Brame 1972: 33)

cf. Hume (1994: 171) for an alternative formulation of this rule.

Hayward & Hayward (1989: 185) argued against the use of [+low, +back] features in the representation of gutturals:

> The class of guttural sounds cannot be equated with the class of [+low] segments, however. As has often been pointed out, the specification [+low] is simply not appropriate for the laryngeals [h] and [ʔ] because the definition of the feature refers to the position of the body of the tongue, and this organ is not involved in any primary way in laryngeal articulations. Furthermore, even if the laryngeals were allowed to be [+low] 'by convention', there are cases, as we have seen, where uvulars need to be included in the class, and these have been classified as [-low]. Chomsky & Halle (cf. 1968: 305).

> Invocation of [+back] is even less useful, for this would not only leave out the laryngeals (for exactly the same reasons as those just considered) but would bring in the velars, which, unless modified in some way [...], do not, as far as we are aware, pattern with gutturals phonologically.

For the authors, who support their analysis by adducing data from several Semitic and Cushitic languages, "crucial to the definition of 'guttural' is a satisfactory distinctive characterization of the laryngeals" (p. 186):

> It seems to us that any attempt at providing a comprehensive solution to the problems raised by the various sorts of behaviours exhibited by [h] and [ʔ] cross-linguistically will in all likelihood be made within the framework of Feature Geometry, in which hierarchical relations between features and classes of features are given explicit recognition (cf., for example, Clements 1985; Sagey 1986). The events involved in producing [h] and [ʔ] would be assigned to a separate 'laryngeal node'. In languages where the laryngeals behaved as 'guttural consonants', it would be necessary to give overt recognition to the relationship existing between the laryngeal node features and

a particular 'zone of constriction', namely the guttural zone. This relation would, of course, obtain in virtue of the location of the larynx within this zone.

In independently conducted research, McCarthy (1991; 1994) recognized the feature [pharyngeal] and bound the representation of emphatics and gutturals in these terms (1994: 219):

> The phonetic evidence establishes important points of similarity between the gutturals and the emphatics. Broadly, the gutturals and the emphatics share constriction in the pharynx, and narrowly, the uvular gutturals share with *q* and the coronal emphatics a constriction in the oropharynx produced by raising and retracting the tongue body. We expect to find two principal types of phonological patterning corresponding to these phonetic resemblances: a class of primary and secondary [pharyngeal] sounds, including gutturals, q̠, and emphatics; and a class of sounds with [pharyngeal] constriction produced by the [dorsal] articulator, including uvular gutturals, q̠, and emphatics.

After a detailed discussion, McCarthy concludes that in Arabic "the laryngeals are classified as [pharyngeal] and so belong to the guttural class" (p. 224). Altogether, medieval Maltese data support McCarthy's analysis on the phonological patterning of emphatics and gutturals, including uvular *q* and laryngeal *h*.

In his dissertation *Towards a Comparative Typology of Emphatics* Bellem (2007) adopted Element Theory. In Harris & Lindsey (1995) the theory includes the resonance 'elements' listed in Table 2.

Table 2: Resonance elements in Harris & Lindsey (1995)

Element	Salient acoustic property	Articulatory target C	Articulatory target V
A	$F_1 \sim F_2$: convergence	pharyngeality	a
I	$F_1 \sim F_2$: wide divergence	palatality	i
U	$F_1 \sim F_2$: downwards shift	(velar-)labiality	u
(@	none (acoustic baseline)	velarity	ə)

Bellem (2007: 131) argues that pharyngeals are {A}-headed, while coronals in languages with a salient contrast 'front–back' are characterized by the presence of {I}. It follows that the element {A} is involved as primary melodic feature for gutturals, and secondary for emphatic coronals. I retain this analysis, rather than that proposed by Backley (2011), where the element {A} may also characterize plain coronals. The formal implications of headedness in elements are analyzed in Breit (2013).

2.2 Medieval Maltese consonants in Element Theory

I propose an architecture in which the elements {C} and {V} play the role of the elements {ʔ}, {H}, and {L} in previous models; cf. Harris & Lindsey (1995); Bellem (2007); Backley (2011); and Puech (2016). A segment in a string is represented as a column organized in two sets of elements. The structural elements {C} and {V} refer to the *manner of articulation*, including laryngeal voice; melodic elements refer to the *place of articulation* through profiles of resonance. The melodic elements are {I}, {U}, and {A}. Headedness (underlined element) expresses the dominance of an element's main property. In the absence of front rounded vowels, {I} and {U} may not combine; thus, they are hosted on the same line. In the presence of mid-vowels, {I} or {U} may combine with {A}: they are hosted on two separate lines.

Consonants are divided into two major categories: obstruents and sonorants. The former includes stops and affricates, spirants and fricatives; the latter includes liquids, nasals and glides. In Jakobson et al. (1952: 24), affricates are considered as "strident stops" and in Clements (1999) as "noncontoured stops". As observed by Bellem (2007: note 176), "the status of pulmonic affricates is also not entirely clear". I propose to represent them as strong stops (headed {C}). Similarly, fricatives may be 'weak', like approximants, or 'strong', like sibilants. They will be represented with headed or headless {C} merged with headless {V}. Sonorants are represented with headed {V} dominated by {C}, which corresponds to segments produced with 'spontaneous voice' in Chomsky & Halle (1968).

Obstruents and sonorants either are underspecified on a third line, or have {V} or {C} as specifier. {V} expresses voice in obstruents. If an obstruent has no voiced counterpart nor a voiced allophone, it is marked with {C} on the third line: this applies in Maltese to the voiceless gutturals *q*, *χ*, and *ħ*. For sonorants, the element {C} on the third line features the absence of oral airflow in nasals; lateral /l/ is unspecified, while the rhotic (plain or emphatic) is specified for {V}.

(2)

	Stops		Fricatives		Sonorants	
	weak /	*strong*	*weak* /	*strong*	*weak* /	*strong*
	C	C̲	C	C̲	C	C
			V	V		V̲
	(C or V)		(C or V)		(V)	C

Studies in Arabic dialectology suggest that the affricate /ʤ/ may also be realized as either /ʒ, g/ or /j/, depending on the geographical region of dialects; cf. Kaye (1972). Maltese retained the post-alveolar affricate pronunciation. Contrary to other 'coronal' consonants, however, Maltese /ʤ/ is not a 'sun letter' to which the definite article *l* assimilates; cf. Sutcliffe (1936: 18), Comrie (1980: 25). This suggests that in Medieval Maltese the phoneme was still 'felt' as a voiced (post)palatal obstruent. On the other hand, prefixed *t* in verbal forms assimilates to /ʤ/, as it does to other coronal obstruents; cf. Sutcliffe (1936: chapter V); concerning regressive rounding vowel harmony, /ʤ/ behaves as other coronal obstruents; cf. Sutcliffe (1936), Puech (1978: 387).

In Arabic dental (weak) fricatives /θ/ and /ð/ are phonemic; cf. Al-Khairy (2005: 2-3). However, I did not include the phonetic symbol *ð* in Table 1 to interpret the transcription of modern *deheb* 'gold' from Arabic *ðahab* as "veheb" by Megiser (1606: 20, word 42). Other words point to *θ* (voiceless interdental fricative). In any case, dental fricatives correspond to the plosives *t* or *d* in (pre)modern Maltese; cf. Aquilina (1961: 127), Cowan (1964: 220), Cassola (1987-88: 82, note 75), Comrie (1991: 241), Kontzi (1994: 17), Brincat (2011: 243-44).

Regarding laryngeal *h*, I follow Laufer (1991: 92) whose observations for Hebrew and Arabic "show that in the production of every [h] there is a narrowing of the glottis. The frication in [h] looks as in any other fricatives, except for the place of articulation". I interpret it as a glottal approximant realized as [h] or [ɦ], which neither triggers nor prevents voicing harmony in an obstruent cluster

For resonance, labials are characterized by {U} and coronals by {I}, as in Bellem (2007). I follow Backley (2011: 75) in considering that fricatives *s* and *z* are characterized by the headless melodic element {I}, while post-alveolar *š* is characterized by headed {I}. The glide *y* and the tense vowel *i* as well are {I}-headed, while lax *ɪ* is characterized by headless {I}.

Emphatics and guttural obstruents form a natural class defined by the presence of element {A}. From his experimental work on Hebrew and Arabic, Laufer (1988: 198) concludes "that emphatic and pharyngeal sounds share, qualitatively, the same pharyngeal constriction. However, the pharyngeal constriction is the primary one for pharyngeal and a secondary one for emphatics". Uvular obstruents *q* and *χ* are characterized by the headless element {A}, pharyngeal consonants *ħ* and *ʕ* by headed {A}; in emphatic coronals the element {I} is combined with {A} (Tables 3 and 4).

Table 3: Obstruents in (post)medieval Maltese

Segment	b f t d ṭ ḍ	ṣ s z š ʤ	k g q χ ħ h

Structure	C C̲ C C C C
	V
	   V V V
		C̲ C̲ C̲ C̲ C
		V V V V
		      V V
			C C C C C̲ C
			         V V V
			V C C C

Melody	U U I I I I A A A	I I I I̲ I̲	A A A̲

Table 4: Sonorants in (post)medieval Maltese

	m	n	l	r	ṛ	y	w	ɣ	ʕ
Structure	C V̲ C	C V̲ C	C V̲	C V̲ V	C V̲ V	C V̲	C V̲	C V̲	C V̲
Melody	U	I	I	I	I A	I̲	U̲	A	A̲

Table 5: Arabic roots, medieval and modern forms

Arabic root	Medieval Maltese	Modern Maltese	Gloss
√ f ṣ d	faṣad	*faṣad*	to bleed
√ χ b ṭ	χabaṭ	*ħabat*	to bump
√ ħ ṣ d	ħaṣad	*ħasad*	to reap
√ χ ṭ f	χaṭaf	*ħataf*	to snatch
√ q b ḍ	qabaḍ	*qabad*	to catch
√ m š ṭ	mašaṭ	*maxat*	to comb
√ n ṣ b	naṣab	*nasab*	to set a net
√ q r ṣ	qaraṣ	*qaras*	to pinch
√ q ṭ r	qaṭar	*qatar*	to fall by drops
√ r b ṭ	rabaṭ	*rabat*	to tie
√ ṭ l b	ṭalab	*talab*	to request

2.3 Loss of emphatic consonants and compensatory effects

In (pre)modern Maltese, forms whose Arabic etymon had an emphatic consonant are characterized by stem vocalism *a*. Other stems have vocalism *i* by default, or *u* for some of them. In Table 5, Arabic roots are given after Aquilina's dictionary (Aquilina 1987; 1990). Medieval forms are reconstructed; modern forms are orthographic.

As is well known, an emphatic consonant prevented 'imaala', i.e. fronting and raising of /ā/ to lax and diphthongized /rᵊ/ (Cowan 1966; Alexander Borg 1976), (Alexander Borg 1997: 271). Even more interesting is the split between two *ū*, represented as *ŭ* and *û* by Vassalli (1796: XVIII) and Vassalli (1827: 11). The author describes the former as the "contraction of *o*, and of *u*", while the latter is the "contraction of *e*, and of *u*". In past participles, the stem-infixed vowel is *ŭ* for 'back' (formerly emphatic) stems, while it is *û* for 'front' stems. The two vowels are merged in Standard Maltese but remain distinct in Gozitan Maltese pausal forms (Alexander Borg 1977):

(3) Arabic root Pf-3-M.SG Gloss   PP-M.SG: Vassalli   Gozitan.   Standard M.
 √ f ṣ d   fasad   'to bleed'   mifsŭd   mifsouḍ   mifsūḍ
 √ f s d   fised   'to spoil'   mifsûd   mifseuḍ   mifsūḍ

Modern Gozitan diphthongized realizations [oĭ] vs. [eĭ] of *ī* in pausal context are also attested by Vassalli (1827: 11) and in Bonelli (1897: vol. IV, 97):[2]

(4) a. √ ṭ l b   taboip (l. 19)   *tabīb*   'doctor'
   b. √qss   qasseis (l. 23)   *qassīs*   'priest'

2.4 Conclusion

In medieval Maltese, the whole stem domain was 'back' in presence of an etymological emphatic consonant, otherwise it was 'front' (except in forms with stem vocalism *u*). We can reconstruct two steps:

- Stem backness is anchored on a radical emphatic consonant, and extended to the whole stem: the element {A} is shared by the emphatic consonant and stem vowels.

---

[2]Bonelli's footnote: "In emphatic position, especially at the end of a sentence, the items *bylli*, *dīn* or similar, will be pronounced in the country *byllei*, *dein* etc.; *bylli ma ġejtš? byllei?* why you did not come, why?". [The term 'emphatic' refers here to phrase focus, not to consonant properties].

- Stem backness is anchored on vowels; emphatic consonants are merged with their plain counterpart: 'back' stem vowels are characterized by a headed element {A}, while {I} is assigned by default to 'front' stem vowels.

3 Gutturals in pre-modern Maltese

Canon Agius de Soldanis (1712-1770), born in Rabat (Gozo), and Mikiel Anton Vassalli (1761-1829), born in Żebbuġ (Malta), were two erudite Maltese scholars. In the eighteenth century, the prevailing opinion was that Maltese ancestors were Punic, Hebrew, Syriac, or even Etruscan; cf. Brincat (2011: chapter 7). Thus, de Soldanis called the book he published in 1750: *Della Lingua Punica, presentamente usata da Maltesi.* In the introduction to his dictionary, Vassalli (1796) suggests that Maltese is a legacy from several Semitic languages: Punic, Phoenician, Hebrew, Chaldean, Samaritan, Syriac, and Arabic. Moreover, he connects these substrata to Maltese dialectal variations. In subsequent work, however, Vassalli (1827) agreed that Maltese is, in fact, an offshoot from Arabic.

3.1 Description of gutturals by A. de Soldanis 1750

In *Alfabeto Punico-Maltese*, Agius de Soldanis (1750) lists 22 symbols. The following excerpts (p. 72-74) have been translated into English; modern orthographic forms are in italics.

(5)   k [k]   Grave, acute as Greek *k*, and more forced than *q*, e.g. *Kaws* 'bow'; *Kera* 'house rent'; *qaws, kera.*

gk [g]   shall be pronounced instead of Hebrew *Ghimel*, and Greek *Gamma* γ,[3] especially if it comes before a vowel as a consonant, e.g. *Gkrieżem* 'throats'; *grieżem.*

q [q]   Thin, acute, is pronounced in the summit of the throat, e.g. *Qolla* 'jar'; *qolla.*

hh [h]   Is pronounced with strong aspiration, e.g. *Hhait* 'wall'; *Hharbiſc* 'to scratch'. If there is a dot on one of the *h*s, then the aspiration should be more open, while always born from the throat with a light or a strong push from the chest, e.g. *Ħhamar*, donkey ~ stupid; *ħmar.*

---

[3]"Gimel" is the third letter of consonantal alphabets in some Semitic languages. Its sound value in Phoenician is the voiced plosive [g]. The Greek letter "gamma" is derived from it.

ch [χ]   Is pronounced grave, hoarse in the summit of the throat, with a bit more force than preceding [hh], e.g. *Chait* 'thread'; *ħajt.*

h [h]   Nicely aspirated, e.g. *Hem* 'there'; with a dot on top, it should be pronounced with more breathing, but gently, e.g. *Ḣem* 'trouble'; *hemm, hemm.*

gh [ʕ/ɣ]   The most difficult letter, which is grave, and is pronounced in the middle of the throat, among modern Arabs and among Punic-Maltese, e.g. *Ghain* 'eye'. If on top of the *g* a dot has been noted, the pronunciation shall be deeper, and if more than one dot, the aspiration is growing, e.g. *Ġhar* 'grotto', *Ğhar* 'shame', *¨Ğhar* 'envious of'; *għar, għar, għer.*

The author distinguishes different realizations of 'għ' (Aain) by diacritic dots (Table 6).

Table 6: Realisations of 'għ'

A. de Soldanis	Gloss	Arabic root	Vassalli (IPA)	Modern spelling
Ġhar	cave	√ ɣ w r	[ɣoːr]	għar
Ğhar	shame	√ ʕ j r	[ʕaːr]	għar
¨Ğhar	he got jealous	√ ɣ j r	[ɣaːr]	għer

Concerning *h*, Agius de Soldanis uses a diacritic dot to distinguish *Ḣem* 'noise' from *Hem* 'there', which may indicate that initial *h* was better preserved in nouns or verbs than in cliticized adverbs. In modern Maltese, intervocalic *h* is dropped: *deheb*, [dēb]) 'gold', except in dialects where *h* is realized as *ħ*: [deħeb].

There is no doubt that Agius de Soldanis was aware of dialectal differences between different varieties of Maltese pronunciations. The distribution of velar *k* and uvular *q* in his work differs from modern mainstream Maltese. The author records the words in his *Dizionario* (1750) listed in Table 7.

The alternation *q ~ k*, well spread at this time, is still attested in Great Harbour (Malta) and Rabat (Gozo). In my fieldwork in the 1980s, I recorded the forms in Table 8 in Rabat (near the hospital) and Xewkija (close to Rabat); cf. Puech (1994).

Vassalli's *Lexicon* (1796) is preceded by a *Preliminary Discourse to the Maltese Nation*, which provides us with reliable dialectal descriptions of gutturals. The following excerpts have been translated from Italian into English:[4]

---

[4]Special thanks to Michelangelo Falco, who assisted me in translating the original text. I am the only one to be held responsible for any error of translation or interpretation.

(6)	LIV	**h** [h]	To the symbol H, I have assigned an aspirated sound and called it He, such as Havn *here*, hynn *there*, hi *she*, ybleh *silly*.
	LXXIV		Among the new symbols added, a majority was necessary to describe GUTTURAL sounds.
	LXXV	**ጰ** [ħ]	To the first guttural sound, called Hha, I assigned a symbol similar to an A compressed in this way **ጰ**. This sound is found in many Oriental languages, and it is very aspirated, profound and dry, like the Arabic ح.
	LXXVI	⦶ [χ]	The second guttural sound, which resembles an O with a perpendicular line down the middle, indicates a hoarse and almost hampered pronunciation. The appropriate sound is Arabic خ: like ⦶ĭa *my brother*.
	LXXVII	∩ [ʕ]	The third guttural sound, called Aajn, is represented by this symbol ∩, which I took from Phoenician, as it is found in the inscriptions, and modified it to better fit with the other letters. It describes a very guttural and slightly husky sound, common among the Oriental languages. Since it is often unpronounced at the end of a word, I marked this instance as ∩¯ to make it distinct; and, therefore, its presence is maintained in order to preserve the root of the word.
	LXXVIII	ɜ [ɣ]	I wanted to describe the fourth guttural sound, which denotes a big, huskier and more guttural sound, with two Aajn united in this way ∩∩, but in order to avoid confusion with the Latin letter m I depicted it as ɜ.
	LXXIX	¢ [q]	There is another sound in our language common among Oriental languages, which is considered by some a guttural sound, and by others a palatal, that is formed in the roof of the mouth, like a K. Nevertheless, it differs for its sharpness of pronunciation, half palatal and half guttural, and produces a certain epiglottal sound, which is very difficult to describe. For this reason, I have included it among the guttural sounds. It is not a low-pitched sound, instead it is harsh and very high-pitched. The symbol that represents it, ¢, is Phoenician as well, but I gave it a better shape more fitting with the present font.

Table 7: Distribution of velar *k* and uvular *q* listed in Agius de Soldanis (1750)

	A. de Soldanis	page	Modern orthography	Gloss
k	kadìm	148	*qadim*	'old'
	kasma	149	*qasma*	'break'
	kaui	149	*qawwi*	'strong'
q	qbir	167	*kbir*	'big'
	Qemmùna	167	*Kemmuna*	'Comino'
	qelp	168	*kelb*	'dog'
	qlàmàr	168	*klamar*	'calamary'
	qtieb	170	*ktieb*	'book'
	qul	170	*kiel*	'he ate'

Table 8: *q ~ k* alternation, after Puech (1994)

Orthography	Gloss	Standard	Rabat	Xewkija
qalb	'heart'	[ʔalb̥]	[qalb̥]	[kalb̥]
kelb	'dog'	[kɛlb̥]	[kælb̥]	[kælb̥]

3.2 Minimal pairs

In *Grammatica della lingua Maltese*, Vassalli (1827: 14-15) gives lists of minimal pairs. Examples below have been transcribed in IPA. Some words are obsolete in modern Maltese (MM):

(7) a.

k	Gloss	MM	*q*	Gloss	MM
karkar	to drag along	*karkar*	qarqar	to rumble	*qarqar*
kiˀs	drinking glass	*kies*	qiˀs	to measure	*qies*
klūbi	ravenous	*klubi*	qlūbi	courageous	*qlubi*
krīb	groaning	*krib*	qrīb	nearness	*qrib*
ʕakar	viscous	*għakar*	ʕaqar	to ulcerate	*għaqar*
joktor	it abounds	*joktor*	joqtor	it leaks	*joqtor*
ħarrīˀk	who prosecutes	*ħarriek*	ħarrīˀq	who ignites	*ħarrieq*

19

b. ħ   χ

ħajjar	to allure	*ħajjar*	χajjar	to let choose	*ħajjar*
ħallæ	breaker, pile	*ħalla*	χallæ	to leave	*ħalla*
ħajt	wall	*ħajt*	χajt	thread	*ħajt*
ħall	to untie	*ħall*	χall	vinegar	*ħall*
ħarat	to plough	*ħarat*	χarat	to strip off leaves	*ħarat*
ħarqa	burn	*ħarqa*	χarqa	a strip of clothes	*ħarqa*
ħazen	to show respect	*ħażen*	χazen	to store	*ħażen*
ħɪlæ	to become sweet	*ħila*	χɪlæ	to waste	*ħela*
baħħar	to sail	*baħħar*	baχχar	to perfume	*baħħar*

c. ʕ   ɣ

ʕabbæ	to load	*għabba*	ɣabbæ	to deceive	*għabba*
ʕalaq	bloodsucker	*għalaq*	ɣalaq	to close	*għalaq*
ʕâli	high	*għali*	ɣâli	expensive	*għali*
ʕâr	shame	*għar*	ɣâr	cave	*għar*
ʕazel	to choose	*għażel*	ɣazel	to spin (wool)	*għażel*
ʕɪraq	to sweat	*għereq*	ɣɪraq	to sink	*għereq*

3.3 Dialectal variation in pre-modern Maltese

Vassalli knew perfectly well that many speakers do not respect what is the 'correct' pronunciation of gutturals for him. In his introduction to the *Lexicon* (1796) he comments on speech habits in different areas in the following terms:

XVII   If we want to explore the subtleties of this language (Maltese), and, so to say, carry out a fine-grained analysis, exploring its dialects, we would also find that they are like the related oriental languages, each with a special and varied inclination to one of these languages. Our language is usually divided into five dialects by the population, using these dialects we jok-ingly make ourselves incomprehensible to each other. They are named as follows in Maltese = Lsŷn tal blŷd , lsŷn tal ∃awdeıɥ, lsŷn tar-rℵajjël t' ys-fel , lsŷn tar-rℵajjël ta fŭq , lsŷn tar-rℵajjël tan-nofs = *Dialect of the city, dialect of the Gozo, dialect of the low villages, dialect of the high villages, and dialect of the middle villages.* Each dialect has its own subdialect of a cer-tain place, and they make it possible to identify which area you come from, since they have appreciable differences. Mainly they are distinguished by pronunciation, that is by the sounds: consonants, or vowels, or both.

XVIII With the *dialect of the towns*, which I call the *dialect of the harbour*, since it is spoken in the towns by the main harbour, we intend to refer to the language of the new capital and its suburb, of the town called l'Isola - since it is a peninsula inside the harbour -, of Bermula, of Borgo-Santangelo, and of the castles around. In the dialect of these places which can be considered as one big town, subdialects can be distinguished: as a matter of fact, the citizens of Isola differ considerably in their speech from the inhabitants of Bermula, and they differ from the people of Borgo-Santangelo, and they all differ from the people of Valletta ...

XIX The defect of this language can be recognized mainly through the lack of the sounds ⊕ ∃ e ¢ [respectively: χ γ q], which are pronounced by the speakers of this dialect as ℵ ∩ e K [respectively: ħ ʕ k], without any real dis-tinction: therefore, they are often confused in the discourse and one word is taken for another. A major part of the speakers naturally lacks these sounds because they did not acquire them in their childhood. Many have these sounds though, but they either abstain from using them, believing to speak in a trendier way, or they use them in the wrong way.

XX The dialect of Gozo Island is little different from those of the countryside of Malta as to the pronunciation ... very ancient Arabic expressions are used there, especially by the peasants, whose speech is Arabized a lot.

XXI Now we come to the dialects of the countryside of Malta. The one which is spoken (fyr-rℵajjël ta fŭq) in the high lands, that is in the West, is the purest dialect of Malta; the ancient capital, called *li Mdina* with its suburbs where a few barbarisms are more widespread than elsewhere is excluded. I cannot hear any defects in the guttural sounds ...

XXII Similarly, in the oriental villages of Malta called (r-rℵajjël t'ysfel) *low vil-lages*, there is a good dialect, undamaged in the guttural sounds ...

XXIII Finally, despite sharing the mistakes of the neighboring areas the best Maltese pronunciation can be found in the middle villages. In this area, the guttural sounds are preserved in their entirety, as can easily be observed by those who have some knowledge of Oriental languages. The very aspirate sound of the root H at the end of the word is pronounced as it is, like Ybleh[5] *silly*, Ykreh[6] *ugly*, Nebbyh[7] *who wakes up*, which differs from Nebbyⱱ[8] *who barks*, though throughout the domain badly pronounced ⱱ ...

I give Vassalli's examples of 'ideal pronunciation' in IPA in Table 9.

Table 9: Examples of Vassalli's 'ideal pronunciation'

Harbour	Vassalli's norm	Modern orthography	Gloss
mʊχrɪɛt	maħrɪ°t	*moħriet*	'plough'
χlʊmt	χolma ħlʊmt ħolma	*ħlomt ħolma*	'I dreamt about'
'nχossni ɣɪrkān	'nħossni ʕɪrqān	*inħossni għarqan*	'I feel sweaty'
qaʕqa	kaʕka	*kagħka*	'ring-cake'
jɪtqaʕweʃ	jɪtkaʕweʃ	*jitkagħweġ*	'he moves (spasm)'
jħoqq	jħokk	*iħokk*	'he rubs'
buqaʕwār	bukaʕwār	*bukagħwar*	'black beetle'

3.4 Allophonic variation in gutturals

According to Vassalli's observations and idealized norm, radical *h* is maintained in uncorrupted dialects in all positions. However, if *h* stands for the 3rd masculine object suffix, it may be realized as [ħ]; cf. Vassalli (1827: §24):

> The He, H, h merely denotes the aspirated and soft sound; such as *il- kerha, u il-belha harbet mal ybleh* 'the ugly and the silly [female] fled with the silly [male]'; *Bhĭma mhejjma* 'spoiled animal'. The same sound is kept at the end of words when it is radical, e.g. *ġieh* 'honor', *mweġġeh* 'honored'; *blyieh*, or *tbelleh* 'he grew foolish'; *ikreh* 'ugly', or derived: *kerreh, tkerreh*. However, if word final h is an affixed pronoun, then it will be pronounced *ħ* ...

---

[5] *ibleh* 'foolish'; cf. *belleh*

[6] *ikreh*: 'ugly'; cf. *kerah*

[7] *nebbieħ* 'that makes one aware of s.th.'; cf. *nebbah* or *nebbeh*

[8] *nebbieħ* 'barker' ('animal that barks'); cf. *nebah*

Vassalli's examples in square brackets have been transposed into IPA:

(8) a. [χallūħ]   ħalla-ɪᴍᴘʀ 2ᴘʟ+Obj 3ᴍ.sɢ   'leave him!'   *ħalluh*

     [χallīħ]   ħalla-ɪᴍᴘʀ 2sg+Obj 3ᴍ.sɢ   'leave him!'   *ħallih*

  b. [fīħ]   fi prep+Obj 3ᴍ.sɢ   'in it'   *fih*

In final position, the 3rd person feminine singular and 3rd person plural are respectively /ha/ and /hom/, with variations in vowel quality which are irrelevant for the representation of /h/. When the stem ends in a guttural consonant, /h/ assimilates the place of articulation of the stem consonant (cf. §25):

(9) a. [selaχχa]   selaχ-ᴘꜰ-3sɢ ᴘꜰ+Obj-3ꜰ.sɢ   'he skinned it'   *selaħha*

  b. [fetaħħa]   fetaħ-ᴘꜰ-3sɢ ᴘꜰ+Obj-3ꜰ.sɢ   'he opened it'   *fetaħha*

To sum up, /h/ has four allophones: [h], [ħ], [χ] and zero. The 3rd person masculine singular object suffix has three allomorphs: /h/, /hū/ or /ū/, whose distribution depends on their position in the word.

Sonorant /ɣ/ is realized as a voiceless uvular fricative [χ] when it is in word final position or followed by a voiceless consonant (cf. §28):

(10) a. [aχsel]   ɣasel-ɪᴍᴘʀ-2sg   'wash!'   *aħsel*

   b. [ferraχχem] ferraɣ-ᴘꜰ-3sɢ+Obj-3ᴘʟ   'wash them!'   *ferraghhom*

Pharyngeal /ʕ/ (cf. §17) has three allophones: [ʕ], [ħ] if followed by suffix -*h*, and zero in word-final position:

(11) a. [samʕet]   sema'-ᴘꜰ-3ꜰ.sɢ   'she heard'   *semghet*

   b. [samaħħem] sema'-ᴘꜰ-3ᴍ.sɢ+Obj-3pl   'he heard them' *semaghhom*

   c. [sama]   sema'–ᴘꜰ-3ᴍ.sɢ   'he heard'   *sema'*

3.5 Conclusion

In eighteenth century Maltese, the sound pattern has a maximal set of six guttural consonants: *q*, χ, γ, ħ, ʕ, and *h*. However, some dialects have velar *k* rather than *q*; γ or zero for ʕ, or ʕ for γ; χ for ħ, or ħ for χ; *h* or χ or zero for *h*.

Dialectal variation and allophonic changes undergone by γ and ʕ in different contexts, and the assimilation of place of articulation by *h* preceded by a guttural, contributed to the loss of identity for these sounds. Such variation induced predictable changes, which, indeed, became established in the nineteenth century.

4 Gutturals in modern Maltese

Different sources contributed to the documentation on Modern Maltese in the twentieth century. First, urban and rural dialects have been documented by Bonelli (1897-1900) and Stumme (1904). Altogether, their descriptions are convergent, even if their perception of guttural sounds is somewhat different. Saada (1986) published ethnotexts recorded in the 1960s by residents in Tunisia from Maltese families. Her transcription of guttural sounds is almost like Bonelli's. Vanhove (1991) described "the survival of [ʕ] in a Maltese idiolect at Mtaħleb in Malta". Schabert (1976) described conservative idiolects in which [ʕ] appears to be an onglide of pharyngealized vowels. Altogether, I call 'modern', as opposed to 'contemporary', varieties which still include a pharyngeal sonorant and/or pharyngealized vowels. Thus, 'modern' Maltese includes conservative Gozitan dialects which have kept [γ] but not [ʕ]; cf. Puech (1994: texts 8 to 10 from Għarb). See also Aquilina & Isserlin (1981).

4.1 Bonelli: Archivio Glottologico Italiano

Bonelli (1897) published Maltese idiomatic expressions, jingles and two traditional narratives recorded during a two-month stay in urban and rural areas of Malta and Gozo. He completed his study on "the Maltese dialect" in 1898 and 1900. His set of guttural sounds includes *q*, ʕ, ħ, *h*. The postvelar stop *q* is general and does not alternate with its mutated form ʔ. This reflects his informants' pronunciation from Valetta and Rabat (Gozo). The pharyngeal sonorant ʕ is the reflex of both ʕ and γ. The pharyngeal fricative ħ is the reflex of both ħ and χ. From Bonelli's transcriptions, it is not clear whether *h* should be granted full phonemic status.

Whether Bonelli's *h* should be granted phonemic status or not, it is present in instances where it is usual in the spelling system:

(12) in final position (3 M.SG direct object after a long or diphthongized vowel):

    a. p. 88 dufrejh   'his nails'   *difrejh*

          p. 98 ḥudowh (Gozo)   'they took him'   *ħaduh*

                saqs^{i}ēh   'he asked him'   *saqsieh*

    b. in internal stem position (alternating with stem final *ħ*):

          p. 89 kerha   'ugly-F.'   *kerha*

          cf.   koroħ   'ugly-pl.'   *koroh*

    c. in intervocalic position (direct object initial h):

                bdī^{e}t yssaqsī^{e}ha   'she began to ask her'   *bdiet issaqsieha*

    d. in personal pronouns:

          p. 89 u hū ma …   'and he did not …'   *u hu ma …*

                u hī'a qaltlu   'and she told him'   *u hija qaltlu*

    e. in adverbs:

          p. 97 beqʻeu sejrīn hekk 'they had continued that way' *baqgħu sejrin hekk*

Notice that Stumme (1904: 78) takes note of Bonelli's retention of *h* but never uses it in his own phonetic transcriptions.

Bonelli transcribes the pharyngeal sonorant by the reversed comma (ʻ) symbol. It is present in radical positions where it is expected:

(13) a. In first radical position:

          p. 88 ʻadda   'he passed'   *għadda*

                š-ʻandek?   'what do you have?'   *x'għandek?*

                naʻmlu   'we do'   *nagħmlu*

          p. 89 ʻaijat   'he shouted'   *għajjat*

    b. In second radical position:

          p. 88 qaʻat   'he stayed'   *qagħad*

          p. 89 weʻda   'a vow'   *wegħda*

    c. In third radical position:

          p. 88 ma satʻouš   'they could not'   *ma setgħux*

          p. 89 semʻou   'they heard'   *semgħu*

In Bonelli's contributions, no vowel is transcribed as pharyngealized.

4.2 Stumme: Maltesische Studien

Stumme (1904) faithfully reports the dialectal variation between (post)velar *q*, maintained in urban areas, and the glottal realization *ʔ* in countryside dialects. He claims that the sound *h* is "totally lacking" (p. 78). Moreover, none of his informants made a distinction between pharyngeal *ḥ* (IPA *ħ*] and velar *ḫ* (IPA [χ]); nor between Arabic ع (IPA [ʕ], transcribed as ꜣ) and غ (IPA [ɣ]). On the other hand, Stumme carefully analyzes vowel pharyngealization in relevant contexts (p. 79).

4.2.1 Dialectal variants of *q*

Post-velar stop *q* contrasts with (post)palatal *k* appears in texts from Valetta:

(14)   *qalb* 'heart' vs. *kelb* 'dog'

Glottal stop *ʔ* contrasts with (post)palatal *k* in texts from countryside towns:

(15)   *ʔalb* vs. *kelb*

Only one *k* in texts from Victoria (Gozo), the contrast being supported by the vowel quality:

(16)   *kalb (qalb)* vs. *kẹlb (kelb)*
    cf. kabdu   for *qabdu*   'they caught'
       fok   *fuq*   'upon'
       fkar   *fqar*   'poor-pl.'

In Maltese, the change from *q* to *ʔ* has spread from peripheral towns and villages to Valetta (*il-Belt*) and its suburbs. It has been generalized in the twentieth century. However, in my own fieldwork in the 1980s, I still heard postvelar *q* in the Great Harbour area, and *k* instead of *q* or *ʔ* in Xewkija, a village close to Victoria (Gozo).

It should also be noticed that in Standard Maltese some speakers use *k* for *q* (realized as a glottal stop) for some words; cf. Albert Borg (2011: 27).

4.2.2 Reflexes of *h*

"The sound *h* is totally lacking in my texts" Stumme (1904: 78). Its reflexes are:

(17) a. no direct correspondence (virtual consonant for stress assignment):

p. 7	joqtólom	'he's killing them'	*joqtolhom*
	fuq-râsom	'on their heads'	*fuq rashom*
p. 9	î	'she'	*hi*

  b. a glottal stop:

p. 5	tara'ómš	'she does not see them'	*tarahomx*

  c. *għajn* in radical position:

p. 19	ḳer3a	'ugly-F.'	*kerha*

  d. a long or diphthongized vowel:

p. 53	dệp/dệĕp	'gold'	*deheb*

  variants: dẹ'ep/dẹ3ẹp

  e. a glide:

p. 27	raptûwom	'they tied them'	*rabtuhom*
p. 47	idéĭja	'her two hands'	*idejha*
p. 5	ḥallîjom	'he left them'	*ħalliehom*

  f. pharyngeal *ḥ*:

p. 9	íkraḥ	'(the) ugliest'	*ikrah*
p. 7	talbûŏḥ	'they asked him for'	*talbuh*
p. 6	taḥḥom	'their'	*tagħhom*

Moreover, Stumme notes that English *h* is pronounced *ḥ*, e.g. [ḥarri] for 'Harry'.

4.2.3 Effect of pharyngeal sonorant 3 on contiguous vowels

Stumme (1904: 75) describes the sound transcribed by the glyph 3 (IPA [ʕ]) as "strongest throat pressure sound (arab ع)". If 3 immediately precedes radical or suffixal *ī* or *ū*, an 'intrusive' vowel is inserted; cf. Hall (2006). The intrusive nucleus and the high long vowel form a diphthong. In other terms, the first element of the diphthong does not stand for the vocalization of sonorant /ʕ/ but for the phonologization of the vocalic transition between the pharyngeal sonorant and *ī* or *ū* (examples from Stumme's first text: *Bočča*, dialect of Valetta):

(18)

	Stumme		Gloss	Modern orth.
tʒeĭt	ʕīd-IMPF.3F.SG		'she says'	tgħid
tîʒeĭ	tīʕ-1SG		'my'	tiegħi
ʒoŭda	ʕūd-noun.F.SG		'(a piece of) wood'	għuda
tîʒoŭ	tīʕ-3M.SG		'his'	tiegħu
jisímʒoŭ	sema'-IMPF-3PL		'they hear'	jisimgħu

ʒ is obligatorily adjacent to a vowel; thus, the stem-initial vowel is not syncopated in (19c):

(19)   a.   čáʒaq   noun-collective   'pebbles'   ċagħak

     b.

ʒámel	ʕamel-PF-3M.SG	'he made'	għamel
ʒámlu	ʕamel-PF-3PL	'they made'	għamlu
ʒámlet	ʕamel-PF-3F.SG	'she made'	għamlet
šʒámel	what-ʕamel-PF-3 M.SG	'What did he make?'	x'għamel?

     c.

ʒamílt	ʕamel-PF-1SG	'I made'	għamilt
cf. contra kitib-	PF-1SG	'I wrote'	ktibt

Adjacent to ʒ, a stem or suffixal mid-vowel is more open:

(20)

bo̦ʒo̦t	noun	'far'	bogħod
sémʒe̦t	sema'- PF-3F.SG	'she heard'	semgħet

4.2.4 Pharyngealized vowels

Stumme (1904: 79) describes some vowels as 'ʒain-retaining' (ʒain-haltig). These vowels, which are noted with a subscribed tilde, keep strong guttural pressure (starke Kehlpressung) during their whole length. They stand for ʒ merged with a low or mid vowel (represented by IPA ɔ and ε below):

(21)

šạ̃mel	š + ʕamel-PF-3M.SG	'what did he make?'	x'għamel
jạ̃mel	ʕamel- IMPF-3M.SG	'he makes'	jagħmel
nạ̃mlu	ʕamel-IMPF 1PL	'we make'	nagħmlu

(22)	milbọt	adverbial locution	'from far'	*mill-bogħod*
	šọl	work-noun M.SG	'work'	*xogħol*

A word-final stem vowel may be pharyngealized, but never a suffixal vowel:

(23) sɛbạ 'seven' *sebgħa*; cf. contra sémȝɛt (not *sémɛt) *semgħet* 'she heard'

4.2.5 Comparison with Tunisian Arabic

A few years before his fieldwork in Malta, Stumme (1896) had published a grammar of Tunisian Arabic. Comparing Stumme's transcriptions for Tunisian Arabic and Maltese is enlightening (Table 10).

Table 10: Comparison between Tunisian Arabic and Maltese

Tunisian Arabic (1896: 9)	Maltese 1904	Gloss
smáʕ	séma *sema'*	hear-PF.3M.SG
smáʕt	smáĭt *smajt*	hear-PF.1/2sg
sémʕat	sémʕet *semgħet*	hear-PF.3F.SG
sémʕu	sémʕoŭ *semgħu*	hear-PF.3pl

4.2.6 Conclusion

Brame (1972: 60) claims that in modern Maltese a rule of "absolute neutralization" changes the 'abstract' sonorant ʕ into vowel *a* (cf. below 6.2). Stumme's transcriptions for Maltese, by contrast with Tunisian Arabic, prove that ʕ followed by long *ī* or *ū* triggered the diphthongization of the vowel. Thus, the path of change has not been the vocalization of the guttural sonorant (ʕ → a) but its deletion in twentieth century Maltese in all contexts (residual idiolectal attestations):

(24) a. 'hear-PF.3pl'   sémʕū (underlying long final vowel)

        ū- diphthongization sémʕoŭ

        ʕ-deletion   sémoŭ (deletion of ʕ and diphthong phonologization)

    b. 'make-IMPF.1SG'   naʕmel

        ʕ-deletion   nạmel (compensatory length and pharyngealization)

4.3 Pharyngealization in the twentieth century

The reference book published by Aquilina (1959) (*The Structure of Maltese*) was first written before the World War as a Ph.D. thesis submitted at SOAS (School of Oriental and African Studies). The author postulates three sets of vowels (Table 11).

Table 11: Three sets of vowels

Short	Long (unpharyngealized)	Pharyngealized	
a	aː	$ˤa \sim aˤ \sim aˤaː$	ạ
e	eː	$ˤe \sim eˤ \sim eˤeː$	ẹ
i	iː	$ˤi \sim iˤ \sim iˤiː$	ị (dialectal)
o	oː	$ˤo \sim oˤ \sim oˤoː$	ọ
u	uː	$ˤu \sim uˤ \sim uˤuː$	ụ (dialectal)

Aquilina, however, adds this important comment:

> The above pharyngealized vowels are classified as special vowels to distinguish them from the unpharyngealized ones. Such differentiation is necessary to maintain the phonetic and historical individuality of the two sets; but it must be borne in mind that pharyngealization is so weakened that although it is dialectally perceptible in some of our villages and towns, it is hardly perceptible in others.

Based on his fieldwork in the 1970s, Schabert (1976) analyzed two conservative varieties of Maltese, one from St Julians (in the periphery of Valetta) and the other from the coastal village of Marsaxlokk. Like Aquilina (1959), Schabert (1976: 16) postulates three sets of vowels as in Table 12:

> Pharyngealization is realized in the following way: the pharyngealized vowel is phonetically longer than its non-pharyngealized counterpart (even in unstressed position), and during the whole length of the vowel or during a portion of its length the pharynx is slightly constricted.

According to Schabert (1976: 18), it sounds as if a faint ˤ slips into part of the vowel. In words which start by a pharyngealized vowel there is no prosthetic glottal stop, but when pharynx constriction occurs in the first part an initial sound like [ˤaː] may be heard. He gives the following examples:

Table 12: Vowels according to Schabert (1976)

short vowels	pharyngealized vowels	long vowels
i u		ī ū
		ɪᵊ
o		ǫ	ō
æ a	æ̣	ạ	ǣ ā

(25) a. Stressed position (glissando towards a centralized non-syllabic vocoid)

/fæ̣ m/	[fɛ̣ ·ẹ̆ m] ~[fɛ̣ :m]	*fehem*	'he understood'
/ʃǫ l/	[ʃǫ ·ọ̆ l] ~[ʃǫ :l]	*xogħol*	'work'
/ʔạ d /	[ʔạ ·ặ t] ~[ʔạ́ :t]	*qagħad*	'he stayed'

b. Unstressed position

/æ líʔi/	[ɛ ·lɪ·ĕʔi]	*għelieqi*	'fields'
/yoʔǫ d/	[jóʔǫ ·t]	*joqgħod*	'he stays'
/nạ mlūh/	[nạ ·mlú·ə̣ ħ]	*nagħmluh*	'we do it-M.SG'

Schabert's description is of great interest although not, in my opinion, representative of the present dialectal situation in the urban area in which St Julians is integrated; neither is the idiolect he recorded from Marsaxlokk representative for this village; cf. Puech (1994: text 43 and 44-50) and Azzopardi-Alexander (2011: 235-253). Finally, we shall mention the very careful description of an idiolect spoken in Mtaħleb (Malta) by Vanhove (1991). This idiolect attests the survival of ʕ and illustrates the complex relationship between vowel length and pharyngealization in the context of phonemic ʕ. See also Camilleri & Vanhove (1994) for a phonetic and phonological analysis of the dialect spoken in Mġarr (Malta).

5 Gutturals in contemporary Maltese

In phonemic terms, contemporary Maltese includes two laryngeal obstruents: /ʔ/ and /h/; the latter may be expressed by a pharyngeal or postvelar voiceless allophone: [ħ, χ]; cf. Alexander Borg (1997: 259). Vowels are no longer pharyngealized. We will distinguish two stages in contemporary Maltese. In more conservative idiolects, formerly pharyngealized vowels keep some degree of length even in unstressed position. In more innovative idiolects vowel length is maintained in stressed position only:

(26) ǽmel   ǽmel   *għamel*   'he did'

      āmɪlt   amɪlt   *għamilt*   'I/you-SG. did'

(27) ḗmes   ḗmes   *hemeż*   'he fastened'

      ēmɪst   emɪst   *hemiżt*   'I/you-SG fastened'

According to Hume et al. (2009: 36-38), length is similar for an underlying long vowel and a short vowel adjacent to *għ* in stressed position:

(28) tǻma   *tagħma*   għama-imperf.3F.SG   'she grows blind'

      tǻma   *tama*   noun F.SG   'hope'

      taʃʃa   *taxxa*   noun F.SG   'tax'

      tǻʃʃaʔ   *tgħaxxaq*   għaxxaq-imperf.3F.SG   'she makes happy'

According to my own observations and phonetic observations in Hume et al., a short vowel adjacent to *għ* is not lengthened in unstressed position:

(29) nɔrbɔt   *norbot*   rabat-imperf.1SG   'I tie'

      nɔbɔt   *nobgħod*   bagħad-IMPF.1SG   'I hate'

(30) tálap   *talab*   talab-perf.3.M.SG   'he asked'

      nɪlap   *nilgħab*   nilgħab-IMPF.1SG   'I play'

There are, however, other idiolects in which a short vowel adjacent to *għ* is lengthened in this position. Thus, Camilleri (2014: 60) gives /nilaːb/ 'I play'. According to Vanhove (1991), the long vowel attracts word stress, which yields [niláp]. Notice also the following variation:

(31)   Hume et al. (2009)   Camilleri (2014)
        [lápt]   [lápt]   *lgħabt*   'I played'
        [láptu]   [láptu]   *lgħabtu*   'you played'

There are two distinct stem pattern classes for 'h-medial' verbs (Camilleri 2014: 66; *Korpus Malti v. 3.0* 2016):

(32)   class 1   class 2
      a. [fḗm] 'he understood' *fehem*   [dḗr]   'he appeared'   *deher*

      b. [fɪmt] 1/2 SG   *fhimt*   [dért] 1/2 SG   *dhert*

Class 2 perfect conjugation is like that of 'għ-medial' verbs, e.g. *xehed* 'to give evidence' and *xegħel* 'to switch on'. Plural imperfect forms, however, are kept distinct; cf. Camilleri (2014: 123).

Hume et al. (2009: 42) evoke the question of a third degree of *phonemic* length. In any case, the actual length of vowels in different contexts depends on several factors, with variation in individual or dialectal speech habits. Main factors are:

1. underlying representation;

2. position in open or closed syllable;

3. word stress position;

4. intonation pattern.

6 On the abstractness of phonology: Maltese ʕ and *h*

Brame (1972) called his main contribution on Maltese: *On the Abstractness of Phonology: Maltese ʕ*. As shown by this title, the focus was on the pharyngeal sonorant. Prior to analyzing Brame's arguments, I will refer to David Cohen's comparison between Jewish Tunis Arabic and Maltese with respect to ʕ and *h*. Finally, I will briefly expose the theoretical background on which my proposal for the representation of ʕ and *h* is based.

6.1 Cohen's virtual phoneme

The loss of the pharyngeal sonorant ʕ and the approximant *h* broke up the unity of morphological paradigms in forms which had either phoneme as a root consonant. Cohen (1966; 1970) compared the Maltese case with that of Tunis, where the loss of phonemic *h* in the Jewish community was compensated by different strategies which maintained the morphophonemic unity of the Arabic dialect spoken in the city by different communities. For Maltese, Cohen (1970: 131) postulated a virtual segment occupying the position of ʕ but never realized as such:

> The non-articulation of a sound corresponding to graphic signs għ and *h* is characteristic of a part of the population. This part is in constant contact with elements of other groups for whom these signs present diverse realizations from mere intervocalic hiatus to the articulation of pharyngeal and laryngeal consonants in some positions. The existence of a phoneme in positions marked in spelling by għ and *h* is felt by all people, at least

in a great number of forms. Apparently, the situation is comparable with Jewish Tunis where the non-articulation of phoneme *h* which still exists in the surrounding Muslim dialect maintains the awareness of a sort of virtual phoneme, pure phonic quantity with no defined form, realized in different ways depending on contexts. [my translation].

In her tribute to Cohen's eminent contribution, Vanhove (2016: 6) concludes that

> the complementary distribution of the various allophones Cohen proposes is not exhaustive because of the limited documentation he had access to, but is accurate for the Maltese language of the first half of the twentieth century.

6.2 Brame's abstract ʕ

Even if the author concedes that "abstract segments and absolute neutralization must be countenanced in linguistic theory", Brame (1972: 60) concludes that the preservation of morphological regularities induces the inclusion of ʕ in the underlying sound system for new generations of language learners:

> Instead, great pains were taken to demonstrate that the evidence for underlying ʕ is in the phonetic data. That is, the child coming to the language-learning situation is capable of inducing ʕ on the basis of Maltese phonetics alone. It would be absurd to ascribe historical knowledge to the language learner. The fact that abstract ʕ must be postulated in the phonological component of Maltese is of consequence for the ultimate formulation of a natural principle of the type some have recently been interested in developing. First, any such condition will have to allow for phonological segments that never show up on the phonetic surface. Second, the condition will have to allow for rules of absolute neutralization, since apparently one of the rules needed to account for the phonetics of Maltese is of this type. This rule is stated as:
> ʕ → a
> Among others, this rule will account for the phonetic reflex of ʕ observed in the derivations listed [above].

Some data quoted by Brame in support of his analysis are well attested in diachrony but not usual any more. Let us take the example of *imgħadt* [imʕatt] 'I chewed'. Prosthetic *i* was motivated by the initial stem cluster [mʕ]; cf. Brame (1972: 46), Comrie (1986: 14). In contemporary Maltese, the form is simply pronounced [mátt]. Conservative realizations with prosthetic *i* are, however, preserved in some expressions, e.g. *bl-imgħarfa* 'with a spoon'. Alexander Borg (1997: 262) is certainly correct in his overall conclusion:

> the generative interpretation of abstract *għajn* may ultimately prove more faithful to historical fact than to the synchrony of M. At all events, the notion that M. speakers perceive an underlying 'pharyngeal segment' *għajn* finds little support in written usage, since the correct assignment of this digraph in written M remains a notorious source of error even among highly literate speakers.

Brame did not investigate *h* reflexes. Logically, the same arguments put forward for ʕ lead to including *h* into the underlying sound system as well.

6.3 Emptiness in CV Phonology

6.3.1 CV-only Phonology

Within the framework of Government Phonology, Lowenstamm (1996) made the radical claim that "syllable structure universally, i.e. regardless of whether the language is templatic or not, reduces to CV." In this model, a Maltese form like *kitbu* 'they wrote' is analyzed as a sequence of three light open syllables, the second of which has an empty nucleus: 'k i t · b u' (the empty nucleus position is here represented by a 'median point'). Words obligatorily start with a C position, and end in a full or empty nucleus, to comply with the CV-only principle.

In other versions, words can start with a V position, or end in a C position; cf. Polgárdi (2012: 111). Independently of Government Phonology, strict C/V alternation may be viewed as an effect of applying the Obligatory Contour Principle (OCP) to syllabic structure. This principle stipulates that, at a given level of structure, adjacent identical elements are prohibited (McCarthy 1986; Odden 1986). In this approach, a sequence of strictly adjacent consonants, like 'C C', or strictly adjacent nuclei, like 'V V' are prohibited. On the other hand, sequences like 'C · C', where the medial position stands for an empty nucleus, and 'V · V', where the medial position stands for an empty consonant, are allowed. Under the OCP application, two adjacent empty positions are also prohibited: a sequence like *'C · · V' is ill-formed.

6.3.2 Segmental length

In Lowenstamm's model, a geminate consonant is represented by two C's straddling an empty nucleus (represented by the zero symbol); conversely, a long vowel is represented by two V's straddling an empty C-position:

(33)   *demmi* 'my blood'

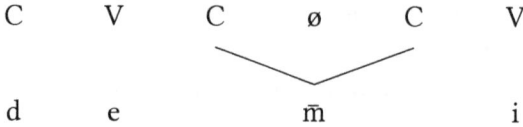

C	V	C	ø	C	V
d	e		m̄		i

(34)   *dāri* 'my house'

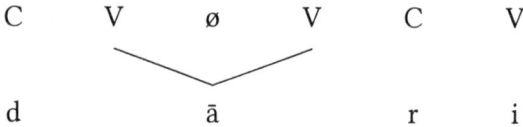

C	V	ø	V	C	V
d		ā		r	i

Alternatively, a long segment may be interpreted as an element {C} or {V} occupying a position and controlling a contiguous empty unit of phonological space; cf. Russo & Ulfsbjorninn (2017). In this view, an empty position precedes the position occupied by the element {C} for geminates; it follows the position occupied by the element {V} for a long vowel:

(35)   C   V   ø   V   V

d	e	m̄	i

(36)   C   V   ø   C   V

d	ā	r	i

The melody of monophthongal long segments occupies the double space of the vertex.

6.3.3 Maltese diphthongs in Element Theory

Maltese has two types of diphthongs: The 'bogus' diphthongs in (31) are in fact a vowel contiguous to the glide *y* or *w*; the type of diphthong in (34) results from melodic *fission* due to an 'intrusive' nucleus between the long vowel and a pharyngeal sonorant; on 'intrusive' vowels, cf. Hall (2006). The diphthong is an allophonic realization of the long vowel in the presence of /ʕ/ and becomes phonologized when the consonant is lost. When /ū/ or /ī/ are followed by *q* or *ħ* the long vowel is also perceived as altered and slightly diphthongized; cf. Aquilina (1959: 38, 54) and Borg & Azzopardi (1997: 304, 305). In this context, however, there is no loss of the consonant and, thus, no phonologization of the diphthong.

6.3.3.1 a- Sequence nucleus+glide

(37)   The vowels *e*, *o*, and *a* merge with glides *y* or *w* to yield a bogus diphthong:

a.	s a y f	*sajf*	'summer'
	b ɛ y t	*bejt*	'roof'
b.	b ɛ w s	*bews*	'kisses'
	d a w l	*dawl*	'light'

The syllabic pattern of these forms is CVCC, like in:

(38)   ħ ɔ b z   *ħobż*   'bread'

6.3.3.2 b- *Complex nucleus melodic fission*   When ʕ immediately precedes a long tense vowel *ī* or *ū*, the long vowel diphthongizes. In (39a) stem initial ʕ is preceded by an empty space to avoid an OCP clash with the prefix *t*, and is immediately followed by an underlyingly long nucleus (step 1); the melody of the long vowel splits: The element {A} is copied from the pharyngeal glide to occupy the first space unit, while the element {I} occupies the second space unit (step 2); in (39b) the diphthong is phonologized.

Melodic fission is illustrated by Stumme's examples where sonorant ʕ triggers the diphthongization of the adjacent vowel, i.e. in 't3eĭd' *tgħid*-IMPF.3 F.SG 'she says' and 'sam3ou' *semgħu*-PF.3PL 'they heard':

(39)   a. Step 1 (etymon)

t		ʕ	ī	d		s	a	m		ʕ	ū
C		C	V	C		C	V	C		C	V
		<u>V</u>				V		<u>V</u>		<u>V</u>	
		V		V				C		V	
I			I	I		I		U			U
		<u>A</u>					A			<u>A</u>	

b. Step 2: diphthongization

t	ʕ	eį	d		s	a	m	ʕ	oų
C	C	V	C		C	V	C		C	V
	V				V		V		V	
	V						C		V	
I		I	I		I		U			U
	A̱	A				A			A̱	A

7 Phonological interpretation of orthographic *h*

In this contribution, I will overlook the residual role of *h* in stems. Some of the relevant paradigms and alternations are commented in Camilleri (2014: 67). Suffice it to say that, in modern Maltese, stem-*h* is most often assimilated to *għ*, or to *ħ*. My focus will be on the representation of *h* in suffixes.

7.1 *h*-initial suffixes

Orthographic *h* behaves as a consonant in object pronouns:

(40)   a.   *ha* (or -*hie*): 3F.SG object (35b) -*na* (or -*nie*): 1PL object

          b.   *hom*: 3PL object -*kom*: 2PL object

In (40a) *h* patterns with suffixes starting by a consonant in (40b) with respect to stem structure and stress assignment but has no surface realization:

(41)   a.   *kitibha* 'he recruited her' [kitíba]

             kitibna 'he recruited us' [kitíbna]

          b.   *kitibhom* 'he recruited them' [kitíbom]

             kitibkom 'he recruited you-all' [kitíbkom]

If the object pronoun is V-initial, the second stem vowel in an open syllable is deleted:

(42)   a.   kitbek 'he recruited you-sg' [kítbek]

          b.   kitbu 'he recruited him' [kítbu]

In (42) the second stem nucleus is syncopated in intervocalic position, while a consonant position blocks stem nucleus syncope in (41). An empty position (represented by a median dot) blocks syncope as well in (43b), since the second stem nucleus is not in intervocalic position:

(43) a. *k i t i b · n a*
      cf. k i t i b · k o m

    b. *k i t i b · a*
      k i t i b · o m

The underlying representation of pronouns with *h* in (40a) above is:

(44)

h	*a*	or	*h*	*ie* …	*h*	*o*	*m*
·	V		·	V̄	·	V	C
							V̲
							C
				I		U	U
	A					A	

Notice that in *kitibna* the suffix consonant is separated from the last stem consonant by an empty position, since a sequence 'CC' would be an OCP violation. Similarly, the representation of *kitibha* as */k i t i b · · a/, with two adjacent empty positions, would be an OCP violation. Orthographic *h* occupies a single space unit left empty, i.e. not occupied by either the element {C} or {V}.

In intervocalic position, the empty space unit is occupied by a palatal or labial glide in agreement with the preceding vowel. According to Alexander Borg (1997: 275), the underlying long vowel is shortened in case of glide insertion:

(45) a. k · s ī · a   [k s í y a]   *ksieha*   'he covered it-F.SG'

    b. y i š · t · r ū · o m [yištrúwom]   *jixtruhom* 'they buy them'

Yet, Borg quotes dialectal forms in which the long vowel and the inserted glide yield a geminate glide; cf. Puech (1994: 87):

(46) t · r ī d ū · i m   [tridúwwim]   *triduhim*   'you-PL want them'

If both vowels are [nonhigh] they are fused (Alexander Borg 1997: 276):

(47) a. š · t · r ā · a   [štrá]   *xtraha*   'he bought it-F.SG'
                   [štrá]

    b. š · t · r ā · o m   [štrá.om]   *xtrahom*   'he bought them'
                   [štrő́m]

In the mirror sequence 'V · V̄' ', due to word-stress shift, glide insertion is optional:

(48) š · t · r ā · ī l i   [štra.íli]   *xtrahieli*   'he bought it for me'
                              [štrayíli]

7.2 Word-final *h*

When the 3M.SG object suffix is immediately preceded by a vowel and is word-final (or only followed by enclitic negation *š*), its allomorphic realization is *ħ*:

(49) *kitbuh*   'they wrote it-M' [k i t b ú ħ]

      ktibnieh   'we wrote it-M'   [k t i b n í ħ]

This applies to stems with etymological *h* in word-final position:

(50) *kerah*   'ugly-M.SG'   [k é r a ħ] cf. *kerha* 'ugly-F.SG'

7.3 Conclusion

Orthographic *h* stands for a virtual consonant, i.e. occupies a C-position whose vertex is empty. Its underlying presence is revealed by its effect on the syllabic structure and stress assignment, or by a glide preventing hiatus. In word-final position (disregarding the negative enclitic) it is represented by an allomorph *ħ*, an instance of phonologically conditioned allomorphy.

8 Phonological interpretation of the digraph *għ*

The sonorants ʕ and ɣ, represented in modern spelling by the digraph *għ*, are etymological in many roots as first, second, or third radical. My focus will be on diachronic changes in stems whose one radical was ʕ or ɣ. I identify four stages, which synchronically correspond to overlapping lengths.

8.1 *Għ* adjacent to a (mid)low vowel

In premodern Maltese, ʕ and ɣ correspond to two distinct sonorants. In most dialects, however, they have been merged. The examples below are drawn from the verb *għamel* 'to make' for two forms in the perfect (3rd M.SG and 1/2 sg). Concerning the quality *i* or *e* of the second stem vowel, suffice it to say that it depends on contexts and dialects; cf. *għamel* 'he made' vs. *għamilt* 'I made':

(51) **Lect A** (lost in contemporary Maltese)

ʕ	á	m	e	l		ʕ	a	m	í	l		t
C	V	C	V	C		C	V	C	V	C	·	C
V̱		V̱		V̱		V̱		V̱		V̱		
C								C				
	U	I		I		U		I		I		I
A̱	A			A		A̱	A					

The loss of articulation of the sonorant is compensated by vowel pharyngealization and length. The initial C-position is represented by an empty vertex associated to a headed element {A}. This position is merged with the adjacent (mid)low nucleus. Pharyngealization results from the embedding of the pharyngeal sonorant in the vowel: it is marked by the element {C} in dependent position under the vertex {V}. Length is kept in the pharyngealized vowel even if it is unstressed:

(52) **Lect B** (conservative lect; cf. Aquilina 1959, Schabert 1976)

	ą́	m	e	l			ą̄	m	í	l		t
·	V̄	C	V	C		·	V̄	C	V	C	·	C
	C	V̱		V̱			C	V̱		V̱		
	C						C					
		U	I		I		U		I		I		I
A̱	A			A		A̱	A					

Pharyngealization has been lost but the vowel retains length, whether it is stressed or not. The paradigm of stems with initial *għ* is similar to that of stems with initial *ħ*, like *ħemeż* 'to pin'; cf. Camilleri (2014: 19). The initial underlying position is represented by an empty vertex associated to a headless melodic element {A}. In being merged with the empty position, this nucleus remains 'long' in all positions:

(53) **Lect C**

	á̄	m	e	l			ā	m	í	l		t
V̄	C	V	C		V	C	V	C	·	C
C	V̱		V̱		C	V̱		V̱		
C		C			C					
	U	I	I		U		I		I		I
A		A			A					

The initial nucleus is long if it is stressed, and short if stress migrates rightward. Thus, the underlying representation is restructured. It starts with an underlying long nucleus which behaves as an ordinary long nucleus with respect to length:

(54) **Lect D**

á	m	e	l		a	m	í	l		t
V̄	C	V	C		V	C	V	C	·	C
V		V				V		V		
C						C				
U	I	I			U	I	I			I
A		A			A					

In the nineteenth century, the conservative lects A and B overlapped; cf. Bonelli (1897; 1898; 1900), Stumme (1904). Lects B and C are well documented in the twentieth century; cf. Aquilina (1959), Schabert (1976), Vanhove (1991). Conservative lect C and innovative lect D are representative of contemporary Maltese.

8.2 *Għ* adjacent to an underlying high vowel

When initial *għ* precedes the vowels *ī* or *ū*, a (pharyngealized) diphthong occurred in most dialects, including Standard Maltese:

(55) a. [áįd] *għid* '(religious) feast' *għ* stands for etymological ʕ
         [záịr] *żgħir* 'small'   ɣ

      b. [áųd] *għud* 'wooden hook' *għ* stands for etymological ʕ
         [áųl] *għul* 'ogre'   ɣ

The diphthong is kept in internal position:

(56) a. [záịra] *żgħira* 'small-F.SG'
      b. [áųda] *għuda* '(piece of) wood-F.SG'

The quality of the nucleus in the diphthong is variable: *aĭ~eĭ~oĭ* for *għī*, *eŭ~aŭ~oŭ* for *għū*; cf. Aquilina (1959: 54), Alexander Borg (1978: 73), Alexander Borg (1997: 270), Borg & Azzopardi (1997: 299). Variations are observed between rural dialects, with several intervening factors, but also within Standard Maltese. Notice also the absence of diphthongization triggered by *għ* in the dialectal area of the Grand Harbour. All realizations below are attested for *żgħir* 'small-M.SG':

(57) a. [zɣaịr], [zoịr] (in Gozo)
      b. [zaịr], [ze̞ịr], [zeịr], [zīr] (in the Grand Harbour)

8.3 Digraph *għ* followed by *h*-suffix

Concerning *għ* as third radical, if the stem is followed by an object suffix starting with -*h*, the sequence 'għ-h' is realized as [ħħ]:

(58) a. *bela'*   [béla]   'he threw'

  b. *belagħha* [beláħħa] 'he threw it'

It should also be noticed that there are innovations in inflections, even more so in the language of young people. For example, Fabri (2011: 99):

(59) a. *raha* [rá]   'he saw her'

  b.   [raħħa]   on the model of (59b)

8.4 Conclusion

In diachrony, the main reflexes corresponding to etymological guttural sonorants are: vowel diphthongization and/or pharyngealization, lengthening, and allomorphic *ħ*. In the synchrony of contemporary Maltese, I claim, using the same terms as Brame, that on the basis of Maltese phonetics and morpho-phonemic patterns, the child coming to the language-learning situation is capable of inducing underlying stems that include an empty vertex associated to the melodic element {A}:

- in position of first radical; cf. *għamel*:

·	V	C	V	C
A	A			

- in position of second radical; cf. *lagħab*:

C	V	·	V	C
	A	A	A	

- in position of third radical; cf. *sema'*:

C	V	C	V	·
		A	A	

Applicable phonological processes are fusion, diphthongization and deletion. Other cases are accounted for by (phonologically-conditioned) suppletive allomorphy.

9 Representation of modern Maltese consonants

Tables 13 and 14 below give the inventory of contemporary Maltese consonants. Compared to the inventory in Tables 1 and 2, there is on the one hand the loss of emphatic and guttural consonants, and, on the other hand, the introduction of new phonemes, due to massive borrowings from Sicilian, Italian and, nowadays, from English; cf. Mifsud (1995). Concerning ħ, Borg & Azzopardi (1997: 301) state:

> Orthographic ħ always corresponds to /h/; orthographic għ and ħ correspond to /h/ in word final position or when they occur together (orthographic għ + ħ). /h/ is articulated as a convexed (central) post-palatal, velar, glottal or pharyngeal voiceless fricative. Its place of articulation varies according to the vocalic context that follows it. However, partially (but often fully) voiced when it precedes voiced obstruents but does not occur in opposition to a voiced velar or post-velar fricative.

Table 13: Obstruents in Modern Maltese

Segment	p b	f v	t d	s z	ts dz	š ž	tʃ dʒ	k g	h ʔ
Structure	C C	C̲ C̲	C C	C̲ C̲	C C	C̲ C̲	C̲ C̲	C C	C̲ C̲
		V V		V V		V V			V
	V	V	V	V	C V	V	C V	V	C C
Melody	U U	U U	I I	I I	I I	I̲ I̲	I̲ I̲		
									A A

Table 14: Sonorants

	m	n	l	r	y	w
Structure	C	C	C	C	C	C
	V̲	V̲	V̲	V̲	V̲	V̲
	C	C				
Melody	U	I	I	I	I̲	U̲
				A		

I repeat for convenience the representation of major categories given in §2.2 in Table 15.

Table 15: Representation of major categories (repeated)

	Stops		Fricatives		Sonorants	
	weak /	*strong*	*weak* /	*strong*	*weak* /	*strong*
	C	C̲	C	C̲	C	C
			V	V	V	V̲
	(C or V)		(C or V)		(V)	C
	Labials	(Denti)alveolar	Post-alveolars		Palato-velar	Guttural
Melody	U	I	I̲		none	A

10 Conclusion

The loss of emphatic consonants in postmedieval Maltese transferred the burden of maintaining lexical contrasts to stem vowels only. Four centuries later, the loss of guttural consonants broke up regular morphophonemic alternations, inducing opacity in the sound pattern. In other words, there has been a trade-off between 'less' on the phonological side and 'more' on the morpho-phonological side. Until the (post)medieval stage the natural class of emphatic and guttural consonants was characterized by the element {A}. In pre-modern Maltese, in which *h* was already on its way out and *q* had not yet been replaced by a glottal stop, the narrow 'guttural' class was characterized by {A}. This class extended from (post)velars to pharyngeal consonants. In modern Maltese, only voiceless pharyngeal *ħ* and glottal stop *ʔ* retain the element {A} in their representation. A further step in the sound pattern shift tends to favor more urban laryngeal *h* over more rural pharyngeal *ħ* as the main allophone for the 'guttural' fricative.

Using the CV framework, I argued that the etymological laryngeal approximant *h* must be analyzed as an empty C-position: its phonotactic behavior is that of a consonant with respect to syllabic structure and stress, but it has no autonomous realization. In some contexts, however, it is directly represented by a glide in intervocalic position, or by the voiceless guttural fricative in word-final position. An empty vertex hosting the melodic element {A} is the direct reflex of former guttural sonorants, indirectly expressed by pharyngealizing and lengthening effects on adjacent vowels. Once pharyngealization has been lost in contemporary Maltese, it is no longer justified to maintain two different underlying representations corresponding to orthographic *h* and *għ*. The sound pattern only requires that underlying representations may include a content-empty unit of phonological space. Surface forms are generated by regular phonological processes, or phonologically-conditioned allomorphy. In Brame's terms, children "coming to the language-learning situation" are endowed by UG with the capacity of inducing the role of empty consonants in the sound pattern they acquire. Yet, some regularities are of an allomorphic rather than a phonological nature. Thus, canonical paradigm acquisition is also necessary in the learning process.

I would like to end this contribution by extending the phonological predictions made by Fabri (2011: 99):

> Bringing in the acquisition perspective once again, another observation is relevant in this context. A diary of language development of my own son, Noah, shows clearly that he often omitted the glottal stop for quite a long time during his acquisition phase. Moreover, even when he learnt how to write at school, he would systematically omit the letter 'q', which represents the glottal, thus implying that he was not even aware of its occurrence. It is, therefore, not implausible to speculate that one way in which Maltese could change is the occurrence of the glottal stop, a change that also affects its phonemic status within the phonological system.

If Noah's children induce a sound pattern without any 'guttural' consonant characterized by the melodic element {A}, the millenary cycle of transferring guttural load from consonants to vowels will have been completed.

Abbreviations

PF	Perfect		M	Masculine
IMPF	Imperfect		F	Feminine
IMPER	Imperative		SG	Singular
PP	Past participle		PL	Plural
1, 2, 3	1st, 2nd, 3rd person		Obj	(suffixed) Object pronoun

Appendix: Diachronic changes in Maltese gutturals

Table 16: Diachronic changes in Maltese gutturals

Pre-modern Maltese

i	$k̲$/q[1]	χ ħ	h~ø	γ[2] ʕ	Agius de Soldanis (1750)
ii	q	χ~ħ	h	γ~ʕ	Vassalli (1796; 1827)

Modern Maltese

			h~ø	ʕ	Bonelli (1897; 1900)
iii	q/ʔ[3]	ħ	ʼ~ø	ʕ	Stumme (1904); Saada (1986)[4]
iv	ʔ	ħ		γ|A|[5] ʕ|A|~|Ạ|[6]	Aquilina 1959 Schabert (1976)
v	ʔ	ħ		ʕ|Ā|~|Ā|	Vanhove (1991) Cohen (1966; 1970)

Contemporary Maltese

vi	ʔ	ħ		|Ā/A|[8]	Aquilina & Isserlin (1981)[7] Puech (1994)
vii		h[9]			Alexander Borg (1997); Borg & Azzopardi (1997); Hume et al. (2009)
	ʔ	h	glide~ø[10]	|Ā/A|	Camilleri (2014)

Notes to Table

[1] Uvular *q* alternates with retracted *k̲* before a [back] vowel. Velar *k* in this environment is still attested in Xewkija (Gozo); e.g. [k̲alp] for *qalb* 'moon' vs. [kælp] for *kelb* 'dog'.

[2] Postvelar *γ* is still attested for older speakers in some Gozitan villages (Għarb, Qala); e.g. [γɑlɑʔ, γlɒʔt] for *għalaq, għalaqt,* 'he / I closed'.

[3] Postvelar *q* is still attested, at least for older speakers, in the Grand Harbour (Malta) and Gozo (Rabat). Phonemic *ʔ* is distinct to the optional glottal prosthetic onset in V-initial words..

[4] Maltese spoken in Tunisia by French citizens from Maltese families until the 1950s.

[5] The author postulates a set of mid- or low pharyngealized vowels (p. 18). These vowels are preceded or followed by the symbol ɣ, corresponding to orthographic *għ* or *h*. The Symbol |A| refers to mid or low vowels whose phonological expression includes element {A}.

[6] Schabert (1976: 19-20) contrasts the mid/low long vowels [ā æ ɔ] with the allophones [ạ̄ æ̣ ọ̣] of pharyngealized vowels; the two dialects described by Schabert are conservative.

[7] Aquilina & Isserlin (1981) "cannot rule out that pharyngealization may actually occur still in Gozitan dialecrs" (p. 137), but "encountered no clear instances of 'pharyngealized' vowels near a no longer pronounced /ʕ/" (p. 114).

[8] At this stage, no pharyngealization, but variable length due to several factors.

[9] Allophones of /h/ are [h, ħ, χ], depending on contexts and speech habits. In urban Maltese, the pharyngeal articulation is less valued than the laryngeal one.

[10] In general, the reflex of etymological *h* is zero; e.g. [nifmu] *nifhmu* 'we understand'. Maltese avoids hiatus by inserting a homorganic glide or by fusing two [nonhigh] vowels. In some dialects proto-*h* has been assimilated to ħ; cf. *fehem*: [fēm] vs. [feħem].

References

Agius de Soldanis, Giovanni Pietro F. 1750. *Della lingua punica presentamente usata da maltese &. C. Overro nuovi documenti, li quali possono servire di lume all'antica lingua etrusca; stesi in due dissertazioni & c.* Roma: Joe Zammit Ciantar. Facsimile edition: Malta 2007.

Aquilina, Joseph. 1959. *The structure of Maltese: A study in mixed grammar and vocabulary.* Malta: The Royal University of Malta.

Aquilina, Joseph. 1961. *Papers in Maltese linguistics.* Malta: The Royal University of Malta.

Aquilina, Joseph. 1987. *Maltese-English dictionary.* Vol. 1. Malta: Midsea books.

Aquilina, Joseph. 1990. *Maltese-English dictionary.* Vol. 2. Malta: Midsea Books.

Aquilina, Joseph & Benedikt Isserlin. 1981. *A survey of contemporary dialectal Maltese, volume 1: Gozo.* Leeds: University of Leeds.

Azzopardi-Alexander, Marie. 2011. The vowel system of Xlukkajr and Naduri. In Sandro Caruana, Ray Fabri & Thomas Stolz (eds.), *Variation and change: The dynamics of Maltese in space, time and society*, 235–253. Berlin: Akademie Verlag.

Backley, Philip. 2011. *An introduction to Element Theory.* Edinburgh: Edinburgh University Press.

Bellem, Alex. 2007. *Towards a comparative typology of emphatics, across Semitic and into African dialect phonology*. London: School of Oriental & African Studies dissertation.

Bonelli, Luigi. 1897. Il dialetto maltese. In Graziadio I. Ascoli (ed.), *Archivio glottologico italiano; supplementi periodici*, vol. sesta dispensa (Nabu Public Domain Reprints), 53–98. Torino: Ermanno Loescher.

Bonelli, Luigi. 1898. Il dialetto maltese (continuazione). In Graziadio I. Ascoli (ed.), *Supplementi periodici all' archivio glottologico italiano*, vol. settima dispensa (Nabu Public Domain Reprints), 37–70. Florence: Ermanno Loescher.

Bonelli, Luigi. 1900. Il dialetto maltese (continuazione): Lessico. In Graziadio I. Ascoli (ed.), *Supplementi periodici all' archivio glottologico italiano*, vol. 7 (Nabu Public Domain Reprints), 1–68. Torino: Ermanno Loescher.

Borg, Albert. 2011. Lectal variations in Maltese. In Sandro Caruana, Ray Fabri & Thomas Stolz (eds.), *Variation and change: The dynamics of Maltese in space, time and society*, 11–31. Berlin: Akademie Verlag.

Borg, Albert & Marie Azzopardi. 1997. *Maltese*. London: Routledge.

Borg, Alexander. 1976. The IMAALA in Maltese. *Israel Oriental Studies* 6. 191–223.

Borg, Alexander. 1977. Reflexes of pausal forms in Maltese rural dialects? *Israel Oriental Studies* 7. 211–225.

Borg, Alexander. 1978. *A historical and comparative phonology and morphology of Maltese*. The Hebrew University dissertation.

Borg, Alexander. 1997. Maltese phonology. In Alan S. Kaye (ed.), *Phonologies of Asia and Africa*, vol. 1, 245–285. Winona Lake, Indiana: Eisenbrauns.

Brame, Michael K. 1972. On the abstractness of phonology: Maltese ʕ. In Michael K. Brame (ed.), *Contributions to generative phonology*, 22–61. Austin, TX: University of Texas Press.

Breit, Florian. 2013. *Formal aspects of element theory*. University College London dissertation.

Brincat, Joseph. 2011. *Maltese and other languages: A linguistic history of Malta*. Malta: Midsea Books.

Camilleri, Antoinette & Martine Vanhove. 1994. A phonetic and phonological description of the Maltese dialect of Mġarr (Malta). *Zeitschrift für Arabische Linguistik* 28. 87–110.

Camilleri, Maris. 2014. *The stem in inflectional verbal paradigms in Maltese*. University of Surrey dissertation.

Cassola, Arnold. 1987-88. Una edizione diversa della lista di voci maltesi del seicento di hieronymus megiser. *Journal of Maltese Studies* 17-18. 72–86.

Chomsky, Noam & Morris Halle. 1968. *The sound pattern of English*. New York: Harper & Row.

Clements, George N. 1985. The geometry of phonological features. In Colin J. Ewen & John M. Anderson (eds.), *Phonology yearbook*, vol. 2, 225–252. Cambridge: Cambridge University Press.

Clements, George N. 1999. Affricates as noncontoured stops. In Osamu Fujimora, Brian D. Joseph & Bohumil Palek (eds.), *Proceedings of LP'98: Item order in language and speech*, 271–299. Prague: The Karolinum Press.

Cohen, David. 1966. Le système phonologique du maltais. *Journal of Maltese Studies* 3. 1–26.

Cohen, David. 1970. *Études de linguistique sémitique et arabe*. The Hague: Mouton.

Cohen, David & Martine Vanhove. 1991. La 'cantilène' maltaise du 15ème siècle: Remarques linguistiques. In *Comptes rendus du GLECs (1984-1986)*, vol. 29-30, 177–200. Paris.

Comrie, Bernard. 1980. The sun letters in Maltese: Between morphophonemics and phonetics. In M. Kenstowicz (ed.), *Studies in African linguistics*, 25–37. Urbana, IL: University of Illinois.

Comrie, Bernard. 1986. The Maltese pharyngeal. *Zeitschrift für Phonetik, Sprachwissenschaft und Kommunikationforschung* 39(1). 12–18.

Comrie, Bernard. 1991. Towards a history of African Maltese. In Alan S. Kaye (ed.), *Semitic studies, in honor of Wolf Leslau*, 234–244. Wiesbaden: Otto Harrassowitz.

Cowan, William. 1964. An early Maltese word-list. *Journal of Maltese Studies* 2. 212–225.

Cowan, William. 1966. Loss of emphasis in Maltese. *Journal of Maltese Studies* 3. 27–32.

Fabri, Ray. 2011. The language of young people and language change in Maltese. In Sandro Caruana, Ray Fabri & Thomas Stolz (eds.), *Variation and change: The dynamics of Maltese in space, time and society*, 89–107. Berlin: Akademie Verlag.

Ghazeli, Salem. 1977. *Back consonants and backing coarticulation in African*. University of Texas at Austin dissertation.

Hall, Nancy. 2006. Cross-linguistic patterns of vowel intrusion. *Phonology* 23. 387–429.

Harris, John & Geoff Lindsey. 1995. The elements of phonological representation. In Jacques Durand & Francis Katamba (eds.), *Frontiers of phonology: Atoms, structures, derivations*, 34–79. London: Longman.

Hayward, Katrina M. & Richard J. Hayward. 1989. 'guttural': Arguments for a new distinctive feature. *Transactions of the Philological Scociety* 87(2). 179–193.

Hume, Elizabeth. 1994. *Front vowels, coronal consonants, and their interaction in nonlinear phonology*. New York: Garland.

Hume, Elizabeth, Jennifer Venditti, Alexandra Vella & Samantha Gett. 2009. Vowel duration and Maltese 'gh'. In Bernard Comrie, Ray Fabri, Elizabeth Hume, Manwel Mifsud, Thomas Stolz & Martine Vanhove (eds.), *Introducing Maltese linguistics*, 15–46. Amsterdam: John Benjamins Publishing Company.

Jakobson, Roman, Gunnar M. Fant & Morris Halle. 1952. *Preliminaries to speech analysis: The distinctive features and their correlates*. Cambridge, MA: MIT Press.

Kaye, Alan S. 1972. Arabic /ž/: A synchronic and diachronic study. *Linguistics* 79. 31–63.

Al-Khairy, Mohamed. 2005. *Acoustic characteristics of African fricatives*. University of Florida dissertation.

Kontzi, Reinhold. 1994. Il-kontribut ta' studjuži Ġermaniži fl-istudju ta' l-ilsien Malti mill-bidu tas-seklu sbatax sal-bidu tas-seklu għoxrin [martin zammit, trans.] *Journal of Maltese Studies* 25. 13–39.

Korpus Malti v. 3.0. 2016. http://mlrs.research.um.edu.mt/.

Laufer, Asher. 1988. The emphatic and pharyngeal sounds in Hebrew and in African. *Language and Speech* 31(2). 181–205.

Laufer, Asher. 1991. The 'glottal fricatives'. *Journal of International Phonetic Association* 21(2). 91–93.

Lowenstamm, Jean. 1996. CV as the only syllable type. In Jacques Durand & Bernard Laks (eds.), *Current trends in phonology, models and methods*, vol. 2, 24–46. Salford: ESRI.

McCarthy, John J. 1986. OCP effects: Gemination and antigemination. *Linguistic Inquiry* 17(2). 207–263.

McCarthy, John J. 1991. Semitic gutturals and distinctive feature theory. In Bernard Comrie & Mushira Eid (eds.), *Perspectives on African linguistics IIi. Papers from the third annual symposium on African linguistics*, 63–91. Amsterdam: John Benjamins Publishing Company.

McCarthy, John J. 1994. The phonetics and phonology of Semitic pharyngeal. In Patricia Keating (ed.), *Phonological structure and phonetic form, papers in laboratory phonology IIi*. Cambridge: Cambridge University Press.

Megiser, Hieronymus. 1606. *Propugnaculum europae*. Leipzig: Kessinger Legacy Reprints.

Mifsud, Manwel. 1995. *Loan verbs in Maltese, A descriptive and comparative study.* Leiden: Brill.

Odden, David. 1986. On the role of the obligatory contour principle in phonological theory. *Language* 62(2). 353–383.

Polgárdi, Krisztina. 2012. The distribution of vowels in English and trochaic proper government. In Bert Botma & Roland Noske (eds.), *Phonological explorations: Empirical, theoretical and diachronic issues*, 111–134. Berlin: Mouton de Gruyter.

Puech, Gilbert. 1978. A cross-dialectal study of vowel harmony in Maltese. In Donka Farkas, Wesley M. Jacobsen & Karol W. Todrys (eds.), *Papers from the fourteenth regional meeting*, 377–389. Chicago: University of Chicago.

Puech, Gilbert. 1994. *Ethnotextes maltais.* Wiesbaden: Harrassowitz.

Puech, Gilbert. 2016. Minimalist representation of sounds. In Gilbert Puech & Benjamin Saade (eds.), *Shifts and patterns in Maltese*, 61–89. Berlin: Mouton de Gruyter.

Russo, Michela & Shanti Ulfsbjorninn. 2017. Breaking the symmetry of geminates in diachrony and synchrony. *Papers in Historical Phonology* 2. 164–202.

Saada, Lucienne. 1986. Maltais en tunisie. In *Atti del congresso internazionale di amalfi, 5-8 dicembre 1983.* Nap;es.

Sagey, Elizabeth. 1986. *The representation of features and relations in nonlinear phonology.* Cambridge, MA: MIT dissertation.

Schabert, Peter. 1976. *Laut- und formenlehre des maltesischen anhand zweier mundarten.* Germany: Palm & Enke Erlanger Studien.

Stumme, Hans. 1896. *Grammatik des Tunischen Arabisch.* Leipzig: J.C. Hinrichs'sche.

Stumme, Hans. 1904. *Maltesische Studien: Eine Sammlung prosaischer und poetischer Texte in maltesischer Sprache, nebst Erläuterungen.* Leipzig: J. C. Hinrichs'sche.

Sutcliffe, Edmund. 1936. *A grammar of the Maltese language, with chrestomathy and vocabulary.* Oxford: Oxford University Press.

Vanhove, Martine. 1991. On the survival of [ʕ] in a Maltese idiolect at Mtaħleb in Malta. *Journal of Afroasiatic Languages* 3. 22–34.

Vanhove, Martine. 2016. From Maltese phonology to morphogenesis: A tribute to David Cohen. In Gilbert Puech & Benjamin Saade (eds.), *Shifts and patterns in Maltese*, 1–18. Berlin: Mouton de Gruyter.

Vassalli, Michael A. 1796. *Ktŷb yl klŷm mâlti, 'mfysser byl-latĭn u byt-taljânm, sive liber dictionum melitensium.* Franz Sammut (ed.). Malta: SKS.

Vassalli, Michael A. 1827. *Grammatica della lingua maltese.* Malta: Nabu Public Domain Reprints.

Wettinger, Godfrey. 1985. *The Jews of Malta in the late middle ages.* Malta: Midsea Books.

Wettinger, Godfrey & Michael Fsadni. 1968. *Peter caxaro's cantilena: A poem in medieval Maltese.* Malta: Self-published.

Chapter 3

Onset clusters, syllable structure and syllabification in Maltese

Luke Galea
University of Malta

Adam Ussishkin
University of Arizona

This chapter aims to describe syllable structure and the phonotactic constraints on onset consonants in Standard Maltese. The current work is based on the phonetic and phonological description of Maltese in Azzopardi (1981) and Borg & Azzopardi-Alexander (1997). The phonological account provided here, however, is grounded in an Onset-Rhyme model. Furthermore, the phonotactics of Maltese are described in terms of sonority. After establishing the nature of onset consonants in Maltese, we address the process of syllabification in Maltese.

1 Maltese syllable structure

Before describing the possible syllable structures in Maltese, it is important to highlight that Maltese monosyllables are restricted by complementary quantity. This means that in monosyllabic words (cf. Table 1), short vowels are either followed by a geminate (G) or by a consonant cluster (CC), and long vowels are followed by a single consonant but never by a geminate (Azzopardi-Alexander 2002). This does not mean that open syllables in Maltese do not occur; however, they are not restricted by quantity.

Therefore, in Maltese the syllable types V:G and V:CC do not occur due to this complimentary quantity restriction, and as a result are not found in syllable structures with added onsets or codas.

Luke Galea & Adam Ussishkin. Onset clusters, syllable structure and syllabification in Maltese. In Patrizia Paggio & Albert Gatt (eds.), *The languages of Malta*, 55–79. Berlin: Language Science Press. DOI:10.5281/zenodo.1181789

Table 1: Complementary quantity in Maltese[1]

CVG	[hɐpp]	*ħabb*	'he loved'
CVCC	[tɐlp]	*talb*	'prayer'
CV:C	[kɐːp]	*kap*	'boss'

Azzopardi (1981) and Borg & Azzopardi-Alexander (1997) present the possible syllable types in Maltese. They argue that the minimal syllable requirement is a vowel. The maximum number of onset consonants is three and the maximum number of coda consonants is two. Thus, a maximal Maltese syllable would have the shape (C)(C)(C)V(C)(C).

A clearer picture of the possible syllable structure of Maltese is presented in (Camilleri 2014: 48), who discusses syllable structures that occur as monosyllables and within word forms. We extend Camilleri (2014)'s list of possible syllable structures, adding additional structures to that list, in order to provide an exhaustive list (cf. Table 2) of the possible syllable structures (both as monosyllables and within word forms). Therefore, the possible syllable structures listed in Table 2 are based on Azzopardi (1981), Borg & Azzopardi-Alexander (1997) and Camilleri (2014). What is presented in this chapter is a first attempt at fully capturing the possible syllabic structures (both onsets and codas) in Maltese (some of this work appears in Galea 2016). However, our focus in this paper is on onsets, and the description in Table 2 is split into four categories: 1) vowel-initial syllable structures: *V-initial*, 2) one-consonant onset syllable structures: *C-initial*, 3) two consonant onset syllable structures: *CC-initial* and 4) three consonant onset syllable structures: *CCC-initial* to show the syllabic nature of onsets in Maltese. A − in Table 2 refers to forms that do not occur as either monosyllables or within-word forms.

---

[1]As noted by a reviewer, some non-standard varieties might have different forms. Furthermore, traditionally the digraph 'gh' in Maltese is linked to vowel lengthening (as discussed in Azzopardi 1981). However, a thorough phonetic/phonological study on this has not been carried out.

Table 2: Possible syllable types and onset distribution in Maltese

Initial	Syllable type	Monosyllable	Within-word forms
V	V[2]	[ʊ] *hu* 'he'	[ʊ.hut] *uħud* 'some'
	VG	[ɔmm] *omm* 'mother'	—
	VCC	[ɛlf] *elf* 'thousand'	—
	VCCC[3]	[ɪntʃ] *int=x* you.2sg/2pl=neg 'aren't you'	—
	V:C	[ɐ:f] *af* know.3sg 'know'	[ɐ:f.sɐ] *għafsa* 'a squeeze'
	V: (e.g., V:CVC)	—	[ɛ:.mɛs] *għemeż* wink.3sgm.perf 'he winked'
	VC (e.g., VC.CVC)	—	[ɔr.bɔt] *orbot* 'tie (imp.)'

---

[2]This category (V) is problematic as it is not clear whether such a monosyllable exists as an autonomous stress bearing unit or not. Furthermore, the language does not provide many examples of this type, which might add to its questionable status.

[3]There is a lack of morpheme-internal triconsonantal codas and the cluster spans two morphemes.

C	CV	[lɛ] *le* 'no'	[lɛ.fɐʔ] *lefaq* 'he sobbed'
	CV:	[dʒɪ:] *ġie* 'he came'	[dʒɪ:.li] *ġieli* 'sometimes'
	CVW	[rɐw][4] *raw* 'they saw'	[rɐw.kɔm] *rawkom* 'they saw you'
	CVC	—	[hɐz.bɛt] *ħasbet* 'she thought'
	CV:C	[tɐ:f] *taf* 'she knows'	[tɐ:f.nɐ] *tafna* 'she knows us'
	CVG	[hɐpp] *ħabb* 'he loved'	[tɪn.hɐpp] *tinħabb* 'to be loved'
	CVGC	[zɐmmʃ] *żammx* 'he didn't hold'	[ɪn.zɐmmʃ] *inżammx* 'it wasn't held'
	CVCC	[bɐrt] *bard* 'cold'	[kɐz.bɐrt] *kasbart* 'I disgraced'
	CVCCC	[mɔrtʃ] *mortx* 'didn't go'	—

---

[4]There is disagreement in the literature on whether this vowel is a long vowel or not (see Borg 1986:231; and Camilleri 2014:48). However, neither of these studies investigated this issue empirically and we suggest that this would be the best way of resolving the issue.

CC	CCV	[blɐ]	[stɐ.hɐ]
		bla	*staħa*
		'without'	'he was shy'
	CCV:	[kjuː]	[kpɪː.pɛl]
		kju	*kpiepel* 'hats'
		'queue'	
	CCVW	[tfɛw]	[tfɛw.kɔm]
		tfew	*tfewkom*
		'they switched sth off'	'they outshone you'
	CCVC	—	[ftɐh.tʊ]
			ftaħtu
			'I opened it'
	CCV:C	[frɐːk]	[kniːs.jɐ]
		frak	*knisja*
		'crumbs'	'church'
	CCVG	[frɔtt]	[ʊ.zuː.frʊtt]
		frott	*użufrutt*
		'fruit'	'usufruct'
	CCVGʃ[5]	[ʔbɐttʃ]	[ɪn.ʔbɐttʃ]
		qbatx	*inqbadtx*
		'didn't catch'	'I didn't get caught'
	CCVCC	[frɪsk]	—
		frisk	
		'fresh'	
	CCVCCC	[hsɪltʃ]	[ɪn.hsɪltʃ]
		ħsiltx	*inħsiltx*
		'didn't wash'	'I didn't shower'

---

[5] This syllable structure can only occur through morphological inflection, through the addition of the negative suffix /-ʃ/.

CCC	CCCV:	[strɔ:]	[zbrɐ:.nɐ]
		straw	*żbrana*
		'straw'	'he exploded'
	CCCVW	[ʃtrɐw]	[ʃtrɐw.nɐ]
		xtraw	*xtrawna*
		'they bought'	'they bought us'
	CCCVC	—	[strɐm.bɐ]
			stramba
			'odd (fem.)'
	CCCV:C	[sptɐ:r]	—
		sptar	
		'hospital'	
	CCCVCC	[strɐmp]	—
		stramb	
		'odd (m)'	
	CCCVG	[ftrɐkk]	—
		f'trakk	
		'in a truck'	

Focusing on the structures CVW, CCVW and CCCVW, Camilleri (2014) claims that the vowel before syllable- or word-final glides (/w, j/) is always a short vowel. Therefore, following Camilleri's (2014) description, this creates the possible syllable structures CVC, CCVC, CCCVC, where the coda consonant is always a glide. We do not fully commit to Camilleri's (2014) claim because sequences such as [ɐw], [ɛw], [ɐj] and so on are what Azzopardi (1981) and Borg & Azzopardi-Alexander (1997) consider to be diphthongs. Therefore, the rhyme of the syllable is a vowel plus a transition to another vowel or a glide (cf. Azzopardi 1981). Bearing this in mind, it is not clear whether the vowel before is short or not. Since there are no empirical studies that show the phonetic realizations of diphthongs in Maltese, we consider these structures to be of the type C(C)(C)VW, where W stands for the glides /w, j/. A glide is part of the nucleus, because if it were a separate consonant we would predict vowel lengthening since a short vowel plus a coda consonant would violate the bimoraic minimum on syllable nuclei (e.g., compare [tɐw] *taw* 'they gave' and [rɐ:t] *rat* 'she saw').

The list of possible syllable structures presented in Table 2 differ from those proposed by Camilleri (2014). Camilleri (2014) lists the syllable structure CCV: as occurring only as a within-word form but not as a monosyllable. Camilleri (2014) illustrated this type through the word /kni:sja/ *knisja* 'church'. We disagree with this description as following the syllabification process in Maltese (which is discussed in §2), the /s/ serves as a coda to the previous syllable (and not as an onset to the following syllable); therefore, the syllable structure of the word /kni:sja/ *knisja* is not CCV:.CCV but CCV:C.CV. In the list in Table 2, we provide the example /kju:/ *kju* 'queue' (another possible example is /blu:/ *blu* 'blue'), which show that that the structure CCV: can also occur as a monosyllable.[6]

Two structures are not reported by Camilleri (2014). First, the structure CCCV: in /strɔ:/ *straw* 'straw' occurs both as a monosyllable and within words. Secondly, a long vowel, V:, can occur as a syllable within words, e.g., /ɛː/ in /ɛː.mɛs/ *għemeż* 'he winked' or /ɐ:/ in /ɐ:.fɐs/ *għafas* 'he pressed'. In (C)CVGC, the C following the geminate is restricted to the occurrence of the morpheme /-ʃ/ used for negation as in the examples: [ɪn.**zɐmm**ʃ] *inżammx* 'it was not held' and [ɪn.**ʔbɐtt**ʃ] *inqbadtx* 'I didn't get caught', or /-s, -z/ as a suffix for English-origin plurals; e.g., /klɐpps/ *clubs* 'clubs'. Furthermore, the syllable type C(C)VCCC as in the examples (from Table 2) [mɔrtʃ] *mortx* 'I didn't go' and [ħsɪltʃ] *ħsiltx* 'I didn't wash' (and other words which include these syllables) are limited to the 1st person and 2nd person negative inflected forms.

In the following subsections, we describe the phonotactic constraints of each syllable structure type from Table 2 in detail. Specifically, we address both phonetic and phonological issues of each syllable structure type. The description of the permissible onset consonants is achieved through the principles of sonority (for codas cf. Galea 2016). In this work, we adopt the sonority scale below. Furthermore, we also adopt Selkirk's Sonority Sequencing Principle (Selkirk 1984), which requires a sonority rise between a left-margin constituent and the syllable peak:

(1)   Vowels   > glides   > sonorants   > obstruents
      High Sonority   Low Sonority

1.1 The nucleus

All vowels in Maltese can serve as a syllable nucleus. As a matter of fact, the language allows vowels on their own to occur as a permissible syllable. This is

---

[6]Nonetheless, these are open empirical questions, which should be investigated in production studies.

restricted to a few words, typically function words and often unstressed, such as /ɪ/ *hi* 'she', /ʊ/ *hu* 'he' or *u* 'and', some exclamations such as /ɔ:/ 'oh', but also, less frequently, content words such as /ɐ:/ 'confusion'.

1.2 Vowel-initial syllable structures

It is debatable whether Maltese allows onsetless syllables. The phonetic realization of onsetless syllables shows that vowels are variably preceded by an epenthetic glottal stop, which constitutes a syllable onset; e.g., /ʊ/ → [ʔʊ] *hu* 'he' (Azzopardi 1981). As a matter of fact, Borg & Azzopardi-Alexander (1997) claim that this insertion is more likely to happen in utterance-initial or in post-pause position.[7] This might suggest that the preferred syllable structure in Maltese requires onsets (i.e., .CV...), and this type of epenthesis occurs in spoken Arabic dialects and dialects of English and German. To illustrate, syllables in Arabic always require an onset. If syllables lack an onset, a glottal stop is inserted (cf. Standard Arabic, Egyptian Arabic: Gadoua (2000); Cairene Arabic: Wiltshire (1998); Youssef (2013)). The preceding context triggers the insertion of a glottal stop; Wiltshire (1998) argued that when the definite article is in phrase-initial position an epenthetic glottal stop is always inserted, as in [ʔil.mu.dar.ris] 'the teacher'. This observation is also put forward by Youssef (2013), who claimed that in Cairene Arabic, the definite article /il/ is always preceded by an epenthetic glottal stop: [ʔil].

Historically, Maltese had a voiced pharyngeal approximant [ʕ], which is no longer present in current Maltese though it is represented in the orthography by the digraph <għ>. Borg (1997) and Brame (1972) argue that vowels adjacent to orthographic <għ> are lengthened, whereas Puech (1979) argues that this vowel duration is context-dependent. Hume et al. (2009) investigated this observation by recording two native speakers of Maltese. They investigated whether the vowels adjacent to <għ> are lengthened in a variety of positions within the word. Focusing on absolute phrase-initial position, Hume et al. (2009) argued that there is increased vowel duration in the <għ> context in monosyllabic words; e.g., in a minimal pair such as [ɐ:tt] *għadd* 'he counted' and [ɐtt] *att* 'act', they showed that the duration of the vowel /ɐ/ is longer in the <għ> context. Nonetheless, even though they had a number of vowel-initial syllables in their corpus, Hume et al. (2009) did not report whether there were any glottal stop insertions before the vowel.

---

[7] Galea (2016) provides similar results to this claim. Some speakers seem to insert a glottal stop before the epenthetic vowel before word-initial geminates. This might suggest that, at least for some speakers, glottal stops before vowels are required by their phonology.

To sum up, potentially underlyingly vowel-initial syllables in Maltese might actually be phonetically realized as .CV..., where the C is an epenthetic glottal stop. If this is true, there are no truly vowel-initial syllables in the language, because the epenthetic glottal stop serves as an onset to a vowel-initial syllable. Words that have orthographic <għ> or <h> in absolute initial position tend to have longer adjacent vowels. However, only the durations of vowels adjacent to <għ> have been investigated empirically (Hume et al. 2009). Furthermore, <għ>-initial words would be preceded by a glottal stop. Related evidence to this can be found in orthography where <għ>-initial words are occasionally misspelled by literate native speakers with the letter <q> (the grapheme used to represent glottal stop); e.g., <qandi> instead of <għandi> 'I have'. This evidence shows that some speakers consider that the glottal stop is part of the phonology of these words. However, production studies need to be carried out to fully understand this phenomenon.

1.3 Permissible onsets in Maltese

Almost all consonants in the inventory of Maltese constitute permissible single onsets; examples are listed in Table 3 below. The status of the phone /ʒ/ in Maltese is unclear (cf. Borg & Azzopardi-Alexander 1997). It occurs in some loan words such as [tɛlɛvɪʒɪn] *televixin* 'television', where the voiced post-alveolar fricative constitutes an onset to the final syllable. Furthermore, it can occur as part of onset clusters such as [ʒbiːɐ][8] *xbiha* 'image'; however, there are no monosyllabic words which have [ʒ] as a single onset consonant. In all of the examples presented in Table 3, there are no sonority violations in the onset consonant. The structure conforms to the SSP, since a single consonant is always less sonorous than a vowel as the nucleus.

1.4 Permissible onset clusters in Maltese

It is generally claimed that the larger the distance in sonority between the first consonant (C_1) and the second consonant (C_2) in a consonant cluster, the more well-formed the onset cluster is (Topintzi 2011). Nonetheless, clusters having the same or similar sonority are allowed to occur in sequence in a number of languages, such as Russian and Bulgarian. This is referred to as the *Minimum Sonority Distance* principle (cf. Selkirk 1984; Levin 1985; Parker 2011). Maltese is one

---

[8]This [ʒ] is only voiced because it is C_1 in a CC onset in which C_2 is voiced, thus triggering regressive voicing assimilation, which operates in Maltese onset clusters and is discussed later on this section.

Table 3: Simple onsets in Maltese

Stops	[pɐːɹ] *par* 'pair' [bɐːɹ] *bar* 'bar' [tɐːɹ] *tar* 'he flew' [dɐːɹ] *dar/dahar* 'back/house' [kɐːp] *kap* 'head of an institution' [gɔst] *gost* 'fun' [ʔɐːm] *qam* 'he woke up'
Fricatives	[fɐːɹ] *far* 'it overflowed' [vɐːɹɐ] *vara* 'statue' [sɐːɹ] *sar* 'it became' [zɐːɹ] *żar* 'he visited' [ʃɐːɹ] *xahar/xagħar* 'month/hair' [ħɐll] *ħall* 'vinegar/ he undid (a knot)'
Affricates	[tʃɐːɹ] *ċar* 'clear' [dʒɐːɹ] *ġar* 'neighbour' [tsɔkk] *zokk* 'branch' [dzɔːnɐ] *żona* 'zone'[9]
Nasals	[mɐːɹ] *mar* 'he went' [nɐːɹ] *nar* 'fire'
Glides	[wɐʔt] *waqt* 'during' [juːm] *jum* 'day'
Liquids	[lɐːt] *lat* 'point of view' [rɐːt] *rat* 'she saw'

of the languages that allows clusters with minimum sonority distance. To compare, Spanish, for example, only allows onset clusters which are made up of an obstruent and liquid; e.g., /kr/ in /krus/ 'cross' (Baertsch 2002), which means that onset clusters in Spanish have a larger distance in sonority between C_1 (e.g., /k/) and C_2 (e.g., /r/). On the other hand, languages such as Russian, Bulgarian and Leti allow onset clusters containing consonants which are closer on the sonority scale; e.g., /kn/ in Russian /kniga/ 'book'. However, Parker (2011: 1168) claims that

---

[9]For some speakers this is pronounced as [zɔːnɐ].

"if a language permits clusters with a lower sonority distance, it allows clusters of all higher distances as well" but not the other way around, which is the case in Maltese. Clusters that have minimum sonority distance give rise to plateaus. Sonority plateaus arise when there is no difference in sonority between the members of a consonant cluster (such as in Maltese /tp/ in /tpɛjjɛp/ 'you/she smokes' or /sf/ in /sfɔrts/ 'effort'). The SSP states that there must be one peak from the onset to the syllable nucleus; thus, plateaus in the onset violate the SSP. Blevins (1995), following Jespersen (1904)'s version of the SSP, accounts for such plateaus, whereas other versions of the SSP do not (e.g. Selkirk 1984; Clements 1990; Zec 2007). A syllable with an onset cluster such as /kl/ in /klɪːm/ *kliem* 'kliem' or /pr/ in /prɛtsts/ *prezz* 'price' has a higher sonority distance, and this leads to a rising sonority profile from the onset to the syllable nucleus. In comparison, consonant clusters such /kt/ in /ktɪːb/ *ktieb* 'book' or /dv/ in /dvɐljɐ/ *dvalja* 'table cloth' lead to a sonority plateau and, thus, a possible violation of the SSP.

In addition to allowing onset consonant clusters with very 'flat sonority' (Zec 2007), Maltese also places a constraint on word-initial tautosyllabic consonant clusters: they are restricted by a voicing assimilation rule which operates regressively. Therefore, consonant clusters are both voiced or both voiceless: e.g., [bdɛw] *bdew* 'we started'; [pkɪːt] *bkiet* 'she cried'.

To give an example of the range of possible clusters from low sonority distance to high sonority distance, we show the spectrum of possible consonant clusters beginning with /p/ in Table 4. The permissible clusters start from those that have a minimum sonority distance (e.g., /pt/, /pk/), which lead to a sonority plateau, which are followed by clusters that have a higher sonority distance (e.g., /pr/ and /pj/).

(2) lists some examples of minimum distance sonority clusters of voiced consonant clusters:

(2)   Voiced consonant clusters
    a. /bd/ in /bdiːl/ bdil 'change'
    b. /dg/ in /dgɔrr/ tgorr 'you complain'
    c. /zb/ in /zbiːp/ żbib 'raisins'

In the case of higher sonority distance onset clusters, Maltese allows: Obstruent + Nasal, Obstruent + Liquid, Obstruent + Glide, as in (3).

Table 4: Permissible /p/-initial clusters

MSD	Cluster	Example	Sonority
Low	/pt/	[ptɐ:.lɐ] btala 'holiday'	
	/pk/	[pkɛw] bkew 'they cried'	Plateau
	/pʔ/	[pʔɐjt] bqajt 'I stayed'	
	/ptʃ/	[ptʃɛj.jɛtʃ] bċejjeċ 'pieces'	
	/pts/	[ptsɪ:.tsɛn] bżieżen 'bread rolls'	
	/ps/	[psɐrt] bsart 'I guessed'	
	/pf/[10]	[pfɔr.mɐ] b'forma 'with a shape'	
	/pʃ/	[pʃɐ:.rɐ] bxara 'announcement'	
	/ph/	[phɐ:l] bħal 'like'	
	/pn/	[pnɪ:.tsɛl] pniezel 'brushes'	
	/pl/	[plɐt:] platt 'plate'	
	/pr/	[prɛts:] prezz 'price'	
	/pw/	[pwɪ:.nɪ] pwieni 'pains'	Increase
High	/pj/	[pjɐ:n] pjan 'plan'	

(3) Examples of higher sonority distance clusters

    a. Obstruent + Nasal
       /tn/ in /tnɛjn/ tnejn 'two'
       /zm/ in /zmɪ:n/ żmien 'time'

    b. Obstruent + Liquid
       /dl/ in /dlɐ:m/ dlam 'darkness'
       /fr/ in /frɐ:r/ Frar 'February'

    c. Obstruent + Glide
       /ʔw/ in /ʔwɪ:l/ qwiel 'idioms'
       /vj/ in /vjɐtʃtʃ/ vjaġġ 'journey'

The voicing assimilation rule is not strictly respected in clusters beginning with /ʔ/ and /h/. When these consonants occur as C_1 in a CC consonant cluster, voicing assimilation is violated when C_2 is a voiced obstruent e.g., /ʔb/ in /ʔbi:l/ qbil 'agreement' and /hd/ in /hdu:t/ ħdud 'Sundays'. Even though the voicing

---

[10] Cluster /pf/ appears only in the case of the preposition b' before /f/. As one reviewer noted, this type of sonority profile is limited to morphologically complex examples (e.g., /fp/ in /fprɔtʃɛss/ f'proċess 'in process'

harmony is violated, the SSP is not; instead, this leads to a sonority plateau. In the opposite case, when a voiced obstruent is in C_1 position and /ʔ/or /h/ is in C_2 (e.g., /bʔ/ in /bʔɐjt/ *bqajt* 'I stayed', and /dh/ in /dhuːl/ *dħul* 'entrances'), such clusters lead to a sonority reversal. Borg & Azzopardi-Alexander (1997) claim that the frequency of consonant cluster onsets with /ʔ/ and /h/ + voiced obstruent (e.g., [hd]) is lower than that of CC onsets of /ʔ/ and /h/ + voiceless obstruent (e.g., [ht]). Furthermore, /ʔ/ and /h/ also cluster with consonants further up in the sonority scale as in (4):

(4) Consonant clusters with /ʔ/ and /h/ as C_1

    a. /ʔl/ in /ʔluːp/ *qlub* 'hearts'

    b. /ʔr/ in /ʔreːr/ *qrar* 'confession'

    c. /hm/ in /hmɐːr/ *ħmar* 'donkey'

    d. /hl/ in /hlɐːs/ *ħlas* 'payment'

1.5 Sibilant onset clusters

Maltese allows sibilant-initial onset clusters. To start with, Maltese permits sibilant-initial clusters which have a high sonority distance and do not violate the SSP as in (5).

(5) Sibilant onset clusters: high sonority distance

    a. /sr/ in /srɪːp/ *sriep* 'snakes'

    b. /zr/ in /zreːr/ *żrar* 'coarse aggregate used in concrete'

    c. /ʃm/ in /ʃmuːn/ *Xmun* 'Simon'

    d. /ʃl/ in /ʃlɔkk/ *Xlokk* 'south east'

    e. /zm/ in /zmɛrtʃ/ *żmerċ* 'awry'

In sibilant obstruent clusters, the voicing assimilation rule still applies in sibilant clusters as in (6).

(6) Sibilant onset clusters: Voicing assimilation

    a. /sk/ in /skuːr/ *skur* 'dark'

    b. /sp/ in /spɪss/ *spiss* 'often'

    c. /ʃt/ in /ʃtɐ:ʔ/ *xtaq* 'he wished'

    d. /ʃk/ in /ʃkɪːl/ *xkiel* 'obstacle'

    e. /zb/ in /zbɐll/ *żball* 'mistake'

    f. /zv/ in /zvɔːk/ *zvog* 'vent'

Clusters such as /sk sp st zb/ in (6), just like in English and Italian, pose a challenge to the Sonority Sequencing Principle since the sibilant is more sonorous than the stop (in the first five examples in (6)) and leads to a sonority plateau in /zv/.

The syllabification of sibilant initial clusters has been a long-standing debate in phonology. Numerous approaches have been proposed: approaches which span from the strictly phonological, such as Kaye (1992), to more experimental approaches such as Browman & Goldstein (1992). Experimental evidence suggests that there is not a universal solution to syllabification: in some languages, like English (Marin & Pouplier 2010), sibilant clusters pattern like non-sibilant clusters and are considered to be tautosyllabic, but in other cases such as Italian, sibilant-obstruent clusters, unlike obstruent-liquid clusters, are heterosyllabic (Hermes et al. 2013). In languages such as Moroccan Arabic, Tashlhiyt Berber and possibly Maltese, sibilant-initial clusters and obstruent-initial clusters are heterosyllabic (see Hermes et al. 2014: for a preliminary articulatory study).

1.6 Sonorant-initial clusters

Maltese has consonantal sequences that have a sonorant (/l m n r/) as C_1. Maltese has combinations of sonorant + stop (e.g., /lp/, /md/, /nt/, /rk/), sonorant + fricative (e.g., /ls/, /ms/, /nz/, /rv/), sonorant + glottal (e.g., /mʔ/ and /nh/) sequences. However, such sequences violate the SSP, as C_1 is more sonorous than C_2. Also, such clusters are examples of sonority reversals, where C_1 is more sonorant than C_2. In order to avoid this sonority reversal one of two strategies can be employed in Maltese. First, Azzopardi (1981) proposes that the realization of sonorants as C_1 in a consonant sequence could be syllabic. Thus, /mʔɐːr/ surfaces as [m̩ .ʔɐːr] *mqar* 'at least'. This realization does not violate the SSP because a syllabic consonant constitutes its own syllable nucleus. The other strategy is to insert a vocalic element of [ɪ]-like quality before the sonorant consonant: [ɪm.ʔɐːr]. In this case, the vowel [ɪ] serves as a syllable nucleus, which is followed by the sonorant [m], which serves as coda to the first syllable. In addition, it is possible for a prothetic glottal stop to be inserted before the vocalic element. If this glottal stop were represented in the phonological structure, then this would constitute a syllable onset. More examples of sonorant-initial clusters are presented in (7):

(7)   Realization of sonorant-initial clusters

    a.   /lp/ → [ɪl.puːp] or [ʔɪl.puːp] or [l̩.puːp] lpup 'wolves'

    b.   /md/ → [ɪm.diː.nɐ] or [ʔɪm.diː.nɐ] or [m̩.diː.nɐ] Mdina 'Mdina (name of town)'

c. /nz/ → [ɪn.ziːt] or [ʔɪn.ziːt] or [n̩.ziːt] nżied 'I add'

d. /rv/ → [ɪr.vɛll] or [ʔɪr.vɛll] or [r̩.vɛll] rvell 'rebellion'

e. /mh/ → [ɪm.ħeːr] or [ʔɪm.ħeːr] or [m̩.ħeːr] mħar 'clams'

Regardless of which strategy is employed, sonorant-initial clusters in Maltese are never tautosyllabic, but rather are always heterosyllabic.

1.7 CCC-initial clusters

As shown in Table 2, Maltese also allows for tri-consonantal word-initial clusters (abbreviated to CCC-initial). Borg & Azzopardi-Alexander (1997) show that the premitted combinations of consnants are very restricted. C_1 is usually a fricative (/s, ʃ, z/) or a bilabial stop (i.e., /p, b/). C_2 can be either an oral stop (i.e., /p, b, t, d, k, g/) or the fricative /f/. C_3 tends to be occupied by a sonorant but can be filled by any other consonants. It is important to note that voicing assimilation still applies in CCC-initial clusters. Furthermore, the prefixes /b-, p-/ 'with', /ʃ-/ 'what' and /f-/ 'in' can contribute to the creation of CCC-initial onsets. In Table 2, we provide the example [ftrɛkk] *f'trakk* 'in a truck', where the first consonant [f] is a prefix, leading to the triconsonantal cluster [.ftr...]. Additional examples of triconsonantal clusters in Maltese are provided in (8).

(8) CCC-initial

a. [stʔɐrr] stqarr 'he confessed'

b. [zbrɔffɐ] żbroffa 'he exploded'

c. [sptɐːr] sptar 'hospital'

2 Syllabification in Maltese

According to Borg & Azzopardi-Alexander (1997), polysyllabic words which have one consonant in medial position, such as CVCVC, are syllabified as CV.CVC, where the medial consonant constitutes a syllable onset to the following syllable, as in (9). This follows the Maximum Onset Principle (MOP) that a consonant flanked between two vowels is more likely to syllabify as an onset rather than a coda (cf. Kahn 1976).

(9) Syllable division of one medial consonant

a. [kɪ.sɛr] kiser 'he broke'

b. [mɪː.tʊ] mietu 'they died'

    c. [lɐ:.pɛs] lapes 'pencil'

    d. [tɪ.fɛl] tifel 'a boy'

In polysyllabic words with structures like CVCCV or CVCCVC, medial consonant sequences are not treated as consonant clusters as they tend to be syllabified
as the coda to the preceding syllable and the onset of the following syllable (cf.
Azzopardi 1981). Therefore, the medial cluster in a CVCCV word split across the
two syllables (CVC.CV); see (10) for examples.

(10)   Syllable division of medial consonant sequences

    a. [hɔl.mɐ] ħolma 'dream'

    b. [tɐh.fɛr] taħfer 'forgiveness'

    c. [ʃɔr.tɐ] xorta 'sameness'

    d. [tɔʔ.bɐ] toqba 'hole'

The same syllable division applies to word-medial geminates as shown in (11).

(11)   Syllable division of word-medial geminates

    a. [hɐf.fɛr] ħaffer 'he dug'

    b. [rɐt.tɐp] rattab 'he softened'

    c. [tɛl.lɛf] tellef 'he disrupted'

    d. [ʔɐtʃ.tʃɐt] qaċċat 'he removed'

Word-initial geminates occur due to morphophonological processes; however,
they are disallowed phonologically. Word-initial geminates tend to be preceded
by an epenthetic vowel, which in Maltese is a vowel of [ɪ]-like quality (see Galea
2016 for results on the production of the epenthetic vowel in different conditions
across a number of speakers). For this reason, we assume that word-initial geminates in Maltese, like word-medial geminates, are ambisyllabic, where the first
part of the geminate serves as a coda to the previous syllable and the second part
of the geminate serves as an onset to the following syllable. Therefore, underlying word-initial geminates surface as word-medial geminates and are syllabified
in the same way as word-medial geminates; see (12).

(12)   Syllable division for word-initial geminates

    a. /ppɐkkja/ → [ɪp.pɐk.kjɐ] ippakkja 'he packed'

    b. /ddɛffɛs/ → [ɪd.dɛf.fɛs] iddeffes 'he poked his nose in s.o. else's affairs'

    c. /ssɛbbɐh/ → [ɪs.sɛb.bɐh] issebbaħ 'he was beautified'

We argue that vowel epenthesis before word-initial geminates allows the syllabification of stray consonants (Itô 1986; 1989).

In the case of three-consonant sequences in word-medial position, Azzopardi (1981) proposed that the preferred syllabification of such sequences is as a consonant syllabified as a coda to the preceding syllable followed by a two-consonant onset cluster to the following syllable, as in (13).

(13) Syllabification of medial clusters

    a. [mɐh.frɐ] maħfra 'forgiveness'

    b. [mɪ.nɪs.trʊ] ministru 'minister'

It is also possible for such clusters to be syllabified in such a way that the first two consonants constitute a consonant cluster in coda position, and the third consonant constitutes a simple onset in coda position, as in (14).[11]

(14) Syllabification of medial clusters

    a. [jɐʔs.mʊ] jaqsmu 'they divide/share'

    b. [hlɪst.kɔm] ħlistkom 'I freed you (pl.)'

There might be a correlation between syllable boundary and morpheme boundary in examples like [hlɪst.kɔm] ħlistkom 'I freed you (pl.)', where the coda consonant cluster [st] belongs to the verb and the initial [k] is part of the clitic. Yet, this is not the case in [jɐʔs.mʊ][12] jaqsmu 'they divide/share', where the suffix -ʊ is not placed in a syllable of it own. It is possible that in cases where the morpheme has a CVC structure (such as /kɔm/ 'you (pl.)', such morphemes could constitute separate syllables. This suggests that morpheme boundaries are respected more than syllable boundaries, and as a result, this would lead to a division of a sequence of three consonants to CC.C.

2.1 Syllabification of sonorant-initial clusters and word-initial geminates

As previously described, sonorant-initial clusters and word-initial geminates in Maltese trigger vowel epenthesis in syllable-initial position (Azzopardi 1981; Borg & Azzopardi-Alexander 1997), as in (15).

---

[11]We acknowledge that this is highly speculative and the implications of our intuitions need to be emperically investigated.

[12]A counterexample of this is the 3F clitic [ɐ], as in [jɐʔ.sɐm.ɐ] jaqsamha 'he breaks her', where the morpheme constitutes a syllable on its own.

(15) Insertion before sonorant-initial clusters and word-initial geminates

    a. /mhɐːr/ → [ɪmhɐːr] imħar 'clams'

    b. /ʃʃɛjjɛr/ → [ɪʃʃɛjjɛr] ixxejjer 'you/she wave(s)'

Here, we discuss the role of the epenthetic vowel in the syllabification of sonorant-initial clusters and word-initial geminates. There seems to be a cross-linguistic consensus on the function of epenthetic vowels: they serve to repair input forms which do not meet a language's structural requirements (Hall 2011). Hall (2011) describes three ways in which epenthetic vowels surface. First, following Itô (1986; 1989) epenthesis allows the syllabification of stray consonants. Second, following Broselow (1982), epenthesis is triggered by a particular sequence of consonants. Finally, following Côté (2000), epenthesis is triggered by the need to make consonants perceptible. The case of epenthesis in word-initial position in Maltese falls into all three categories. Here, we describe how the epenthetic vowel in Maltese syllabifies stray consonants.

First, the location of the epenthetic vowel before sonorant-initial and word-initial geminates in Maltese is fixed: the epenthetic vowel always precedes a sonorant–initial consonant cluster (e.g., /nt/, /lt/, /ms/)[13] or word-initial geminate (e.g., /dd/, /vv/, /ss/). As the examples in Table 5 show, the epenthetic vowel is fixed both in position and also in quality as it always surfaces as a vowel of /ɪ/-like quality.

Table 5: Epenthetic vowel before sonorant-initial consonant clusters and word-initial geminates

Sonorant initial consonant clusters			Word-initial geminates		
/nfɐʔt/→[ɪn.fɐʔt]	*infaqt*	'I spent'	/ddɐhhal/→[ɪd.dɐh.hal]	*iddaħħal*	'to be inserted'
/rbɐht/→[ɪr.bɐht]	*irbaħt*	'I won'	/vvɔtɐ/→[ɪv.vɔː.ta]	*ivvota*	'to vote'

Unlike word-initial geminates and sonorant-initial clusters, obstruent-initial clusters do not trigger epenthesis. Obstruent + obstruent (e.g., /pt, bd, sf/) or obstruent + sonorant (e.g., /tl, km/) do not trigger epenthesis before the first consonant or between the two consonants. This is in contrast to other varieties of Arabic, which break up word-initial clusters by inserting an epenthetic vowel between C_1 and C_2 in the cluster (cf. Watson 2007; Kiparsky 2003). In addition there are other dialects in which the epenthetic vowel is before C_1, e.g., [ismiʕt] 'I heard' in Cyrenaic Arabic (cf. Mitchell 1960).[14]

---

[13]Unless such the sonorants are treated as syllabic.

[14]We would like to thank one of our reviewers for pointing out this reference.

Following the principle of Prosodic Licensing, which "requires all phonological units [to] belong to higher prosodic structure" (Itô 1986: 3), epenthesis allows the syllabification of otherwise unsyllabifiable consonants. Furthermore, the principle of Prosodic Licensing ensures that each segment in the phonological string is syllabified. Therefore, for syllabification to take place, segments must belong to higher prosodic structures such as syllables. Any segments that are not linked to syllables must be dealt with in order to satisfy Prosodic Licensing. Epenthesis can be explained through the syllabification of stray consonants as posited by Itô 1986; 1989. Following Itô's directionality of syllabification, we postulate that syllabification takes places from right to left. The process of syllabification in Maltese allows for Stray Epenthesis (Itô 1986), where stray consonants are syllabified precisely because a vowel is inserted, providing a new syllable for such consonants to be parsed by. Maltese, unlike Korean or Attic Greek, does not allow for Stray Erasure, where stray consonants are deleted from the phonological string. Evidence for this comes from production studies of word-initial geminates in Maltese, which shows that the duration of the geminate is longer than that of singletons (cf. Galea et al. 2015).

Therefore, the sonorant in sonorant-initial consonant clusters and the first part of the geminates in word-initial geminates trigger Stray Epenthesis (Itô 1986). These segments are not deleted but trigger epenthesis as all segments in a phonological string have to be syllabified. Following Stray Epenthesis, the sonorant in the consonant clusters (e.g., /lt/ in (16)) and the first part of the geminate (e.g., /ff/ in (17)) become the coda of a preceding syllable. The epenthetic vowel fills in the nucleus of the preceding syllable (cf. (17) below).

(16) Right-to-left syllabification of sonorant-initial clusters

    [ltɪːm]   ltiem 'orphan'

      .tɪːm

    *l.tɪːm

    ɪl.tɪːm

(17) Right-to-left syllabification of word-initial geminates

    [ɪffɪrmɐ]   ffirma 'to sign'

        .mɐ

      fɪr.mɐ

    *f.fɪr.mɐ

    ɪf.fɪr.mɐ

In addition, any of the prefixes that can be added to a verb serve as an onset to this added syllable (cf. Figure 1). For instance, the first person imperfect prefix

σ   σ   σ

O   R   O   R   O   R

N   C   N   C   N

n   ɪ   f   ɪ   r   m   ɐ

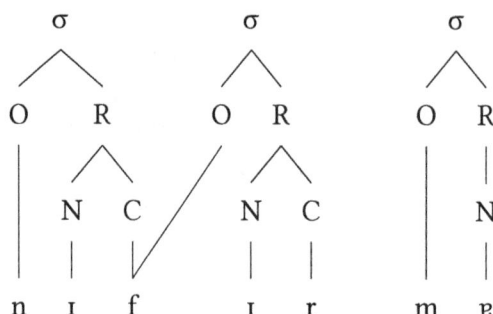

Figure 1: Syllabification of the inflected verb form [nɪffɪrmɐ] 'I sign'
In the representation of geminates, geminates are associated to the
coda and onset slots; and it is assumed that these double associations
represent the geminates. Such a representation is widespread within
the literature on geminates, and we follow Davis (2011) with respect
to conventions for geminate representations with respect to syllable
structure.

/n-/ can only be added before the epenthetic vowel, thus a form like *nffirma is
banned (cf. (18)). The result is a syllable with an epenthetic vowel as its nucleus
and the prefix as an onset.

(18)   Syllabification of imperfect prefix /n-/ 'n'
     [n-ffɪrmɐ]   niffirma 'I sign'
        .mɐ
      fɪr.mɐ
    nɪf.fɪr.mɐ

A reviewer points out that this rule does not explain why *inffirma is ruled
out given that in Maltese there is a comparable form *nfired* 'to be separated'.
However, Maltese syllable structure does not allow for a cluster made up of a
morphological prefix and a word-initial geminate (i.e., such as *inffirma); on the
other hand, it allows for a cluster made up of a morphological prefix and a sin-
gleton (such as *nfired* 'to be separate').

Following Nespor & Vogel (1986) we take this to be the domain of the prosodic
word as it consists of a stem (i.e., the verb) and a prefix which is added as a result
of morphological inflection (as in the case of *niffirma* in (20)) or derivation. This
is also reinforced by Selkirk (1996)'s proposal that the left and the right edges
of words coincide with the left and right edges of the prosodic word, which was
subsequently adopted for Maltese by Kiparsky (2011) and Wolf (2011). Therefore,
word-initial geminates which result due to a morphophonological process are
part of a single prosodic word, as in (19).

(19) Prosodic Word (PWd)

  a. [ɪffɪrmɐ]_{PWd}
  ffirma
  'to sign'

  b. [nɪffɪrmɐ]_{PWd}
  niffirma
  'I sign'

Furthermore, the application of Stray Epenthesis applies in phonological-initial position and when the previous word ends in a consonant (as in (20)):

(20) Syllabification of word-initial geminates
  [luːk.ɪv.vɔː.tɐ]
  Luke ivvota
  'Luke voted'

In cases where the word before sonorant-initial and word-initial geminates ends in a vowel, a number of strategies can be invoked. Hoberman & Aronoff (2003) claim that the prothetic vowel before word-initial geminates does not occur when the preceding word ends in a vowel. We claim that in such cases, we find cross-morpheme and cross-word boundary syllabification. When a previous word ends in a vowel, the stray consonant in the following word serves as a coda to that syllable, which results in cross-word syllabification, as in (21).

(21) Cross-word syllabification: word-initial geminates
  [.(ʔ)ɐn.dɐd.dɐħ.ħɐl.]
  għandha ddaħħal
  'she has to enter'

Another strategy is Stray Epenthesis, resulting in an inserted vowel before the word-initial geminate, as in (22).

(22) Across word syllabification: word-initial geminates
  [.(ʔ)ɐn.dɐ.ɪd.dɐħ.ħɐl.]
  għandha ddaħħal
  'she has to enter'

On the other hand, unlike sonorant-initial clusters or word-initial geminates, Stray Epenthesis does not operate with obstruent-initial consonant clusters. Obstruent-initial consonant clusters are tautosyllabic and the first consonant is not syllabified as the coda of a previous vowel-final word, as in (23).

(23) Onset clusters
[hɐf.nɐ.ptɪː.hɪ]
ħafna btieħi
'a lot of inner courtyards'

2.2 Summary

In this chapter, we have presented an overview of some of the key phenomena related to the phonetics and phonology of Maltese syllables. More concretely, we outlined the possible syllable structures that can occur as monosyllables and within words in Maltese. As a matter of fact, this can be directly compared with the possible syllable structures of some vareites of Arabic, Italian, and English (the languages from which Maltese originates). Therefore, we propose that a fruitful future study would involve comparing descriptions of syllable structures in Maltese and of the languages Maltese originates from.

This chapter also showed that the possibilities of onset clusters in Maltese are not very heavily restricted. Specifically, Maltese allows for both low sonority distance (e.g., /.pt.../) and high sonority onset clusters (e.g., /.tl.../). Moreover, in the low sonority distance onset clusters, Maltese permits sonority reversals and sonority plateaus. Therefore, even though the sonority framework was used to describe the possible clusters in Maltese, some problems remain. A thorough phonetic analysis using experimental techniques such as an articulography can shed light on the syllable affiliation and possible syllabification of such different clusters by looking at the gestural overlap and the timing of the gestures.

In comparing onset clusters and word-initial geminates, we have shown that word-initial geminates (e.g., /.pp.../) behave similarly to sonorant-initial clusters (e.g., /.lt.../), where they tend to be preceded by an epenthetic vowel. We argued that sonorant-initial clusters and word-initial geminates in Maltese are banned in the phonology and the presence of a preceding vocalic insertions leads to a process of resyllabification.

Acknowledgements

We would like to thank two anonymous reviewers for their comments. Thanks are also due to Marie Alexander, Albert Gatt, Michael Spagnol and Alexandra Vella for reading earlier versions of this paper.

References

Azzopardi, Marie. 1981. *The phonetics of Maltese: Some areas relevant to the Deaf.* University of Edinburgh dissertation.

Azzopardi-Alexander, Marie. 2002. The vowel system of Maltese: From production to perception. In *Proceedings of the 5th Conference of the Association Internationale de Dialectologie Arabe (AIDA)*, 321–333. Cádiz, Spain: AIDA.

Baertsch, Karen. 2002. *An optimality theoretic approach to syllable structure: The split margin hierarchy.* Indiana University dissertation.

Blevins, Juliette. 1995. The syllable in phonological theory. In John Goldsmith (ed.), *The handbook of phonological theory*, 206–244. Cambridge, Mass. & Oxford: Blackwell.

Borg, Albert & Marie Azzopardi-Alexander. 1997. *Maltese. (Descriptive grammars).* London & New York: Routledge.

Borg, Alexander. 1986. *Lehrbuch der Phonetik.* Leipzig, Germany: Teubner.

Borg, Alexander. 1997. Maltese phonology. In Alan S Kaye (ed.), *Phonologies of Asia and Africa.* 245–285. Winona Lake, IN: Eisenbrauns.

Brame, Michael K. 1972. On the abstractness of phonology: Maltese. In Michael K. Brame (ed.), *Contributions to generative phonology*, 22–61. Austin, TX: University of Texas Press.

Broselow, Ellen. 1982. On predicting the interaction of stress and epenthesis. *Glossa: An International Journal of Linguistics* 16(2). 115–132.

Browman, Catherine P & Louis Goldstein. 1992. Articulatory phonology: An overview. *Phonetica* 49(3-4). 155–180.

Camilleri, Maris. 2014. *The stem in inflectional verbal paradigms in Maltese.* University of Surrey dissertation.

Clements, George N. 1990. The role of the sonority cycle in core syllabification. *Papers in laboratory phonology* 1. 283–333.

Côté, Marie-Hélène. 2000. *Consonant cluster phonotactics: A perceptual approach.* Massachusetts Institute of Technology dissertation.

Davis, Stuart. 2011. Geminates. In Marc van Oostendorp, Colin J Ewen, Elizabeth Hume & Keren Rice (eds.), *Geminates*, 837–859. Oxford,UK: Wiley-Blackwell.

Gadoua, Abdulhamid Hadi. 2000. Consonant clusters in Quranic African. *Cahiers Linguistiques d'Ottawa* 28. 59–86.

Galea, Luke. 2016. *Syllable structure and gemination in maltese.* University of Cologne dissertation.

Galea, Luke, Anne Hermes, Albert Gatt & Martine Grice. 2015. Cues to gemination in word-initial position in Maltese. In *Proceedings of the 18th international congress on phonetic sciences (ICPhS)*. Glasgow,UK: University of Glasgow.

Hall, Nancy. 2011. Vowel epenthesis. In Marc van Oostendorp, Colin J. Ewen, Elizabeth Hume & Keren Rice (eds.), *The Blackwell companion to phonology*. 1576–1596. Oxford, UK: Wiley-Blackwell.

Hermes, Anne, Bastian Auris & Doris Mücke. 2014. In *Computational modelling for syllabification patterns in Tashlhiyt Berber and Maltese*. Vol. Proceedings of the 10th International Seminar on Speech Production, 186–189. Cologne, Germany: ISSP.

Hermes, Anne, Doris Mücke & Martine Grice. 2013. Gestural coordination of Italian word-initial clusters: The case of 'impure s'. *Phonology* 30(1). 1–25.

Hoberman, Robert D. & Mark Aronoff. 2003. The verbal morphology of Maltese. *Language Acquisition and Language Disorders* 28. 61–78.

Hume, Elizabeth, Jennifer Venditti, Alexandra Vella & Samantha Gett. 2009. Vowel duration and maltese 'għ'. In *Introducing Maltese Linguistics: Selected Papers from the 1st International Conference on Maltese Linguistics*. Amsterdam: John Benjamins Publishing.

Itô, Junko. 1986. *Syllable theory in prosodic phonology*. University of Massachusetts, Amherst dissertation.

Itô, Junko. 1989. A prosodic theory of epenthesis. *Natural Language and Linguistic Theory* 7(2). 217–259.

Jespersen, Otto. 1904. *Lehrbuch der Phonetik*. Leipzig, Germany: Teubner.

Kahn, Daniel. 1976. *Syllable-based generalizations in English phonology*. Cambridge, Mass.: Massachusetts Institute of Technology dissertation.

Kaye, Jonathan. 1992. Do you believe in magic? The story of s+ C sequences. *Working Papers in Linguistics and Phonetics* 2. 293–313.

Kiparsky, Paul. 2003. Syllables and moras in African. In Carline Fery & Ruben van de Vijver (eds.), *The syllable in Optimality Theory*, 147–182. Cambridge, UK: Cambridge University Press.

Kiparsky, Paul. 2011. *Chains or strata? The case of Maltese*. http://ling.auf.net/lingbuzz/001379.

Levin, Juliette. 1985. *A metrical theory of syllabicity*. Massachusetts Institute of Technology dissertation.

Marin, Stefania & Marianne Pouplier. 2010. Temporal organization of complex onsets and codas in American English: Testing the predictions of a gestural coupling model. *Motor Control* 14(3). 380–407.

Mitchell, Terence F. 1960. Prominence and syllabification in African. *Bulletin of the School of Oriental and African Studies* 23(2). 369–389.

Nespor, Marina & Irene Vogel. 1986. *Prosodic phonology.* Dordrecht, Holland: Foris Publications.

Parker, Steve. 2011. Sonority. In Marc van Oostendorp, Colin J Ewen, Elizabeth Hume & Keren Rice (eds.), *The Blackwell companion to phonology.* 1160–1184. Oxford, UK: Wiley-Blackwell.

Puech, Gilbert. 1979. *Les parlers Maltais: Essai de phonologie polylectale.* Université Lyon II dissertation.

Selkirk, Elisabeth. 1984. On the major class features and syllable theory. In Mark Aronoff & Richard T. Oerhle (eds.), *Language sound structure: Studies in phonology dedicated to Morris Halle by his teachers and students.* 107–113. Cambridge, MA: MIT Press.

Selkirk, Elisabeth. 1996. The prosodic structure of function words. In James L. Morgan & Katherine Demuth (eds.), *Signal to syntax: Bootstrapping from speech to grammar in early acquisition*, 214. Mahwah, NJ: Lawrence Erlbaum Associates.

Topintzi, Nina. 2011. Onsets. In Marc van Oostendorp, Colin J. Ewen, Elizabeth Hume & Keren Rice (eds.), *The Blackwell companion to phonology.* 1285–1308. Oxford, UK: Wiley-Blackwell.

Watson, Janet CE. 2007. *The phonology and morphology of African.* Oxford, UK: Oxford University Press.

Wiltshire, Caroline. 1998. Extending ALIGN constraints to new domains. *Linguistics* 36(3). 423–468.

Wolf, Matthew. 2011. *Cyclicity and non-cyclicity in Maltese: Local ordering of phonology and morphology in OT-CC.* Manuscript, Yale University.

Youssef, Islam. 2013. *Place assimilation in Arabic: Contrasts, features, and constraints.* Universitetet i Tromsø dissertation.

Zec, Draga. 2007. The syllable. In Paul De Lacey (ed.), *The Cambridge handbook of phonology*, 161–194. Cambridge, UK: Cambridge University Press.

Chapter 4

Prosodic and gestural marking of complement fronting in Maltese

Patrizia Paggio
University of Copenhagen and University of Malta

Luke Galea
University of Malta

Alexandra Vella
University of Malta

This paper deals with the use of complement fronting in a corpus of Maltese conversations. Four different kinds of constructions are distinguished based on the discourse status of the fronted complement: focus movement, topicalisation and two types of left dislocation. A discussion is carried out of the ways in which suprasegmental features, both in terms of prosody and gestures, underpin the discourse functions of the four construction types. Our findings show that a falling pitch accent is nearly always present on the fronted complement, and that there is a tendency for gestures to accompany this same complement. We also show that the four construction types can be ordered on the basis of suprasegmental complexity with focus movement as the least complex, followed by topicalisation, and finally both types of left dislocation as the most complex.

1 Introduction

Maltese is often characterised as a language in which word order is relatively free, and largely determined by information structure rather than grammar constraints. The option of placing a sentence complement sentence-initially, in other words fronting it, is one of the possibilities available to Maltese speakers to mark this complement with respect to its discourse and information structure status.

/l\l Patrizia Paggio, Luke Galea & Alexandra Vella. Prosodic and gestural marking of complement fronting in Maltese. In Patrizia Paggio & Albert Gatt (eds.), *The languages of Malta*, 81–116. Berlin: Language Science Press.
DOI:10.5281/zenodo.1181805

Patrizia Paggio, Luke Galea & Alexandra Vella

In this paper, we investigate the use of complement fronting in a corpus of Maltese conversations. Based on the different types of discourse status carried by the fronted complement in context, we posit four different kinds of constructions. We then analyse the prosodic contours of the examples as well as the gestures produced by the speakers in conjunction with the fronted complement. Our aim is to show how suprasegmental features, such as prosodic and gestural features, underpin the discourse functions of the four construction types.

To our knowledge, this is the first study of complement fronting in Maltese building on empirical multimodal data, in other words the first study using non-constructed data which allow us to study this phenomenon as it occurs in real conversations, and to include gestural features in the analysis.

It was in fact the availability of the conversational multimodal data, which will be described below, and the initial observation that gestures seemed to be very prominent in conjunction with fronted constituents in those data, which provided the motivation for this study. It is a generally accepted generalisation that hand gestures, when they occur, are temporally aligned with the main sentence accent (Kendon 1980; McNeill 1992; Loehr 2004; Alahverdzhieva & Lascarides 2010), which is in turn associated with sentence focus (Lambrecht 1994; Vallduví & Engdahl 1995). However, we are not aware of any previous attempt at enriching this body of work with knowledge of how gestures may be used in conjunction with complement fronting, and their relation to prosodic features in these constructions.

The structure of the paper is as follows. In §2 we define complement fronting and give an overview of the literature on relevant constructions mostly based on a discussion of English examples. Based on the literature, we distinguish a number of different constructions all involving complement fronting, i.e. topicalisation, focus movement, and two types of left dislocation. In §3 we give an account of previous studies of this phenomenon in Maltese, and explain how the examples discussed in these studies fit the different constructions we are considering. We then describe our data in §4, in particular how the data have been annotated from the point of view of prosody, gestures, and discourse status. We also provide some counts of the annotated categories for each annotation level. §5 presents the results, both in terms of quantitative analyses and qualitative discussions of chosen examples. The two different analysis methods serve different purposes. While frequency counts are presented to make generalisations about how different features are represented in the different constructions, qualitative descriptions and discussions of a choice of representative examples are intended to offer a more detailed understanding of the data. Finally, §6 contains the conclusion.

2 Complement fronting

Complement fronting is a syntactic mechanism whereby a non-subject constituent[1] is placed *sentence-initially* out of its canonical position, and thereby acquires a special status in terms of the information structure of the sentence. An example from English is the song title in example (1a), where the fronted object is enclosed in square brackets, and the canonical object position is indicated by an underscore. The non-fronted counterpart of the same sentence is shown in (1b).

(1) a. [*This one thing*] *I know* ___.
     b. *I know this one thing.*

The term *topicalisation* has often been used to refer to this construction at least in English, see e.g. Lambrecht (1994), based on the fact that the initial position in a sentence is often occupied by the sentence topic.[2] However, in terms of information packaging this syntactic structure corresponds to at least two different constructions. One is topicalisation proper, in which the fronted complement indeed corresponds to the sentence topic, while the rest of the sentence predicates new information about the complement. The other is a different construction in which the fronted complement corresponds to the focus of the sentence rather than its topic. The latter construction has been called *focus topicalisation* (Gundel 1974), *focus movement* (Prince 1981), *focus preposing* (Vallduví 1992; Ward 1996), and *linksrhematisierung* (Stempel 1981). In addition to being different from the point of view of information packaging, in English the two constructions are also associated with different prosodic contours (Chafe 1976), in that topicalisation exhibits two focal accents, and focus movement[3] only one. Compare sentences (2a) and (2b) below, where small caps have been added to the phrases that receive focal accent[4].

---

[1]The subject of a sentence can also be fronted in conjunction with left dislocation, as will be discussed further on. The same is also possible with subject extraction as in 'This I hope will never happen'. The focus of this paper is, however, on complement fronting.

[2]We follow here Lambrecht (1994) and many others in understanding *topic* as that part of the sentence-presupposed information which the rest of the sentence predicates something about. According to the same framework, *focus* is defined as the non-presupposed, new part of the sentence.

[3]From here on, we will use the term *focus movement* to refer to the construction in which the fronted complement corresponds to the focus of the sentence. However, we are not hereby assuming a transformational approach, according to which the complement would be base-generated in one position and moved to the front.

[4]In (2b), small caps are exactly as in the original source. In (2a), on the contrary, they were added. Prince uses a graphical notation showing the FALL FALL contour characteristic of topicalisation constructions in English.

(2) a. (Prince 1981: 251)

  STARDUST MEMORIES I saw YESTERDAY.

  b. (Lambrecht 1994: 295)

  FIFTY-SIX HUNDRED DOLLARS *we raised yesterday.*

The two constructions are also different in terms of their pragmatic function. The main pragmatic function of topicalised constructions in English is to mark a partially-ordered set relation, or *poset* relation, between the denotation of the topicalised complement and a previously evoked discourse entity (Prince 1981). New information about this entity is predicated in the open proposition corresponding to the rest of the sentence. In (2a), for example, *Stardust memories* is contrasted with other films and *yesterday* contributes the new, focal information. In focus movement, on the other hand, the denotation of the fronted complement is discourse-new information, and it corresponds in fact to a new attribute assigned to an otherwise salient referent (here, the amount of money raised).

In addition to topicalisation and focus movement, a third construction type needs to be mentioned because it will be relevant to our discussion of complement fronting in Maltese. This is *left dislocation*, which in English and other languages is distinguished from topicalisation and focus movement both in syntactic and pragmatic terms. Syntactically, the difference consists in the fact that the fronted constituent (often co-referential with the subject of the sentence), is resumed by a pronoun that occurs in the canonical position this constituent would have in the non-dislocated counterpart of the sentence. Even though left dislocation often involves the detachment of a subject, complement dislocation is also possible, as shown by the following example (coindexation indices are ours):

(3) Gregory & Michaelis 2001: 27

  [*Smiley Burnette*]$_i$, *I don't remember if you were old enough to remember* [*him*]$_i$.

According to some authors (Lambrecht 2001; Gregory & Michaelis 2001), the main pragmatic function of left dislocation is to promote a discourse-new referent to topic status. Since the initial position in a sentence, however, is 'reserved' for topical information, the expression denoting the discourse-new referent is detached from the rest of the sentence by means of syntactic as well as prosodic means. The rest of the sentence contains a pronoun that is coreferential with the dislocated constituent, and in fact if this constituent is dropped, the sentence is still well-formed. Geluykens (1992) describes left dislocation as an interactional device for introducing referents. In his analysis, the left dislocated expression is a complete move which calls for acknowledgement from the listener, as shown by the fact that it is often associated with a falling tone, and followed by a prosodic boundary and a pause. However, another type of left dislocation has also been described (Prince 1997; Geluykens 1992; Gregory & Michaelis 2001) where the dislocated object involves a *poset* relation, similarly to what happens in topicalisation constructions.

Lambrecht (2001) notes that a dislocated constituent may also be coindexed with an affix in Romance, Bantu and, interestingly for the present study, Semitic languages. He quotes the following example from Classical Arabic, in which the clitic pronoun *hu* refers back to *Halid* in the initial sentence position (the glossing of the example – including the separation into morphemes – is our adaptation of the original to the conventions used here):

(4)   Classical Arabic (Moutaouakil 1989: 109)
      Halid-un,   qābal-tu-hu   l-yawm-a
      Halid.NOM met.1SG>3SG the-day.ACC

      'Halid, I met him today.'

In Moutaouakil's original account, the fronted complement is categorised as being the *theme*, which the author describes as a predication-external pragmatic function, to be distinguished from topic, which is predication-internal.

3 Complement fronting in Maltese

The literature on complement fronting in Maltese is relatively sparse. Borg & Azzopardi-Alexander (2009) give an account of topicalisation, which they describe as a process whereby constituents are moved to the leftmost initial position in the sentence, away from their canonical position. One of the examples they give is in (5),[5] where *il-ġurdien* 'the mouse' is fronted, as opposed to what the same authors call "an unmarked reporting of the same situation" (p.72) in (6). The fronted version of this example also shows the use of the pronominal clitic *u* attached to the main verb, which agrees in number and gender with the fronted object.

---

[5]Maltese examples are glossed following the Leipzig glossing rules (https://www.eva.mpg.de/lingua/resources/glossing-rules.php). Thus, '-' separates segmentable morphemes, but is also used in Maltese writing, and therefore in the examples, to attach the definite article to the relevant noun, '=' separates a clitic, including the definite article in the gloss (DEF), and '∴' is used to list non-segmentable meta-linguistic elements. A list of the abbreviations used is provided at the end of this paper.

(5) (Borg & Azzopardi-Alexander 2009: 71)
    Il-ġurdien,   il-qattus-a   qabd-it=u.
    DEF=mouse.SG.M DEF=cat.SG-F caught.3.PRF-3.SG.F=3.SG.M
    'As for the mouse, the cat caught it.'

(6) (Borg & Azzopardi-Alexander 2009: 72)
    Il-qattus-a   qabd-et   il-ġurdien.
    DEF=cat.SG.F caught.3.PRF-3.SG.F DEF=mouse.SG.M
    'The cat caught the mouse.'

A number of examples are given in this work to illustrate that under certain conditions not only object complements, but also adverbials, prepositional complements, and even subjects can be fronted, and that chains of fronted constituents are also possible, as in (7).

(7) Borg & Azzopardi-Alexander 2009: 76
    Jien, oħt=i,   l-ittra,
    I   sister.SG.F=1.SG.POSS DEF=letter.SG.F
    ktib-t=hie=l=ha   lbieraħ.
    wrote.PRF-1.SG=3.SG.F=INDR=3.SG.F yesterday
    'I, my sister, the letter, I wrote it to her yesterday.'

Crucially, the authors claim that this type of construction, which they call topicalisation, is characterised in Maltese by a specific prosodic contour, in that i) the fronted constituent constitutes its own tone group starting on a High pitch on the first stressed syllable and moving to a Low pitch on the last stressed syllable; ii) the rest of the sentence can receive an unmarked intonation pattern with nuclear stress on the last stressed syllable, or a contrastive intonation pattern with a nuclear stress placed elsewhere; iii) a pause may be observable between the two tone groups. In the case of multiple topicalisations, each topicalised constituent involves its own separate tone group.

In example (5), thus, it is argued that there are two distinct tone groups, and that as a consequence, the fronted object is separated from the remaining part of the sentence. In the second tone group, nuclear stress would either fall on the final verb in the unmarked case, or on *il-qattusa* 'the cat' in a contrastive focus reading of the subject.

An additional piece of evidence is given to support the idea that the fronted constituent is somehow detached, or, as the authors put it, "not strictly speaking in a grammatical relation to the rest of the sentence" (Borg & Azzopardi-Alexander 2009: 73), namely the fact that the object marker *lil* 'to', which is normally obligatory with person names functioning as objects, is no longer obligatory if a person name is fronted. Finally, the authors claim that, when an object is fronted, the main verb has to bear a pronominal clitic co-referential with this object.

In other words, the definition of topicalisation they propose is based on syntactic and prosodic characteristics all pointing to the fact that the fronted constituent does not belong to the main sentence predication. These characteristics, however, rather seem to correspond to those mentioned earlier in our account of left dislocation. As far as the discourse status of the fronted constituent is concerned, the authors seem to assume that it always expresses given information, while the rest of the sentence predicates something new about the fronted element. In other words, a fronted constituent in Maltese, in this account, always seems to correspond to a topic, and fronting of one or more constituents thus seems never to involve focus movement.

In an earlier work on word order in Maltese, Fabri & Borg (2002) investigate which order combinations of S, V, and O are grammatically possible in Maltese in contexts where each of the three constituents is either the focus, the topic, or a contrastive focus. In general, it is not clear whether, according to Fabri and Borg, one can assume a canonical, or unmarked word order for Maltese. Clearly, however, not all word orders are possible in all discourse contexts. For our purposes, the two orders OSV and OVS, both involving object fronting, are interesting. Unfortunately, the authors do not provide naturally occurring examples to illustrate the different contexts, but from the tables in which their claims are summarised, it would seem that in both OSV and OVS the object can be focus or topic depending on the prosody.

Vella (1995) also examines the different word order possibilities in Maltese with respect to their prosody. In this early work, and in contrast to Fabri & Borg (2002), she restricts her analysis to structures not involving cliticisation, attempting, in so doing, to come up with a phonological explanation for the word order possibilities in Maltese. Vella invokes the notion of *focus* and the related assignment of [±focus] (Vella 1995; 2009) suggesting that the latter results from speakers' manipulation of semantic material in different discourse contexts. She follows Gussenhoven (1983)'s use of the term *variable* to refer to the material to which speakers obligatorily assign [+focus], and the term *background* to refer to that stretch of speech assigned [-focus]. Gussenhoven (1983: 283) provides the following formulation: "[+focus] makes the speaker's declared contribution to the conversation whilst [-focus] constitutes his cognitive starting point". Apart from a brief reference to left dislocation in Vella (1995) Vella does not attempt to distinguish between different types of complement fronting (topicalisation, focus movement or left dislocation) as elaborated in the literature. Nevertheless her examples, especially the constructed ones, appear to fit better into the category involving focus movement than into either of the two other categories. The Map Task data examples in Vella (2003; 2009) are similarly used to illustrate different instances involving focus movement resulting from a variety of conditions such as changes in word order, cliticisation, negation and the presence of indefinite pronouns, all of which appear to trigger the assignment of [+focus] to the variable. In terms of prosody, the clear conclusion of all of Vella's work is that statements[6] involving focus movement and therefore an early [+focus], are characterised prosodically by a falling pitch accent. This falling pitch accent is followed by a movement involving a slight rise, which she analyses as a sequence consisting of a phrase accent linked to a secondary prominence and a boundary tone rising to the edge of the phrase.

Left dislocation in Maltese is discussed in Bezzina (2015), who examines the different properties of left dislocation examples in spoken data. Interestingly for our discussion, Bezzina refers to the examples in Borg & Azzopardi-Alexander (2009) as examples of left dislocation, even though the authors use the term topicalisation. She claims that the general purpose of the construction is that of promoting new referents to topic status, and notes that the dislocated constituent is perceived as detached from the rest of the sentence. Her main interest is in the way the degree of formality of the data affects the construction. She shows, in fact, that a formal style may allow for syntactically rather complex dislocated elements.

At least two of the characteristics noted by Borg & Azzopardi-Alexander (2009) with respect to the constructions they refer to as instances of topicalisation – which Bezzina (2015) refers to as examples of left dislocation – do not seem to occur in the focus movement examples which feature in Vella's work. These are separation into different tone groups by means of a pause and the accompanying, also separate, falling intonational movements.[7] The focus movement examples described by Vella, by contrast, involve a falling pitch accent only on the [+fo-

---

[6]A parallel construction has been described to occur in questions having an early [+focus]. In this case, a rising pitch accent is followed by an upstepping phrase accent linked to a secondary prominence and a boundary tone which continues on a level high to the edge of the phrase.

[7]It is worth noting that the 'chains of fronted constituents' noted by Borg and Azzopardi-Alexander (2009) in their examples are mirrored by a similar effect noted in particular in Vella's (2003) work. This is the possibility of 'tone copying' as described by Grice et al. (2000) in the case of phrase accents. This phenomenon involves a pitch accent assigned to an early [+focus] element being followed by not one, but many, phrase accent and boundary tone sequences (see examples in 2003: 1778).

cus] element; any post-focal elements usually involve a slight rise consisting of the phrase and boundary tone sequence mentioned earlier.

To sum up, previous studies of complement fronting in Maltese provide evidence for the fact that any of the constructions described in the previous section, i.e. topicalisation, left dislocation, and focus movement, may be at play when a complement is fronted. However, to our knowledge no systematic data-driven account has been given so far of what distinguishes these constructions in terms of their syntax, the discourse status of the fronted constituent, and the suprasegmental features associated with them. It is the aim of this article to fill this gap by proposing such an account based on multimodal data, in other words spoken language data and accompanying gestural behaviour. We will be concerned with complement fronting as exemplified in (8), to be compared with the non-fronted counterpart in (9). We will, on the other hand, not be concerned with examples involving fronting of adverbials, or subject fronting.

(8) MAMCO: 19_g_148
il-Baileys   *in-ħobb*   *ukoll*
DEF=Baileys-SG.M 1-love.IPFV.SG as.well
'Baileys I like as well.'

(9) *in-ħobb*   *il-Baileys*   *ukoll*
1-love.IPFV.SG DEF=Baileys-SG.M as.well
'I like Baileys as well.'

4 Corpus data

The data described in this paper were taken from the multimodal corpus of Maltese MAMCO (Paggio & Vella 2014). This corpus is made up of twelve video-recorded first encounter conversations. Twelve speakers (six males, six females) participated in two sets of recordings, all of which were made in Malta. At the time of recording, all speakers were students at the University of Malta. All speakers were Maltese dominant speakers and had not met prior to the experiment. They were instructed to get to know each other. The set up for the collection of this corpus was the same as was previously used for the Nordic multimodal corpus of first meeting dialogues NOMCO (Paggio et al. 2010), and involves pairs of speakers standing in a studio conversing freely for about 5 minutes.

In this study, our focus is on constructions displaying complement fronting. In particular, we investigate what prosodic contours are associated with the constructions, whether the fronted complement in these examples is accompanied by hand gestures, and what the discourse status of the fronted complement is. A total of 36 examples involving complement fronting were selected manually from the 24 dialogue recordings. Some of the examples contain a clitic pronoun coreferential with the fronted complement, others don't. In (10) and (11) we show two examples: in the former, the clitic *h* refers to and agrees with the fronted complement.[8] In the latter, the fronted element *second year* involves a code-switch into English of a structure which, in Maltese, would have been a prepositional phrase *fit-tieni sena* 'in the second year': no clitic is involved (and none would have been involved had there been no code-switch).

(10) MAMCO: 20_g_165

    it-tequila   j-rid   j-koll-i   burdata għali=h

    DEF=tequila.SG.M 1-want 1-have-1SG mood   for=3.SG.M

    'Tequila I need to be in the mood for it.'

(11) MAMCO: 10_f_31

    second year għad-ni

    second year still-1SG

    'In my second year, I am.'

A first summary of the data showing the distribution of clitics and gestures is provided in Table 1.

Table 1: Corpus data statistics: gestures and clitics (absolute counts)

fronted complement	with gesture	without gesture
with clitic	11	0
without clitic	16	9
total	27	9

The sound files were transcribed and annotated in PRAAT (Boersma & Weenink 2009). Gestures, where present, were annotated using the ANVIL tool for multimodal annotation (Kipp 2004). In addition, the examples were also coded in a separate text file with categories referring to the discourse status of the various referents. Transcriptions and annotations are described in detail in what follows.

---

[8]Note that in example (10) the speaker treats *tequila* as a masculine noun, probably associating it with the masculine *drink*, even though the 'correct' grammatical gender is feminine.

The annotated data can be obtained through the authors. A complete list of the examples from the corpus is included at the end of this paper together with their semi-literal translation.

4.1 Annotation of prosody

The main purpose of the annotation and subsequent analysis of the prosody of the selected structures was to test the claims advanced in Borg & Azzopardi-Alexander (2009) about the prosodic characteristics of fronted complements in Maltese, and at the same time to explore the question whether different constructions might be distinguished in Maltese based on their different intonation patterns, as is the case for topicalisation vs focus movement in English.

The annotation was carried out following Vella (1995; 2003; 2009). It is couched in the Autosegmental-Metrical framework of Intonational Phonology, see e.g. Pierrehumbert (1980) and Ladd (2008). It involved the identification of tunes consisting of sequences of pitch or phrase accent and boundary tones. Tones can be H(igh) or L(ow). Pitch accent tones are those associated with prominent syllables having nuclear status and are marked by means of an asterisk, *[9]. Phrase accent tones are those having a secondary association of the sort described by Grice et al. (2000: 180) as tones which "resemble ordinary pitch accents, but do not signal focus or prominence in the same way [as ordinary pitch accents] reflecting their essentially peripheral nature". These are marked by means of a hyphen, -, following the relevant tone. Boundary tones are marked as **p** or **i** depending on whether they are associated with a phonological phrase boundary or an intonational phrase boundary.

In the prosodic annotation of example (12), for instance, corresponding to (11) discussed earlier, we see a falling tune H*+L starting on the accented syllable *SE of the fronted complement *SEcond year*, and falling to the edge of the phonological phrase (Lp). In instances where a boundary target might be expected but where its realisation may be difficult to determine or tease out as a separate tonal target (separate in this case from the following L phrase accent), parentheses are used. This is the case here. The fall is followed by a phrase accent L- on the accented syllable of *GĦADNi* rising slightly to the boundary at the edge of the intonational phrase Hi. In the textual rendering of this and the succeeding examples, the syllable carrying the sentence accent is shown in small caps and preceded by

---

[9]Tones can also be associated with prominent syllables which are prenuclear, hence H*. An instance of this can be found on *NIES* in the second, w(eak)-branching of the two phonological phrases in example (16): nuclear prominence in this example falls on *In*GLIż* in the first phonological phrase within the intonational phrase.

Patrizia Paggio, Luke Galea & Alexandra Vella

an asterisk, whilst any syllables carrying a secondary accent in postnuclear position are shown in small caps without additional marking. Boundaries are shown by means of a bar, '|', and are indicated even in the absence of a physical break. A list of the symbols used in the annotation is provided at the end of this paper.

(12)   *sEcond year | GĦAD ni |
        H*+L   (Lp)   L-   Hi

Figure 1 displays the PRAAT screen dump corresponding to the same example.

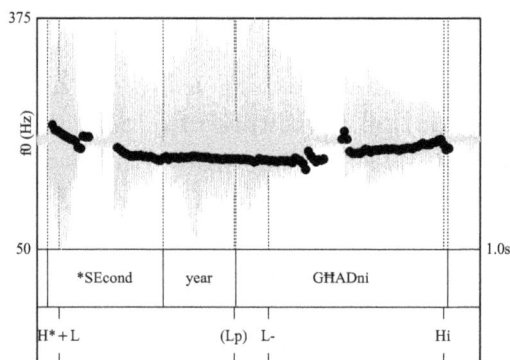

Figure 1: PRAAT screen dump showing the prosodic annotation of the example *Second year għadni.*

Counts of the various prosodic patterns found in the corpus are shown in Table 2. The majority of our examples (i.e. 27/36, or 75%) have one nuclear pitch accent on the fronted complement. The remaining examples (i.e. 9/36, or 25%) have two or three nuclear pitch accents, the first of which is also on the fronted complement. The second nuclear pitch accent (and the third in the one example involving three consecutive pitch accents) is on a following element in the rest of the utterance, either within the same intonational phrase (although a separate phonological phrase), or in a separate intonational phrase. The nuclear pitch accent on the fronted complement in all except one example is followed by the phrase accent and boundary tone sequence, L- Hi. Such a pattern is described by Vella (2009: 51), who states that a nuclear pitch accent is "followed by a L phrase accent linked to the stressed syllable closest to the edge of the intonational phrase and a final Hi boundary tone". A yes-no question is involved in one of the examples, shown in (13).

Table 2: Frequency counts of different combinations of one or more nuclear pitch accent (fall or rise) and post-nuclear phrase accent + boundary sequences

Nuclear pitch accent type	Post-nuclear phrase accent + boundary sequence type			
	–	L-Hi	L-Hi L-Hi	L-Hi L-Hi L-Hi
Fall				
H*+L (Lp)		15	10	1
H*+L (Lp) H*+L (Lp)	1	5	2	
H*+L (Lp) H*+L (Lp) H*+L (Lp)		1		
Total Fall				35
Rise				L+H-Hi
L* H				1
Total Rise				1
Grand total				36

(13) MAMCO: 23_f_22
l-universita'   *qiegħed inti?*
DEF=university.SG.F stay3.SG you

'The university do you attend (it)?'

Yes-no questions in Maltese have a different tonal structure as compared to statements, see Vella (1995; 2009: 51). The fronted complement in the question carries a nuclear pitch accent (just as statements do). However, the nuclear pitch accent in this case is rising (i.e. L* Hp) rather than falling (i.e. H*+L). In postnuclear position, the phrase accent and boundary tone sequence is L+H- Hi. The prosodic annotation of the example is shown in (14).

(14)   l-universi *TA' | qiegħed INti?
                    L*   Hp L+H-   Hi

To sum up, there is a clear tendency in our data for fronted complements to carry their own nuclear falling pitch accent. The tendency for the intonation of elements which follow the fronted complement to carry the phrase accent and boundary tone sequence L- Hi described for example (12) is also clear. Only a very small number of examples in the data analysed, in fact, involve more than one falling pitch accent.

4.2 Annotation of hand gestures

In this study, hand gestures are considered to be suprasegmental features on a par with prosodic features. There are good reasons for this assumption. There is large agreement in the literature that hand gesture strokes are temporally aligned (or slightly precede) the main sentence accent (Kendon 1980; Bolinger 1986; McNeill 1992; Alahverdzhieva & Lascarides 2010), and it has been observed and verified on annotated multimodal data (Loehr 2004; 2007) that gesture phrases are temporally coordinated with intermediate phrases in the sense of Pierrehumbert (1980). In an empirical study of German data (276 examples), Ebert et al. (2011) find that gesture strokes tend to precede sentence accent by 0.36s on average, in other words they confirm what seems to be generally acknowledged in the literature. However, the authors of this study make the claim that whatever alignment is observed between gesture phrases and intonationally motivated stuctures is a by-product of an interdependence between gestures and focus phrases, which in turn is motivated by information structure. They do find evidence to confirm this claim, since they observe that the onsets of gesture phrases in their data align with new-information foci with a time lag of only 0.31s on average (and a small standard deviation). The same kind of temporal interdependence is not found, on the other hand, between gesture phrases and contrastive focus phrases.

To our knowledge, no one has investigated whether hand gestures play a role in conjunction with complement fronting. Since we have seen that fronted complements in Maltese are accompanied by pitch accents, we would expect that hand gestures, if present, would be likely to align with them. However, finding that hand gestures are coordinated with fronted complements would seem to contradict Ebert et al. (2011)'s claim that gesture phrases align with focus phrases in that fronted complements, as we have seen, do not necessarily correspond to sentence foci. In fact, a first look at the data gave us the impression that there was a tendency for fronted complements to be accompanied by gestures. The goal of the gesture annotation was to verify this expectation in a systematic way and to provide a new perspective from which to look at the relation between gestures and discourse structure.

For each of the examples under discussion, if a hand gesture by the speaker overlaps the fronted complement, this hand gesture was annotated as a temporal element associated with the corresponding video frames. The annotation procedure and the labels used to annotate gestures are taken from the MUMIN coding

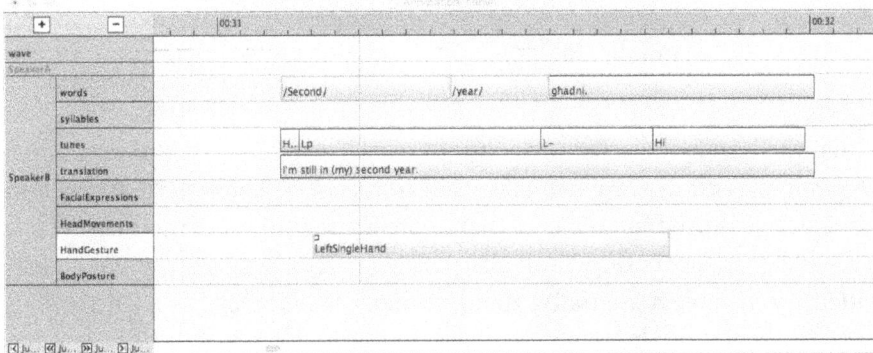

Figure 2: Annotation of a hand gesture in ANVIL: gesture element with link to corresponding words.

scheme (Allwood et al. 2007), an annotation scheme for multimodal behaviour which provides attributes for the annotation of shape, dynamics and function of head movements, facial expressions, hand gestures, and body posture. The scheme has been successfully used to code multimodal behaviour in several languages, e.g. in the NOMCO project, which has developed annotated conversational data for Danish, Swedish, Finnish and Estonian (Paggio et al. 2010; Paggio & Navarretta 2017).

According to what the MUMIN scheme prescribes, we do not explicitly mark gesture strokes, which we understand as the most dynamic parts of the gestures, nor do we mark the internal structure of a gesture in terms of its preparation, prestroke hold, stroke, and retraction (see e.g. McNeill 1992). Instead, we create temporal elements in the annotation that correspond to the whole duration of the gesture from the beginning of the movement to its completion. In a series of gestures, we follow Kipp (2004)'s recipe to distinguish the various gestures: essentially, we draw a boundary every time a gesture changes direction and velocity, and a new stroke is visible.

Only two types of attributes were selected from the MUMIN scheme and annotated in our data. There are attributes that indicate which hand was used as well as whether the hands in a two-handed gesture are used symmetrically, and others that specify the semiotic type of the gesture. They are shown in Table 3.

Table 3: Hand gesture annotation attributes

Attribute	Values
Handedness	BothHandsAsymmetric, BothHandsSymmetric RightSingleHand, LeftSingleHand
Semiotic type	Symbolic, Iconic, Deictic, IndexicalNonDeictic

Whilst the handedness features should be self-explanatory, the semiotic ones deserve some comment. *Symbolic* is used to annotate conventional emblematic gestures; *iconic* is used for gestures that express the content of their object by similarity – either in a concrete or an abstract way; *deictic* is used for hand gestures that identify an object spatially; finally *IndexicalNonDeictic* is used for batonic gestures, or beats. We have not yet analysed how the two sets of attributes are used in the data: in future, we intend to investigate whether semiotic type interacts in systematic ways with discourse features of the associated referents.

The gesture annotation of an example discussed previously, see (12), is illustrated in Figure 2. The video frame shows the point of maximal extension of the hand gesture performed by the speaker on the right. Below the frame is a section of the ANVIL annotation board displaying the word transcription, the prosodic annotation, the English translation, and the hand gesture element, which is linked to the words *second year*. The gesture is categorised as a *LeftSingleHand* one, and the annotation also contains the semiotic feature *Symbolic* (not visible in the figure), which is reserved for conventionalised, emblematic gestures like the 'two' gesture in question. The annotation also shows additional tracks (syllables, FacialExpressions, HeadMovements, and BodyPosture) that were not used for this study and are therefore left empty.

A total of 30 hand gestures are present in the fronted complement example dataset. Of these, 27 (90%), occur in conjunction with the fronted complement. This looks like a pattern, indicating a strong tendency for fronted complements to be accompanied by gestures. To check that this is a real tendency, we also analysed all the hand gestures produced by two of the MAMCO speakers in two different conversations. Both speakers produce 80 hand gestures for which the

whole extension from the beginning of the movement to its end has been annotated as described earlier. Of the 80 gestures, only 17 (21%) in the case of one
speaker, and 13 (16%) in the case of the other, are aligned with the initial sentence constituent. Six of these cases (2 and 4, respectively) involve fronting. The
remaining gestures occur in the middle of the sentence, towards the end, or span
the whole sentence. The last type makes up a large portion of the gestures (63
and 67, respectively). These gestures have a long duration, either because they are
repeated or because they have a long prestroke hold, and their extension spans
the duration of the whole sentence.

These numbers seem to provide a more complex picture than the one described
by Ebert et al. (2011) for German, and call for a detailed analysis of the alignment
between gesture strokes and pitch accents in Maltese. For the present study, however, it suffices to note that in general, the probability for a gesture to align with
the initial sentence constituent in our data (without spanning the rest of the sentence at the same time) is relatively low. This probability increases in sentences
where the initial constituent is a fronted complement.

4.3 Annotation of discourse status

The purpose of annotating the fronted complement with respect to the discourse
status of the corresponding referent was to use discourse status to distinguish
between the constructions discussed previously.

The discourse referent corresponding to the fronted complement was annotated using one of the three categories *new, poset,* or *old. New* means that the
referent has not been mentioned earlier and is not implied, in other words that
it is referentially new;[10] *poset* that it has not been mentioned, but stands in what
Prince (1981) calls a partially-ordered set relation with an already mentioned or
implied referent (for instance by expressing contrast or by referring to a more
specific but related concept); finally *old* means that the referent has already been
mentioned. The distribution of the three categories is shown in Table 4.

---

[10]For a discussion of the difference between referentially and relationally new, see e.g. Gundel
& Fretheim (2008).

Table 4: Corpus data statistics: discourse status of the fronted complement (absolute counts)

Discourse status	Counts
new	15
poset	7
old	14
total	36

5 Results

In this section we analyse the way in which the different contructions involving fronting which we described earlier are realised in the corpus data. We start by providing some corpus statistics intended to give a quantitative view of different properties of these constructions in our data, and we then analyse examples which we consider typical of these tendencies in a qualitative fashion.

5.1 Corpus statistics

Based on the overview of the literature, we distinguish four different constructions based on the discourse status of the fronted complement. In addition, the presence or absence of a clitic or a pronoun coreferential with the fronted complement is used as a diagnostic to keep topicalisation and left dislocation apart.

- By definition, in focus movement (FM) constructions the fronted complement is *new*. Following Prince (1981)'s analysis, we expect it often to be an attribute that is added as new information to an otherwise presupposed referent.

- In left dislocation constructions, there are two possibilities, as we saw earlier. The fronted complement can be *new*, and introduced as a new topic for subsequent reference. It can, however, also be *old*. Following Geluykens (1992), we will call the two types of left dislocation LD1 and LD2, respectively. In either case, there is always a clitic or a pronoun in the rest of the sentence which has the same referent as the fronted complement and syntactically agrees with it.

- Finally in topicalisation constructions (TOP), the fronted complement is either *old* or it stands in a *poset* relation with an already introduced referent.

There is no clitic or pronoun in the rest of the sentence that agrees with the topicalised complement. Note that examples of topicalisation without a following clitic in our data also include PP fronting. This seems to confirm that cliticisation is linked to a specific construction rather than to syntactic properties of the fronted constituent.

Table 5 shows counts of the four constructions in the corpus together with a specification of the discourse label of the fronted complement, which was used for the construction classification. Given this taxonomy and the distribution of the data shown in the table, the question we ask in this section is whether the suprasegmental characteristics provided by prosody and gestures to some extent differ depending on the construction type.

Table 5: Constructions and discourse status of the fronted complement (absolute counts)

Construction type	new	poset	old
FM	11	0	0
LD1	4	0	0
LD2	0	0	7
TOP	0	7	7
total	15	7	14

We saw earlier that the majority of our examples (27) are characterised by the occurrence of a single pitch accent on the fronted complement, whilst the remaining 9 examples display two pitch accents (three in one single case). If we look at how the two prosodic patterns map onto the different construction types (Table 6), an interesting tendency seems to emerge.

The numbers show that the tendency for topicalisation and focus movement constructions to be accompanied by only one pitch accent is inverted in the case of left dislocation, where we see a slight preponderance of the two-accent pattern (7 vs 4). The differences are statistically significant (Fisher's exact test, p-value = 0.004918). The different pattern displayed by left dislocation reflects the fact that the fronted complement in this construction is somehow detached from the rest of the construction, as also indicated by the presence of a clitic or pronominal reference. The length of the utterance (in the sense of the number of words used), may also, however, in itself contribute to the presence of an additional pitch accent. In fact, most of the cases in which two pitch accents occur, but also most

Patrizia Paggio, Luke Galea & Alexandra Vella

Table 6: Constructions and pitch accent (counts and proportions)

Construction type	One accent	Two accents
FM	10 (.91)	1 (.09)
LD1	1 (.25)	3 (.75)
LD2	3 (.43)	4 (.57)
TOP	13 (.93)	1 (.07)
total	27 (.75)	9 (.25)

of the left dislocation constructions, are relatively long. This makes sense in terms of discourse strategy. Left dislocation constructions introduce the referent in a more elaborate way, and therefore often have more substantial material in the clause.

Turning now to gestures (Table 7), we see here that left dislocation and top-icalisation constructions seem to fall into a different category in that they are always or nearly always characterised by the presence of a gesture (100% of the LD1 and LD2 cases, and 75% of the TOP ones), against a more or less 50/50 distri-bution in the case of focus movement. The differences, once the two LD types are collapsed, are significant (Fisher's exact test, p-value = 0.01135). It is tempting to advance the tentative explanation that gestures are instrumental in marking the topical nature of the fronted complement in left dislocation and topicalisation constructions.

Table 7: Constructions and pitch accent (counts and proportions)

Construction type	Gesture yes		Gesture no	
FM	5	(.46)	6	(.54)
LD1	4	(1)	0	(0)
LD2	7	(1)	0	(0)
TOP	11	(.75)	3	(.21)
total	27	(.75)	9	(.25)

5.2 Analysis of four examples

To provide a more detailed analysis of the tendencies identified in the statistical analysis, we give below what we consider particularly illustrative examples of the four construction types from our corpus. Given our focus on both prosody and gestures, we have chosen examples where gestures are always produced in conjunction with the fronted complement, even though about half of the examples of focus movements do not contain a gesture. For each example we describe the way prosodic and gestural characteristics have been annotated.

(15) MAMCO: 18_g_116
      sa l-aħħar ta-x-xahar   għand=hom
      till DEF=end of-DEF=month have=3.PL
      'Till the end of the month they have.'

Example (15) is a focus movement construction. The two speakers are talking about how much time students have left to prepare for their exams. The fronted complement *sa l-aħħar tax-xahar* 'till the end of the month' is a temporal expression that provides a new attribute to the presupposed timeframe of the action, and is thus annotated as *new*.

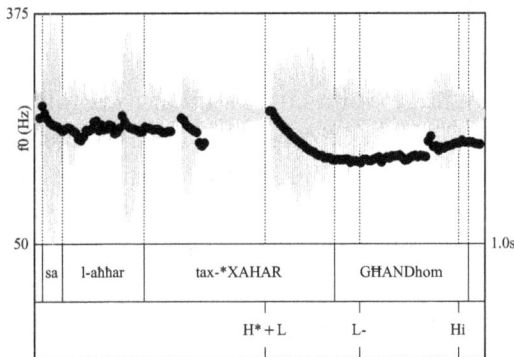

Figure 3: PRAAT screen dump showing the prosodic annotation of example (15) *sa l-aħħar tax-xahar għandhom* 'Till the end of the month they have'.

The prosody is characterised by a falling pitch accent, H*+L, on the nuclear accented syllable of the fronted complement, *XAHAR. Pitch continues to fall to a Low phrase accent. L-, associated with the secondary accent on GħAND in *għandhom*, followed by a slight rise to a Hi boundary at the end of the phrase. There

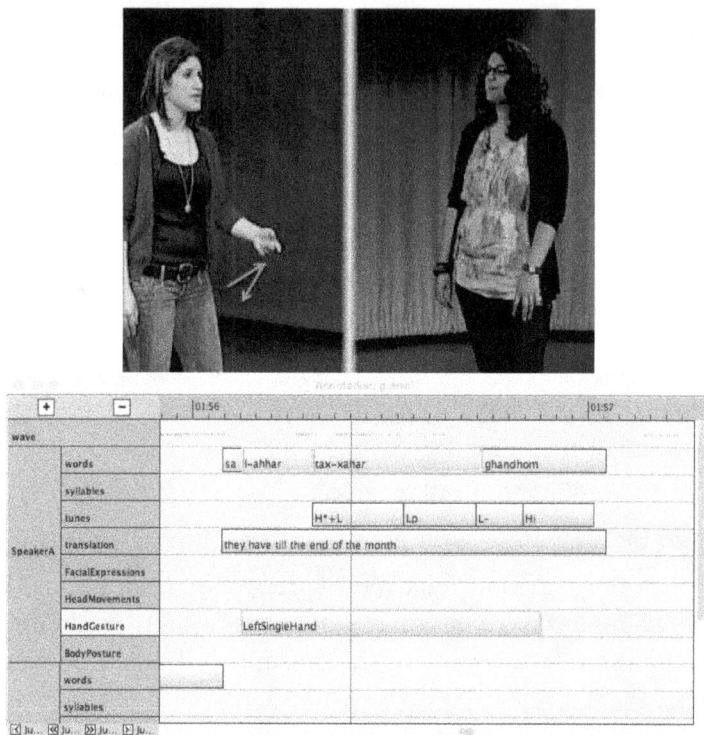

Figure 4: Focus movement and gesturing in example (15)

is no clear intermediate target for a Low boundary, Lp, following the H*+L pitch accent, in this example. Figure 3 displays the PRAAT screen dump showing the prosodic contour and annotation. The gesture performed by the speaker on the left, and shown in Figure 4, is a batonic gesture (*IndexicalNonDeictic*) performed with the left hand. The arrows in the figure are intended to show the trajectory of the gesture: the hand starts from a resting position close to the body, is lifted forward and brought back to its initial position. The segment corresponding to the gesture in the annotation board shows the entire extension of the movement, which overlaps with the fronted focus carrying the pitch accent.

(16)   MAMCO: 36_k_105
       Malti   u   Ingliż   ħafna nies   ikoll=hom
       Maltese and English many people have=3.PL
       'Maltese and English many people have them'

Example (16) is a left dislocated construction of the LD1 type. The two speakers are discussing course requirements, and one of them mentions Maltese and English as being subjects that a lot of people meet the requirements for. Maltese and English have not been mentioned previously and are not contrasted with other subjects or requirements. They have therefore been labelled as *new*. The verbal affix *-hom* agrees in number with the fronted complement.[11] The discourse function of LD1 is, as we saw earlier, to promote a new referent to being the topic of the sentence. Interestingly, the other speaker acknowledges the introduction of the new referent by nodding, thus making this example neatly conform with Geluykens (1992)'s view of left dislocation as an interactional device.

The prosody in this case, see Figure 5 is again characterised by a falling pitch accent, H*+L, on the fronted element, *In*GLIŻ*. In this case the fall is not visible (although it is auditorily perceptible) due to the presence of the obstruent (/z/ in word-final position in Maltese is devoiced to a [s]). The phonological phrase containing the fronted complement in this case is followed by another phonological phrase having a H tone, H*, on the accented syllable NIES, followed by a phrase accent, L-, on the syllable carrying secondary prominence KOL of *ikollhom* and a slight rise to a High boundary tone, Hi, at the end of the phrase. The main difference here is that the fronted element gets its own separate pitch accent, which is not the case for the focus movement case illustrated earlier.

---

[11]It can also be argued, however, that *hom* in this example agrees with the plural subject. Were such an analysis to be chosen, the example would have to be re-categorised as a focus movement example rather than a case of LD1.

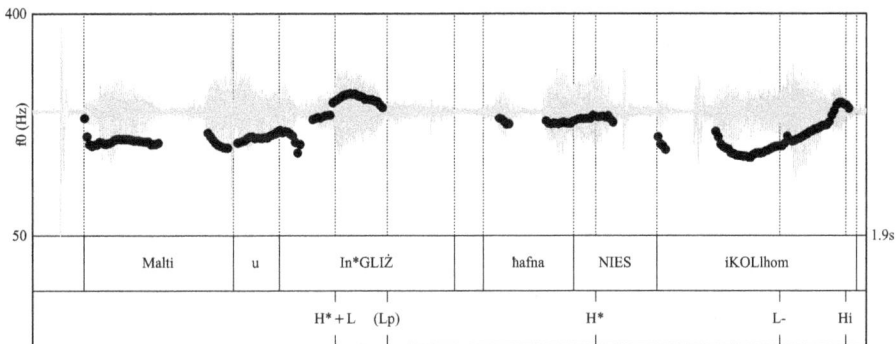

Figure 5: PRAAT screen dump showing the prosodic annotation of example (16) *Malti u Ingliż ħafna nies ikollhom* 'Maltese and English many people have them'.

As for the gestural behaviour, the speaker actually produces two hand gestures, one for each of the nouns in the fronted complement. Both are symmetrical two-handed gestures, where the hands move together first to the left, and then to the right, as can be seen in Figure 6. In the annotation board, the red vertical line corresponding to the mouse position highlights the second gesture, which overlaps with the fronted complement that carries the pitch accent. The first gesture, in turn, aligns temporally with the unaccented *Malti* 'Maltese', the other noun in the fronted complement. In other words, we see here an example where gestures accompany the fronted complement, but where there isn't a complete correspondence between the gestural and the prosodic features.

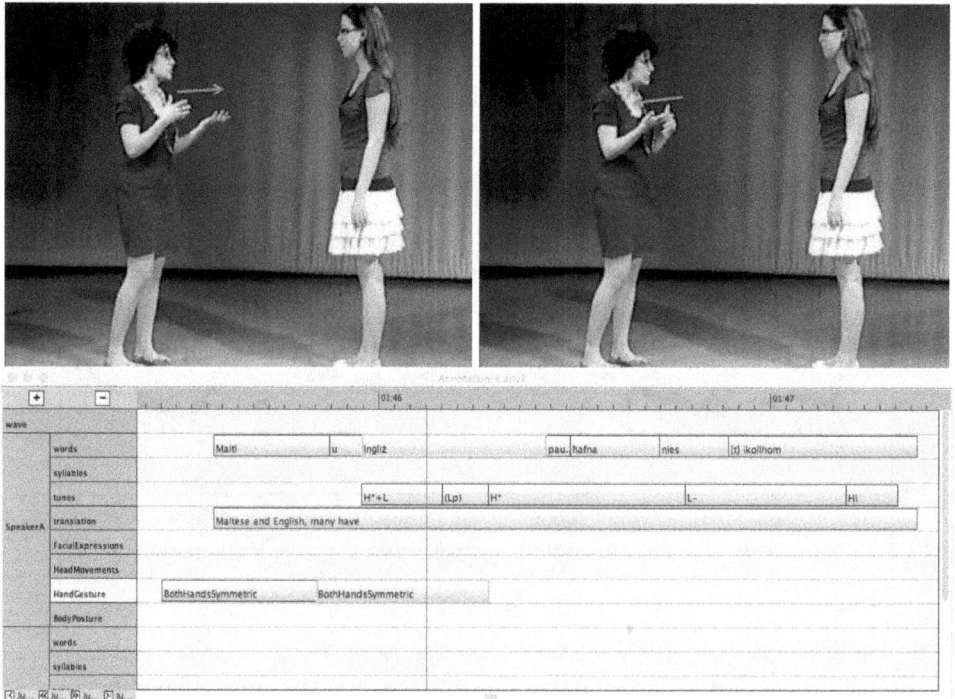

Figure 6: Left dislocation (LD1) and gesturing in example (16)

(17) MAMCO: 20_g_165

    it-tequila   *j-rid*   *j-koll-i*   *burdata għali=h*

    DEF=tequila.SG.F 1-want 1-have-1.SG mood   for=3.SG.M

    'Tequila I need to be in the mood for it.'

Example (17), which was also mentioned earlier as example (10), is a left dislocated construction of the LD2 type. The referent of the fronted complement,
it-tequila 'tequila' has just been mentioned by the other speaker in the context
of a discussion of various alcoholic drinks. The discourse status label used is
therefore *old*. The current speaker, on the left in Figure 7, makes this referent the
topic of her utterance and states her attitude towards it. Note that there is a lack
of agreement between the fronted complement *it-tequila*, which is feminine, and
the masculine clitic in *għalih*.[12]

---

[12] One of the reviewers of this paper considered the error in this example a slip on the part of the
speaker. Another, however, noted that tequila is often considered masculine in Maltese speech,
on a par with *wiski, vodka* etc.

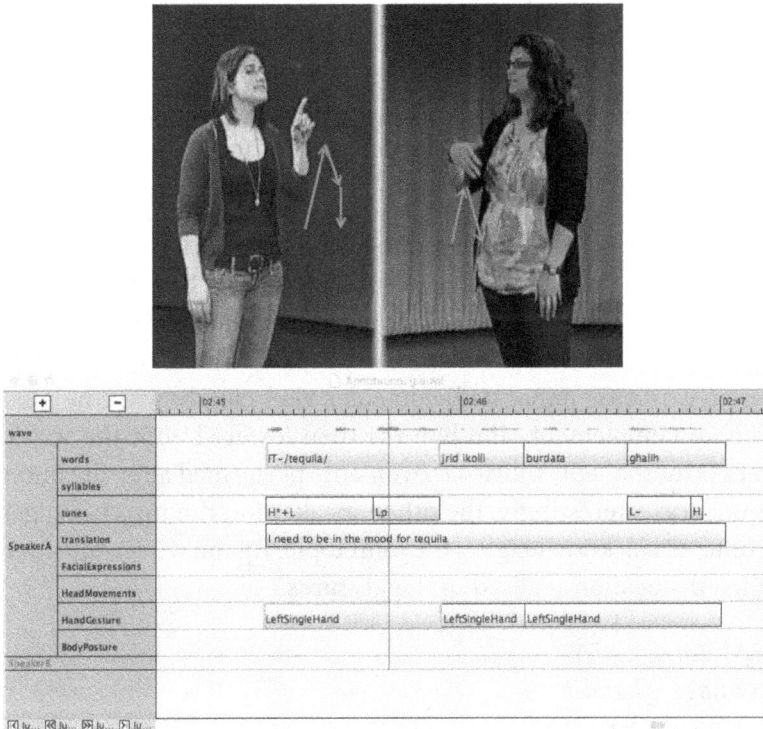

Figure 7: Left dislocation (LD2) and gesturing in example (17)

The prosody of the example, shown in Figure 8, is characterised by a falling pitch accent, H*+L, on the fronted element *te*QUIla*, with a clear Low phrase boundary, Lp at the end of this element. Pitch continues to fall to a Low phrase accent, L-, on the secondary accent on *ghaLIH*, and there is a final slight rise to a High boundary tone, Hi. In this case, although there is no clear pause following the fronted complement, a phonological phrase boundary, Lp, does seem to be present.

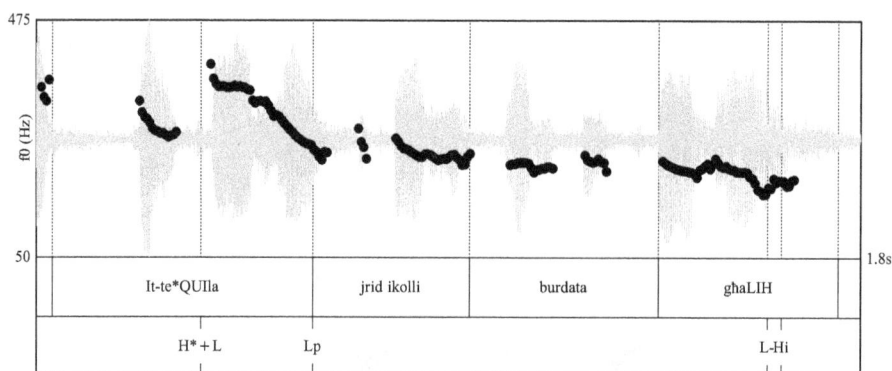

Figure 8: PRAAT screen dump showing the prosodic annotation of example (17) *it-tequila jrid jkolli burdata ghalih* 'Tequila I need to be in the mood for it'.

On the gestural level the speaker (on the left) performs what looks like a deictic gesture, as if pointing at an imaginary tequila in the air. The dynamic of this gesture corresponds to the upward arrow in the figure, and the first gestural element in the annotation board. The point of maximal extension of the gesture (which is not, however, explicitly annotated) coincides very clearly with the pitch accent on the fronted complement. The hand is then lowered with the index still extended in two subsequent, shorter movements performed after the phonological phrase boundary. Interestingly, the other speaker (on the right) also gestures at the same time, as if acknowledging the joint topic. Again, we see the interactional nature of left dislocation realised in the gestures.

(18)   MAMCO: 4_b_155
       recordings ghand-i
       recordings 1-have-1.SG
       'Recordings I have.'

Finally, an example of a topicalised construction is shown in (18). The speakers are discussing the methods they used in their dissertations. The male speaker explains that he conducted interviews. The female speaker then says that she does not have data from interviews, but that instead she has some recordings. The referent corresponding to the fronted object, *recordings*, stands in a *poset* relation to *interviews* which both speakers have just mentioned: more specifically, it marks a contrast between the two referents.

The prosody is characterised by a falling pitch accent, H*+L, on the nuclear accented syllable of the fronted complement *re*CORdings*, as shown in Figure 9. It is difficult to ascertain whether there is an L boundary tone, Lp, separating the phrase containing the fronted complement from the phrase accent and boundary tone sequence, L-Hi, on GHAN of *għandi*.

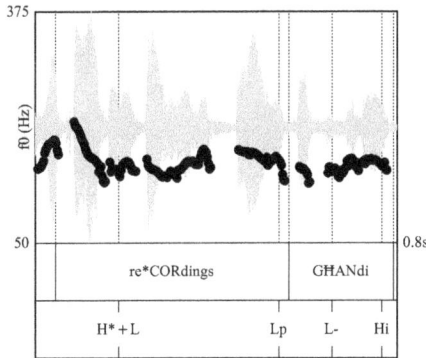

Figure 9: PRAAT screen dump showing the prosodic annotation of example (18) *recordings għandi* 'recordings I have'.

As for the gestures, the speaker (on the right) accompanies the topicalised object (and the corresponding pitch accent) with a batonic gesture performed with the right hand, as can be seen in Figure 10. From the annotation board in the same figure it can also be seen that this gesture is immediately preceded by another one in correspondence with the negated 'interviews' in the preceding sentence.

To sum up, the examples discussed above show what seems to be a rather fundamental difference between left dislocation constructions on the one hand, and topicalisation and focus movement on the other, a difference which is also indicated by the quantitative analysis of the prosodic features. Left dislocation examples display a more complex suprasegmental structure, more often charac-

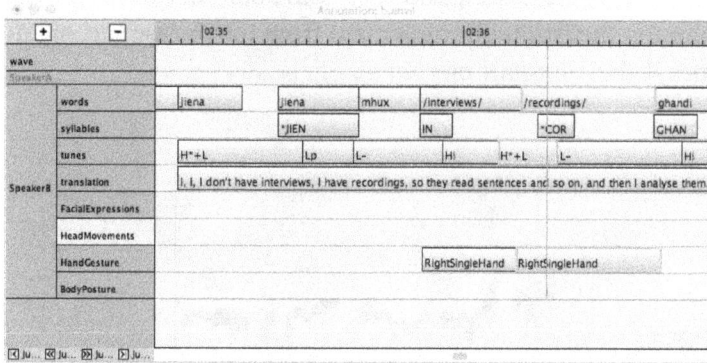

Figure 10: Topicalisation and gesturing in example (18)

terised by two pitch accents and the presence of multiple gestures, sometimes on the part of both speakers. There are, however, more initial gestures in topicalisation than in focus movement constructions.

6 Conclusions

This paper deals with complement fronting in Maltese, and examines the interface between syntax, prosody, discourse and gestures by discussing the temporal alignment of pitch accents and gestures with the fronted complement, as well as the discourse status of the referent denoted by this same complement in different contexts. This study is the first of its kind in that it uses data taken from a corpus of spoken Maltese (MAMCO). Our results contribute to what previous research has shown, but also give a more detailed analysis by providing an account of four different constructions all involving complement fronting: focus movement, topicalisation and two types of left dislocation.

Overall, the results show that, unless the example is a question, the fronted complement has a falling nuclear pitch accent, annotated as H*+L (Lp). However, there is a tendency for left dislocation to have two falling nuclear pitch accents, one on the fronted complement and the other on another complement following it. In the majority of the examples, the nuclear pitch accent on the fronted complement was followed by a low boundary phrase accent, L- Hi. As for the realisation of gestures, our results show that left dislocation and topicalisation constructions have a clear tendency (75-100%) to be accompanied by a hand gesture on the fronted complement. In the case of focus movement, on the other hand, the likelihood of a gesture occurring is much less (about 50%). These figures contrast with the much lower probability of sentence-initial gestures (10-21%) in a baseline of 160 non-fronted examples from the same corpus.

Keeping in mind that this was a corpus-based investigation using limited spoken data and, therefore, the number of examples was small, we make the following tentative conclusions. Firstly, the prosody on fronted complements is similar across the four types of construction (unless the fronted complement involves a question which in turn has a different prosodic structure than statements); however, the presence of an additional pitch accent in left dislocation examples seems to strengthen the detached nature of the fronted complement, which is also signalled in some cases by the presence of verbal or gestural feedback by the interlocutor. Secondly, the occurrence of gestures partitions the constructions in a slightly different way, with left dislocation and topicalisation on the one hand, and focus movement on the other. In this connection, it is noteworthy that gestures align more readily with topics than foci in constructions involving fronting.

The two sets of findings seem to point to the fact that the four construction types can be placed on a continuum as regards the complexity of the suprasegmental structure, with focus movement and both types of left dislocation on the two ends of the scale, and topicalisation in the middle, sharing some features with focus movement (prosodic structure) and others with left dislocation (presence of gestures). This continuum is illustrated in Figure 11.

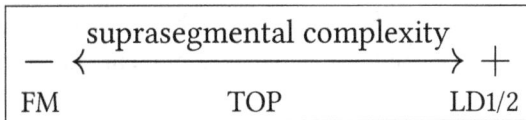

Figure 11: Maltese fronted complement constructions ordered on a continuum of suprasegmental complexity

An aspect which has not been analysed in depth, and which could constitute a direction for future work, relates to the transition between the fronted complement and the rest of the sentence. In left dislocated constructions, in contrast to focus movement ones, the transition seems to be characterised by some sort of discontinuity. Such discontinuities are often perceptually noticeable but not necessarily easy to identify acoustically, thus rendering phonological interpretation difficult.

In addition, a more thorough analysis of the temporal coordination between gesture phrases and speech in the entire corpus would provide a more solid basis to understand the relation between gestures and discourse in more general terms.

Acknowledgements

We would like to thank the students from the Institute of Linguistics at the University of Malta who helped with the transcription and annotation of the MAMCO corpus. We also thank Marie Azzopardi-Alexander, Elisabet Engdahl and the external reviewer for their comments on the first version of this article.

Abbreviations

Abbreviations used in the glosses

1	First person	IPFV	Imperfect Verb
3	Third person	M	Masculine
DEF	Definite	POSS	Possessive
F	Feminine	PRF	Perfect Verb
INDR	Indirect Object	SG	Singular

Individual symbols used in the prosodic annotation

H   High tone
L   Low tone
*   prominence marker, e.g. H* represents a High tone associated with a prominent (accented) syllable usually in nuclear position, but possibly also in prenuclear position.
-   secondary prominence marker, e.g. L- represents a Low tone associated with a syllable having a secondary prominence in post-nuclear position.

p   phonological phrase boundary marker,
        e.g. Lp is a phonological phrase boundary Low tone.
i   intonational phrase boundary marker,
        e.g. Hi is an intonational phrase boundary High tone.
( )   marker of a phonologically expected tonal target
        which does not seem to be realised phonetically.

Patterns used in the prosodic annotation

Examples of patterns combining the symbols above are the following:

H* + L (Lp)   Falling pitch accent with a Low boundary tone phonological
                 target which may or may not be realised.
L- Hi   Low phrase accent and slight rise to an H boundary tone
                 associated with a secondary prominence in postnuclear
                 position.

Fronted complement examples corpus

1. *bl-interviews għamiltha*
   'with interviews I do it'

2. *Ħaż-Żabbar għandi kuġin minn hemmhekk jien*
   'Ħaż-Żabbar I have [a] cousin from there'

3. *Wied il-Għajn ija immur ta*
   'Wied il-Għajn yes do I go [there]'

4. *jiena mhux interviews recordings għandi differenti 'iġifieri*
   'I don't have interviews recordings I have I mean'

5. *emozzjonijiet qiegħda nagħmel infatti*
   'emotions I'm doing in fact'

6. *linguistics jiena*
   'linguistics I do'

7. *imma dil-water fight qatt ma mort*
   'this water fight never I went'

8. *proċedura u hekk tal-qorti għa'na m'għamilnihomx*
   'procedures and so on of the courts still we haven't done them'

9. *id-dar ta' ħdejha toqgħod iz-zija tiegħi fiha*
   'the house next to it lives my aunt in it'

10. *second year għadni*
    'second year I'm still [in]'

11. *opra ma taraħħiex bil-wiefqa taraha bil-qiegħda*
    'an opera you don't see it standing you see it sitting down'

12. *tipo mużika tal-parties ma nħobbhiex*
    'as in music for parties I don't like it'

13. *twenty two ħa nagħlaq*
    'twenty two I'm going to be'

14. *picnic u hekk ħa nitħajjar immur*
    'picnic and such I'm going to be tempted to go [to]'

15. *practicals u hekk għadna għaddejjin s'issa*
    'practicals and such still we are carrying on till now'

16. *u n-nagħġu ilni ma nara'*
    'and the goat [nickname] for a while I haven't seen'

17. *Martini per eżempju jogħġobni*
    'Martini for example I like'

18. *sa l-aħħar tax-xahar għandhom*
    'till the end of the month they have'

19. *il-Baileys inħobb ukoll*
    'Baileys I like as well'

20. *it-tequila jrid jkolli burdata għalih*
    'tequila I need to be [in the] mood for it'

21. *i... i... ije l-università qiegħed*
    'ye... ye... yes [at] the University I am [there]'

22. *ħafna nies it-tequila jdejjaqhom ħafna*
    'a lot of people tequila they dislike [it] a lot'

23. *l-università qiegħed inti?*
    'the university do you attend [it]?'

24. *twenty għalaqna*
'twenty we turned'

25. *sentej' iżgħar minnek jien kont*
'two years younger than you I was'

26. *il-Fabian anka jien ili ma narahom ta*
'Fabian also I in a while haven't seen them too'

27. *il-tagħkom naħseb il-ħadd m'għadni nara jie'a*
'your class-mates I think none of them I see'

28. *outskirts ħafna noqgħod*
'outskirts a lot I live [there]'

29. *ee Antonia jisimni jien*
'uh Antonia my name is me'

30. *l-filosofija kelli intermediate*
'philosophy I had [at] intermediate'

31. *u Chetcuti tgħidx k'm konna nittnejku bih miskin*
'and Chetcuti you don't say how much we used to make fun of him poor [him]'

32. *sal-erba u nofs għandna*
'until 4:30 we have'

33. *ma ma Dr. Moses kont*
'oh dear with Dr Moses I was'

34. *dak il-hassle m'għandix aptit jien*
'that hassle I don't fancy it'

35. *l-għadam ta' Novembru qatt m'għamilthom u qatt ma doqthom 'iġifieri on-estament*
'the bones of November never I made them and never I tasted them I mean honestly'

36. *Malti u Ingliż ħafna nies ikollhom*
'Maltese and English many people have them'

References

Alahverdzhieva, Katya & Alex Lascarides. 2010. Analysing speech and co-speech gesture in constraint-based grammars. In Stefan Müller (ed.), *Proceedings of the HPSG10 Conference* (CSLI Publications), 6–26.

Allwood, Jens, Loredana Cerrato, Kristiina Jokinen, Costanza Navarretta & Patrizia Paggio. 2007. The MUMIN coding scheme for the annotation of feedback, turn management and sequencing phenomena. In Jean-Claude Martin, Patrizia Paggio, Peter Kuehnlein, Rainer Stiefelhagen & Fabio Pianesi (eds.), *Multimodal corpora for modelling human multimodal behaviour*, vol. 41 (Special issue of the International Journal of Language Resources and Evaluation 3–4), 273–287. Berlin: Springer.

Bezzina, Anne-Marie. 2015. La dislocation à la gauche comme manifestation de la variation stylistique en Maltais. *Studii de linguistica* 5. 91–113.

Boersma, Paul & David Weenink. 2009. *Praat: Doing phonetics by computer.* Retrieved May 1, 2009, from http://www.praat.org/.

Bolinger, Dwight. 1986. *Intonation and its parts: Melody in spoken English.* Stanford: Stanford University Press.

Borg, Albert & Marie Azzopardi-Alexander. 2009. Topicalisation in Maltese. In Bernard Comrie (ed.), *Introducing Maltese linguistics*, 71–81. Amsterdam: Amsterdam: John Benjamins.

Chafe, Wallace. 1976. Givenness, contrastiveness, definiteness, subjects, topics, and point of view. In Charles N. Li (ed.), *Subject and topic*, 25–55. New York: Academic Press.

Ebert, Cornelia, Stefan Evert & Katharina Wilmes. 2011. Focus marking via gestures. In *Proceedings of Sinn und Bedeutung 15*, 193–208. Saarbrücken, Germany: Universaar - Saarland University Press.

Fabri, Ray & Albert Borg. 2002. Topic, focus and word order in Maltese. In Abderrahim Youssi, Fouzia Benjelloun, Mohamed Dahbi & Zakia Iraqui-Sinaceur (eds.), *Aspects of the dialects of African today*, 354–363. Rabat: Amapatril.

Geluykens, Ronald. 1992. *From discourse process to grammatical construction: On left-dislocation in English* (Studies in discourse and grammar). Amsterdam: John Benjamins.

Gregory, Michelle L & Laura A Michaelis. 2001. Topicalization and left-dislocation: A functional opposition revisited. *Journal of pragmatics* 33(11). 1665–1706.

Grice, Martine, D. Robert Ladd & Amalia Arvaniti. 2000. On the place of phrase accents in intonational phonology. *Phonology* 17(02). 143–185.

Gundel, Jeanette K. 1974. *The role of topic and comment in linguistic theory*. University of Texas at Austin dissertation. Published by Garland in 1989.

Gundel, Jeanette K. & Thorstein Fretheim. 2008. Topic and focus. In Laurence Horn & Gregory Ward (eds.), *The handbook of pragmatics*, 175–196. London: Blackwells.

Gussenhoven, Carlos. 1983. Focus, mode and the nucleus. *Journal of Linguistics* 19. 377–417. DOI:10.1017/S0022226700007799

Kendon, Adam. 1980. Gesture and speech: Two aspects of the process of utterance. In Mary Ritchie Key (ed.), *Nonverbal communication and language*, 207–227. Berlin: The Hague: Mouton.

Kipp, Michael. 2004. *Gesture generation by imitation - from human behavior to computer character animation*. Boca Raton, Florida, dissertation.com: Saarland University, Saarbruecken, Germany dissertation.

Ladd, D. Robert. 2008. *Intonational phonology* (Cambridge Studies in Linguistics). Cambridge: Cambridge University Press.

Lambrecht, Knud. 1994. *Information structure and sentence form: Topic, focus, and the mental representations of discourse referents*. Cambridge: Cambridge University Press.

Lambrecht, Knud. 2001. Dislocation. In Martin Haspelmath (ed.), *La typologie des Langues et les universaux linguistiques* (Handbücher zur Sprach- und Kommunikationswissenschaft), 1050–1078. New York: De Gruyter.

Loehr, Daniel P. 2004. *Gesture and intonation*. Georgetown University dissertation.

Loehr, Daniel P. 2007. Aspects of rhythm in gesture and speech. *Gesture* 7(2). 179–214.

McNeill, David. 1992. *Hand and mind: What gestures reveal about thought*. Chicago: University of Chicago Press.

Moutaouakil, A. 1989. *Pragmatic functions in a functional grammar of African* (Functional grammar series). Berlin: Walter de Gruyter.

Paggio, Patrizia, Jens Allwood, Elisabeth Ahlsén, Kristiina Jokinen & Costanza Navarretta. 2010. The NOMCO multimodal Nordic resource - goals and characteristics. In Nicoletta Calzolari, Khalid Choukri, Bente Maegaard, Joseph Mariani, Jan Odijk, Stelios Piperidis, Mike Rosner & Daniel Tapias (eds.), *Proceedings of the seventh conference on International Language Resources and Evaluation (LREC'10)*. Valletta, Malta: European Language Resources Association (ELRA).

Paggio, Patrizia & Costanza Navarretta. 2017. The Danish NOMCO corpus of multimodal interaction in first acquaintance conversations. *Language Resources and Evaluation* 51. 463–494.

Paggio, Patrizia & Alexandra Vella. 2014. Overlaps in Maltese conversational and task oriented dialogues. In Patrizia Paggio & Bjørn Nicola Wessel-Tolvig (eds.), *Proceedings from the 1st European Symposium on Multimodal Communication*, 55–64. Valletta, Malta: Linköping University Electronic Press.

Pierrehumbert, Janet Breckenridge. 1980. *The phonology and phonetics of English intonation*. Massachusetts Institute of Technology, Dept. of Linguistics & Philosophy dissertation.

Prince, Ellen. 1981. Topicalization, Focus-Movement, and Yiddish-movement: A pragmatic differentiation. In *Proceedings of the seventh annual meeting of the Berkeley Linguistics Society*, 249–264.

Prince, Ellen. 1997. On the functions of left-dislocation in English discourse. In Akio Kamio (ed.), *Directions in functional linguistics*, 117–143. Amsterdam: Philadelphia: John Benjamins.

Stempel, Wolf-Dieter. 1981. L'amour elle appelle ca – L'amour tu ne connais pas. In Jürgen Trabant, Horst Geckeler & Eugenio Coseriu (eds.), *Studia linguistica in honorem Eugenio Coseriu*, vol. 4, 351–367. Berlin: de Gruyter.

Vallduví, Enric. 1992. *The informational component*. New York: Garland.

Vallduví, Enric & Elisabet Engdahl. 1995. The linguistic realisation of information packaging. *Linguistics* 34. 459–519.

Vella, Alexandra. 1995. *Prosodic structure and intonation in Maltese and its influence on Maltese English*. University of Edinburgh dissertation.

Vella, Alexandra. 2003. Phrase accents in Maltese: Distribution and realisation. In *Proceedings of the 15th International Congress of Phonetic Sciences*, 1775–1778. Barcelona.

Vella, Alexandra. 2009. Maltese intonation and focus structure. In Ray Fabri (ed.), *Maltese linguistics: A snapshot. In memory of Joseph A. Cremona*, 63–92. Bochum: Brockmeyer.

Ward, Gregory L. 1996. *The semantics and pragmatics of preposing*. New York: Garland.

Chapter 5

Conditions on /t/-insertion in Maltese numeral phrases: A reassessment

Christopher Lucas
SOAS, University of London

Michael Spagnol
University of Malta

There has, for a considerable period, been disagreement and confusion as to the conditions governing the appearance of the /t/ morpheme that sometimes intervenes between the numerals 2–10 and a following plural noun in Maltese, as in *ħames skejjel / ħamest iskejjel* 'five schools' (e.g. Aquilina 1965: 118; Borg 1974; Cremona 1938: 204–205). In recent work (Lucas & Spagnol 2016) we reported on a native-speaker production experiment designed to improve our understanding of this issue. The results of that experiment suggested that the key factor determining /t/-insertion was onset of the plural noun: CV-initial plurals virtually never permit /t/-insertion, whereas CC-initial and V-initial plurals at least sometimes do. Number of syllables also appeared to be a relevant factor, in that, e.g., monosyllabic CC-initial plurals were found to strongly favour /t/-insertion, disyllabic CC-initials less so, and polysyllabic CC-initials not at all.

The present work builds on this earlier research, arguing that a more accurate and more general statement of the conditions on /t/-insertion is one that makes reference primarily to morphological pattern, rather than to onset and number of syllables. This conclusion stems from a new production experiment focusing specifically on /t/-insertion with CC-initial disyllabic plurals. The experiment tested combinations of numerals with a number of both "sound" (suffixing, non-stem-altering) plurals and "broken" (non-suffixing, stem-altering) plurals. The latter fell into one of three patterns: CCVVCV(C), CCVjjVC and CCVCVC. The basic prediction was that the broken plurals would, in general, be much more favourable to /t/-insertion than the sound plurals. This prediction was borne out (broken plural mean insertion rate: 32%; sound plural mean insertion rate: 5%). Additionally, we predicted

Christopher Lucas & Michael Spagnol. Conditions on /t/-insertion in Maltese numeral phrases: A reassessment. In Patrizia Paggio & Albert Gatt (eds.), *The languages of Malta*, 117–141. Berlin: Language Science Press.
DOI:10.5281/zenodo.1181791

that broken plurals of the CCVCVC pattern, such as *gwerer* 'wars', in which two consonants occupy the initial root-consonant slot in the basic, highly /t/-resistant, CVCVC pattern (cf. Mifsud 1994), would be less favourable to /t/-insertion than the other CC-initial broken plural patterns tested. This too was borne out (mean insertion rates: CCVCVC 23%; CCVjjVC 37%; CCVVCVC 55%). Taken together, these two findings show that morphological pattern should be taken as the key determinant of /t/-insertion, with onset and number of syllables contributing only secondarily.

1 Introduction

1.1 Overview

In a recent article (Lucas & Spagnol 2016), the present authors made a first attempt at a definitive statement of the conditions governing so-called /t/-insertion in Maltese numeral phrases. We provided experimental evidence that the incidence of /t/-insertion correlates strongly with phonological properties of the nominal head of a numeral phrase. The present article shows, on the basis of new experimental data, that, notwithstanding our earlier findings, /t/-insertion is better seen as a morphologically-governed phenomenon, and that the apparent role of phonology is at least partly epiphenomenal.

1.2 What is /t/-insertion?

Maltese cardinal numerals from 'two' to 'ten' have two main forms: a DEPEN-DENT form, used when the numeral modifies a following plural noun, and an INDEPENDENT form for non-modifier uses. While there is only one version of the independent form, the dependent form comes in two versions: with or without /t/.[1] This is illustrated in Table 1 and the example in (1), in which it can also be seen that /t/-insertion before a plural noun beginning with a consonant cluster triggers insertion of a prothetic /i/.

(1) a. *ħames skejjel*
     b. *ħamest iskejjel*
         'five schools'

As can be seen from (1), *skejjel* 'schools' is an example of a Maltese plural for which /t/-insertion with a preceding numeral is optional, at least for some speak-

---

[1]Maltese orthography treats this /t/ as a suffix on the numeral, but phonologically it behaves as a prefix on the following plural noun (see Lucas & Spagnol 2016 for details). We follow Maltese orthography here, but will refer to this morpheme simply as /t/, not as a suffix.

ers. As we will see, there are dozens of Maltese plurals with this property, though the previous literature on /t/-insertion sometimes gives the impression that this is a non-optional process (e.g. Cremona 1938: 204–205; Sutcliffe 1936: 188–189). In fact, this literature (e.g. Borg 1974, Cremona 1938; Fabri 1994) is characterized by a remarkable lack of consensus on the details of what triggers /t/-insertion. To take the most striking example: Aquilina (1965: 118) suggests that /t/-insertion is licit with any plural with a vocalic onset, while Borg (1974: 294) claims that plurals with vocalic onsets are the precise context in which /t/-insertion does not occur. Despite this lack of consensus, there is nevertheless general agreement that the most important factors governing /t/-insertion are the onset and number of syllables of the plural noun (for further details on the previous literature on this topic, see Lucas & Spagnol 2016).

Table 1: Independent, bare dependent and dependent /t/-form cardinal numerals 2–10 in Maltese.

	Independent form	Bare dependent form	Dependent form with /t/
'two'	tnejn	żewġ / ġiex	żewġt / ġixt
'three'	tlieta	tliet	tlitt / tlett
'four'	erbgħa	erba'	erbat
'five'	ħamsa	ħames	ħamest
'six'	sitta	sitt	sitt
'seven'	sebgħa	seba'	sebat
'eight'	tmienja	tmien	tmint
'nine'	disgħa	disa'	disat
'ten'	għaxra	għaxar	għaxart

1.3 Previous experiment

Our aim in Lucas & Spagnol (2016) was to put the description of this construction on a firmer footing by testing these two factors experimentally with multiple native speakers. All earlier work on this topic had depended on authors' personal intuitions or informal observations. Accordingly, we recruited 35 native speakers of Maltese for a production experiment. In this experiment the test items were pairings of a numeral between 'two' and 'ten' (presented as a figure) and one of 56 singular nouns whose plurals fell into eight different categories: mono-, di- and polysyllabic (3+) CC-initial words; mono-, di-, and polysyllabic CV-initial words; and di- and polysyllabic V-initial words (there being no monosyllabic V-initial plurals in Maltese). The subjects' task was then to produce what they saw, as the phrase would naturally occur in context, i.e. with the numeral in the dependent form, the noun in the plural, and with /t/-insertion if considered appropriate.[2] For example, if our target were as in example (1) above, the test item would appear as in (2), *skola* being the singular 'school'.

(2)   *5 skola*

The results of this experiment showed that, among our 56 test items, there was indeed a very strong main effect of both onset and number of syllables in the incidence of /t/-insertion.[3] This can be clearly seen from Figure 1.

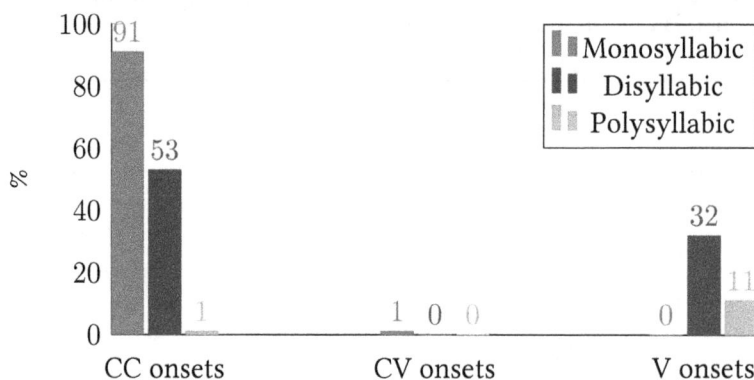

Figure 1: /t/-insertion rates (%) by onset and number of syllables (adapted from Lucas & Spagnol 2016)

In this dataset, /t/-insertion is essentially absent with plurals with CV onsets, no matter the number of syllables. With CC onsets the picture is entirely different, and number of syllables appears to be crucial: monosyllabic CC-initial plurals tested trigger /t/-insertion approximately 90% of the time, disyllabic CC-initial plurals approximately 50% of the time, and polysyllabic CC-initial plurals

---

[2] The task was demonstrated by means of examples, not explained conceptually. Subjects were asked after the test (which included equal numbers of test and filler items) whether they had any idea what it was investigating. None realized that /t/-insertion was the topic of investigation.

[3] The experiment also tested a third factor: choice of specific numeral between 2 and 10. We found no main effect of this factor, though there was an interaction of all three factors. See §2.2 of the present article and Lucas & Spagnol (2016) for further details.

essentially never. With V initials, matters are much less clear cut: neither disyllabics nor polysyllabics particularly favour /t/-insertion, but polysyllabics do so noticeably less than disyllabics, though without disallowing it altogether.

As we noted in the earlier article, however, there is likely more to these results than meets the eye. In the previous literature on this topic, Borg (1974: 297) and Ambros (1998: 91) both suggest that the distinction between SOUND and BROKEN plurals plays an important role in the occurrence of /t/-insertion. This distinction, which Maltese inherits from Arabic, concerns the morphological means by which plural number is indicated on nouns and adjectives. Sound plurals are those in which plural is indicated by suffixation of a plural morpheme to the singular form, with little or no alteration to the stem, as in *kelma* 'word', *kelm-iet* 'word-PL'. Broken plurals, by contrast, are those in which plural is indicated by means of an abstract PATTERN morpheme – a vocalic melody that combines with the root consonants of the word in question, as in *kelb* 'dog', *klieb* 'dog.PL'. Borg (1974: 297) claims that "sound plurals do not take /t/".

It was not possible to include the sound vs. broken plural distinction as another factor in the experiment reported on in Lucas & Spagnol (2016), as this would have necessitated an impractically large number of test items. We did, however, ensure that both sound and broken plurals were represented as test items in all the conditions where this was possible, so as to gain some preliminary insights as to the relevance of this factor. For example, a /t/-insertion rate across all 35 subjects of 20% with the sound plural *ajruplani* 'aeroplanes' (sg. *ajruplan*), and 26% with the sound plural *idejn* 'hands' (sg. *id*), suggests that Borg's claim cannot be completely correct, at least as far as vowel-initial plurals are concerned. Regarding CV-initial plurals, we have already seen that none of these were favourable to /t/-insertion, and this was true for both sound and broken plurals. The most interesting case was that of the CC-initial plurals. Recall that, with these, the incidence of /t/-insertion varied sharply according to the number of syllables, with /t/-insertion rates of around 90% with monosyllabics, around 50% with disyllabics, and essentially zero with polysyllabics. A crucial point to realise here, however, is that, among CC-initial plurals in Maltese, there are no polysyllabic broken plurals and no monosyllabic sound plurals. So the results for these two conditions cannot help us determine the relative importance to /t/-insertion of number of syllables and the sound vs. broken plural distinction. With disyllabic CC-initials, on the other hand, both sound and broken plurals are amply represented. Table 2 shows the CC-initial disyllabic plurals tested in Lucas & Spagnol (2016) along with the frequency with which our test subjects inserted /t/ with these items.

Table 2: /t/-insertion rates for CC-initial disyllabic plurals (adapted from Lucas & Spagnol 2016).

	Test items	**/t/-insertion frequency (%)**
Broken plurals	*ljieli* 'nights'	80
	ġranet 'days'	77
	bramel 'buckets'	74
	kmamar 'rooms'	71
	skejjel 'schools'	56
Sound plurals	*platti* 'plates'	7
	stampi 'pictures'	6

We see that /t/-insertion rates for the two sound plurals are close to zero, while for the broken plurals they are much higher. It therefore seems that Borg's (1974: 297) claim (that /t/-insertion is incompatible with sound plurals), while not absolutely correct, is certainly on the right track. This and related issues were investigated in detail in the experiment reported on in the following sections.

2 New experiment

2.1 Rationale and predictions

The purpose of the follow-up experiment that we report on here was twofold: a) to investigate the relevance of the sound vs. broken plural distinction to /t/-insertion rates; and b) more generally, to tease apart the relative importance to /t/-insertion of phonological and morphological factors. We approached these problems by focusing in detail on just one of the seven conditions investigated in the first experiment: CC-initial disyllabic plurals (both broken and sound). Restricting our investigations to these was the natural choice for a variety of reasons. Since we have already established that onset and number of syllables correlate strongly with patterns of /t/-insertion, it makes sense to hold these constant while examining whether other factors play a role. We have already seen that CV-initial plurals – both broken and sound – are very hostile to /t/-insertion no matter the number of syllables, so these are not useful for further investigation (but see the discussion below of the morphologically related *gwerer*-type broken plurals), while the lack of monosyllabic CC-initial sound plurals and polysyllabic CC-initial broken plurals rules these out too. It would certainly be interesting to investigate further what combination of factors regulates /t/-insertion with V-initials, but since there is a relative paucity of V-initial broken plurals, we leave these aside for present purposes to focus on the disyllabic CC-initials, of which there is an abundance, both broken and sound.

Focusing on disyllabic CC-initial plurals allows us to test a number of hypotheses. First, and most straightforwardly, that broken plurals of this type are more favourable to /t/-insertion than phonologically equivalent sound plurals.

Second, it may be that not all broken plural patterns are favourable to /t/-insertion. There are three Maltese broken plural patterns that are CC-initial disyllabic: CCVVCV(C), with a long medial vowel, as in *bramel* 'buckets' (sg. *barmil*) and *qsari* 'flower pots' (sg. *qasrija*); CCVjjVC, with a medial geminate glide, as in *knejjes* 'churches' (sg. *knisja*); and, most significantly, CCVCVC, with two short vowels, as in *gwerer* 'wars' (sg. *gwerra*). This final pattern is significant because it features an initial consonant cluster in a morphophonological slot that in other Arabic and Semitic varieties, and most of the Maltese lexicon, would usually host just a single root consonant. The pattern CCVCVC is therefore one sub-type of the more general pattern (C)CVCVC, of which a more prototypical example than *gwerer* is *bozoz* 'bulbs' (sg. *bozza*), with three straightforward candidates for the three root consonants that this pattern typically requires. As can be seen from Table 2, we tested four plurals of the CCVVCV(C) type in the first experiment, and recorded /t/-insertion rates from 71% to 80% with these, and one of the CCVjjVC type, for which the /t/-insertion rate was 56%. We did not test any of the CCVCVC (*gwerer*) type. Among our CV-initial disyllabic test items, however, we tested one plural of the CVCVC type: *bozoz*. In keeping with all the other CV-initial plurals in the first experiment, there were no instances of /t/-insertion with *bozoz*. What this means is that CC-initial plurals of this pattern – like *gwerer* – are therefore an ideal testing ground for the idea, universal in the previous literature, that all CC-initial broken plurals are favourable to /t/-insertion. Our hypothesis is that, in reality, onset, like number of syllables, is only of secondary importance to /t/-insertion: we predict that plurals of the *gwerer*-type, despite being CC-initial, will, like their CV-initial counterparts of the *bozoz*-type, be unfavourable to /t/-insertion, due to their membership of the same basic (C)CVCVC pattern.

Third, we saw from the results of the first experiment that /t/-insertion with CC-initial disyllabic broken plurals is by no means obligatory (see Table 2). This raises the question of whether any factors in addition to the specific broken plural pattern influence the frequency of /t/-insertion where this is optional. It seems plausible that various factors do indeed play a role. For example, we hypothesized in Lucas & Spagnol (2016) that the string frequency in corpora (Krug 1998) of specific numeral–noun combinations would positively correlate with frequency of /t/-insertion for nouns where this is optional. This is something we are investigating in presently ongoing work and will not take further here. Another factor that could plausibly play a role here is the precise phonetic composition of the onset. As shown in (1), /t/-insertion also triggers insertion of a prothetic /i/ with non-V-initial plurals. Prothetic /i/-insertion elsewhere in Maltese grammar is sensitive to the precise composition of initial consonant clusters, so it would not be a surprise to find that this also has an effect on rates of /t/-insertion where this is optional. We had no grounds to formulate a specific hypothesis in relation to this point, but we made sure to test plurals with as wide a range of CC onsets as possible (see §2.2 for more details), so that we could discover any structured variation that does exist in this domain.

From another perspective, it also seems likely, given the findings of half a century of variationist sociolinguistics (cf. Chambers 2003), that, where /t/-insertion is optional, this linguistic variation will have been co-opted to index one or more social variables. In the experiment reported in Lucas & Spagnol (2016), we found no effect of gender or age, but recall that in that experiment we found little or no optionality of /t/-insertion for the majority of conditions (see Figure 1 above), meaning the scope for sociolinguistic variation was limited. What optionality we did observe in that experiment was concentrated, as noted above, in the CC-initial disyllabic condition that is the focus of the present investigation. It makes sense, therefore, to revisit the possibility of sociolinguistic variation here. We cannot know at present whether variable /t/-insertion is stable or represents a change in progress. If it is the latter, we would expect to find that /t/-insertion behaviour varies according to the speakers' age, as well as their gender, since it is a well-established finding of variationist sociolinguistics (e.g. Labov 2001) that females tend to be more linguistically innovative than males. As a practical matter, it proved impossible in the period available for this research to recruit adequate numbers of subjects representing age groups higher than that of undergraduate university students. We ensured, however, that males and females were equally represented among our subjects, so that any gender-based differentiation in /t/-insertion could also be readily discovered.

Finally, while our principal hypothesis is that sound plurals will be relatively unfavourable to /t/-insertion, research into exemplar-based linguistic processing (e.g. Rumelhart & McClelland 1986; Bod 1998; Eddington 2009) leads us to hypothesize that sound plurals will not be totally incompatible with /t/-insertion (cf. also the non-zero results from the previous experiment for the sound plurals *platti* 'plates' and *stampi* 'pictures' shown in Table 2), and, moreover, that /t/-insertion with sound plurals will be sensitive to their phonological similarity to the broken-plural patterns that favour /t/-insertion. We therefore selected plurals to test that varied according to two parameters. First, suffix type: we ensured that all three of the most frequently occurring sound plural suffixes for disyllabic plurals – *-iet*, *-i* and *-s* – were represented among the test items. Note that the items taking the *-iet* plural suffix, such as *brimbiet* 'spiders' (sg. *brimba*), have final stress, whereas items taking the other two suffixes, such as *gruppi* 'groups' (sg. *grupp*) and *stejpils* 'staples' (sg. *stejpil*), have initial stress. All CC-initial disyllabic broken plurals have initial stress, so we predict that sound plurals with the *-iet* suffix will be less favourable to /t/-insertion than those with the suffixes triggering initial stress. Second, we chose sound-plural items that varied according to the nature of the first syllable, specifically whether or not it resembled that of the two broken plural patterns we predicted would favour /t/-insertion: CCVVCVC and CCVjjVC. Thus we had items with a long vowel in the first syllable, e.g. *stili* 'styles' (sg. *stil*), or with a medial geminate, e.g. *vjaġġi* 'journeys' (sg. *vjaġġ*), and others without these properties, e.g. *spaners* 'spanners' (sg. *spaner*). Since a number of the items that fall into the latter category have a light first syllable (i.e. a short vowel and no coda), for convenience we henceforth refer to the whole category as "light first syllable", as opposed to "heavy first syllable" for items of the *stili/vjaġġi* category.[4] These research questions and hypotheses are summarized in Table 3. The following section gives details on the design of the experiment.

2.2 Experiment design

The basic design of the experiment followed that of the first experiment, reported on in §1.3. Subjects were recruited from the University of Malta, their ages ranging from 18 to 22. The experiment was split into a broken-plural section and a sound-plural section. 20 subjects (10 male, 10 female) took the sound-plural part. The same 20, and 10 more (5 male, 5 female) took the broken-plural part. In the

---

[4]Note, however, that a number of items in the "light" category do, in fact, have a coda (e.g. *flipflops*). The label is thus for brevity and convenience only. The key distinguishing feature for this factor is resemblance to the broken plural patterns CCVVCVC and CCVjjVC.

Table 3: Summary of research question and hypotheses

Factor	Predicted pattern	Type of factor
General		
Plural type	Broken > sound	Morphological
Broken plurals		
Broken plural pattern	CCVCVC > CCVVCV(C), CCVjjVC	Morphological
Phonetic properties of onset	Exploratory	Phonological
Gender	Exploratory	Social
Sound plurals		
Suffix type/stress position	Non-stress-attracting suffixes > *-iet*	Morphophonological
Weight of first syllable	Heavy > light	Phonological

broken-plural part there were 70 test items and an equal number of fillers, and in the sound-plural part there were 49 test items and an equal number of fillers.[5]

As in the first experiment, test items consisted of a pairing of a numeral between 'two' and 'ten', presented as a figure, and the singular form of the plural

---

[5]The decision was made to split the experiment into a sound-plural and a separate broken-plural section, rather than combining them into a single dataset, because we were confident, based on the previous literature and informal observation, that the difference in /t/-insertion rates between the two plural types would be totally apparent, removing the necessity to analyse the broken/sound distinction as an additional fixed effect within a single dataset. This confidence was borne out by the results reported in §3.1. Splitting the experiment in this way had two advantages. First, it meant that in each of the two sections the test items could be coded differently, and different hypotheses could be tested. Second, it meant that we could collect more data without having to ensure equal numbers of subjects for both sections. Limited time to carry out this research imposed constraints on the preparation and use of test materials. The broken-plural test materials were ready first and were used to collect data from ten subjects immediately. At the next opportunity for data collection, the sound-plural materials were ready, and so both sets of materials were then used to collect data from 20 further subjects. These 20 took the broken-plural test first, then the sound-plural part after a short break, so that all 30 subjects took the broken-plural test under identical conditions. It is possible that having subjects take the sound-plural test after the broken-plural one resulted in some sort of learning effect, but note that all subjects were asked after completing both tests what they thought the topic of the investigation was, and none ascertained its true purpose.

noun we were targeting, the task being to realise the phrase as it would be in context: the noun in the plural and the numeral in the dependent form, and /t/ optionally inserted between the two. Refer to Table 1 for all forms of the Maltese numerals 'two' to 'ten'. In the experiment, the numeral was in fact just one of the following seven: 2, 4, 5, 7, 8, 9, 10. *Tliet* 'three' (/t/-form *tlitt/tlett*) and *sitt* 'six' (/t/-form *sitt*) were not included because, in the case of the former, the /t/-form and non-/t/-form are too similar phonetically to reliably tell apart phonetically every time, and, in the case of the latter, the two forms are identical.

Since our aim in this second experiment was primarily to investigate the effect of phonological and morphological properties of the plural noun itself, holding other factors constant as far as possible, we considered pairing the different nouns with the same numeral every time: *ħames(t)* 'five', for example. We decided against this, however, for two reasons. First, as noted in footnote 3, the results of the first experiment showed there was no main effect of numeral choice on rates of /t/-insertion. So including various numerals in the test stimuli or always just the same one ought not to have a meaningful effect on the variable we are investigating. Second, we suspected that always having the same single numeral in the stimuli would make it too easy for test subjects to correctly guess precisely what the experiment was designed to investigate – something we successfully avoided (cf. footnote 5). As such, we used the seven numerals specified above and each was used an equal number of times: with ten nouns in the broken-plural part (70 test items ÷ 7) and seven nouns in the sound-plural part (49 test items ÷ 7).

As in the first experiment, fillers, which alternated regularly with test items, consisted of pairings of a numeral between 'eleven' and 'nineteen' and a noun, the nouns varying widely according to onset and number of syllables. Note that the noun following a numeral from the 11–100 set is always in the singular, and thus never triggers /t/-insertion.

The first six stimuli (including fillers) that subjects encountered in the broken-plural and sound-plural parts of the experiment are illustrated in (3) and (4), respectively. Stimuli were presented in a PDF file on a laptop, with one stimulus per page, a page filling the screen. Subjects had to produce the appropriate form in response to the onscreen stimulus and scroll down to the next page of the PDF having done so. Their responses were given orally and the audio recorded. Responses were categorized independently by both authors, according to whether each one featured /t/-insertion or not. If the presence of /t/-insertion in an individual response was unclear to one or both authors it was excluded from analysis. In total, 15% of responses in the broken-plural data and 13% in the sound-plural data were excluded for this reason, or because subjects gave responses featuring non-target plurals.

(3)   Broken-plural test items and fillers

      a. 12 qasba

      b. 2 qasrija (target: *żewġ(t i)qsari*)

      c. 13 bandiera

      d. 5 raħal (target: *ħames(t i)rħula*)

      e. 15 għalqa

      f. 10 xkora (target: *għaxar(t i)xkejjer*)

(4)   Sound-plural test items and fillers

      a. 19 bniedem

      b. 4 kwadru (target: *erba(t i)kwadri*)

      c. 16 ħabsi

      d. 5 brama (target: *ħames(t i)bramiet*)

      e. 11 gallarija

      f. 4 slogan (target: *erba(t i)slogans*)

The nouns to be tested were selected as follows (a full list can be found in Table 5 and Table 6 in §3). With the broken plurals first of all, the three patterns CCVVCV(C), CCVjjVC, and CCVCVC had to be represented. It should be noted here that plurals from the first of these patterns are far more numerous than plurals from the other two (and CCVjjVC is much more frequent than CCVCVC). Since the plurals selected had to be fairly frequent and familiar to our young, mostly town-dwelling subjects, and we also wanted a reasonable balance of different onset types, we chose not to have equal numbers of test nouns from each of the three patterns. Instead, there were ten plurals of the CCVCVC pattern, 15 of the CCVjjVC pattern, and 45 of the CCVVCV(C) pattern.

Regarding onset, the 70 broken-plural test items selected fell into the 12 categories listed in Table 4.[6] This categorization also entails less fine-grained categorizations of course, such as a three-way division into stop-initial (including affricate-initial; 29 tokens), fricative-initial (26 tokens), and sonorant-initial (15 tokens), or a binary division into sonorant-initial (15 tokens) and others (55 tokens).

---

[6]Given the presence of the /sk/–SONORANT-initial items, the abbreviation "CC" in this article should be understood as standing for "consonant cluster" in general, rather than for a cluster of exactly two consonants. That said, two-consonant onset clusters are much more numerous than three-consonant onset clusters, both in our test items and in Maltese generally.

Table 4: The broken plural test items by onset type

Onset types	No. of Items	Example	
STOP-STOP	6	*qtates*	'cats'
STOP-FRICATIVE/AFFRICATE	6	*gżejjer*	'islands'
STOP-SONORANT	9	*drabi*	'times'
AFFRICATE-STOP	2	*ġkieket*	'jackets'
AFFRICATE-SONORANT	6	*ċwievet*	'keys'
FRICATIVE-STOP	8	*stilel*	'stars'
FRICATIVE-FRICATIVE/AFFRICATE	5	*ħxejjex*	'vegetables'
FRICATIVE-SONORANT	9	*flieles*	'chicks'
SONORANT-STOP	5	*mkatar*	'handkerchiefs'
SONORANT-FRICATIVE/AFFRICATE	6	*rġejjen*	'queens'
SONORANT-SONORANT	4	*mrietel*	'hammers'
/sk/-SONORANT	4	*skrapan*	'shoemakers'

Turning to the sound-plural test items, we extracted all 225 CC-initial disyllabic sound plurals recorded in Aquilina's (1987–1990) dictionary. Most of these were archaic and/or infrequent and had to be discarded. Among the remainder, the most commonly represented plural suffix was *-i*, as in *sferi* 'spheres' (sg. *sfera*), followed by *-iet*, as in *brimbiet* 'spiders' (sg. *brimba*), then *-s*, as in *slogans* 'slogans' (sg. *slogan*). We selected all tokens of the latter two plural types that we judged sufficiently frequent and familiar (11 tokens of each type) and 27 of the more familiar tokens of *-i* plurals, choosing items with a range of onset types and initial-syllable weights. Of this total of 49 sound-plural tokens, 19 had a light initial syllable, and the remaining 30 had a heavy initial syllable.

2.3 Statistical analysis

The two experimental data sets (broken and sound plurals) were analyzed separately using hierarchical (mixed-effects) logistic regression models with random intercepts for test item and subject. The models were fit in R (Team 2016) using the function "glmer" in the "lme4" package (Bates et al. 2015). As summarized in Table 3, the objective of this study was to investigate one primary factor (the distinction between sound and broken plurals), and five additional factors (3 for broken, 2 for sound plurals). The latter factors were added as fixed effects to the models for the two data sets. The presentation of results in the following sections proceeds as follows. First, the statistical significance of the individual factors is reported in a table listing the results of Wald Chi-square tests calculated with the function Anova in the "car" package (Fox & Weisberg 2011). These tests reveal whether – based on the data at hand – a predictor may be considered as contributing information about the distribution of /t/ insertion in Maltese plurals. Next, a graphical summary of the internal structure of the factors is given using effect displays. These provide estimates about /t/-insertion rates in the different conditions (e.g. male vs. female subjects, heavy vs. light initial syllable). All graphs include 95% confidence intervals and show estimates while holding other factors at their means. The effect displays were constructed with the packages "effects" (Fox 2016), "lattice" (Sarkar 2008), and "latticeExtra" (Sarkar & Andrews 2016). The figures plotted in the effect displays are also provided in tabular form. Finally, technical details about the model coefficients are given in the appendix.

3 Results

3.1 Basic finding

The headline result is that the key hypothesis – that /t/-insertion rates are sensitive to the sound vs. broken plural distinction – is strongly confirmed. The mean /t/-insertion rate for all broken plurals tested was 32%, while for all sound plurals tested it was 5%. However, the results are far from uniform in either set of test items, and particularly with the broken plurals, as can be seen in Figure 2. The

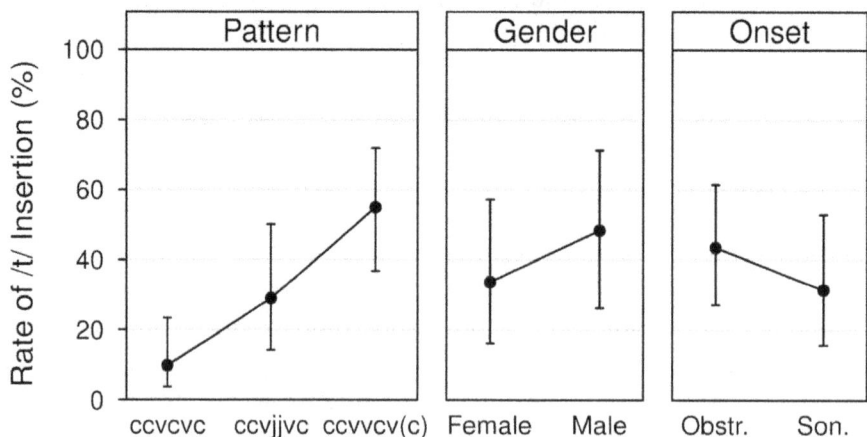

Figure 2: Effect displays showing estimated /t/-insertion rates in broken plurals. In each panel, other variables are held at their means (error bars: 95% confidence intervals)

reasons for this heterogeneity are explored in the following sections. The full list of items tested, together with the per item results, can be found in Table 5 and Table 6.

3.2 Broken plurals

Table 7 shows the statistical significance of the three factors investigated in relation to broken plurals: pattern (i.e. CCVVCV(C), as in *bramel*, CCVjjVC, as in *knejjes* and CCVCVC, as in *gwerer*); phonetic properties of the onset; and gender of the test subject. We can see that pattern is a statistically significant factor, as we predicted it would be, while the factors of onset and gender of subject (about which we had no specific hypotheses) turn out not to be statistically significant.[7]

The internal structure of these three factors is shown in Figure 2 and Table 8. Note that the prediction that the *gwerer*-type CCVCVC pattern is less favourable to /t/-insertion than the other two is confirmed: there was a statistically significant difference both between the CCVjjVC pattern and the CCVCVC pattern (z = 2.56, p = 0.01), and between the CCVVCV(C) pattern and the CCVCVC pattern (z = 5.39, p < 0.0001).[8]

3.3 Sound plurals

As noted in §3.1 and illustrated in Table 6, although rates of /t/-insertion were generally much lower with sound plurals than with broken plurals, rates were not consistent across all the sound plural items tested. While 25 of the 49 items tested triggered no /t/-insertion at all, the other 24 did at least 5% of the time, and the item with the highest rate of /t/-insertion was *sferi* 'spheres' (sg. *sfera*), at 31%. We suspected before collecting the data that any such differences would be due to morphophonological properties of the plurals, specifically: 1) the nature of the first syllable (i.e. heavy, due to a long vowel or a word-medial geminate, and thus phonologically similar to the /t/-favouring broken-plural patterns, or otherwise light), and 2) the position of stress (i.e. on the initial syllable, in the case of items with the plural suffixes -*i* and -*s*, or on the final syllable, in the case of items with

---

[7]Table 7 shows that the factor of onset does not contribute useful information to an understanding of how /t/-insertion is distributed among the broken plurals tested, when onset is coded as a binary distinction between initial sonorant and initial obstruent consonants. Onset is similarly not useful with a more fine-grained coding, as in Table 4 and the accompanying discussion.

[8]The difference between the CCVVCV(C) and CCVjjVC patterns was also found to be statistically significant (z = -2.39, p = 0.02).

Table 5: CC-initial disyllabic broken plurals – test items and /t/-insertion rates. Key: CCVVC(C): plain typeface; CCVjjVC: **bold italics**; CCVCVC: **BOLD CAPS**.

Test items	Meaning	% /t/	Test items	Meaning	% /t/
qsari	flower pots	87%	skieken	knives	46%
slaleb	crosses	87%	skrataċ	cartridges	45%
ħnieżer	pigs	87%	rwiefen	gales	44%
qtates	cats	86%	sfafar	whistles	44%
flieles	chicks	85%	ċrieket	rings	43%
ġkieket	jackets	79%	bziezen	bread rolls	43%
kpiepel	hats	76%	msielet	earrings	41%
żwiemel	horses	73%	*ħxejjex*	vegetables	*41%*
qniepen	bells	73%	*ħrejjef*	fables	*39%*
dbielet	skirts	72%	ċpiepet	bracelets	37%
drabi	times	67%	**MĦADED**	pillow	**37%**
blalen	balls	67%	*xmajjar*	rivers	*36%*
ċmieni	chimneys	67%	*skejjel*	schools	*33%*
kwiekeb	stars	65%	ktieli	kettles	33%
sħaħar	wizards	64%	bdiewa	farmers	32%
mwejjed	tables	*64%*	mkatar	handkerchiefs	31%
bżieżaq	balloons	63%	ċraret	pcs of cloth	30%
ħbula	ropes	62%	*nbejjed*	wines	*30%*
skrejjen	propellers	*62%*	zlazi	sauces	30%
xfafar	blades	62%	*xkejjer*	sacks	*29%*
skrapan	shoemakers	59%	**GWERER**	wars	**28%**
knejjes	churches	*57%*	*stejjer*	stories	*27%*
ċwievet	keys	56%	rkiekel	bobbins	26%
rdieden	sp. wheels	56%	*gżejjer*	islands	*23%*
ġrieden	mice	54%	msiemer	nails	20%
ħwienet	shops	53%	**SKWERER**	set-squares	**19%**
rziezet	farms	53%	**PLAKEK**	plugs	**17%**
XKAFEF	shelves	**53%**	**VLEĠEĠ**	arrows	**15%**
mrietel	hammers	53%	*rġejjen*	queens	*15%*
qżieqeż	piglets	52%	**STILEL**	stars	**13%**
ktajjen	chains	*50%*	twieqi	windows	13%
rħula	villages	48%	**SPONOŻ**	sponges	**13%**
mqaret	date pastries	48%	**PJAZEZ**	squares	**10%**
rwejjaħ	smells	*46%*	*ħsejjes*	sounds	*3%*
kxaxen	drawers	46%	**FLOTOT**	fleets	**0%**

Table 6: CC-initial disyllabic sound plurals – test items and /t/-insertion rates. Key: light first syllable: plain typeface; heavy (long vowel): **_bold italics_**; heavy (medial geminate): **BOLD CAPS**

Test items	Meaning	% /t/	Test items	Meaning	% /t/
sferi	spheres	*31%*	bramiet	jellyfish	0%
FJAMMI	flames	22%	**TNALJI**	tongs	**0%**
pjagi	plagues	*21%*	stensils	stencils	0%
friżers	freezers	*20%*	ħjariet	cucumbers	0%
bdoti	pilots	*17%*	qronfliet	carnations	0%
xkupi	brooms	*14%*	briksiet	bricks	0%
skedi	cards	*12%*	**PLATTI**	plates	**0%**
GRUPPI	groups	11%	drillers	drills	0%
stili	styles	*11%*	**TRAĊĊI**	traces	**0%**
travi	beams	*11%*	*gradi*	grades	*0%*
ŻBALJI	mistakes	10%	skandli	scandals	0%
pruniet	plums	9%	brimbiet	spiders	0%
DVALJI	tab. cloths	7%	blackboards	blackboards	0%
drogi	drugs	7%	*cruises*	cruises	*0%*
kwoti	shares	6%	*stejpils*	staples	*0%*
GRAMMI	grams	6%	**ĦNEJJIET**	arches	**0%**
ħġiġiet	panes	6%	spagiet	pcs of string	0%
SKOSSI	bumps	5%	ġbejniet	small cheeses	0%
skużi	excuses	*5%*	stampi	pictures	0%
flipflops	flipflops	5%	**VJAĠĠI**	journeys	**0%**
FROTTIET	fruits	5%	brackets	brackets	0%
slogans	slogans	*5%*	brushes	brushes	0%
spaners	spanners	5%	pjanti	plants	0%
DRAMMI	dramas	5%	statwi	statues	0%
kwadri	paintings	*0%*			

Table 7: Contribution of the factors to /t/-insertion in broken plurals: Wald Chi-square tests

Factor	Levels	Wald Chi-square	*df*	*p*	
Broken plural pattern	CCVCVC, CCVVCV(C), CCVjjVC	32.67	2	<0.0001	***
Phonetic properties of onset	obstruent, sonorant	2.11	1	0.15	
Gender	female, male	0.83	1	0.36	

Table 8: Estimated /t/-insertion rates in broken plurals

		95% confidence interval	
Factor	**Estimated /t/-insertion rate**	**Lower limit**	**Upper limit**
Pattern			
CCVCVC	10%	4%	23%
CCVjjVC	29%	14%	50%
CCVVCV(C)	55%	37%	72%
Gender			
Female	34%	16%	57%
Male	48%	26%	71%
Onset			
Obstruent	44%	27%	61%
Sonorant	31%	16%	53%

the plural suffix -iet). As can be seen from Table 9, only initial syllable weight turned out to be a significant predictor of /t/-insertion rates. Specifically, while /t/-insertion was low or very low across the board with the sound plural items tested in this experiment, it was significantly less low with those items with a heavy initial syllable. This is illustrated in Figure 3 and Table 10.

Table 9: Contribution of the factors to /t/-insertion in sound plurals: Wald Chi-square tests

Factor	Levels	Wald Chi-square	df	p	
Weight of first syllable	heavy, light	7.59	1	0.006	**
Suffix type / stress position	-iet, non-stress-attracting suffixes	0.00	1	0.95	

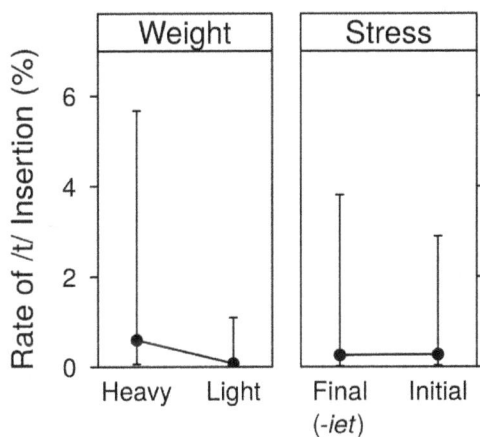

Figure 3: Effect displays showing estimated /t/ insertion rates in sound plurals. In each panel, other variables are held at their means (error bars: 95% confidence intervals)

135

Table 10: Estimated /t/ insertion rates in sound plurals

Factor	Estimated /t/-insertion rate	95% confidence interval	
		Lower limit	Upper limit
Weight			
Heavy	0.6%	0.1%	5.7%
Light	0.1%	0.0%	1.1%
Stress			
Final (-*iet*)	0.3%	0.0%	3.8%
Initial	0.3%	0.0%	2.9%

3.4 Summary of results

In this new experiment on /t/-insertion behaviour with CC-initial disyllabic plurals we found, in line with our predictions, that broken plurals trigger /t/-insertion much more often than sound plurals, even when onset and number of syllables – the two factors generally cited in the previous literature as most significant to /t/-insertion – are held constant.

Also in line with our predictions was the finding that broken plurals of the *gwerer*-type CCVCVC pattern trigger /t/-insertion significantly less often than the other two CC-initial disyllabic broken plural patterns.

We suspected that the gender of our test subjects and the precise nature of the onset might have an influence on rates of /t/-insertion. This proved not to be the case, however.

Finally, we suspected that /t/-insertion behaviour with sound plurals would be influenced by the weight of the initial syllable, and the position of stress, in the plural items tested. Stress position was found not to be a significant factor, but we found that items with a heavy initial syllable were associated with significantly higher rates of /t/-insertion than those with a light initial syllable. This should not, however, obscure the fact that overall the rate of /t/-insertion with the sound plural items tested was close to zero.

4 Discussion

We have seen that the two main predictions were borne out: when we hold onset and number of syllables constant (at CC and two, respectively), broken plurals are much more favourable to /t/-insertion than sound plurals, and broken plurals of the *gwerer*-type CCVCVC pattern are much less favourable than plurals of other patterns. This is clear confirmation that /t/-insertion cannot be understood purely in phonological terms, such as the onset type and number of syllables of plural nouns: their morphological profile is at least as important.

As explained in §2.1, the genesis of the hypothesis that *gwerer*-type CCVCVC plurals would be unfavourable to /t/-insertion, despite beginning with a consonant cluster, was the insight that they belong to the same basic (C)CVCVC pattern as plurals such as *bozoz* 'bulbs' (sg. *bozza*), which, like all CV-initial plurals, seems to be particularly hostile to /t/-insertion. If onset type had been more important, we would have expected *gwerer*-type plurals to pattern with other CC-initial broken plurals and be favourable to /t/-insertion. In the event, it was the morphological identity of these items – their membership of the /t/-resistant (C)CVCVC pattern – that proved decisive, not their onset.

We must be careful not to take this line of argument too far, however. Our results show that the kinds of phonological factors considered in the literature to date clearly cannot do all the work of explaining what governs /t/-insertion. But our results also indicate that phonology has a role to play. This is perhaps easiest to see by considering the sound-plural items with the highest rates of /t/-insertion. These show that Borg's (1974: 297) blunt claim that "sound plurals do not take /t/" is too sweeping: they certainly do not favour /t/-insertion, but they do not rule it out altogether. Consider in particular items such as *pjagi* 'plagues' (sg. *pjaga*), with a /t/-insertion rate of 21%, and *travi* 'beams' (sg. *travu*) with a rate of 11%. These have an identical phonological profile to broken plural items we tested, such as *qsari* 'flower pots' (sg. *qasrija*), with a /t/-insertion rate of 87%, and *drabi* 'times' (sg. *darba*), with a rate of 67%. More generally, note the following parallels between the broken and sound plurals that we tested. The two broken plural patterns in our data that were more favourable to /t/ were CCVVCVC, as in *bramel* 'buckets' (sg. *barmil*), with a long vowel in the first syllable, and CCVjjVC, as in *knejjes* 'churches' (sg. *knisja*), with a medial geminate; and it was also the sound plurals with either a long vowel in the initial syllable or a medial geminate that triggered /t/-insertion significantly more frequently than the others. It is unlikely that this is a coincidence. Rather it seems that phonology is playing a secondary role here: an item's morphological identity as a sound plural ensures it will be basically hostile to /t/-insertion, but this hostility can be lessened to a limited extent, just in case its phonology closely resembles that of an appropriate broken plural pattern.

A similar dynamic seems to hold with the *gwerer*-type CCVCVC broken plurals. One might have expected these to be totally incompatible with /t/-insertion, rather than permitting it with an average frequency of 23%. After all, these have the same basic pattern as CV-initial plurals such as *bozoz*, which seem to totally exclude the possibility of /t/-insertion.[9] Instead it seems that, as with the sound plurals such as *sferi*, the morphological pressure on plurals such as *gwerer* to resist /t/-insertion is mitigated somewhat by their phonological similarity (having a CC onset) to the broken-plural patterns which actively favour /t/-insertion.

It is noteworthy, finally, that we found no significant effect of gender on speakers' /t/-insertion behaviour. With linguistic variation of this kind, where, in a sufficiently well-defined context (e.g. with broken plurals of the CCVVCV(C) type) there seems to be total optionality from a linguistic point of view, it is natural to expect that inter-speaker variation might be invested with social meaning. But this is especially likely to be the case with variation that is the result of changes in progress, and it could be that the optionality of /t/-insertion, at least in the restricted domain of disyllabic CC-initial plurals investigated here, is in fact a system that has been stable for several generations or more. Future studies could investigate this issue by repeating the kind of experiment described here, with test subjects stratified by age, gender, and perhaps other sociolinguistic variables.

5 Conclusion

This article has provided evidence that, contrary to previous work on the topic, it is morphological, not phonological properties of the plural noun that should be seen as the prime determinants of whether /t/-insertion is triggered in the presence of an accompanying numeral. Specifically, at least as far as CC-initial plurals are concerned, /t/-insertion is favoured only by particular broken-plural patterns. On the other hand, we have seen that phonology does seem to play a secondary role. While sound plurals are, on the whole, very hostile to /t/-insertion, there are some whose phonology happens to closely resemble that of the /t/-favouring broken-plural patterns, and it seems to be this which causes them to trigger /t/-insertion, if only rarely.

---

[9] A degree of caution is required here. In the first experiment, *bozoz*, which never triggered /t/-insertion, was the only plural of this type that we tested. Since a) it has never been suggested in the previous literature that /t/-insertion is possible with CV-initial items in general, and b) we found in our first experiment that CV-initial items, including other broken plurals such as *kotba* 'books' (sg. *ktieb*), were uniformly hostile to /t/-insertion, it is reasonable to extrapolate that this generalises to all broken plurals of the CVCVC pattern. But we do not, at present, have the data to prove that this is the case.

This is by no means all there is to be said on this topic. Aside from the sociolinguistic dimension suggested above, there are several aspects of the grammar of /t/-insertion that remain unclear, for example the conditions determining /t/-insertion with vowel-initial plurals, and whether the frequency of a plural noun (or a numeral–noun string) has an effect on its /t/-insertion behaviour. It is to be hoped that puzzles such as these can be solved in future work.

Acknowledgements

The authors would like to sincerely thank Lukas Sönning for his generous assistance and input into the analysis and presentation of this research, which was made possible by means of a Humboldt research fellowship for postdoctoral researchers. Any shortcomings of this work are entirely the responsibility of the authors.

Appendix

Table 11: Parameter estimates for the broken-plural model

Fixed effects	β	SE	z	p
Intercept (CCVCVC, Obstruent, Female)	−2.42	0.63	−3.87	0.0001
Pattern: CCVjjVC	1.32	0.52	2.56	0.01
Pattern: CCVVCVC	2.42	0.45	5.39	<0.0001
Onset: Sonorant	−0.52	0.36	−1.45	0.15
Gender: Male	0.61	0.67	0.91	0.36

Random effects	Variance	SD		
Item	1.22	1.10		
Subject	3.24	1.80		

Table 12: Table A2. Parameter estimates for the sound plural model

Fixed effects	β	SE	z	p
Intercept (Heavy, Final)	−5.17	1.43	−3.61	0.0003
Weight: Light	−2.08	0.75	2.76	0.006
Stress: Final	0.05	0.90	0.06	0.95

Random effects	Variance	SD
Item	1.21	1.10
Subject	7.32	2.71

References

Ambros, Arne. 1998. *Bon Ġornu, kif int: Einführung in die maltesische Sprache.* Wiesbaden: Reichert.

Aquilina, Joseph. 1965. *Teach yourself Maltese.* London: The English Universities Press.

Bates, Douglas, Martin Maechler & Ben Bolker. 2015. Fitting linear mixed-effects model using lme4. *Journal of Statistical Software* 67(1). 1–48.

Bod, Rens. 1998. *Beyond grammar: An experience-based theory of language.* Stanford: CSLI Publications.

Borg, Alexander. 1974. Maltese numerals. *Zeitschrift der Deutschen Morgenländische Gesellschaft* 124(2). 291–305.

Chambers, Jack K. 2003. *Sociolinguistic theory: Linguistic variation and its social significance.* 2nd edn. Oxford: Blackwell.

Cremona, Antonino. 1938. *Tagħlim fuq il-Kitba Maltija.* Oxford: Oxford University Press.

Eddington, David. 2009. Linguistic processing is exemplar-based. *Studies in Hispanic and Lusophone Linguistics* 2. 420–33.

Fabri, Ray. 1994. The syntax of numerals in Maltese. In Joseph M. Brincat (ed.), *Languages of the Mediterranean: Proceedings of the Conference held in Malta, 26–29 September 1991,* 228–239. Msida: University of Malta.

Fox, John. 2016. R package 'effects'. *R package version 3.* https://cran.r-project.org/web/packages/effects/effects.pdf, accessed 2016-12-08.

Fox, John & Sanford Weisberg. 2011. *An R companion to applied regression.* Thousand Oaks: Sage.

Krug, Manfred. 1998. String frequency: A cognitive motivating factor in coalescence, language processing and linguistic change. *Journal of English Linguistics* 26. 286–320.

Labov, William. 2001. *Principles of linguistic change, vol 2: Social factors.* Oxford: Blackwell.

Lucas, Christopher & Michael Spagnol. 2016. Connecting /t/ in Maltese numerals. In Gilbert Puech & Benjamin Saade (eds.), *Shifts and patterns in Maltese,* 260–290. Berlin: De Gruyter.

Mifsud, Manwel. 1994. Internal pluralization in Maltese: Continuity and innovation. In Dominique Caubet & Martine Vanhove (eds.), *Actes des premières journées de dialectologie Arabe,* 91–105. Paris: INALCO.

Rumelhart, David E. & James L. McClelland. 1986. On learning the past tenses of English verbs. In David E. Rumelhart, James L. McClelland & The PDP Research Group (eds.), *Parallel distributed processing: Explorations in the microstructure of cognition, vol. 2: Psychological and biological models,* 216–271. Cambridge, MA: The MIT Press.

Sarkar, Deepayan. 2008. *Lattice: Multivariate data visualization with R.* New York: Springer.

Sarkar, Deepayan & Felix Andrews. 2016. *latticeExtra: Extra Graphical Utilities Based on Lattice, version 6.28.* Online manual. https://CRAN.R-project.org/package=latticeExtra.

Sutcliffe, Edmund. 1936. *A grammar of the Maltese language, with chrestomathy and vocabulary.* Oxford: Oxford University Press.

Team, R Core. 2016. *R: A language and environment for statistical computing.* Vienna, Austria: R Foundation for Statistical Computing. www.R-project.org.

Chapter 6

Borrowed affixes and morphological productivity: A case study of two Maltese nominalisations

Albert Gatt

Institute of Linguistics and Language Technology, University of Malta

Ray Fabri

Institute of Linguistics and Language Technology, University of Malta

Among the derivational processes that have been adopted into Maltese based on the Romance model, there are processes to derive nouns from verbs which are relatively recent developments. Examples include the use of the suffix *-Vr* (e.g., *spara/sparar* 'shoot'/'(the) shooting'), and the use of *-(z)zjoni* (e.g., *spjega / spjegazzjoni* 'explain'/'explanantion'). This paper discusses these processes in the context of Maltese derivation in general. After a brief theoretical exposition and an overview of Maltes derivation, we present a corpus-based analysis of the productivity of *-Vr* and *-(z)zjoni* derivations, followed by an analysis of the evidence for indirect borrowing in these two cases, based on the work of Seifart (2015). We show that, while there is evidence that both are productive, the statistical evidence suggests that *-Vr* processes are more likely to result in novel forms. By the same token, *-Vr* nominalisations more clearly represent cases of indirect borrowing, as evidenced by the greater number of types which have corresponding simplex forms, and by the greater probability that the simplex forms are more frequent than the nominalisations.

1 Introduction

The morpho-phonological system of Modern Maltese is the result of intensive contact involving an Arabic stratum, a Romance (Sicilian, Italian) superstratum

Albert Gatt & Ray Fabri. Borrowed affixes and morphological productivity: A case study of two Maltese nominalisations. In Patrizia Paggio & Albert Gatt (eds.), *The languages of Malta*, 143–169. Berlin: Language Science Press.
DOI:10.5281/zenodo.1181793

and an English adstratum (Brincat 2011; Mifsud 1995b). The result is a hybrid morphological system incorporating both root-based and stem-based forms (see, among others, Drewes 1994; Mifsud 1995b; Fabri 2010; Spagnol 2013).

The extent to which the Semitic or Romance components predominate in the Maltese lexicon is something of an open question. For example, Brincat (2011) suggests that the Romance component accounts for some 52% of the lexicon, based on counts obtained from a standard dictionary. By contrast, Comrie & Spagnol (2016) restrict their counts to a small sample of lexical items and find that Romance etymology accounts for some 30%.

Whatever the actual predominance of Romance versus Semitic, the hybridity of the Maltese morphological system raises a number of empirical questions which have broad theoretical significance. Among these is the question of productivity. The term 'productivity' is here operationally defined as referring to the extent to which morphological processes are used by speakers to generate novel forms. This criterion – i.e. the use of a process to generate novel forms – is widely adopted in many discussions of morphological productivity (including Aronoff & Schvaneveldt 1978; Cutler 1980; Aronoff & Anshen 1998; Bauer 2001; Dressler 2003; and Plag 2004, among others.)

In earlier work on Maltese (for example by Mifsud 1995b; Hoberman & Aronoff 2003), it has sometimes been argued that the Semitic/Arabic derivational component is relatively unproductive, with novel word forms being largely created through stem-based processes ultimately arising from Romance. Indeed, some recent work by Saade (2016) has suggested that quantitative measures of the productivity of a subset of Romance-derived derivational affixes in Maltese yield a ranking comparable to that found for their Italian cognates in a earlier work by Gaeta & Ricca (2006), although the absolute productivity values found are lower for Maltese processes compared to their Italian counterparts.

These views and findings motivate the decision in the present study to focus primarily on comparison of two non-Arabic deverbal suffixes, namely *-(z)zjoni* and *-Vr* (where *V* is either /a/ or /i/), as a test case. Thus, certain derivational processes of Arabic origin fall outside the scope of the present paper, though we discuss them briefly in order to situate our study within the broader context of the Maltese morphological system.

We conduct a corpus-based analysis of *-Vr* and *-(z)zjoni* to address two related issues: (a) to what extent these affixes are productive, based on statistical criteria formulated by Baayen (2009); and (b) whether there is evidence for their status as directly or indirectly borrowed affixes, in the sense discussed by Seifart (2015). Individually, these two questions shed light on the nature of the morphological system in Maltese and the extent to which empirical evidence justifies claims that certain processes are in greater use than others in modern Maltese. However, the questions of productivity and of whether an affix is in/directly borrowed are also complementary in another important sense. Following Seifart (2015) we view indirect borrowing as a process involving the importation of complex forms having an affix from a source language, followed by the use of that affix on novel forms, thus implying parsing or decomposition. This implies that productivity is part and parcel of the definition of indirect borrowing. As Hay & Baayen (2001) argue, the extent to which a lexical item can be parsed in perception (for example, into a stem and its affixes) can help in predictions of the productivity of the processes giving rise to that item in the first place. By the same token, the ability to place an affix (or morphological process) somewhere along the continuum between direct and indirect borrowing complements the statistical evidence for productivity that can be derived from corpora along the line suggested by Baayen (2009), among others.

This chapter is structured as follows. We first briefly introduce the theoretical framework within which we view derivational morphological processes. Next (§3), we discuss derivation in Maltese, with particular reference to nominalisation and stem-based processes. §4 gives a descriptive overview of the two affixes under consideration, with remarks concerning their status as directly or indirectly borrowed affixes. §5 describes a corpus-based investigation of productivity of -*Vr* and -*(z)zjoni* forms, followed by an empirical investigation of the evidence in favour of indirect borrowing in the two cases. §6 concludes with some remarks on possible future research directions.

2 Some theoretical preliminaries

In the present study, the term 'derivation' is not meant to imply a process that has a direction, as in 'x is derived from y' (as opposed to 'y is derived from x'). In other words, we do not adopt a procedural approach to derivational morphology, which would require a commitment as to the precedence of certain forms from which others are derived. Even for the linguist, the decision as to which lexemes in a pair has (diachronic) priority is often a matter of approximate reasoning (as Ellul 2016, for example, shows in connection with Maltese deverbal nominalisations).

Rather, we propose to think of derivation in terms of links between forms that have a formal and semantic relationship, that is, between words/lexemes. The term 'derivation' is used here simply to distinguish one type of lexical relation from other relations, in particular from inflection, which is a relation between grammatical word forms instantiating a lexeme, as opposed to a relation between lexemes. In the following, we use a double arrow (↔) to express the idea that in x ↔ y, x and y are derivationally related to each other. Thus, for example, in English, REVOLT ↔ REVOLUTION means that *revolt* and *revolution* are two lexemes that have both a formal and a semantic relationship.

One way to conceive of such derivational relationships in a non-procedural fashion is with reference to what we call *derivational families*, i.e., words/lexemes that are related to each other through a common, shared base. Cases that involve allomorphic variation of the base (including stem allomorphy) are also included within a derivational family. To take an example, the base form KOMPO 'compose/make up' relates the following forms to each other: *(ik)kompo(n)-a* 'compose', *kompo(n)-iment* 'essay', *kompo(n)-enti* 'component', *kompo(ż)-izzjoni* 'composition' and *kompo(ż)-itur* 'composer'.

The assumption is that the base in all of these forms somehow expresses some common underlying, basic meaning, or at least serves to index a cluster of related basic meanings. To the native speaker, the relationships would be intuitively obvious for *kompożizzjoni* 'composition' in relation to *kompożitur* 'composer', though perhaps less obvious for *komponent* 'component' relative to *komponiment* 'essay'. At the same time, the relationship between the latter two, while semantically more opaque than in the case of KOMPOŻIZZJONI ↔ KOMPOŻITUR, is nevertheless quite clear from a formal perspective (i.e. the shared stem is intuitively obvious to the native speaker). This suggests that there may be a disjuncture between the semantic and formal links, so that one could conceive of a combination of at least two criteria governing the intuition of a relationship, one based on form and another on meaning, where the strength of the relation between two forms can vary as a function of the strength of the formal and semantic relations. Thus, a more tenuous link would be perceived between two forms if, say, they share a base but the meaning deviates considerably (see Bybee 1995 for a network model of morphology developed along these lines).

A gradient of associative strength among related forms would also be able to account for derivational relationships among forms which are related by a common root via processes of Arabic origin, as in the case of $\sqrt{b\text{-}j\text{-}d}$ in (1) and $\sqrt{\hbar\text{-}d\text{-}m}$ in (2).

(1) (Second verbal form (CVCCVC), from *abjad*, root $\sqrt{b\text{-}j\text{-}d}$;)
     abjad ↔ *bajjad*
     white ↔ paint/whitewash
     to whitewash

(2)   (Deverbal noun from root $\sqrt{\hbar\text{-}d\text{-}m}$;)
     ħadem ↔ *ħaddiem*
     work ↔ worker
     worker

These might be presumed to constitute families in which the root indexes a cluster of basic meanings, though there is considerable semantic variation among related forms. This need not imply that the processes involved are productive (Mifsud 1995b; Hoberman & Aronoff 2003), or that all relationships among lexemes sharing a root are equally transparent – indeed, as we have seen, some arguments to the contrary have been advanced. It does, however, imply that the root itself has some psychological reality for the native speaker. It is worth noting that some psycholinguistic evidence does point towards a role for the root as an index for lexical retrieval by native Maltese speakers (see e.g. Twist 2006; Ussishkin et al. 2015).

Another frequently observed phenomenon is that derivational families (unlike inflectional families, generally) display gaps, that is, not all the theoretically or potentially possible forms actually occur in everyday use. To take an example, the Korpus Malti, a corpus of Maltese (described in Gatt & Čéplö 2013 and introduced more fully in §5 below), yields examples of a number of forms for the base DIMOSTR- 'demonstrate', including *dimostrazzjoni* 'demonstration', *dimostrant* 'demonstator', *(i)ddimostra* 'demonstrate', and even one occurrence of *dimostratur* 'demonstrator' (the more frequently attested form being *dimostrant*). The corpus does not, however, attest to the use of potential formations such as *#dimostrist* or *#dimostrament*, though the suffixes *-ist* and *-ment* are productively used in Maltese. The established family networks provide the potential for new creations, but many factors play a role in determining which are actually formed and used, including phonological restrictions on the base, blocking through an already available form, and other constraints which have been discussed extensively in the theoretical literature (e.g. Spencer 1991; Spencer & Zwicky 1998; Aronoff & Fudeman 2011; and Haspelmath & Sims 2010, among others.)

3 Derivational morphology in Maltese

As noted in the introductory section, at different phases of its history, Maltese borrowed lexically from a number of languages. Its early sources were mainly Sicilian, Tuscan, and Modern Italian; in recent times, English has become an additional source (for discussion of these various influences see Mifsud 1995b; Borg &

Azzopardi-Alexander 1997; Fabri et al. 2013; Spagnol 2013; and Brincat & Mifsud 2016). As a result, Maltese displays a great deal of lexical and morphological variety, and derivation also reflects this rich historical background, displaying both non-concatenative (templatic, root-based) forms (exemplified in 1 and 2 above), which are generally older forms historically going back to Arabic, and concatenative (affixal, stem-based) forms, which are generally historically of non-Arabic origin, i.e., Sicilian, Italian or English.

In this section, we first give a brief overview of the types of derivational processes available, before turning to a consideration of the status of stem-based derivational processes, in anticipation of the study presented in §5.

3.1 Verbal derivation

The historically older derived verbal forms are based on the conjugation system typical of Arabic, often referred to with the term *binyanim* from Hebrew, and known as *forom* 'forms' in Maltese. Traditional descriptive grammars list 10 derivational verbal forms, though the vast majority of Maltese verbs do not conjugate in all forms (in fact, the majority have only between two and three forms, as shown by Spagnol 2013) and at least one form – form ɪᴠ – has only a single attested entry and thus cannot really be considered a derivational form in modern Maltese. The roots are generally assumed to be triliteral, as in the case of $\sqrt{d\text{-}ħ\text{-}l}$ 'enter'; or quadriliteral, as in the case of $\sqrt{ħ\text{-}r\text{-}b\text{-}t}$ 'spoil/ruin'. The derived forms are characterised either by changes in the cᴠ template (i.e., non-concatenative processes), by affixation, or both. Table 1 displays a few examples in addition to those given in (1) and (2) above.

Table 1: Examples of root-based verbal derivations.

Root	Derived form	Form #	Gloss
$\sqrt{d\text{-}ħ\text{-}l}$	daħħal	II	'let in'
$\sqrt{f\text{-}h\text{-}m}$	fiehem	III	'explain'
$\sqrt{k\text{-}s\text{-}r}$	tkisser	V	'get broken'
$\sqrt{d\text{-}ħ\text{-}l}$	ndaħal	VII	'interfere'

The productivity of these derivational forms in modern Maltese, which evince a lot of gaps and are often semantically idiosyncratic, is a matter of discussion (see, e.g., Mifsud 1995b and Hoberman & Aronoff 2003). There appears to be general agreement, based mainly on intuition, that these forms are fossilised and not generally productive, that is, new formations in the templatic system are rare to non-existent. A separate issue, which we noted in our theoretical outline in §2, is whether the root has any psychological reality. Evidence from studies of lexical access has suggested that this is the case (Twist 2006; Ussishkin et al. 2015).

Note that, although new verbal forms are not being created within the templatic system, new verbs, especially from English, are being created in Maltese (these verbs are referred to as Type D verbs by Mifsud 1995a). These are created on the pattern of a particular declensional class of verbs, namely, verbs with a final weak consonant, that is, *j* or *w*. The new forms are characterised by the suffix *-ja* attached to a borrowed base form, which is either verbal or nominal in origin, to produce a verbal stem for inflection. Often this process is also accompanied by gemination of the initial consonant, which then requires *i*-epenthesis for syllabification, as in *immoniterja* 'monitor', from English *monitor*; and *iċċekkja* 'check', from English *check*. This process appears to be highly productive, with new verbs continually being produced according to this pattern, as shown by Mifsud (1995a). These verbs, in turn, become candidates for deverbal derivation in forms such as *iċċekkjar* 'checking', formed using -*Vr*, which will be discussed below.

3.2 Nominal derivation

Derived nominals (nouns and adjectives) also consist of formations that display both concatenative (i.e., affixal) and non-concatenative (i.e., templatic) patterns. Table 2a shows a few examples of noun patterns that are derivationally related to other forms via templatic processes. Table 2b gives some examples of nominal derivations which arise from affix-based processes.

There are indications that, just as in the case of verbal derivation based on templatic patterns, templatic nominal derivation is not productive anymore.

3.3 The status of stem-based derivational processes

Many of the stem-based derivational processes outlined above raise the question whether they involve 'real' affixes. Clearly, whether or not they are productive is an important consideration here. Justification for treating such affixes as productive morphemes generally comes from cases of local formations which do not have cognates in a source language, since this means that they could not have been absorbed whole but must have been created locally.

Obvious examples of local creations are derived forms which have a lexical base from one language source but which make use of a derivative feature (affix-

Table 2: Examples of templatic (root-based) and affix-based nominal derivation patterns.

Template	Root	Root Gloss	Example	Gloss
cvcc/a	$\sqrt{s\text{-}r\text{-}q}$	steal	serq/a	(a) theft
t-vcciic/a	$\sqrt{\hbar\text{-}w\text{-}d}$	mix up	taħwid/a	(a) mix-up
ccvvc	$\sqrt{\dot{z}\text{-}f\text{-}n}$	dance	żfin	(the) dancing
cvc_ic_ivvc	$\sqrt{\hbar\text{-}d\text{-}m}$	work	ħaddiem	worker

(a) Template-based patterns

Affix	Base	Base Gloss	Example	Gloss
-ment	aġġorna	to update	aġġornament	the/an update
-tur/a	ċċekkja	to check	ċekkjatur/a	checker/a check
-ist	arti	art	artist/a	artist
-vġġ	arpa	harp	arpeġġ	arpeggio
-vr	spara	to shoot	sparar	the/a shooting
-(z)zjoni	kkonserva	to conserve	konservazzjoni	conservation

(b) Affix-based patterns

ation, templatic arrangement) from a different language source. The examples in (3) show the well-known case of the Italian origin suffix *-ata* being attached to stems of words of Arabic origin to create new lexemes.

(3) (Suffix *-ata* applied to stems of Arabic origin;)
fenek ↔ *fenkata*
rabbit ↔ rabbit meal
xemx ↔ *xemxata*
sun ↔ sunstroke

At first blush, this suggests that such affixes have made their incursion into Maltese through what Seifart (2015) calls *indirect borrowing*, which Seifart places at one end of a continuum, at the other end of which is *direct borrowing*. In the latter case, 'an affix is recognized by speakers of the recipient language ...and used on native stems as soon as it is borrowed, with no intermediate phase of occurrence in complex loanwords only' (p. 512). By contrast, the paradigm case of indirect borrowing occurs where a number of lexical items with a particular affix are first borrowed into the target language, with the affix gradually coming into productive use on native stems following a process of analysis of the borrowed items. Note that this characterisation of direct versus indirect borrowing is diachronic in flavour. However, Seifart also suggests a number of criteria for identifying an indirectly borrowed affix in a language at a given stage of development. We turn to these in §4.2 below, where we discuss the question of whether the two nominalising affixes under discussion are best thought of as examples of direct or indirect borrowing.

4 -*Vr* and -*(z)zjoni* nominalisations

Following the overview above, we now turn our attention to a case study involving two nominalisation suffixes in Maltese: -*Vr* and -*(z)zjoni* . Before we present the results of a quantitative investigation, we give a descriptive outline.

4.1 Descriptive outline

-*Vr* is usually classified as -*ār*, with long /a/, and traced back to the Italian infinitive ending -*āre*, as in *amare* 'love' (Mifsud 1995a: 249). Indeed, in Italian the infinitive form can function as a noun, as shown by the use of *dire* 'say' and *fare* 'do' in the following proverb: *tra il dire e il fare c'è di mezzo il mare* (literally: 'there is an ocean between the said and the done'). However, while the -*are* ending (equivalently -*ere* and -*ire*) in Italian is not specifically a nominaliser, but marks the verb as infinitive, though it can then be used as a (verbal) noun, -*Vr* in Maltese is specifically and exclusively a nominaliser. Indeed, Maltese, like other Semitic languages, does not have a morphological infinitive.

The -*Vr* ending can be found both with Italian stems, as in *issorveljar* '(the) overseeing' from Italian *sorvegliare* 'oversee', and with English stems, as in *ibbrejkjar* '(the) braking' and *ipparkjar* 'the parking', from English *brake* and *park*, respectively. Given that, in these cases, the Maltese verbal form ends in short /a/ (e.g. *ipparkja* and *ibbrejkja*), the assumption is usually that the -*Vr* nominal is related to a verbal stem which already displays the /a/. There are however a few forms which display an -*īr* in place of -*ār*. Examples are *aġir* 'action', *servir* 'serving', *avvertir* 'warning', *riferir* 'referral', *esegwir* 'execution (of an action)' and *distribwir* 'distribution' (see Camilleri 1993 for a complete listing). To be sure, these are far less frequent than the forms involving /a/.

Like *-ār* forms, *-īr* forms are assumed to be related to a verbal stem ending in /a/, as in *irrefera* 'refer' or *esegwixxa* 'execute'. Interestingly, although these forms end in *-a* in the perfect third person masculine singular, in the imperfect singular they end in /i/, thus, *tirreferi* 'you refer', *tesegwixxi* 'you execute/she executes'. Moreover, these verbs are historically derived from verbs which in Italian end in *-ire* (*riferire, eseguire*). On being integrated into the Maltese inflectional system, they came to be conjugated on the pattern of a set of verbs of Arabic origin, such as *ħeba* 'hide' and *qela* 'fry', which end in /i/ in the imperfect singular (cf. *naħbi* 'I hide', *taħbi* 'you hide/she hides', *jaħbi* 'he hides'). Arguably, the *-i* in these cases can be taken as an inflectional suffix for the imperfect singular, as opposed to *-u* for plural (cf. *tirreferu* 'you (plural) refer', *taħbu* 'you (plural) hide'). In any case, these verbs contrast with the more common stem ending in *-a*, such as *tissorvelja* 'you oversee' and *tibbrejkja* 'you brake'.

Although traditionally the third person masculine singular perfect form (called *il-mamma* in Maltese pedagogical grammars) is taken as the citation form and often as the base form, speakers more naturally produce the second person singular as citation form when asked to give a Maltese equivalent for a foreign verb. This might be taken as an indication that, to the native speaker, the intuitive base form is indeed the second person singular, with the stem ending in /i/ or /a/ explaining the difference between forms such as *ibbrejkjar* 'to brake' (from second person *tibbrejkja*) and *avvertir* 'to warn' (from second person *tavverti*). This is why we use *-Vr* rather than *-ār* to indicate the relevant morph. Nevertheless, as noted by Camilleri (1993), *-īr* forms are comparatively rare.

The suffix *-(z)zjoni* comes from Italian *-zione* (compare: *ġeneralizzazzjoni* 'generalisation', from Italian *generalizzazione*) and has probably been 'strengthened' by English *-ation*. Thus, for example, the Maltese forms *afforestazzjoni* 'afforestation' and *aġġudikazzjoni* 'adjudication' do not have obvious cognates in Italian but they do have English equivalents in *-ation*. Here, too, there are candidates for allomorphic variants of the suffix, whose status is however unclear. Relevant examples are *manutenzjoni* 'maintenance', *intenzjoni* 'intention', and *prekawzjoni* 'precaution', all of which have a singulative /z/, rather than a geminate. (Note that this is not an orthographical but a phonological effect.) The former are preceded by a stem-final consonant, the latter by a stem-final vowel; cf. *manuten-zjoni* vs. *assoċja-zzjoni*. For this reason, we characterise the suffix as *-(z)zjoni* rather than *-zzjoni*.

There are a number of cases where *-Vr* and *-(z)zjoni* forms share the same base. Examples include, *istallar* and *istallazzjoni* 'installation', both of which are related to *i(n)stalla* 'to install'. The difference in meaning is not always clear, though generally it appears that the *-Vr* version refers to a process or event (close to English *-ing* formation, as in 'installing'), while *-(z)zjoni* can refer to either a process/event or an entity (similar to English *installation*, i.e., the result of an installation process; see Ellul 2016 and references therein for a resultative analysis of such forms). This observation is not without exceptions, however, as shown by examples such as *armar* 'decoration/decorating' and *tellar* 'panel beater', neither of which have a corresponding *-(z)zjoni* form. In any case, though there are cases where both an *-Vr* and a *-(z)zjoni* form coexist with the same base, most are found exclusively in either one or the other form. Table 3 gives examples of bases which nominalise exclusively in one or the other form.

Table 3: Bases which nominalise using *-Vr* or *-(z)zjoni*, but not both.

-Vr Nominalisation	*-(z)zjoni* Nominalisation	Gloss
ibbukkjar	*ibbukkjazzjoni	booking
depożitar	*depożitazzjoni	depositing
ittestjar	*testazzjoni	testing
*traduttar	traduzzjoni	translation
*assumar	assunzjoni	assumption
*affaxxinar	affaxxinazzjoni	fascination

4.2 Direct or indirect borrowing?

In the previous section, we observed that certain affixes borrowed from Italian may be cases of what Seifart (2015) calls indirect borrowing, since they are used on native stems. Here, we revisit this question in connection with *-Vr* and *-(z)zjoni*.

There are various cases of *-Vr* being used on stems of Arabic origin, as shown below.

(4) (Suffix *-Vr* applied to stems of Arabic origin; personal knowledge)
    ittama ↔ *ittamar*   *tkaża*   ↔ *tkażar*
    to hope ↔ hope   be shocked ↔ shock

By contrast, the suffix *-(z)zjoni* does not seem to be used with stems of Arabic origin. In our corpus data (§5), we have been unable to identify a single case, nor does our intuition as native speakers suggest any examples. However, there are several cases where the affix is used with stems of non-Romance origin, especially English, as shown below.

(5) (Suffix *-(z)zjoni* applied to stems of English origin; Michael Spagnol, pc.)
   esplojta ↔ *esplojtazzjoni* *immoniterja* ↔ *moniterizzazzjoni*
   to exploit ↔ exploitation   to monitor ↔ monitoring

More clearly 'local' in origin are formations where *-(z)zjoni* is applied to lex-emes ending in *-izza* (roughly, the equivalent of English *-ise* or Italian *-izzare*), which are in a derivational relationship to a proper name. These complex forma-tions are frequently candidates for nominalisation using *-(z)zjoni* .[1]

(6) (Suffix *-(z)zjoni* applied to proper names; personal knowledge)
   Xarabank ↔ *Xarabankizzazzjoni* *Dubaj* ↔ *Dubajizzazzjoni*
   Xarabank ↔ Xarabankisation   Dubai ↔ Dubaification

It is possible that rather than being clear-cut cases of direct or indirect borrow-ing, the suffixes under consideration should more accurately be placed some-where along the continuum between these two extremes. This can be done by weighing the empirical evidence for indirect borrowing in the two cases, using the following criteria provided by Seifart (2015: p. 513):

1. A set of complex loanwords with the borrowed affix share a meaning com-ponent;

2. There exists a set of pairs of loanwords, with one element of each pair with the affix and one without, with constant, recognisable changes in meaning between them;

3. Within pairs of complex loanwords and their corresponding simplex loan-words, the former have a lower token frequency.

Of these, the first criterion seems easily satisfied by both *-Vr* and *-(z)zjoni* , insofar as the many forms with these borrowed affixes do share a meaning component, as well as a formal relationship by virtue of having the same nomi-nalising suffix. It is the second and third criteria that are clearly testable. Below, we present a quantitative analysis of the productivity of these affixes, and then turn to the evidence for or against these two criteria. As noted in §1, we view the corpus-based investigation of in/direct borrowing and its implications for the parseability of forms (Hay & Baayen 2001) as complementary to the question of productivity.

---

[1]In the example below, Xarabank is the name of a discussion programme on Maltese national television.

5 An empirical investigation

We now turn to a quantitative analysis of the productivity of the two nominalisation affixes under discussion. We take a corpus-based approach to address the following question: *How productive are -Vr and -(z)zjoni nominalisations in Maltese, that is, to what extent are the two processes likely to contribute novel forms?* We then turn to the criteria for indirect borrowing, and the extent to which we find evidence for them in the two cases.

In quantifying productivity, we take inspiration from the statistical account offered by Baayen (Baayen 1994; 2009) and developed in subsequent work (for example, Lüdeling et al. 2000 and Pustylnikov & Schneider-Wiejowski 2010). We first discusss Baayen's theoretical framework, before describing the data used for this analysis.

5.1 Baayen's productivity measures

Baayen (2009) distinguishes between three conceptions of productivity. The *realised productivity* (RP) of a morphological process is defined as the number of types in a corpus that have been formed using this process. By contrast, *expanding productivity* (P^*) refers to the extent to which a process contributes to the growth rate in the total vocabulary, as reflected in a particular corpus. It is computed as the proportion of hapax legomena formed via the process in question, out of the total number of hapaxes in the corpus. As such, it is intended to reflect the number of 'novel' forms that the process has contributed, where 'novel' is operationally defined as a one-off occurrence, under the assumption that a word with a frequency of 1 is potentially a newly coined form.

Both RP and P^* are strongly dependent on corpus size, since both the total vocabulary size and the number of hapax legomena tend to grow – albeit asymptotically – with corpus size (see Baroni 2008 for discussion). Baayen's final measure of productivity – referred to as *potential productivity* or *category-conditioned productivity* and denoted P – focusses instead on the proportion of hapax legomena formed using the process in question, out of the total number of tokens that are formed using that process. This is less susceptible to variation due to corpus size, since it is related to the total number of tokens arising from a given process. P is usually taken to be the most reliable quantitative indicator of productivity out of the three. It is also interpreted as an indicator of the rate at which the morphological process could be used to create novel or 'potential' forms. In particular, the number of one-off occurrences out of the total number of tokens formed using a process should give us some indication of the relative prevalence of coinages or new usages.

There have been some criticisms of the use of P as formulated by Baayen (2009). In particular, Gaeta & Ricca (2006) argue that because P relies on the number of tokens created via a morphological process, it tends to underestimate the productivity of processes with high token frequency, while overestimating the productivity of forms with lower token frequency. For example, Gaeta & Ricca (2006) find that the Italian nominalising suffix -*tore* would be estimated as much more productive than its feminine counterpart -*trice*, which has a lower token frequency. As a corrective measure, Gaeta & Ricca (2006) suggest using the *variable-corpus* approach, in which morphological processes are compared for their productivity at varying token frequencies. By this argument, given two processes A and B, with token frequencies N_A and N_B such that $N_A < N_B$, the comparison of P would be more meaningful if N_A is used in the denominator. This method has also been used by Saade (2016) for his comparison between Maltese and Italian derivations.

While these arguments are well-taken, they are nevertheless subject to counter-arguments. In particular, since P is by definition estimated relative to token frequency, it is to be expected that as a process becomes more frequent and exhausts its domain of potential application, its productivity will be reduced. A similar argument has been put forward by Baayen (2009).

In the present paper, we will stick to the original proposals made by Baayen for the estimation of P, which we take to be indicative of the likelihood that a morphological process will yield novel forms in future. However, we also take the following additional methodological steps:

1. We estimate productivity over multiple, equal-sized corpus samples. This does not imply that we restrict the denominator in the estimation of P to the minimum token frequency for -*Vr* and -*(z)zjoni*; rather, we obtain multiple measures that also allow the investigation of the effect of increasing corpus size.

2. We consider both vocabulary growth and productivity for -*Vr* and -*(z)zjoni* as a function of increasing corpus size, as well as over the entire corpus.

3. We consider the correlation between the three measures of productivity.

Before turning to the analysis, we give a description of the data used.

5.2 Corpus data

The present analysis draws on data from the Korpus Malti v2.0 Beta, a corpus of ca. 125 million tokens developed and distributed as part of the Maltese Language

Table 4: Distribution of texts in the MLRS Korpus Malti v2.0 Beta, after Gatt & Čéplö (2013).

Text type	Number of tokens
Journalistic texts	68.800.000
Parliamentary debates	43.400.000
Belles lettres	375.000
Academic texts	170.000
Legal texts	4.800.000
Religious texts	403.700
Speeches	18.000
Web pages (blogs, Wikipedia articles, etc)	6.500.000
Miscellaneous other texts	123.000

Resource Server (MLRS).[2] The corpus is tagged with part of speech information, and contains texts from a variety of genres, as shown in Table 4 (Gatt & Čéplö 2013).

For the purposes of our analysis, we took 15 random samples of 1000 sentences each from the corpus. The decision to use multiple samples rather than conduct a single analysis on the corpus as a whole was motivated by three factors. First, using relatively small samples facilitates the manual pruning of false positives from search results (a well-known problem in analyses of morphological productivity; see Pustylnikov & Schneider-Wiejowski 2010). In the present case, for example, false positives include lexemes which end in -ar but are not derived nominals, such as *mar* 'go'; *parpar* 'scarper'; and *għargħar* 'deluge'.[3] Second, the ability to compute the productivity measures over multiple samples provides us with multiple data points, enabling a correlational analysis between the productivity measures, as presented in §5.5 below. Finally, multiple samples also allow the estimation of vocabulary and productivity curves over samples of increasing size, as presented in §5.4 and §5.5 below.

---

[2]http://mlrs.research.um.edu.mt

[3]There seems to be no straightforward way of automating the detection of false positives based on simple criteria such as length. While it would be possible to train a classifier to distinguish true from false positives, it was deemed better, on balance, to apply manual filtering, since the accuracy of automatic classification would in any case probably not reach 100%, and furthermore, an investigation of the features necessary to distinguish true and false positives is well beyond the scope of the present paper.

Each of the 15 random samples was pre-processed as follows:

1. Extraction of tokens tagged as nouns and ending in *-Vr* or *-(z)zjoni*: for the former, we restricted attention to the form *-ār* since the alternative form seems to be restricted to only a few types (cf. the discussion in §4 and the work of Camilleri 1993);

2. Manual pruning of false positives, specifically, nouns with these endings that are not the outcomes of the derivational processes under discussion (e.g. *għar* 'cave', which is not a derived nominal);

3. Extraction, from each sample, of the frequency distribution of types belonging to each process.

5.3 The distribution of *-Vr* and *-(z)zjoni* nominalisations

Table 5 gives an overview of the main characteristics of the samples under analysis, as well as the mean size and vocabulary, number of hapax legomena, and frequencies of *-ar* and *-zjoni* derivations overall.

A few observations are worth making at the outset. First, the 15 corpus samples are relatively homogeneous, with sizes ranging from 257,586 to 264,482 tokens and vocabulary sizes ranging from 23,788 to 24,345. Second, it is immediately clear that the incidence of *-(z)zjoni* nominalisations is far higher than that of *-Vr*

Table 5: Basic statistics for the samples used in the analysis. All figures average over the 15 random samples of 1000 sentences each.

	Mean	St. Dev	Min	Max	Median
Tokens	260,533	1655	257,586	264,482	260,186
Types	24,092	169	23,788	24,345	24,132
Hapaxes	12,611	155	12,340	12,872	12,617
Tokens: *-zjoni*	3,519	137	3,234	3,712	3,512
Types: *-zjoni*	325	20	305	382	325
Hapaxes: *-zjoni*	114	17	93	161	109
Tokens: *-ar*	256	21	227	288	258
Types: *-ar*	61	6	49	73	62
Hapaxes: *-ar*	35	5	25	43	35

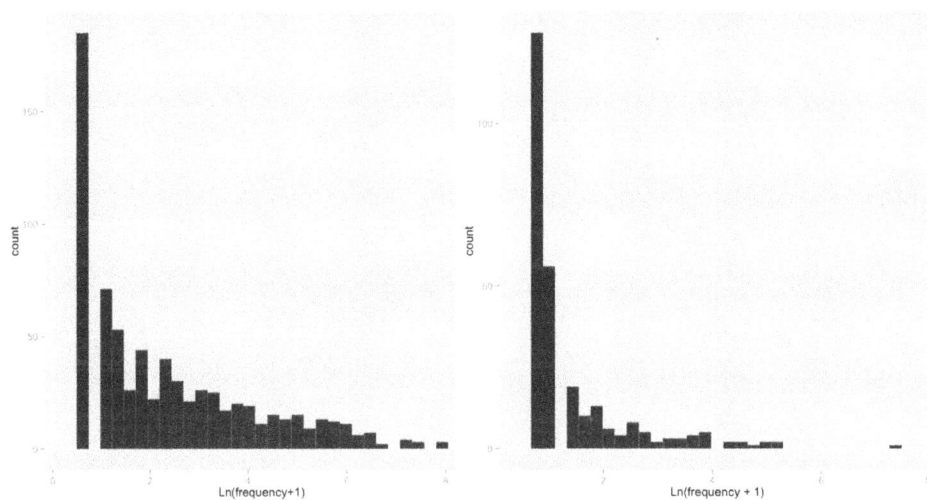

(a) *-(z)zjoni* nominalisations   (b) *-Vr* nominalisations

Figure 1: Frequency histograms for *-Vr* and *-(z)zjoni* nominalisations. Frequencies are plotted on a logarithmic scale on the x-axis, adding 1 to avoid zero frequencies for hapax legomena.

nominalisations: On average, there are 13 times as many tokens of the former as there are of the latter, and 5 times as many types.

Figure 1 displays the type frequency histograms, on a logarithmic scale, for the two processes. Interestingly, *-Vr* nominalisations tend to exhibit a much steeper drop in frequency, and a more uneven distribution, with a substantial gap between the hapax legomena and the next highest frequency. By contrast, *-(z)zjoni* nominals tail off more evenly. In general, not only are there more *-(z)zjoni* types, but there are more types within each frequency interval.

5.4 Vocabulary growth

A useful way to obtain a preliminary indication of the productivity of the nominalisation processes *-Vr* and *-(z)zjoni* is to look at their vocabulary growth curves. These display the size of the vocabulary (that is, the number of types V) as a function of increasing numbers of tokens (denoted N), generated using those processes.

As Lüdeling et al. (2000) note, a relatively unproductive process will tend to exhibit a shallow or asymptotic $N \times V$ curve, with vocabulary size no longer increasing as tokens increase in number. This means that beyond a certain point, as tokens increase, there tend not to be so many instances of novel, previously

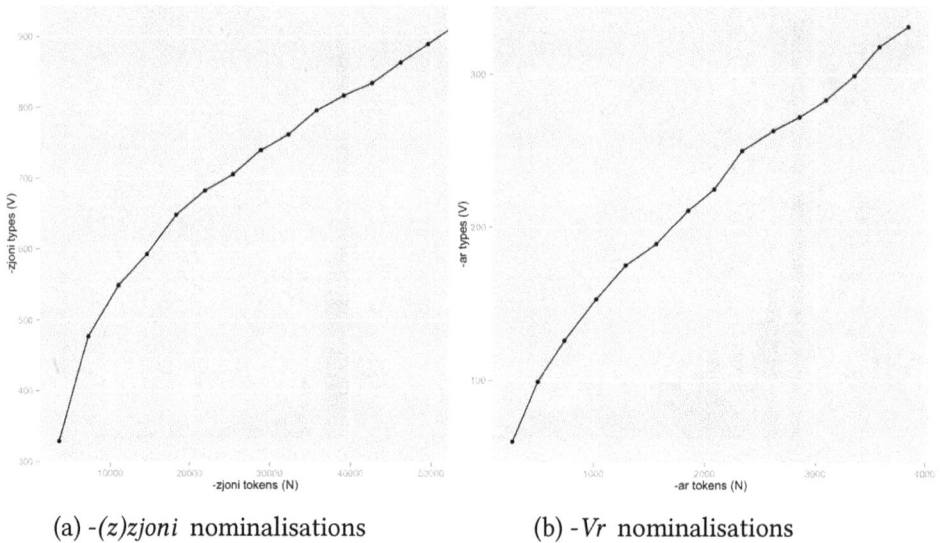

(a) *-(z)zjoni* nominalisations   (b) *-Vr* nominalisations

Figure 2: Vocabulary growth curves for *-Vr* and *-(z)zjoni* as a function of increasing number of tokens. Types are plotted on the y-axis, with tokens on the x-axis.

unattested types. By contrast, the more productive a process is, the steeper the $V \times N$ curve is expected to be.

Vocabulary growth curves were obtained for both *-Vr* and *-(z)zjoni* nominalisations by computing the number of different types over increasingly large samples, obtained by cumulatively merging the data from our 15 random samples and recomputing the token and vocabulary counts at each step. The curves are displayed in Figure 2. The vocabulary growth curves have a similar shape, showing a steep increase in both cases. This provides some *prima facie* evidence that both processes are productive, despite the much higher relative frequency of *-(z)zjoni* formations compared to *-Vr* formations noted in §5.3 above. As the histograms in Figure 1 confirm, this is due to the greater number of high-frequency types in the case of *-(z)zjoni*, also shown by the more even shape of the distribution in Figure 1a. The evidence therefore suggests that the productivity of these processes is independent of their absolute frequency.

5.5 Productivity analysis

We turn now to the quantification of productivity of the two derivational processes, using the measures proposed by Baayen (2009). For the purposes of this part of the analysis, the three measures, RP, P^* and P, were computed sepa-

Table 6: Productivity measures for the two derivational processes. All figures average over the 15 samples; numbers in parentheses are standard deviations.

	Proportional RP	P*	P
-*Vr* nominalisations	0.00245 (0.0002)	0.00275 (0.0004)	0.136 (0.02)
-*(z)zjoni* nominalisations	0.0135 (0.0008)	0.00904 (0.001)	0.033 (0.005)

rately for each sample. This gives us 15 data points, which can be used to correlate the three measures. Table 6 summarises the findings, showing the mean of each of the three measures, across samples. In these figures, RP is estimated as the proportion of types out of all the types in the sample.

Although, as noted in the introduction to this subsection, the three productivity measures are intended to reflect different perspectives on productivity, we nevertheless expect them to be correlated since they each depend on the overall vocabulary size (or on that part of the vocabulary that consists of one-off occurrences, or hapax legomena).

The three productivity measures are highly positively correlated, as shown in Table 7. One partial exception is the correlation between RP and P for -*Vr* nominalisations, which is only marginally significant at $p \approx 0.06$. Over all, however, there is systematic covariation between the three quantitative perspectives on productivity.

However, what is perhaps most interesting from the perspective of this analysis is that while -*(z)zjoni* exhibits greater realised productivity (RP) and expanding productivity ($P*$) than -*Vr* does, the trend is reversed where potential

Table 7: Pearson's correlation coefficients between the productivity measures for each nominalisation process.
* indicates that the correlation is significantly different from 0 a $p \leq 0.001$; [†] indicates that the correlation approaches significance at $p \approx 0.06$.

	-*Vr* Nominalisations		-*(z)zjoni* Nominalisations	
	P*	P	P*	P
Proportional RP	0.80*	0.50[†]	0.94*	0.87*
P*	–	0.86*	–	0.97*

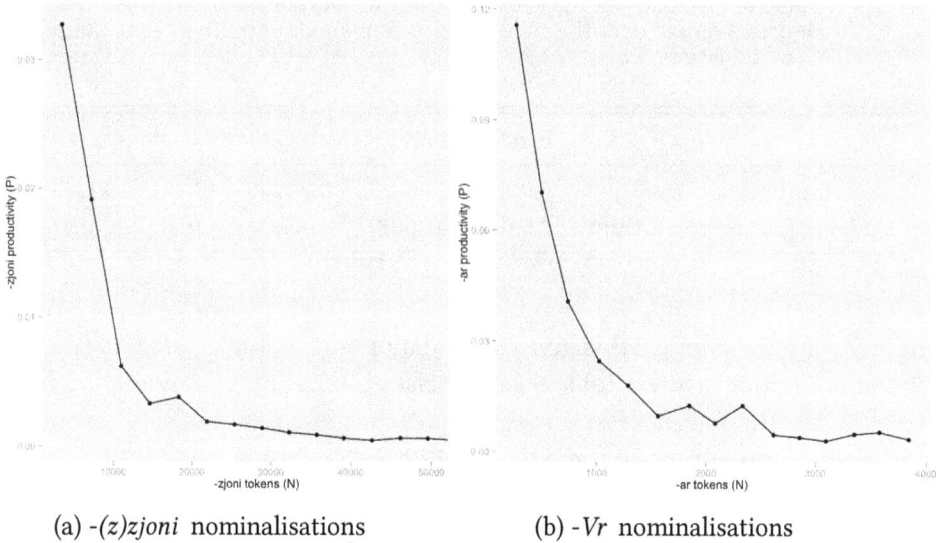

(a) -*(z)zjoni* nominalisations   (b) -*Vr* nominalisations

Figure 3: Productivity (P) of -*Vr* and -*(z)zjoni* as a function of increasing numbers of tokens.

productivity (P) is concerned, as shown in Table 6 above: Potential productivity is greater for -*Vr* than for -*(z)zjoni*. On the basis of this data, then, -*Vr* would be expected to contribute a greater proportion of new vocabulary than -*(z)zjoni*. This is interesting in light of the fact – evident from Figure 2b – that unlike in the case of -*(z)zjoni*, the distribution of -*Vr* types shows a gap between hapaxes and the preceding frequency intervals in the histogram. Taken together, the evidence points towards -*Vr* having a tendency to be used to create novel types, which are reflected as 'one-offs' in the corpus.

As with the vocabulary growth curves in Figure 2 above, we successively merged samples to create larger corpora and re-estimated the number of hapaxes for -*Vr* and -*(z)zjoni*, estimating P as the total number of tokens formed via a particular process increases. The resulting curves are displayed in Figure 3. As expected, both processes show a decrease in P with increasing number of tokens. This is expected, since the proportion of hapaxes tends to decrease as corpus size grows. However, the potential productivity of -*(z)zjoni* drops to a value close to 0 more steeply than does that of -*Vr*.

5.6 Evidence for indirect borrowing

We now turn to the two (out of three) criteria for indirect borrowing outlined by Seifart (2015) and singled out in §4.2. Recall, from our discussion in that section, that our concern is to determine whether *on balance* the evidence points towards these affixes being indirectly borrowed.

This part of the analysis proceeded as follows:

1. We determined, for each lexeme in our sample, its corresponding verbal baseform, if any. For example, the nominalisation *sparar* 'shooting' has a corresponding verbal baseform *spara* 'shoot'. Similarly, *informa* 'inform' corresponds to *informazzjoni*. On the other hand, a number of nominalisations do not have corresponding baseforms in Maltese. For example, there is no verb derivationally related to *devozzjoni* 'devotion'; *demozzjoni* 'demotion'; or *inġunzjoni* 'injunction', though these nominals are all attested in the corpus.

2. We compared the number of types formed with *-(z)zjoni* and *-Vr*, across the entire corpus (i.e. combining all 15 samples), which have corresponding simplex (verb) forms. This sheds light on the evidence for Seifart's second criterion, which stipulates that in case of indirect borrowing, loanwords will typically occur in pairs, where one element has the affix and one does not. The results are displayed in Figure 4a.

3. We also compared the token frequency of forms with and without the affix (i.e. complex and simplex verb forms). Here, we are interested in the number of types formed with a given affix which have lower token frequency than their corresponding simplex forms, as predicted by Seifart's third criterion. For this part of the analysis, we therefore only focus on that subset of the nominalisations identified in the previous step for which corresponding simplex forms are attested. We used the whole of Korpus Malti v2.0. Using the frequency list for this corpus, we extracted the frequency of the nominalisations and that of their corresponding verb forms. Given that verbs in Maltese can be inflected for person, number and gender, and that, furthermore, they can take a set of enclitic object pronouns, the verb forms were identified heuristically by finding all the lexemes in the frequency list which contained the verb stem as a substring, excluding the *-Vr* or *-(z)zjoni* nominalisations themselves.[4] The results are displayed in Figure 4b.

---

[4]This heuristic therefore only gives an approximate estimate of the verb frequency. False negatives are possible for those words which are misspelled in the corpus, as when an author uses *iccekkja* instead of *iċċekkja* 'check'. False positives are in principle possible insofar as a word may have the verb stem as a substring, but be unrelated to it. Though possible, this is relatively unlikely, given that the verb forms have a fairly clear structure and are regular, with little stem allomorphy.

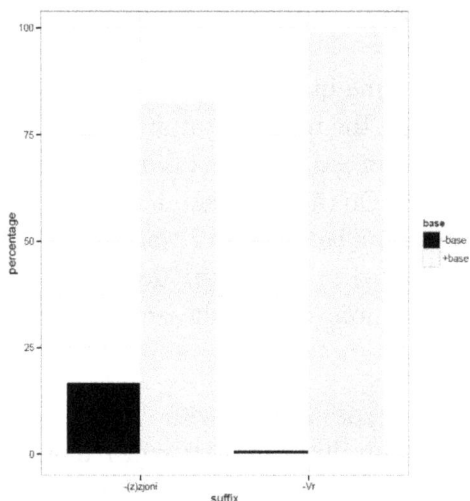

(a) Proportions of *-Vr* and *-(z)zjoni* nominalisations that have corresponding verbal baseforms. Dark bars represent types with no corresponding baseform; light bars reflect types with a corresponding baseform.

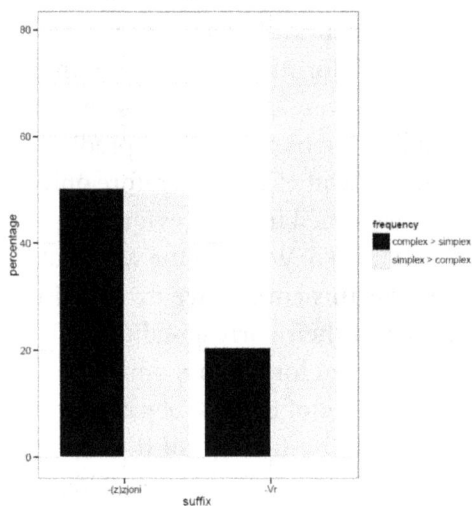

(b) Comparison of the frequency of complex and simplex forms. Dark bars: complex > simplex; light bars: simplex > complex.

Figure 4: Evidence for indirect borrowing: Nominalisations and corresponding baseforms

Two observations can be made from this analysis. First, as far as Seifart's second criterion goes, both nominalisation processes evince a majority of types with corresponding simplex forms. However, this is far more likely with -*Vr* nominalisations (ca. 99% of cases) than -*(z)zjoni* nominalisations (ca. 83% of cases). This suggests that there are more cases of -*(z)zjoni* lexemes which were borrowed wholesale, rather than produced 'online' from stems by native speakers. This conclusion is strengthened by the apparent absence of -*(z)zjoni* forms involving native Semitic stems, observed in §4.2.

Second, as far as token frequency is concerned, -*(z)zjoni* hardly satisfies Seifart's third criterion: with this form, the proportion of cases where the simplex form is more frequent than the nominalised form is roughly equal to the proportion of cases where the opposite holds (both are around 50%). By contrast, over 79% of types formed using -*Vr* are less frequent than their simplex forms.

On balance, therefore, the evidence for indirect borrowing is much more clear in the case of -*Vr* than -*(z)zjoni* .

5.7 Summary

This corpus-based analysis sheds light on the productivity of the two nominalisation processes from two different perspectives. First, the productivity analysis suggests that both -*Vr* and -*(z)zjoni* are productive to some degree. This is reflected both by their vocabulary growth curves and by their non-zero estimates for potential productivity (P). At the same time, it is noteworthy that the process whose formations are most frequently attested – namely, -*(z)zjoni* – turns out to have a lower potential productivity, despite its apparently higher realised (RP) and expanding productivity (P^*). As noted above, the latter two measures are more strongly dependent on corpus size (Baayen 2009).

What could account for the higher P measure for -*Vr*, when -*(z)zjoni* has higher RP and P^*? One possible reason, alluded to in §2, is that, despite the larger number of attested -*(z)zjoni* types, there are also more forms without corresponding simplex forms, because a larger proportion of these types was imported wholesale, so that these types are not derivationally related to an attested verb. Hence, the more corpus-dependent (as opposed to category-conditioned) productivity measures would be inflated by a greater proportion of types that are in fact not derivationally related to bases in the native speaker's mental lexicon.

The second part of the analysis, focussing on the criteria outlined by Seifart (2015) for indirect borrowing, strengthens this position. Specifically, we find that -*Vr* lexemes are more likely to have corresponding simplex forms. Furthermore, a comparison of the frequency of complex and simplex forms shows that the latter are more likely to be used with greater frequency in the *-Vr* case, compared to *-(z)zjoni* . This provides further evidence for wholesale importation of *-(z)zjoni* forms, suggesting that the greater productivity of *-Vr* is in part due to its large-scale re-use on novel, including native, stems, possibly following a process of reanalysis of forms originally imported from Italian, after which the affix became available for use on a broader domain.

In any case, to the extent that the domains of application of the two derivational processes overlap (cf. §4 above), the figures for potential productivity (P) suggest that there will be a greater preference among speakers for forming nominalisations using *-Vr* rather than *-(z)zjoni* in the future. Clearly, this conclusion can only be tentatively reached on the basis of corpus data, especially since such data, by definition, is 'historical' and restricted to already-attested, rather than potential forms.

6 Conclusions

This paper began with an outline of morphological derivation in Maltese, couched within a theoretical framework that is agnostic as to the procedural nature of the derivational process, focussing instead on the relation between two lexemes. Following an outline of both Semitic and Romance derivational processes, we focussed on two derivational suffixes – *-Vr* and *-(z)zjoni* – which appear to share a number of semantic and distributional characteristics. A corpus-based analysis showed that one of them, namely *-Vr*, is likely to emerge as more productive in the long-term. The evidence further points to a greater likelihood that *-Vr* was indirectly borrowed into Maltese, coming to be used on a broader range of stems, including native stems.

The snapshot provided by the present analysis opens up various avenues for future research. An important one is the in-depth analysis of a greater variety of derivational processes, with a view to providing a deeper understanding of derivational morphology in contemporary Maltese as well as gaining a better understanding of the extent to which the domains of such processes overlap. A second important direction for future work is the exploitation of different methodological tools. As the present paper showed, corpus analysis can provide substantial insights into questions related to morphological productivity. However, we believe that such analyses need to be complemented by experimental techniques, which can shed a more direct light on the processing implications of the trends observed in corpora.

Acknowledgements

This work forms part of the project *Morphological Productivity and Language Change in Maltese: Corpus-based and experimental evidence*, supported by a grant from the University of Malta Research Fund. We thank Michael Spagnol, Manwel Mifsud, Benjamin Saade and two anonymous reviewers for helpful comments on earlier drafts of this paper.

References

Aronoff, Mark & Frank Anshen. 1998. Morphology and the lexicon: Lexicalization and productivity. In Andrew Spencer & Arnold Zwicky (eds.), *The handbook of morphology*, 237–247. Oxford: Blackwell.

Aronoff, Mark & Kirsten Fudeman. 2011. *What is Morphology?* 2nd edn. Oxford: Wiley-Blackwell.

Aronoff, Mark & Roger Schvaneveldt. 1978. Testing morphological productivity. *Annals of the New York Academy of Sciences* 318. 106–114.

Baayen, R. Harald. 1994. Productivity in language production. *Language and Cognitive Processes* 9(3). 447–459.

Baayen, R. Harald. 2009. Corpus linguistics in morphology: Morphological productivity. In Anke Lüdeling & Merja Kytö (eds.), *Corpus linguistics. An international handbook*. Chap. 43, 900–919. Berlin: de Gruyter.

Baroni, Marco. 2008. Distributions in text. In Anke Lüdeling & Merja Kytö (eds.), *Corpus linguistics: An international handbook*, chap. 37, 803–821. Berlin: Mouton de Gruyter.

Bauer, Laurie. 2001. *Morphological Productivity*. Cambridge: Cambridge University Press.

Borg, Albert & Marie Azzopardi-Alexander. 1997. *Maltese*. London: Routledge.

Brincat, Joseph. 2011. *Maltese and other languages: A linguistic history of Malta*. Malta: Midsea Books.

Brincat, Joseph & Manwel Mifsud. 2016. Maltese. In Peter O. Müller, Ingeborg Ohnheiser, Susan Olsen & Franz Rainer (eds.), *Word-formation: An international handbook of the languages of Europe (vol. 5)*, 3349–3366. Berlin: De Gruyter Mouton.

Bybee, Joan. 1995. Regular morphology and the lexicon. *Language and Cognitive Processes* 10(5). 425–455.

Camilleri, Edel. 1993. *Is-Suffissi Nominali Rumanzi fil-Malti (Romance nominal suffixes in Maltese)*. University of Malta B.A. Honours Dissertation.

Comrie, Bernard & Michael Spagnol. 2016. Maltese loanword typology. In Gilbert Puech & Benjamin Saade (eds.), *Shifts and patterns in maltese*, 315–330. Berlin: De Gruyter Mouton.

Cutler, Anne. 1980. Productivity in word formation. In *Papers from the sixteenth regional meeting, Chicago Linguistic Society*, 45–51. Chicago, Ill: CLS.

Dressler, Wolfgang. 2003. Degrees of grammatical productivity in inflectional morphology. *Rivista di Linguistica* 15(1). 31–62.

Drewes, A.J. 1994. Borrowing in Maltese. In Peter Bakker & Maarten Mous (eds.), *Mixed languages: 15 case studies in language intertwining*, 83–111. Amsterdam: Ifott.

Ellul, Leanne. 2016. *In-Nomi Verbali fil-Malti (Verbal nouns in Maltese)*. University of Malta Masters Thesis.

Fabri, Ray. 2010. Maltese. *Revue Belge de Philologie et d'Histoire* 88(3). 791–816.

Fabri, Ray, Michael Gasser, Nizar Habash, George Kiraz & Shuly Wintner. 2013. Linguistic Introduction. In Zitouni, I. (ed.), *Semitic language processing*, 16–21. Berlin: Springer.

Gaeta, Livio & Davide Ricca. 2006. Productivity in Italian word formation: A variable-corpus approach. *Linguistics* 44(1). 57–89. DOI:10.1515/LING.2006.003

Gatt, Albert & Slavomír Čéplö. 2013. Digital corpora and other electronic resources for Maltese. In *Proceedings of the International Conference on Corpus Linguistics*. Lancaster, UK: University of Lancaster.

Haspelmath, Martin & Andrea Sims. 2010. *Understanding Morphology*. 2nd edn. London: Routledge.

Hay, Jennifer & R. Harald Baayen. 2001. Parsing and productivity. In Geert Booij & Jaap van Marle (eds.), *Yearbook of morphology 2001*, 203–235. Dordrecht: Kluwer. DOI:10.1007/978-0-387-93837-0

Hoberman, Robert D. & Mark Aronoff. 2003. The verbal morphology of Maltese: From Semitic to Romance. In J. Shimron (ed.), *Language processing and acquisition in languages of Semitic, root-based morphology*, chap. 3, 61–78. Amsterdam: John Benjamins Publishing Company.

Lüdeling, Anke, Stefan Evert & Ulrich Heid. 2000. On Measuring Morphological Productivity. In Werner Zühlke & Ernst G. Schukat-Talamazzini (eds.), *KONVENs-2000 sprachkommunikation*, 57–61. Germany: VDE-Verlag.

Mifsud, Manwel. 1995a. *Loan verbs in Maltese: A descriptive and comparative study*. Leiden: Brill.

Mifsud, Manwel. 1995b. The productivity of African in Maltese. In Joseph Cremona, Clive Holes & Geoffrey Khan (eds.), *Proceedings of the 2nd International*

Conference of the International Association for African Dialectology (AIDA), 151–160. Cambridge, UK: University Publications Centre.

Plag, Ingo. 2004. Productivity. In Bas Aarts & April McMahon (eds.), *Handbook of English linguistics*, 537–556. Oxford: Blackwell.

Pustylnikov, Olga & Karina Schneider-Wiejowski. 2010. Measuring morphological productivity. *Studies in Quantitative Linguistics* 5. 1–9.

Saade, Benjamin. 2016. Assessing productivity in contact: Italian derivation in Maltese. *Linguistics* to appear.

Seifart, Frank. 2015. Direct and indirect affix borrowing. *Language* 91(3). 511–532. DOI:10.1353/lan.2015.0044

Spagnol, Michael. 2013. *A Tale of Two Morphologies: Verb Structure and Argument Alternations in Maltese*. University of Konstanz PhD Thesis.

Spencer, Andrew. 1991. *Morphological theory*. Oxford: Blackwell.

Spencer, Andrew & Arnold Zwicky. 1998. *The Handbook of Morphology*. Oxford: Blackwell.

Twist, Alina. 2006. *A Psycholinguistic Investigation of the Verbal Morphology of Maltese*. University of Arizona, Tucson (AZ) PhD Thesis.

Ussishkin, Adam, Colin Dawson, Andrew Wedel & Kevin Schluter. 2015. Auditory masked priming in Maltese spoken word recognition. *Language, Cognition and Neuroscience* January 2015. 1–20.

Chapter 7

On raising and copy raising in Maltese

Maris Camilleri

University of Essex

This paper seeks to describe and account for the (morpho)syntactic behaviour of lexically determined raising predicates and constructions, and will be considering a list of properties that characterise these. Different raising-to-SUBJ constructions available in Maltese are discussed, and eventually formalised within the Lexical Functional Grammar framework. We will argue that raising constructions in Maltese can be divided into two analyses: raising that involves a structure-shared dependency, and raising that involves an anaphoric binding dependency between the matrix SUBJ and any embedded grammatical function, subject to the identified constraints that will be discussed. We illustrate how in Maltese, raising structures are of the former type, while copy raising is of the latter.

1 Introduction

To date, there has not been any descriptive account of the different properties and behaviours that characterise raising constructions in Maltese, except initial discussions of various behaviours in Camilleri et al. (2014) and an account of the raising behaviours of various aspectual auxiliaries in Camilleri (2016), as well as a mention of these structures in Fabri (1993). The main aim of this study is to discuss alternations of the sort in (1), where (1a) involves a default 3SGM matrix form, while (1b) involves the raising of the 3PL embedded subject (SUBJ), and where in the latter structure, an overt DP/SUBJ in the embedded clause is not possible, hence the ungrammaticality of (1c).[1]

---

[1]Unless specified, the data should be understood as being provided by the author, a native speaker.

Maris Camilleri. On raising and copy raising in Maltese. In Patrizia Paggio & Albert Gatt (eds.), *The languages of Malta*, 171–201. Berlin: Language Science Press. DOI:10.5281/zenodo.1181795

(1) a. *J-i-dher*   *(li)* *(it-tfal)*   *sejr-in*   *tajjeb*
    3M-FRM.VWL-appear.SG COMP DEF-children go.ACT.PTCP-PL good.SGM
    (it-tfal)[2]
    DEF-children

    'It seems that the children are doing well'

  b. *It-tfal*   *j-i-dhr-u*   *(li)* *sejr-in*
    DEF-children 3-FRM.VWL-appear.IMPV-PL COMP go.ACT.PTCP-PL
    tajjeb
    good.SGM

    'The children seem to be doing well'

  c. **J-i-dhr-u$_i$ li t-tfal/huma$_i$ sejr-in tajjeb*

We here start our discussion with an example from the Culicover (2009: 244) textbook in order to better understand what we are to understand when we say that a verb is a raising predicate. In English, given the contrast in (2), the fact that 'something can be a subject of *appear to* VP whenever it can be a subject of a *that*-complement containing VP' suggests that *appear* is a raising predicate. When raising is not present, as in (2a), what we have is the formation of what is referred to as an *It*-Extraposition structure. While the sentences in (2) are syntactically distinct, the semantic composition is the same. This follows from the fact that since *appear* is a raising predicate and only selects for a clausal argument, the non-thematic external argument function is filled in by the semantically vacuous pronoun *it*, which in turn has no effect whatsoever on the semantic interpretation of the construction.

(2) a. It appears that I have forgotten to do my work

  b. I appear to have forgotten to do my work

The predicates that are able to license raising structures are idiosyncratic, and one has to specifically determine these on the basis of a number of syntactic properties that may well be language internal. However, crosslinguistically one finds that similar and corresponding lexical items keep displaying the same behaviour (Stiebels 2007). In this study we aim to provide an overview of the raising predicates available, whilst identifying which syntactic properties are associated with raising predicates and structures in Maltese. Reference to the term *raising* with respect to the set of lexical items and constructions we will be discussing here comes from the transformational rule used in Rosenbaum (1967) to account

---

[2]The segmentation followed in this study is based on the account in Camilleri (2014).

for SUBJ-to-SUBJ raising construction alternations, such as the one illustrated in (2b). Postal (1974), on the other hand, generalised over this rule to account for all sort of raising constructions, including SUBJ-to-OBJ (ECM) constructions. Another term provided in the literature for verbs which display raising behaviours and involve a one-place predication that is a clausal argument, is that of 'aspectualisers' in Newmeyer (1975: 8).[3] While we choose to refer to the predicates under discussion as 'raising' predicates, we won't be employing any transformational sort of analysis. Rather, we will formalise our account within the Lexical Functional Grammar (LFG) framework, where all constructions are assumed to be base-generated, and the relationship between the semantically equivalent but syntactically distinct sentences in the pairs in (1) and (2) in Maltese and English, respectively, boils down to the presence or absence of functional binding/structure-sharing via a functional equation that defines the equivalence between the SUBJ in the main clause and the embedded clause. Rather than movement, relations and dependencies in LFG are understood 'in terms of relations between functions' and not structural positions (Bresnan 1982: 400). In (1b) and (2b), there thus holds an interpretive/referential dependency between the SUBJ in the matrix and the unexpressed external argument of the predicate in the embedded clause. This relation is referred to as *control*. As we will discuss, raising constructions in Maltese differ as to whether they involve functional control or anaphoric control. The former involves structure-sharing between the SUBJ grammatical functions (GFs) across both clauses, while anaphoric control involves binding, i.e. a co-referential dependency.

The paper proceeds as follows: In §2 we provide a very brief overview of the framework of LFG and how raising is dealt with. In §3 we delve further into the details of the basic properties of raising constructions in Maltese, and the predicates involved. We provide evidence as to why it is believed that they should be analysed as raising predicates. §4 discusses copy raising and how it involves a distinct mechanism, when compared with non-copy raised structures. §5 then concludes the paper.

---

[3]Here we choose not to use this term, as "aspectualisers" elsewhere in the literature refer to a set of predicates, auxiliaries, light verbs and particles which provide information with respect to PHASAL ASPECT (Binnick 1991; Michaelis 1998); and Vanhove 1993 and Camilleri 2016 for specific reference to phasal verbs or aspectualisers in Maltese.

2 Raising in LFG

2.1 LFG: The theory

LFG employs a parallel architecture/correspondence (Kaplan & Bresnan 1982) and models a theory of language analysis. Such an architecture allows for distinct co-present projections that relate to one another via functional correspondences modelling different representations of linguistic analysis, each having their own rules and constraints. LFG is primarily a lexicalist theory that relies heavily on lexical entries and the information present in them. Lexicalist approaches are thus based on an underlying assumption that it is not syntax which should deal with a number of structures and relations. Rather, these are best left to the morphological domain and the lexicon, including the argument-structure. The argument-structure essentially represents predicate-argument relations. The arguments and their thematic roles are then mapped onto grammatical functions (GFs). What concerns us most, for the purpose of this study, is where in the model, syntactic analyses take place.

LFG employs two representational levels where syntactic analyses can be done, based on an important principle whereby syntactic functions are analysed independently of any sort of configurational structure (Bresnan 2001; Dalrymple 2001; Falk 2001; Bresnan et al. 2015). This split between function and constituency translates into the constituent-structure (*c*-structure) and the functional-structure (*f*-structure). The *c*-structure has to do with the external properties related with syntax, which allow and account for the variation that exists across languages. It takes into account word order considerations, constituency, syntactic categories, dominance and precedence. Through the use of phrase structure rules that build up syntactic trees, the surface linear order configurationality (or the lack of it), is represented. While X-Bar syntax (Chomsky 1970) is used for configurational or semi-configurational languages, flatter *c*-structures that do not need to be restricted to binary branched tree structures are also available. The other level of syntactic representation, i.e. the *f*-structure, is concerned with internal syntactic properties, which are believed to be more universal in nature. The *f*-structure thus represents the relevant GFs, i.e. SUBJ, OBJ etc., as well as other syntactically relevant features involved in any syntactic construction.

Every level of linguistic representation in the parallel architecture that constitutes the LFG model makes use of a distinct language. The *f*-structure, which is our main concern here, makes use of hierarchical attribute value matrices (AVMs). The information necessary for the *f*-structure comes from the lexical entry as well as information coming from the annotation on *c*-structure nodes. The functional head of an *f*-structure is a PRED feature, which takes a list of semantic/thematic arguments represented through their enclosure in angle brackets. These are then mapped onto GFs on the basis of a default hierarchy of mappings (Kibort 2004; Kibort 2007) or through lexical specifications, if necessary. While these two levels of syntactic representation feed information into one another, agreement, binding, complementation, local dependencies including raising and control, long distance dependencies and other such constructions, are all done at the *f*-structure level, on the basis of a reference to the different relations and dependencies that are present across and amongst the GFs.

For what concerns us in this study, the relevant constraints include those related with the *f*-structure, which is constrained by the Uniqueness, Completeness and Coherence conditions. Uniqueness requires that there be no duplication in the *f*-structure, such that every attribute/feature is itself unique and takes its own unique value. In the case of unbounded discourse functions (UDFs) such as TOPIC and FOCUS and adjuncts (ADJs), set values for these do not violate Uniqueness. As a result, many of these could be co-present. The Completeness condition requires that the PRED's argument-structure requirements be satisfied within the *f*-structure, while Coherence checks that every GF present in the *f*-structure is one that is selected by the PRED. UDFs as well as other 'syntactic functions requiring that they be integrated appropriately into the *f*-structure' (Bresnan 2001: 63), partake in the Extended Coherence Condition (Bresnan & Mchombo 1987: 746), which states that: 'Focus and Topic must be linked to the semantic predicate argument structure of the sentence in which they occur, either by functionally or anaphorically binding an argument.'

2.2 The theory of raising in LFG

A constraint imposed on raising constructions in LFG is that the 'raised' GF be a *term*/core-argument, and should thus be an embedded SUBJ, OBJ, or OBJθ (Bresnan 1982: 419; Dalrymple 2001: 10) and that 'lexically controlled local dependencies [...] involve simultaneous instantiations of two grammatical functions to a single *f*-structure value' (Asudeh & Toivonen 2012: 6). This is thus a 'functional predication relation' (Bresnan 2001: 270), and can be defined as a relation that 'involves a dual assignment of grammatical relations: a single NP functions as an argument of both the subordinate clause and the matrix clause, and bears a grammatical relation in both clauses' (Kroeger 2004: 107). This view of control thus entails a symmetrical relation between the GFs involved, and is referred to as functional-identity, token-identity or structure-sharing. Unlike unbounded distance dependency constructions, where one finds dependencies involving UDFs occupying multiple instantiations, in the case of raising (and control), there is a limitation to the 'sentence node', and the dependency is hence bounded/local. Having said this, however, it is possible to also have 'multiple structure-sharing, resulting from [...] further embedding' (Asudeh 2005: 491; Asudeh & Toivonen 2006: 22; Alsina 2008: 18), as long as the clauses proceed locally. See (3) for an illustration of chained raising cascades in Maltese.

(3) *Laħq-u   dehr-u   qis-hom   donn-hom*
     reach.PFV.3-PL appear.PFV.3-PL as.though-3PL.ACC as.though-3PL.ACC
     ħa   j-i-bde-w   j-e-rġgħ-u   j-morr-u[4]
     PROSP 3-FRM.VWL-start.IMPV-PL 3-FRM.VWL-repeat.IMPV-PL 3-go.IMPV-PL

     'They did happen to have appeared as though they will start going again.'

In raising constructions of the type in (1b) and (2b) the complement clause is mapped onto an XCOMP GF. A GF of this type, as opposed to the COMP GF is an open complement, and licenses structure-sharing between the relevant matrix and embedded GFs to take place. The XCOMP embodies distinct *c*-structure constituents that function predicatively, such that XCOMP ≡ {NP | VP | AP | PP} (and CP under Falk's (2001) view based on his account of *to*). The XCOMP clausal argument is thus the only GF which these raising verbs subcategorise for. The SUBJ's 'appearance outside the brackets' (Zaenen & Kaplan 2002: 12) represents the fact that the external argument is not selected by the predicate, i.e. ⟨XCOMP⟩SUBJ. The

---

[4] An anonymous reviewer questions the acceptability of this construction: 'The co-occurrence of *qis-hom* and *donn-hom* next to each other is unacceptable since one of them is redundant.' I assure the reader that this sentence is pretty acceptable for the author, with the presence of **both** the predicates *qis-* and *donn-*, although of course this chained cascade is not obligatory and indeed only one of them may be present. Furthermore, neither of them, for that matter, need be present, given that they simply reinforce the same interpretation which *deher* 'seem' itself renders in the overall structure. Data from the MLRS further support this claim (as in (a)), including data involving the reversed order of these same predicates.

(i) (MLRS; v3.0)
     qis-u   donn-u   in⟨t⟩esa
     as.though-3SGM.ACC as.though-3SGM.ACC forget.PASS.PFV.3SGM
     koll-u
     all-3SGM.GEN

     'it's as though all has been forgotten'

Additionally I point out that redundancy at the syntactic level, which is what we have here, should not entail, or be equated to unacceptability, as is being implied by the reviewer. Redundancy can in fact be observed in several aspects of a language's grammar.

brackets are what would otherwise 'enclose the semantically selected arguments of the lexical form' (Bresnan 2001: 283). This formal distinction, i.e. between GFs within, or external to the brackets, functions as a means with which to represent whether the matrix imposes restrictions on such GFs or not.

In the absence of raising, the semantically vacuous position of the external argument is filled by dummy/expletive pronouns, since these lack a semantic PRED value (Bresnan 2001: 283). The availability of such pronouns is itself lexically specified (Kroeger 2004: 123). When raising is not available, and hence no structure-sharing is involved, the lexical entry is: $\langle \text{COMP} \rangle \text{SUBJ}$. This distinction at the lexical entry level is summarised as follows from Bresnan (1982: 404): 'Unlike XCOMPs, closed COMPs may undergo *It* Extraposition ...' in English. The raising/non-raising ambiguity of English *seem* is in Asudeh & Toivonen (2012: 14) reduced to the following constraint in the lexical entry: $(\uparrow \text{SUBJ EXPLETIVE}) = {}_c\text{IT} \wedge \neg (\uparrow \text{XCOMP}) \mid (\uparrow \text{SUBJ}) = (\uparrow \text{XCOMP SUBJ})$. This constraint states that we either have a constraining equation that requires the presence of an expletive *it* when the complement clause's function is not an XCOMP; or, in the absence of the expletive as the matrix SUBJ, equality between matrix SUBJ and XCOMP SUBJ applies.[5] With this brief introduction to the classic LFG treatment of raising, we can now proceed to characterise in more detail, raising in Maltese.

3 Raising in Maltese

In this section we first highlight the main raising predicates in the language, and then provide morphosyntactic behaviours that serve as evidence sustaining our claim that these predicates are raising predicates.

3.1 Raising predicates

The primary raising predicate in Maltese is *deher* 'appear, seem'. The data in (4), exemplified through the behaviour associated with *deher*, illustrates the array of phrasal categories that can function as a complement of *deher*: CP/VP (4a); NP (4b); AP (4c); PP (4d).

(4) a. *T-i-dher*   *(li)*   *miexj-a*   *'l*   *quddiem*
      3F-FRM.VWL-appear.IMPV.SG COMP walk.ACT.PTCP-SGF ALL front

      'She/It seems to be moving forward'

---

[5]Falk (2001: 137) approaches this ambiguity by positing a 'Functional Control Rule' which states that: 'If $(\uparrow \text{XCOMP})$ is present in a lexical form, add the equation: $(\uparrow \text{SUBJ} \mid \text{OBJ}) = (\uparrow \text{XCOMP SUBJ})$. When this rule is not present, we get the non-thematic argument filled by an expletive (p. 138).

b. *Marija t-i-dher   tifla bilgħaqal[6]*
Mary 3F-FRM.VWL-appear.IMPV.SG girl with.DEF.wisdom

'Mary seems to be a good girl'

c. *T-i-dher   tajb-a*
3F-FRM.VWL-appear.IMPV.SG good-SGF

'She/It seems good'

d. *T-i-dher   bil-bajda   m-dawwr-a*
3F-FRM.VWL-appear.IMPV.SG with.DEF-egg.SGF PASS.PTCP-turn-SGF

Lit: She seems with the egg turned

'She seems to be grumpy (today)'

In this paper we will not delve into issues that have to do with finite raising, i.e. hyperraising, which Landau (2011) refers to as 'non-ordinary raising'. Maltese does employ finite morphological forms even in the embedded clause, apart from the predicate types just considered, which are also available in the embedded clause (as one may have already noticed in e.g. (3)). However, one should make it clear that as discussed in Sells (2006), there need not be an isomorphic relationship between morphological and syntactic finiteness. Clear, unambiguous instances of finite embedded clauses are (5), where the presence of *kont* in (5a) provides a TENSE feature with value PAST. In (5b), we then have an epistemic modal value realised syntactically. We take both these instances to suggest that the embedded complement in Maltese can map onto an IP, which is itself indicative of a finite clause. We will here say nothing more about such construction types and how they may be the same or different from non-finite raising structures. For more discussion on hyperraising in Maltese, refer to Camilleri (2017).

---

[6]It should be mentioned that if we had the construction in (i) instead, *hija* in this context would not be functioning as the SUBJ, but rather as the copula. This data should therefore not be confused with what has been said with respect to the ungrammaticality of (1c). Furthermore, it is clear from such a context that the XCOMP GF which maps onto a CP embeds a sentential complement (S) headed by the pronominal copula.

(i) *Marija t-i-dher   li   hija   tifla bilgħaqal*
Mary 3F-FRM.VWL-appear.IMPV.SG COMP COP.3SGF girl with.DEF.wisdom

'Mary seems that she is a good girl'

(5) a. *N-i-dher*   *(li)*   *kon-t*   *mor-t*   *tajjeb,*
       1-FRM.VWL-appear.IMPV.SG COMP be.PFV-1SG go.PFV-1SG good.SGM
       id-darba   *l-oħr-a*
       DEF-once.SGF DEF-other-SGF

       Lit: 'I seem that I had done well last time'

       'I seem to have done well, the last time'

     b. *Dehr-et*   *(kien)*   *kel-l-ha*   *mnejn*
       appear.PFV.3SGF be.PFV.3SGM be.PFV.3SGM-have-3SGF.GEN from.where
       semgħ-et   *mingħand-hom, dakinhar*
       hear.PFV-3SGF from.at-3PL.GEN DEM.SGM.DEF-day

       'She seemed she had perhaps heard from them that day'

On the basis of the overview of the analysis of SUBJ-to-SUBJ raising in LFG, presented briefly in the previous section, we provide the lexical entry associated with *deher* 'seem' that allows for the expletive and raising alternation. Following Berman (2003) we account for the default 3SGM agreement in the matrix as being itself indicative of a PREDless SUBJ analysis. Although never discussed previously, an expletive pronoun, namely *huwa*, which is equivalent in form to the long version of the 3SGM subject pronoun, alternating with the short form *hu*, could be said to exist in Maltese. In (6) it is not as controversial to assume that the pronoun *huwa* is functioning as a semantically vacuous pronoun filling in a non-thematic SUBJ position. In the data in (7), on the other hand, we find that *huwa* must have another function, and could well be some sort of clause force that provides an exclamative interpretation and sarcastic tone to this sort of construction.[7]

(6) *Huwa   j-i-dher*   *li/kemm sejr-a*   *tajjeb!*
     he.EXPL 3.M-FRM.VWL-appear.IMPV.SG COMP   go.ACT.PTCP-SGF good.SGM

     'It shows that she is doing well!'

     'It shows how good she's going!'

(7) a. *Huwa   t-i-dher*   *kemm sejr-a*   *tajjeb!*
       he.EXPL 3F-FRM.VWL-appear.SG COMP go.ACT.PTCP-SGF good.SGM

       'It is clearly showing how well she is going (sarcastic)'

---

[7]Parallel structures are mentioned in passing in Borg & Azzopardi-Alexander (1997: 195). For want of a better translation, I gloss *huwa* in such constructions as: he.EXPL so that it is not confused with the syncretic form *huwa* when being used referentially as the pronoun meaning 'he'.

   b. *Huwa   intom t-i-dhr-u*   *li   nisa,*
      he.EXPL you.PL 2-FRM.VWL-appear.IMPV-PL COMP women
     t-af-x!
     2-know.IMPV.SG-NEG

    Lit: 'It is clearly showing that you are women, don't you know'

The conflated lexical entry for *deher* is the following:

deher: I/V $(\uparrow \mu$ PRED VFORM$)$ = Perfective
           $(\uparrow \mu$ PRED VFORM POL$)$ = POS
           $\{(\uparrow$ PRED$)$ = $\langle$XCOMP$\rangle$SUBJ
           $((\uparrow$ XCOMP COMPFORM$)$ = LI$)$
           $(\uparrow$ SUBJ$)$ = $(\uparrow$ XCOMP SUBJ$)$
           $(\uparrow$ SUBJ PERSON$)$ = 3
           $(\uparrow$ SUBJ NUM$)$ = SG
           $(\uparrow$ SUBJ GEND$)$ = M
           |
           $(\uparrow$ PRED$)$ = $\langle$COMP$\rangle$SUBJ
           $((\uparrow$ COMP COMPFORM$)$ = LI$)$
           $\{\neg(\uparrow$ SUBJ PRED$)$
           $(\uparrow$ SUBJ PERSON$)$ = 3
           $(\uparrow$ SUBJ NUM$)$ = SG
           $(\uparrow$ SUBJ GEND$)$ = M
           |
           $\neg(\uparrow$ SUBJ PRED$)$
           $(\uparrow$ SUBJ$)$ = PRO
           $(\downarrow$PRONTYPE$)$ = EXPLETIVE
           $(\downarrow$FORM$)$ = *huwa*$\}\}$

(9) represents the SUBJ-to-SUBJ raising construction in (1b), repeated in (8) below.

(8) *It-tfal   j-i-dhr-u*   *(li)   sejr-in   tajjeb*
     DEF-children 3-FRM.VWL-appear.IMPV-PL COMP go.ACT.PTCP-PL good

    'The children seem to be doing well'

(9)

$$
\begin{bmatrix}
\text{PRED} & \text{`}jidhru\ \langle\text{XCOMP}\rangle\text{SUBJ'} \\
\text{SUBJ} & \begin{bmatrix} \text{PRED} & \text{`}tfal\text{'} \\ \text{PERS} & 3 \\ \text{NUM} & \text{PL} \\ \text{DEF} & + \end{bmatrix}[1] \\
\text{XCOMP} & \begin{bmatrix} \text{PRED} & \text{`}sejrin\langle\text{SUBJ}\rangle\text{'} \\ \text{SUBJ} & \begin{bmatrix} \quad\quad\quad\quad\quad \end{bmatrix}[1] \\ \text{ADJ} & \left\{ \begin{bmatrix} \text{PRED} & \text{`}tajjeb\text{'} \end{bmatrix} \right\} \end{bmatrix}
\end{bmatrix}
$$

The index [1] in the *f*-structure in (9) represents the functional identity between the SUBJ in the matrix and the SUBJ in the embedded clause. This dependency is therefore not achieved via movement, but rather via structure-sharing, i.e. where one and the same syntactic item takes on two distinct functions, which in this context are the matrix SUBJ and the embedded SUBJ. The Uniqueness constraint then ensures that the identical material only be overt in one position. Since (9) accounts for the forward raising present in (8), we observe how the expressed argument is in the matrix. This then controls the relation/dependency with the SUBJ in the embedded clause.

While *deher* and other raising predicates idiosyncratically display an alternation with the expletive construction, this is not necessarily the case for all raising predicates in the language. Similarly, it is neither the case that all raising predicates available in the language necessarily display the array of *c*-structure complement types listed in (4). Furthermore, the availability of a complementiser introducing the clausal complement is itself a lexical restriction imposed by the clause-taking raising predicate.[8] *Beda* 'begin', which has in Camilleri (2016) been shown to function as a raising predicate, along with other aspectualisers in the language, such as *qabad* lit. 'catch, start', *reġa'* 'repeat' and *qagħad* 'fit, endure', does not allow its embedded clause to be introduced by a complementiser. Syndetic marking is thus not allowed, as the ungrammaticality of (10a) illustrates. Nevertheless, changes in the canonical constituent order, such as the preposing of the ADJunct in (10b), results in the obligatory presence of the complementiser.

---

[8]See Camilleri (2016: 288-292) for additional discussion, including a reference to complementiser forms other than *li*, including *billi* and *biex*.

(10) a. **Bdie-t   li   t-mur*
   start.PFV-3SGF COMP 3F-go.IMPV.SG
   Intended: 'She started to go'

  b. *Bdie-t   li,   kuldarba *(li) n-e-rsaq*
   start.PFV-3SGF COMP every.time COMP 1-FRM.VWL-get.close.IMPV.SG
   lej-ha,   t-i-tlaq
   towards-3SGF.GEN 3F-FRM.VWL-leave.IMPV.SG
   t-i-ġri
   3F-FRM.VWL-run.IMPV.SG
   'She started that, every time I draw close to her, she runs away'
   (Camilleri 2016: 242)

A parallel behaviour with respect to the obligatory or optional presence of the complementiser also follows for *deher*. Although *li* is optional, as in (4a), this becomes obligatory in contexts where there is a FOCUS discourse function in the embedded clause, as in (11a), or when there is a right-dislocation of the (matrix) SUBJ, as in (11b), for example, where here we observe how as a consequence, the complement clause itself becomes right-dislocated.

(11) a. *T-i-dher   *(li)* HI *marr-et   tajjeb*
   3F-FRM.VWL-seem.IMPV.SG COMP she go.PFV-3SGF good.SGM
   'She seems that as for her, she did well'

  b. *T-i-dher,   Marija, *(li) marr-et   tajjeb*
   3F-FRM.VWL-seem.IMPV.SG Mary   COMP go.PFV-3SGF good.SGM
   'As for Mary, she seems that she did well'

Apart from *deher* and aspectualiser predicates, other raising predicates in Maltese include the pseudo-verbs *qis-* and *donn-*, as discussed in Camilleri et al. (2014).[9] These two forms easily co-occur with, or substitute *deher* except in two identified contexts, as we will see. Other pseudo-verbs such as *għand-* 'have', *għodd-* 'almost', *għad-* 'still; just' and *il-* 'have', were also shown shown to display behaviours attributed to raising predicates in Camilleri (2016).[10] The set of rais-

---

[9]We do not here engage in a discussion on pseudo-verbs and what they are. For more information the reader can refer to Comrie (1982); Fabri (1987); Vanhove (1993); Peterson (2009); Camilleri (2016).

[10]Evidence includes agreement facts; subcategorisation-frame requirements; and other independent evidence that has to do with evidence that favours a matrix verb – complement clause analysis, as opposed to a complex predicate analysis, or an analysis where the pseudo-verbs simply come to render a feature value in the *f*-structure. Under this analysis, the lexical predicate does not function as a complement, but as the clause's head.

ing predicates which have not been described previously, are happenstance verbs. These include *inzerta* (12), *seħel* (13), *laħaq* (14) and *ħabat* (15).[11] The paradigm in (12) is made up of data from the MLRS Corpus (Gatt & Čéplö 2013). In (12a) we have a structure which can be interpreted as an *It*-Extraposition, (although one can argue that it is structurally ambiguous), while the constructions in (12b) and (12c) are SUBJ-to-SUBJ raising structures (SSR).

(12) a. *Inzerta*   *li*   *j-a-qa'*   *taħt*   *il-...*
          happen/occur.PFV-3SGM COMP 3M-FRM.VWL-fall.IMPV.SG under DEF

          'It happens that he falls under ... (He is managed by)'   (MLRS v2.0)

     b. *Inzertaj-t*   *li*   *ħdim-t*   *ħafna fuq dak*
          happen/occur.PFV-1SG COMP work.PFV-1SG a.lot on DEM.SGM

          il-proġett   *u*   *...*
          DEF-project.SGM CONJ

          'I happened such that I have worked a lot on that project' (MLRS v2.0)

     c. *Inzertaj-t*   *n-af*   *xi*   *wħud minn-hom*
          happen/occur.PFV-1SG 1-know.IMPV.SG some some from-3PL.GEN

          'I happened to know a few of them'   (MLRS v2.0)

(13) *Ma šhel-t-x*   */ ma sehil-x*   *ġej-t*
       NEG happen.PFV-2SG-NEG / NEG happen.PFV.3SGM-NEG come.PFV-2SG

       magħ-na   *dakinhar,*   *int.*
       with-1PL.GEN DEM.DEF.SGM.day you

       'You didn't happen to have come with us that day'   SSR

       'It happened that you weren't with us that day'   (*It*-Extraposition)

(14) *Laħq-et*   *għaml-et*   *lumi*   *i-kbar,*   *is-siġra*
       achieve.PFV-3SGF do.PFV-3SGF lemons COMPAR-big, DEF-tree.SGF

       Lit: 'She achieve she did bigger lemons, the tree'

       'It happened that (at some point earlier in the past), the tree produced bigger lemons'

---

[11]Note that *ħabat* in Maltese also functions as an INCEPTIVE aspectualiser. See Camilleri (2016) for more detail.

(15) a. *Kien   ħabat   tajjeb   li   l-parlament*
          be.PFV.3SGM crash.PFV.3SGM good.SGM COMP DEF-parliament.SGM
          Malt-i   beda   j-i-ddiskuti   ...
          Maltese-SGM start.PFV.3SGM 3M-EPENT.VWL-discuss.IMPV.SG ...

          'It happened well that the Maltese parliament started to
          discuss/started discussing ...'   (MLRS v2.0)

      b. *għax   ħbat-t   qbad-t   lilu*
          because happen.PFV-1SG catch.PFV-1SG him

          'because I happened to have caught him'

3.2 Evidence in favour of a raising analysis

Raising tests vary. Primarily, one needs to establish that a dependency exists
between the matrix and the embedded clause. In instances of (forward) SSR, one
needs to establish that the SUBJ is indeed present within the embedded clause,
for this to then also function as the SUBJ of the matrix clause, which is where it
is overtly expressed or pronominally incorporated. Additionally, one also needs
to establish that the matrix SUBJ position is indeed non-thematic.

Establishing that the SUBJ of the embedded clause is still salient in the overall
dependency, and that it in fact exists even though it may not be pronounced,
would verify the expectation that if an embedded SUBJ is indeed available, then
this should be able to reflexively bind a local direct object. This is the case in (16).

(16) *Aħna n-i-dhr-u   n-ħobb-u$_i$ lilna nfus-na$_i$*
      we   1-FRM.VWL-appear.IMPV-PL 1-love.IMPV-PL us   self.PL-1PL.GEN

      'We seem to love ourselves'

Another argument in support of the fact that the SUBJ is also available in the
embedded clause comes from the behaviour of floating quantifiers: The quantifier
kollha 'all.PL' can appear in the matrix or the embedded clause, as illustrated
through (17).

(17) *(Kollha) j-i-dhr-u   li   (kollha) marr-u   (kollha)*
      all.PL   3-FRM.VWL-appear.IMPV-PL COMP all.PL   go.PFV.3-PL all.PL
      flimkien
      together

      'All appear to have gone together'

A piece of evidence that suggests that the SUBJ in the matrix *is* non-thematic, as expected of the external argument of a raising predicate, is the fact that it is possible for the SUBJ to be PREDless as a consequence of the raising of the 3SGM impersonal morphology of the embedded impersonal verb. Instances such as (18) are in principle ambiguous as to whether this sort of raising is involved, given that the raising predicates *donn-* 'as though', *seħel* 'happen' and *deher* 'appear' all allow for an alternation with the *It*-Extraposition construction.

(18) a. *Hawn donn-u/donn-ok*   *qiegħd-a*
    EXIST as.though-3SGM.ACC/as.though-2SG.ACC PROG-SGF
    j-fettil-l-ek   *għaċ-ċikkulata*
    3M-decide.abruptly.IMPV.SG-DAT-2SG for.DEF-chocolate
    'Here it seems/you seem to be craving for chocolate all of a sudden'

  b. *Jekk seħel/sħil-t*   *irnexxie-l-ek,*
    if happen.PFV.3SGM/happen.PFV-2SG manage.PFV.3SGM-DAT-2SG
    għala ma ħad-t-x   *iċ-ċans?*
    why NEG take.PFV-2SG-NEG DEF-chance
    'If it/you happened to have managed, why didn't you take the chance?'

  c. *J-i-dher/t-i-dher*
    3M-FRM.VWL-appear.IMPV.SG/2-FRM.VWL-appear.IMPV.SG
    għand-ek/kel-l-ek   *bżonn ftit mistrieħ*
    have-2SG.GEN/be.PFV.3SGM-have-2SG.GEN need a.little rest
    'You seem to need/have needed some rest'

On the other hand, if we consider what takes place in the case of aspectualiser predicates such as REPETITIVE-expressing *reġa'* and INCEPTIVE-expressing *qabad* lit. 'catch' and *beda* 'start', the ungrammaticality of the sentences in (19), shows that they are not able to display an alternation with an *It*-Extraposition, i.e. they do not take an alternative non-raised structure involving a default 3SGM form.

(19) a. **J-e-rġa'*   *n-a-għmel*   *xi ħaġa*
    3M-FRM.VWL-repeat.IMPV.SG 1-FRM.VWL-do.IMPV.SG some thing
    Intended: 'I do something again'

  b. **J-a-qbad/j-i-bda*
    3M-FRM.VWL-catch.IMPV.SG/3M-FRM.VWL-start.IMPV.SG
    n-a-għmel   *xi ħaġa*
    1-FRM.VWL-do.IMPV.SG some thing
    Intended: 'I start to do something'

Due to the inability of aspectualiser predicates to alternate with the Expletive construction, the availability of the data in (20), consisting of sentences involving a number of stacked aspectualisers, clearly suggests that what is taking place is the chained raising of the default non-referential 3SGM morphology of the impersonal verb at the bottom of the dependency. We take this to imply that aspectualisers also allow for PREDless non-thematic SUBJs, at least in specific constrained contexts such as this, i.e. ones involving impersonal verb-forms in the embedded clause (and predicates with non-canonically indexed SUBJs more broadly).

(20) a. *Qorob/qrob-t* *biex*
  draw.close.PFV.3SGM/draw.close.PFV-1SG in.order.to
  j-e-rġa' *j-a-qbad*
  3M-FRM.VWL-repeat.IMPV.SG 3M-FRM.VWL-catch.IMPV.SG
  j-i-bda *j-kol-l-i* *mara*
  3M-FRM.VWL-start.IMPV.SG 3M-be.IMPV.SG-have-1SG.GEN woman
  t-għin-ni *fid-dar*
  3F-help.IMPV.SG-1SG.ACC in.DEF-house

  Lit: 'He was close/I was close in order to he repeats he starts he be to-me woman she helps me in the house'

  'I am close to once again start having a woman helping me in the house' (Camilleri 2016: 294)

  b. *Rama/ħasel* *qis-u* *ħabat*
  arm.PFV.3SGM/wash.PFV.3SGM as.though-3SGM.ACC crash.PFV.3SGM
  ħa *j-i-ftil-l-i* *għal biċċa*
  PROSP 3M-EPENT.VWL-decide.abruptly.IMPV.SG-DAT-1SG for piece
  ċikkulata
  chocolate

  Lit: 'He started as though he was on the verge of long.for.all.of.a.sudden for piece of chocolate'

  'I started as though I was on the verge of craving for a piece of chocolate' (Camilleri 2016: 294)

Additional evidence in support of the non-thematic status of the matrix SUBJ comes from the free availability of idiom chunks in this position.[12]

---

[12]Differing behaviours will be discussed in §4 with respect to the data in (42).

(21) a. *Daqqa t'id   t-i-sħel   t-a-għmel*
hit.SGF of.hand 3F-FRM.VWL-happen.IMPV.SG 3F-FRM.VWL-do.IMPV.SG
il-ġid,   kultant
DEF-benefit sometimes

Lit: 'A hit of hand happens it does the benefit sometimes'

'Providing help or advice does well every now and then'

  b. *Naħqa ta' ħmar dehr-et   (li) qatt m'hi   se*
bray.SGF of donkey appear.PFV-3SGF COMP never NEG.COP.3SGF PROSP
t-i-tla'   s-sema, biss,   żied-u
3F-FRM.VWL-go.up.IMPV.SG DEF-sky, however add.PFV.3-PL
j-i-sfida-w,   u   rnexxie-l-hom.
3-EPENT.VWL-defy.IMPV-PL CONJ manage.PFV.3SGM-DAT-3PL

Lit: 'A bray of a donkey appeared that never it is going to reach the sky/heaven, but/however they increased they defy, and they managed'

'The cry of the poor or someone insignificant appeared that it was not going to reach far, however, they increased in their defiance, and they managed (to get what they wanted)'

  c. *Riħ   ta' siegħa deher   għodd-u*
wind.SGM of hour   appear.PFV.3SGM almost-3SGM.ACC
naddaf   qiegħa
clean.CAUSE.PFV.3SGM trashing.floor

Lit: 'Wind of an hour appeared almost cleaned the place where wheat is scattered'

'An instant/moment can and may seem to result in more important things'

As discussed in the literature (e.g. Davies & Dubinsky 2008), if the matrix predicate is a raising one, semantic equivalence is expected, irrespective of whether the predicate in the (deepest) embedded clause is active or passive. Observe this behaviour through the constructions below.

(22) a. *Beda/baqa'*   *j-i-ġbor*
          start.PFV.3SGM/remain.PFV.3SGM 3M-FRM.VWL-collect.IMPV.SG
          l-iltiema
          DEF-orphan.PL
          'He started/continued gathering the orphans'   (Active)

      b. *Bde-w/baqgħ-u*   *j-i-n-ġabr-u*
          start.PFV.3-PL/remain.PFV.3-PL 3-EPENT.VWL-PASS-gather.IMPV-PL
          l-iltiema
          DEF-orphan.PL
          'The orphans started/continued to be gathered' Passive: (Alotaibi et al.
          2013: 20)

(23) a. *T-i-dher*   *donn-ha/donn-u*
          3F-FRM.VWL-appear.IMPV.SG as.though-3SGF.ACC/as.though-3SGM.ACC
          ta-t   xi   flus   għall-karitá
          give.PFV-3SGF some money for.DEF-charity
          'She seems as though she gave some money to charity'   (Active)

      b. *J-i-dhr-u*   *donn-hom/donn-u*
          3-FRM.VWL-appear.IMPV-PL as.though-3PL.ACC/as.though-3SGM.ACC
          n-għata-w   xi   flus   għall-karitá
          PASS-give.PFV.3-PL some money for.DEF-charity
          'Some money for charity seem to have been given'   (Passive)

Passivisation data also provides yet another context where idiom chunks can come to function as the matrix SUBJ, once passivisation promotes the idiom from OBJ to SUBJ position.

(24) a. *T-i-dher/donn-ha*
          3F-FRM.VWL-appear.IMPV.SG/as.though-3SGF.ACC
          dahħl-et   fellus   f'mohħ-ha
          enter.CAUSE.PFV-3SGF chick.SGM in.brain-3SGF.GEN
          Lit: 'She seems/She's as though she caused to enter a chick in her
          brain'
          'She seems to have fixed an idea/doubt in her mind'

    b. *Fellus   kbir   j-i-dher*
       chick.SGM big.SGM 3M-FRM.VWL-appear.IMPV.SG
       d-daħħal   f'moħħ-ha
       PASS-enter.CAUSE.PFV.3SGM in.mind-3SGF.GEN
       Lit: 'A big chick appears to have been entered in her mind'
       'A fixed idea seems to have got to her mind'

(25)   a. *Hawn donn-u   qatgħa-l-hom   iż-żejża*
       here   as.though-3SGM.ACC cut.PFV.3SGM-DAT-3PL DEF-breast.SGF
       Lit: 'Here it seems he cut on-them the breast'
       'It seems that their illegal source has been cut'

      b. *Hawn iż-żejża   donn-ha*
       here   DEF-breast.SGF as.though-3SGF.ACC
       n-qatgħ-et-i-l-hom
       PASS-cut.PFV-3SGF-EPENT.VWL-DAT-3PL
       Lit: 'Here the breast seems it has been cut on-them'
       'The illegal source has been cut'

Further evidence in support of the claim that the constructions under discussion involve raising predicates comes from scoping effects and the availability of both a narrow and wide reading of a quantified SUBJ. A narrow reading would not have been available for a control/equi predicate, since the SUBJ of such predicates does not originate in the embedded clause, but is in fact a thematic argument of the matrix itself.

(26) *ħadd   ma j-i-dher/qis-u*
     no.one NEG 3M-FRM.VWL-appear.IMPV.SG/as.though-3SGM.ACC
     j-o-qgħod   hemm
     3M-FRM.VWL-live.IMPV.SG there
     'It seems to be the case that no one lives there'

                      (*seem* scopes over *no one*: Narrow Scope)
     'There is no one such that he/she seems to live there'

                      (*no one* scopes over *seem*: Wide Scope)

Having established a number of properties that provide evidence for raising constructions, there remains another, which essentially deals with meteorological SUBJs. The availability of such SUBJs (as in (27)) uncontroversially implies a non-thematic SUBJ status.

(27) a. *Ix-xita   donn-ha   ma t-rid-x*
DEF-rain.SGF as.though-3SGF.ACC NEG 3F-want.IMPV.SG-NEG
t-e-hda
3F-FRM.VWL-relent.IMPV.SG

'The rain appears as though it does not want to relent'

b. *Il-kesħa   t-i-dher   qiegħd-a ż-żid*
DEF-cold.SGF 3F-FRM.VWL-seem.IMPV.SG PROG-SGF 3F-increase.IMPV.SG

'The cold seems to be increasing'

Such constructions appear to be the usual forward raising constructions we have been considering up till now, i.e. raising constructions where the expressed SUBJ, be it overt or an incorporated pronoun, is in the matrix. It however seems to us that backward raising also exists in Maltese, as argued in Camilleri (2016: 292), following data such as that in (28) below.

(28) a. *Baqgħ-et   nieżl-a   ħafna xita*
remain.PFV-3SGF down.ACT.PTCP-SGF a.lot   rain.SGF

Lit: 'She remained downing the rain'

'It kept raining'

b. *Bdie-t   t-a-għmel   xebgħa   sħana*
begin.PFV-3SGF 2-FRM.VWL-do.IMPV.SG smacking heat.SGF

Lit: 'She started she does smacking heat'

'It started being very hot'   (Alotaibi et al. 2013: 19)

In both instances in (28), the phrases *ħafna xita* and *xebgħa sħana*, which are the respective SUBJs shared between the matrix aspectualiser and the lexical predicate, are not able to neutrally occur in front of the aspectualiser in the matrix, and can thus only ever surface in the embedded clause. We suggest in passing that this data may display instances of backward raising structures (Potsdam & Polinsky 2012), where only 'covert' raising to the matrix is involved. Linearly, on the other hand, the SUBJ is retained as an overt DP in the embedded clause. If our hypothesising of a backward raising analysis is on the right track, then it would account for why we are not able to get neutrally ordered pre-verbal SUBJs in (28), but yet we still get the agreement matching on the aspectualiser in the matrix. The agreement available comes about as a result of the structure-sharing of the SUBJ in the embedded clause with that in the matrix.

4 Copy raising

We consider another type of raising structure in Maltese: copy raising. Copy raising (CR) involves 'a construction in which some constituent appears in a non-thematic position with its thematic position occupied by a pronominal copy' (Potsdam & Runner 2001). In English, unlike what is the case 'in infinitival SSR, in CR, the predicate takes a tensed clause complement introduced by one of the particles *like, as if,* or *as though*' (Potsdam & Runner 2001: 433) which, following Maling (1983) and Heycock (1994), are prepositions. The same view is upheld in Asudeh & Toivonen (2012) and Landau (2011). Such prepositions are then assumed in Fujii (2007) to take a complement clause, given that these complements display the same conditions as the *that*-trace effect (p. 301). A CP complement analysis is motivated, and is in turn taken to imply an account where 'copy raising involves overt raising out of a finite CP' (p. 302). In Asudeh & Toivonen (2012) the *in-situ* copy pronouns are analysed just as other resumptive pronouns. As stated in Asudeh & Toivonen (2012: 325), the difference between resumptives in copy raising constructions vs. those in unbounded discourse dependency structures is that the relation between the matrix non-thematic SUBJ and the embedded copy pronoun is 'lexically-controlled', as opposed to what is the case in unbounded discourse dependencies. Illustrations of CR constructions in English are provided in (29), with the copy pronoun represented in bold.

(29) a. There seems like **there** are problems   (Potsdam & Runner 2001: 454)

b. Tom seemed to me as if **he** had won   (Asudeh & Toivonen 2012: 332)

c. Tom seemed like Bill hurt **him** again   (Asudeh & Toivonen 2012: 346)

Apart from the presence of a pronoun in the embedded clause, and the finiteness of the clause (at least in English), another property that distinguishes raising or *it*-expletive constructions from copy raising ones is that the SUBJ in the latter must be obligatorily interpreted as a perceptual source (PSOURCE): 'a copy raising subject is interpreted as the PSOURCE – the source of perception – and ascribing the role of PSOURCE to the subject is infelicitous if the individual in question is not perceivable as the source of the report' (Asudeh & Toivonen 2012: 334). *It*-expletive and non-CR constructions allow for both an Individual or Event Psource reading. In (30) below, where we have a usual non-copy raised construction, the available Event Psource reading is made obvious by the ADJ complement involved.

(30) *Donn-hom/-u*   */ qis-hom/-u*   *qed*
as.though-3PL.ACC/-3SGM.ACC / as.though-3PL.ACC/-3SGM.ACC PROG
j-a-qra-w   *ktieb*   *tajjeb*   *xi*   *kwiet*   *hawn!*
3-FRM.VWL-read.IMPV-PL book.SGM good.SGM what silence EXIST

'It's as though they are reading a good book, how quiet it is!/They're as
though they're reading a good book'   (Camilleri 2016: 181)

A CR structure with an obligatory PSOURCE rendering of the SUBJ is (31). 'This
is infelicitous if inferred from a pile of files on the desk, but fully appropriate
if she is present and looking panicky and stressed. That is, this sentence is only
appropriate then if 'she' is the direct source of perception' (Camilleri et al. 2014:
193).

(31) *T-i-dher*   *ġà*   *ta-w-ha*   *xebgħa*
3F-FRM.VWL-appear.IMPV.SG already give.PFV.3-PL-3SGF.ACC smacking
xogħol x't-a-għmel
work what.3F-FRM.VWL-do.IMPV.SG

'She seems as though they already gave her a lot of work to do'   (COMP
OBJ; Camilleri et al. 2014: 192)

While Maltese copy raising constructions can simply involve the 'seem; appear; as though' predicate(s) discussed so far, it is also possible to have a structure that is closer to CR constructions in English, in the presence of the (optional)
preposition *bħal* 'like' or the preposition-headed complementiser *bħallikieku* 'as
though', built out of the preposition *bħal* 'like', the usual complementiser *li* and
the counterfactual complementiser *kieku*, as illustrated in (32).[13]

(32) *Qis-ha*   *(bħal(likieku))* *ta-w-ha*   *xebgħa*
as.though-3SGF.ACC as.if   give.PFV.3-PL-3SGF.ACC smacking

'She's as though they gave her a smacking'

---

[13] One could argue that *li kieku* is the full form of the counterfactual complementiser. This complementiser without the P head is not able to occur in CR constructions, as the ungrammaticality
of (i) below, suggests.

(i)   **It-tifla qis-ha*   *(li)*   *kieku ma ta-t-x*   *kas*
DEF-girl as.though-3SGF.ACC COMP COMP NEG give.PFV-3SGF-NEG notice
Intended: 'The girl's as though she didn't bother'

In the presence of this fused grammatical form, which provides an evidential-like interpretation, it becomes possible to even drop the raising predicate itself, as in (33), for example.

(33) a. *It-tifla   bħal(likieku) ma ta-t-x   kas*
          DEF-girl as.though   NEG give.PFV-3SGF-NEG notice

      'The girl's as though she did not bother'

   b. **It-tifla bħal ta-w-ha**   *xebgħa*
          DEF-girl like give.PFV.3-PL-3SGF.ACC smacking

      'The girl's as though they gave her a smacking'

CR in Maltese comes in two flavours. It is not necessarily the case that it should always include an embedded clause that maps onto a COMP GF, which is otherwise what we have when anaphoric-binding is involved. If a P like *bħal* or its fusion with the counterfactual complementiser *(li)kieku* is present, then we can argue that this is functioning as the PRED of the complement that mediates between the matrix raising predicate and the clausal COMP GF argument which the P then subcategorises for. In such an instance we would then have an analysis where *deher*$_{bħal}$ is associated with the lexical entry: $\langle$XCOMP$\rangle$SUBJ, but where the SUBJ is in an anaphorically-bound relation, which in this case would be: ($\uparrow$SUBJ)σ= (($\uparrow$XCOMP COMP GF)σ Antecedent). Independent proof that suggests that *bħal* can function as a PRED that in turn subcategorises for an embedded clause comes both from examples such as (33) as well as from data such as (34), where raising is not even involved.

(34) *J-i-dher   bħal(likieku) marr-u   weħid-hom*
       3M-FRM.VWL-seem.IMPV.SG like   go.PFV.3-PL alone-3PL.GEN

      'It seems they went on their own'   (No raising)

Additional evidence in favour of our account that *bħal* does indeed function as a PRED comes from the availability of verbless constructions such as the one in (35). The difference between (35) and (33) simply boils down to the fact that *bħal* displays a distinct subcategorisation frame in each: An OBJ argument in (35) and a complement clause in (33). (See Dalrymple & Lødrup (2000) for a discussion of such sorts of alternations in English).

(35) *It-tifla   bħal-ek*
       DEF-girl like-2SG.GEN

      'The girl is like you'

The data in (36) illustrate a number of CR constructions with copies in different GFs within the structure.[14]

(36) a. *T-i-dhr-u*   *bḥallikieku xi   ħadd*
2-FRM.VWL-appear.IMPV-PL like.that   some no.one
qal-i-l-kom   *biex   t-i-tilq-u*
say.PFV.3SGM-EPENT.VWL-DAT-2PL in.what 2-FRM.VWL-leave.IMPV-PL
'You appear as if someone told you to leave'
(Embedded COMP OBJ;$_\theta$ Camilleri et al. 2014: 192)

    b. *Dehr-et*   *qis-ha*   *donn-ha*
seem.PFV-3SGF as.though-3SGF.ACC as.though-3SGF.ACC
għajt-u   *magħ-ha*
shout.PFV.3-PL with-3SGF.GEN
'She seemed as though they shouted at her'
(Chained raising + Embedded COMP OBL OBJ; Camilleri et al. 2014: 193)

    c. **Marija** *qis-ha*   *bħal t-i-dher*   *li*
Mary   as.though-SGF.ACC as 3F-FRM.VWL-seem.IMPV.SG COMP
żewġ-ha   *reġa'*   *lura d-dar,*   *x'inhi*
husband-3SGF.GEN return.PFV.SGM back DEF-house, what.COP.3SGF
ferħan-a
happy-SGF
'Mary's as though her husband returned back to the house, how happy she is'
(Embedded COMP SUBJ POSS)

(37) illustrates a CR construction with the presence of the happenstance predicate *seħel* 'happen'.

(37) *Kollha seħl-u*   *qabad-hom*   *in-ngħas*
all.PL   happen.PFV.3-PL catch.PFV.3SGM-3PL.ACC DEF-sleepiness.SGM
'All happened to be overcome by sleepiness'   (Alotaibi et al. 2013: 24)

The *f*-structure in (38) is the one associated with (36a), and illustrates an instance of a mediated CR structure, along with an anaphoric dependency between the matrix SUBJ and the XCOMP COMP OBJ$_\theta$ that is accounted for at the semantic-structure.

---

[14]Note that it is not possible to have a SUBJ copy in the highest embedded SUBJ. See Camilleri et al. (2014) for more detail.

(38)

$$
\begin{bmatrix}
\text{PRED} & \text{`}tidhru\ \langle\text{XCOMP}\rangle\text{SUBJ'} \\
\text{SUBJ} & \begin{bmatrix} \text{PRED} & \text{`PRO'} \\ \text{PERS} & 2 \\ \text{NUM} & \text{PL} \end{bmatrix}[1] \\
\text{XCOMP} & \begin{bmatrix} \text{PRED} & \text{`}b\hbar al\ \langle\text{SUBJ, COMP}\rangle\text{'} \\ \text{SUBJ} & [\quad][1] \\ \text{COMP} & \begin{bmatrix} \text{COMP FORM} & \text{`}likieku\text{'} \\ \text{PRED} & \text{`}qal\ \langle\text{SUBJ, OBJ}_\theta,\ \text{XCOMP}\rangle\text{'} \\ \text{SUBJ} & \begin{bmatrix} \text{PRED} & \text{`}\hbar add\text{'} \\ \text{SPEC} & [\text{PRED}\ \ \text{`}xi\text{'}] \end{bmatrix} \\ \text{OBJ}_\theta & \begin{bmatrix} \text{PRED} & \text{`PRO'} \\ \text{PERS} & 2 \\ \text{NUM} & \text{PL} \\ \text{CASE} & \text{DAT} \end{bmatrix}[2] \\ \text{XCOMP} & \begin{bmatrix} \text{COMP FORM} & \text{`}biex\text{'} \\ \text{PRED} & \text{`}titilqu\ \langle\text{SUBJ}\rangle\text{'} \\ \text{SUBJ} & [\quad][2] \end{bmatrix} \end{bmatrix} \end{bmatrix}
\end{bmatrix}
$$

Constraints on the path of the anaphoric dependency in CR constructions are present. As identified in Camilleri (2016: 179), the availability of optionally up to three 'seem/as.though/as.if' predicates simultaneously, as in (39), allow us to clearly demonstrate their existence. The ungrammaticality of (39) illustrates that it is not possible to have the matrix SUBJ being anaphorically bound with the COMP XCOMP (XCOMP) non-SUBJ GF when a local or optionally chained SUBJ-to-SUBJ raising is nested within.

(39) *Dehr-et   donn-hom   (qis-hom)   qed
      appear.PFV-3SGF as.though-3PL.ACC as.though-3PL.ACC PROG
      j-kellm-u-ha   ħażin
      3-talk.IMPV-PL-3SGF.ACC   bad.SGM
      Intended: 'She seemed as though they talked badly to her'

                                                    (Camilleri 2016: 179)

CR is not only available with *deher* and happenstance verbs. It is also present with aspectualiser predicates. The restriction identified in Camilleri (2016) with respect to such constructions is that for the SUBJ of aspectualisers to display anaphoric binding, the PRED value of the highest embedded clause must be either the pseudo-verb *qis-* or *donn-*. The path for the anaphoric dependency associated with aspectualiser predicates as opposed to the 'seem/appear/as.though' and 'happenstance' predicates obligatorily involves a COMP|XCOMP^{+} path, and where the PRED of the highest COMP|XCOMP must be *qis-* or *donn-*, and cannot be substituted by *deher*. Alternatively, the CR structure can be mediated through *bħal*. These facts can be compared and contrasted through the data in (40).

(40) a. **Bde-w   j-i-dher   qabad-hom*
           start.PFV.3-PL 3M-FRM.VWL-appear.IMPV.SG catch.PFV.3SGM-3PL.ACC
           in-ngħas
           DEF-sleepiness.SGM
           Intended: 'They started seeming as though sleepiness came on-them'

      b. *It-tfal   **bde-w**   qis-u/-hom*   /
           DEF-children start.PFV.3-PL as.though-3SGM.ACC/-3PL.ACC /
           donn-u/-hom   dejjem qed   j-a-sl-u
           as.though-3SGM.ACC/-3PL.ACC always PROG 3-FRM.VWL-arrive.IMPV-PL
           tard
           late
           'The children started as though they are arriving always late'   (SUBJ)

      c. *Reġgħ-et   bħal   qabad-ha   uġigħ*
           repeat.PFV-3SGF as.though catch.PFV.3SGM-3SGF.ACC pain.SGM
           fl-istonku
           in.DEF-stomach
           'She again started feeling pain in her stomach'   (OBJ)

Another property associated with CR constructions, at least in English, is that idiom chunks as matrix SUBJs are not possible, as the ungrammaticality of (41) illustrates, unlike normal raising constructions (Lappin, 1984, p. 241).

(41) a. *Much headway appears as if **it** had been made on the project

      b. *Advantage seems as if **it** has been taken of John

Parallel facts are also present in Maltese, except that instead of being ungrammatical, the idiomatic reading of an idiom chunk is entirely lost in CR constructions, giving way to a literal reading only, as illustrated in the data in (42), since the matrix SUBJ must itself be a PSOURCE, in such constructions.

(42) a. *Iż-żejża*   *donn-ha*   *qatgħ-u-**hie**-l-hom*
               DEF-breast.SGF as.though-3SGF.ACC cut.PFV.3-PL-3SGF.ACC-DAT-3PL
               'The breast seems as though they cut-it on-them'

                                                 (Literal interpretation)

               *'The illegal source appears as though they cut-it on-them'

                                        (*Idiomatic interpretation)

    b. *Il-fellus*   *j-i-dher*
               DEF-chick.SGM 3M-FRM.VWL-appear.IMPV.SG
               *daħħl-u-**hu**-l-ha*   *f'moħħ-ha*
               enter.CAUSE.PFV.3-PL-3SGM.ACC-DAT-3SGF in.mind-3SGF.GEN
               'The chick seems like they put it inside her mind'

                                                 (Literal interpretation)

               *'The doubt seems like they put it inside her head'

                                        (*Idiomatic interpretation)

    c. *Qalb-hom*   *qis-ha*   *qatgħ-u-**ha***
               heart.SGF-3PL.GEN as.though-3SGF.ACC cut.PFV.3-PL-3SGF.ACC
               'They seem to have cut their heart'   (Literal interpretation)
               *'They seem to have lost hope'   (*Idiomatic interpretation)

With this we conclude our discussion on CR in Maltese, and how it is distinct from SSR.

5 Conclusion

In this paper we concentrated on raising-to-SUBJ structures in Maltese highlighting the (morpho)syntactic properties and the constraints that characterise raising and copy raising in the language. Working within the LFG framework, we analysed SSR differently from copy raising at the *f*-structure level. Broadly speaking, the former always involves functional control, while the latter will always have to resort to anaphoric binding, at some level, even if the matrix raising predicate can associate its clausal complement with an XCOMP GF, and not a COMP GF, in CR contexts, especially as a result of our discussion of what *bħal(likieku)* imparts to the structure.

In this overview of raising-to-SUBJ in Maltese we have considered various raising predicate types available in the language, whilst highlighting how their behaviour is not necessarily homogeneous, and the different predicates them-selves impose distinct (morpho)syntactic constraints. While we have left ques-tions unanswered, such as whether Maltese does indeed have backward SUBJ raising structures, or whether raising-to-non-SUBJ constructions exist, our aim in this paper was to provide a first approximation and advance our knowledge on the broad behaviour of raising in Maltese.

Acknowledgements

The research work disclosed in this work is partially funded by the REACH HIGH Scholars Programme – Post Doctoral Grants. The grant is part-financed by the EU, Operational Programme II – Cohesion Policy 2014 - 2020 "Investigating in human capital to create more opportunities and promote the well being of society" – ESF.

References

Alotaibi, Yasir, Muhammad Alzaidi, Maris Camilleri, Shaimaa ElSadek & Louisa Sadler. 2013. Psychological predicates and verbal complementation in African. In Miriam Butt & Tracy Holloway King (eds.), *Proceedings of the LFG 2013 Conference*. Stanford, CA: CSLI Publications.

Alsina, Alex. 2008. A Theory of Structure Sharing: Focusing on Long-Distance Dependencies and Parasitic Gaps. In Miriam Butt & Tracy Holloway King (eds.), *Proceedings of the LFG 2008 Conference*, 5–25. Stanford, CA: CSLI Publications.

Asudeh, Ash. 2005. Control and semantic resource sensitivity. *Journal of Linguistics* 41. 465–511.

Asudeh, Ash & Ida Toivonen. 2006. Expletives and the syntax and semantics of copy raising. In Miriam Butt & Tracy Holloway King (eds.), *Proceedings of the LFG 2006 Conference*, 14–29. Stanford, CA: CSLI Publications.

Asudeh, Ash & Ida Toivonen. 2012. Copy raising and perception. *Natural Language and Linguistic Theory* 30(2). 321–380.

Berman, Judith. 2003. *Clausal syntax of German*. Stanford, CA: CSLI Publications.

Binnick, Robert I. 1991. *Time and the verb: A guide to tense and aspect*. Oxford, UK: Oxford University Press.

Borg, Albert & Marie Azzopardi-Alexander. 1997. *Maltese (Descriptive Grammar)*. London: Routledge.

Bresnan, Joan. 1982. Control and complementation. In Joan Bresnan (ed.), *The mental representation of grammatical relations*, 282–390. Cambridge, MA: The MIT Press.

Bresnan, Joan. 2001. *Lexical Functional Syntax*. Oxford, UK: Blackwell.

Bresnan, Joan, Ash Asudeh, Ida Toivonen & Stephen Wechsler. 2015. *Lexical-functional syntax*. Vol. 16. Hoboken, NJ: John Wiley & Sons.

Bresnan, Joan & Sam Mchombo. 1987. Topic, pronoun and agreement in Chicheŵa. *Language* 63. 741–82.

Camilleri, Maris. 2014. *The stem in inflectional verbal paradigms in Maltese*. University of Surrey dissertation.

Camilleri, Maris. 2016. *Temporal and aspectual auxiliaries in Maltese*. University of Essex dissertation.

Camilleri, Maris. 2017. *Hyperraising in Maltese*. Manuscript, University of Essex. To appear in *Journal of Linguistics*.

Camilleri, Maris, Shaimaa ElSadek & Louisa Sadler. 2014. Perceptual reports in (varieties of) Arabic. In Miriam Butt & Tracy Holloway King (eds.), *Proceedings of the LFG 2014 Conference*, 179–199. Stanford, CA: CSLI Publications.

Chomsky, Noam. 1970. Remarks on nominalization. In Roderick Jacobs & Peter Rosenbaum (eds.), *Readings in English transformational grammar*, 143–160. Waltham, MA: Ginn & Company.

Comrie, Bernard. 1982. Syntactic-morphological discrepancies in Maltese sentence structure. *Communication and Cognition* 15. 281–306.

Culicover, Peter W. 2009. *Natural language syntax*. Oxford, UK: Oxford University Press.

Dalrymple, Mary. 2001. *Lexical functional grammar* (Syntax and Semantics). New York: Academic Press.

Dalrymple, Mary & Helge Lødrup. 2000. The grammatical functions of complement clauses. In Miriam Butt & Tracy Holloway King (eds.), *Proceedings of the LFG 2000 Conference*. Stanford, CA: CSLI Publications.

Davies, William D & Stanley Dubinsky. 2008. *The grammar of raising and control: A course in syntactic argumentation*. Oxford, UK: Blackwell.

Fabri, Ray. 1987. *An analysis of grammatical agreement in Maltese*. University of Düsseldorf MA thesis.

Fabri, Ray. 1993. *Kongruenz und die grammatik des Maltesischen*. Tübingen: Niemeyer.

Falk, Yehuda. 2001. *Lexical-Functional Grammar: An introduction to parallel constraint-based syntax*. Stanford, CA: CSLI Publications.

Fujii, Tomohiro. 2007. Cyclic chain reduction. In Norbert Corver & Jairo Nunes (eds.), *The copy theory of movement*, 291–326. Amsterdam/Philadelphia: John Benjamins.

Gatt, Albert & Slavomír Čéplö. 2013. Digital corpora and other electronic resources for maltese. In. Lancaster, UK.

Heycock, Caroline. 1994. *Layers of predication*. New York: Garland.

Kaplan, Ronald M. & Joan Bresnan. 1982. Lexical-Functional Grammar: A formal system for grammatical representation. In Joan Bresnan (ed.), *The mental representation of grammatical relations*, 173–281. Cambridge, MA: The MIT Press.

Kibort, Anna. 2004. *Passive and passive-like constructions in English and Polish*. University of Cambridge dissertation.

Kibort, Anna. 2007. Extending the applicability of Lexical Mapping Theory. In Miriam Butt & Tracy Holloway King (eds.), *Proceedings of the LFG 2007 Conference*, 250–270. Stanford, CA: CSLI Publications.

Kroeger, Paul. 2004. *Analyzing syntax: A Lexical-Functional approach*. Cambridge, UK: Cambridge University Press.

Landau, Idan. 2011. Predication vs aboutness in copy raising. *Natural Language and Linguistic Theory* 29(3). 779–813.

Maling, Joan. 1983. Transitive adjectives: A case of categorial reanalysis. In Frank Heby & Barry Richards (eds.), *Linguistic categories: Auxiliaries and related puzzles, volume 1*, 253–289. Dordrecht: D. Reidel.

Michaelis, Laura A. 1998. *Aspectual grammar and past-time reference*. New York: Routledge.

Newmeyer, Frederick J. 1975. *English aspectual verbs*. Vol. 203. Berlin: de Gruyter Mouton.

Peterson, John. 2009. "Pseudo-verbs": An analysis of non-verbal (co-)predication in Maltese. In Bernard Comrie, Ray Fabri, Elizabeth Hume, Manwel Mifsud, Thomas Stolz & Martine Vanhove (eds.), *Introducing Maltese linguistics*, 181–205. Amsterdam/Philadelphia: John Benjamins.

Postal, Paul M. 1974. *On raising*. Cambridge, MA: The MIT Press.

Potsdam, Eric & Maria Polinsky. 2012. Backward raising. *Syntax* 15(1). 75–108.

Potsdam, Eric & Jeffrey T Runner. 2001. Richard Returns: Copy Raising and Its Implications. In *Papers from the 37th Chicago Linguistic Society, Main Session*, vol. 1. Chicago, Ill: CLS.

Rosenbaum, Peter. 1967. *The grammar of English predicate complement constructions*. Cambridge, MA: The MIT Press.

Sells, Peter. 2006. Using subsumption rather than equality in functional control. In Miriam Butt & Tracy Holloway King (eds.), *Proceedings of the LFG 2006 Conference*. Stanford, CA: CSLI Publications.

Stiebels, Barbara. 2007. Towards a typology of complement control. *ZAS Papers in Linguistics* 47. 1–80.

Vanhove, Martine. 1993. *La langue maltaise: Etudes syntaxiques d'un dialecte arabe "périphérique"*. Wiesbaden: Harrassowitz.

Zaenen, Annie & Ronald M. Kaplan. 2002. Subsumption and equality: German partial fronting in LFG. In Miriam Butt & Tracy Holloway King (eds.), *Proceedings of the LFG 2002 Conference*. Stanford, CA: CSLI Publications.

Chapter 8

Rhythm in Maltese English

Sarah Grech

Alexandra Vella
University of Malta

There is evidence to suggest that rhythm may be a key element in the identification of Maltese English, MaltE. A number of characteristics at different levels of structure have been noted in research on this variety. These include a number of phonetic and/or phonological features, some of which may combine to trigger the perception of a pronunciation which is identifiably MaltE. Amongst these features, examining aspects of duration and/or timing has been shown to be a worthwhile starting point in understanding the nature of the rhythm of MaltE. Such elements include, but may not be limited to, the preference for full over reduced vowels, the tendency to production of post-vocalic 'r', and gemination of consonants (Calleja 1987; Vella 1995; Debrincat 1999; Grech 2015). It has been pointed out in research to date (Arvaniti 2009; 2012; Nokes & Hay 2012), that while durational characteristics cannot be assumed to be entirely responsible for different rhythm patterns, they remain pivotal, together with features including pitch, or intensity, in the perception of patterns of prominence which collectively could be referred to as rhythm. Following previous research by Grech (2015) and Grech & Vella (2015), there are indications that a Pairwise Variability Index (Grabe & Low 2002) can capture aspects of vowel duration and timing which can, in turn, translate into some measure of lesser or greater degrees of identifiability of this variety of English. This paper therefore reports on a study carried out using a normalised Pairwise Variability Index, nPVI, to measure local patterns of variability in vowel duration, as an indicator of rhythm patterns in 6 MaltE speakers. These speakers were rated in an earlier study (Grech 2015) as representing different degrees of identifiability as MaltE speakers on a continuum of variation. The extent of identifiability of these speakers is correlated to the nPVI results obtained in an attempt at addressing the matter of the extent to which rhythm characteristics may trigger listener perceptions of this variety.

Sarah Grech & Alexandra Vella. Rhythm in Maltese English. In Patrizia Paggio & Albert Gatt (eds.), *The languages of Malta*, 203–223. Berlin: Language Science Press. DOI:10.5281/zenodo.1181797

Sarah Grech & Alexandra Vella

1 Introduction: Describing a new variety of English

Native speakers of Maltese English (MaltE) frequently report recognising another MaltE speaker within a few seconds of speech, even if that speech is decontextualised, such as in an online video clip, or at an airport. The speed and certainty with which such instances of recognition are reported hints at predictable and systematically realised characteristics and features of speech at various levels of linguistic structure, but possibly most noticeably, at the phonetic and/or the phonological levels. A recent study, Grech (2015), taps into this intuitive recognition in an attempt at beginning to determine more precisely which phonetic/phonological features may be likely to trigger such perceptions in the first place.

The presence of characteristics and features serving to distinguish this variety from other varieties of English would hardly be considered unusual, given that some form of English, alongside other languages, has been widely used throughout the Maltese islands since the British established a colony there in the early 1800s. However, there has been – and to a large extent there still is – hotly debated discussion surrounding the kind of English that is actually developing, with the 'complaint tradition' (Milroy & Milroy 2012) about failing standards, and broadly termed 'bad' English frequently being very much at the heart of such debates. Traditionally dismissive attitudes towards the variety of English used in Malta have perhaps until more recently, stymied focused research on variation in MaltE and any of the socially meaningful patterns some of its features and characteristics might present.

The English language first became relevant in Malta in the context of some 200 years of colonial rule, making it the latest in a range of languages adopted alongside Maltese as the island sought to tap into the Mediterranean trade routes and socio-political dynamics (Brincat 2011). Increasingly rooted in Maltese society, English has become established as part of the bilingual reality of the islands' inhabitants, and as such it can be shaped and moulded to suit different contexts and social situations. It has therefore become increasingly important to be able to recognise the emerging MaltE not simply in relation to an established 'other', such as Southern Standard British English, SSBE, closely associated with school models of English, but more pertinently, in relation to the potentially socially meaningful range of variation within the variety itself. With the island's geo-political position making it a feasible location for economic migrants, and an inevitable staging-post for refugees fleeing war, poverty and climate change in Africa and the Middle East, MaltE also sometimes takes on the role of a lingua franca, as new communities seek access to employment, healthcare and school-ing. Thusat et al. (2009), Vella (2013), and Camilleri-Grima (2013) all refer to use of English as evident across different strata of Maltese society, and this, together with Bonnici's (2010) in-depth sociolinguistic study of communities where MaltE is the primary means of communication, suggests that this variety is on the cusp of an endonormative stage of development, which Schneider (2003) refers to as 'nativisation'.

A study in Grech (2015) sought to circumvent the more strongly held attitu-dinal stances towards MaltE by drawing on introspective perception judgments instead. An experimental study with 28 native MaltE listeners judging ten speak-ers, was designed in such a way as to bypass more overtly held attitudinal po-sitions towards MaltE, and to focus instead on its structure. In each case, the 28 listeners were presented with ten 12-15 second clips involving ten different MaltE speakers. While the speakers were all Maltese, one of the speakers had also lived in England for a few years, and was therefore expected both to have acquired some new features or to have modified some of the expected MaltE features, and to be identified by native MaltE listeners as a little different from the rest of the cohort. The remaining speakers were all Maltese, having grown up, been schooled and then established themselves in Malta. Nevertheless, they also displayed different degrees of linguistic variation, due to a number of social and linguistic factors widely recognised as having an impact on language usage in Malta, such as type of schooling, social background, or peer group identity (Vella 2013; Camilleri-Grima 2013). The recorded clips prepared were extracted from longer conversations and tasks designed to generate a similar range and type of lexis and use of language across speakers. All the clips contained pho-netic/phonological features which an earlier study (Grech 2015) had identified as relevant to the identification of MaltE.

It is important to recognise that MaltE is not a homogenous entity, but in fact also presents variation within the variety, what Mori (forthcoming) refers to as a "continuum of continua". Findings in Grech (2015) echo aspects of earlier research on the variety of English used in Malta to suggest that variation can be found at all levels of linguistic analysis. However, it is also suggested (see also Vella 1995; Bonnici 2010 that while variation at the phonetic/phonological levels is likely to cut across different social groups and linguistic backgrounds, variation at other levels is likely to be more contained within a particular subgroup of the variety. In particular, Bonnici (2010) found this to be the case with respect to the question of rhoticity. She suggests that earlier generations may have aimed at a less rhotic variety in a semi-conscious effort to emulate perceived standards of

Sarah Grech & Alexandra Vella

correctness in relation to SSBE, possibly also an impression which might have been transmitted through schooling. Conversely, younger generations may be adopting a more rhotic accent in an effort to distance themselves precisely from too close an association with this variety. Figure 1 below describes a possible schema for some of the characteristics which have featured most prominently in research on MaltE. Those features related to phonetics/phonology have so far been reported to be the ones most likely to be present to some extent across all varieties of MaltE (Vella 1995); by contrast features in other domains, such as pragmatic features, for example, may be drawn on in more specific or restricted contexts.

	Syntax/Morphology	Semantics/Lexicon	Pragmatics
Different features can be present **to varying degrees** including **not at all**	Pronoun copying	*even I* ('me too')	Complimentation
	Sentence final *but*	*pocket* ('pencil case')	Discourse markers *mela, ta*
	Topicalisation/fronting	*slipper* ('running shoes')	Phatic communication
	Variant use of modals	*stay+ing* (continuity)	Politeness strategies
	Variant question formation	periphrastic *of* for possession	Register (formal, careful vs. casual speech)
	...	...	...
Usually present **to some degree** even in the absence of other features	Segmental features such as neutralization or variant pronunciation of /θ/-/ð/ contrast, absence of dark 'l', pronunciation of /ŋ/ in *ing* as [ŋg]		
	Features such as vowel quality and duration, rhoticity, consonant gemination		
	Reflex of the above on rhythmic characteristics		
	Idiosyncratic stress patterns		
	Idiosyncratic intonation		
	Phonology/Phonetics		

Figure 1: Two dimensions of variation in MaltE

We can therefore consider the notion of MaltE as one which operates more on a continuum of variation, particularly in the case of phonetic and phonological features which may serve to identify the speaker to a greater or lesser extent as a speaker of MaltE as opposed to as a speaker of some other variety of English. This view takes its cue from the notion of a 'cline' proposed in earlier sociolinguistic accounts of world varieties of English (Braj 1992: 57), where the different functional uses of English in a given community may generate variation within that particular variety of English. For MaltE, Borg (1980: 4) also makes reference

206

to the presence of such intra-variety variation in the English used in Malta when he talks of 'gradation' of usage across different social strata (but again, see also Mori, forthcoming).

In this respect, one of the richest levels of linguistics to yield evidence of variation which both distinguishes MaltE from other varieties, and also distinguishes individual MaltE speakers from each other, involves the phonetic/phonological. The rest of this chapter reports on a study investigating durational characteristics in MaltE, using the so-called Pairwise Variability Index (Grabe & Low 2002), as a means of measuring variation in the rhythm of MaltE. §2 presents the background to the study, beginning with an overview of rhythm and its measurement, and continuing with a brief investigation of other structural features evident in MaltE which are likely to influence the overall perception of rhythm. The methodology and design of the experimental study are presented in §3, while §4 describes the findings and preliminary indications for further study to be carried out as we move in the direction of a more comprehensive description of MaltE.

2 Rhythm and durational characteristics

2.1 Rhythm and its measurement

When attempting to identify characteristic features of the speech of a newly emerging language variety such as MaltE, an approach accounting for both the localised, physical events of speech as well as their "symbolic value" (Ladd 2011: 348) is crucial to a more holistic understanding of the variety. Thus, the actual phonetic realisation of phonemic categories, and the abstract phonemic categories themselves both require investigation. The study of variation in rhythm presents itself as an ideal domain for combining a phonetic analysis with a phonological one. The combined approach advocated here and highlighted in Ladd (2011) assumes an understanding of the relationship between phonetics and phonology as being two related facets of the same broad area of study. Rhythm may be one of those domains where it is useful to keep in mind this constant interplay of phonetics and phonology.

The study of rhythm has seen a good deal of progress especially concerning the relationship between the occurrence of specific and measurable linguistic elements in context on the one hand, and the more abstract global characterisation that such linguistic elements might come to symbolise in listener perception on the other. Studies in the area of linguistic rhythm have investigated the connection between the phonetic realisation of duration and timing, for example, alongside the broader phonological classification of languages into "stress-timed" or "syllable-timed" languages, as originally proposed by Abercrombie in 1967.

Rhythm has been described recently by Nokes & Hay (2012) as "the patterning of prominent elements in spoken language, as perceived by the listener" (2012: 1). Besides providing a succinct description of the essence of rhythm in language, this definition also focuses on the notion that understanding rhythm is as much about understanding listeners' perceptions of the patterns of prominent and non-prominent elements, as it is about these elements themselves.

Traditionally, definitions of different rhythm patterns across languages are credited to Pike (1945) and Abercrombie (1967: 96) who first presented the notion that languages could be typologically distinguished on the basis of their rhythm patterns. Since then, this view has gone full circle from being gradually debunked, to being more recently partly restored in modified form. The original views expressed by Pike and by Abercrombie resulted in the division of languages into "syllable-timed" or "stress-timed" according to whether all syllables, stressed or unstressed, are produced with more or less even timing (syllable-timed) or whether timing is organised primarily around stressed syllables, with any intervening syllables being modified through reduction or weakening as compensation (stress-timed). Abercrombie (1967: 97) also described rhythm in terms which suggest an observable activity complete with corresponding physiological correlates as "Speech rhythm is essentially a muscular rhythm". Although this suggests that rhythm is essentially something that a speaker produces, Abercrombie also goes on to give a surprisingly prescient suggestion that the notion of rhythm might be better typified if viewed in terms of a combined understanding between the speaker and listener "empathetically" in tune with one another, where, if the speaker/listener pair does not share the same mother tongue, "the sounds will not be recognized as accurate clues to the movements that produce them" (Abercrombie 1967: 97).

This hint of a linguistic element not being exclusively governed by a speaker's output is echoed years later by Roach, who observes that "the distinction between stress-timed and syllable-timed languages may rest entirely on perceptual skills acquired through training" (Roach 1982: 73). The underlying belief, up to the 1990s, remained that perhaps rhythm was best studied within the domain of perception. Nokes and Hay in fact quote Beckman (1992) who refers to the attempts to capture rhythm patterns as "one of the most persistent metaphors in the history of our struggle to understand speech rhythms" (2012: 3). The word 'metaphor' might give an indication as to why some linguists have preferred to treat rhythm as a perceptual phenomenon, rather than as an objectively measurable one in temporal terms. Couper-Kuhlen (1986), for example, takes this route while noting that "it is a natural human tendency to impose structure on perceptual stimuli" (1986: 52).

Nevertheless, Roach also hints at another route to understanding rhythm better when he suggests that "there is no language which is totally syllable-timed or totally stress-timed" (1982: 79). This latter perspective involving a continuum, rather than mutually exclusive categorisation, also encouraged subsequent research into the domain of phonetic, as well as phonological, interpretations of rhythm, where discrete events such as pitch change, or the durational features of different segments, for example, could be measured and correlated with the perceptions of rhythm being more or less syllable- or stress-timed.

The assumption is then that identifying how prominent elements are ordered in speech (Nespor et al. 2011) will yield information about the rhythm as it is perceived. This at last, allows at once for both a broader, and also a more refined understanding of rhythm. Rhythm is accounted for at its most generic as patterned sequences of prominent and non-prominent elements, with prominence here not necessarily being defined any further. Alternatively, we can try to identify some or all of those elements considered to generate a perception of prominence, and isolate them to study their behaviour further. Nokes & Hay (2012) did just that in their real-time study of the duration of segments in New Zealand English. As the authors describe it, New Zealand English is understood to be more syllable-timed than other varieties of English, and further, this current observation is seen as a shift from earlier rhythm patterns, observed to have been much more stress-timed.

A series of studies now widely regarded as pivotal in trying to capture the acoustic correlates of rhythm manifested in durational characteristics are reported on in Grabe & Low (2002) and Low et al. (2000). The analyses in these papers are based on a formula developed to calculate the durational variability of successive pairs of phonological units. In these studies, in order to account for differing speech rates across individual speakers, a version of the Pairwise Variability Index (PVI) referred to as the normalised Pairwise Variability Index (nPVI) was used when measurements of vocalic and intervocalic intervals were carried out. nPVI analyses of a number of languages including both those identified as syllable- or stress-timed and those hitherto unclassified were carried out resulting in the pegging of these languages to different points on the continuum of stress- and syllable-timed languages. The emphasis here is on durational features, in response to the notion that the perception of rhythm can be correlated to a series of measurable events. In this case, the measurable events are successive pairs of intervals either vocalic – and therefore syllabic – or intervocalic, which, while not syllabic, may still affect perceptions of duration. If successive pairs of vowel duration measurements vary considerably, then the resulting index will be higher than if vowel duration is more uniform. A language variety like SSBE, for example, with its notable tendency to having weak or reduced vowels in unstressed positions, contrasted with full vowels, long vowels or diphthongs in stressed syllables, could be expected to have a high nPVI index of variability. Conversely, a language such as Maltese, which is normally said to be a language which does not tend to weaken or reduce vowels in unstressed positions (Borg & Azzopardi-Alexander 1997; Azzopardi 1981) might have a lower nPVI index, also indicating that the variability in duration across successive vowels is not as high as it might be in SSBE.

Other contemporary studies measuring different aspects of duration and timing have produced similar results. Ramus et al. (1999: 265) measured vowel and consonant intervals, based on the premise that "the measurements suggest that intuitive rhythm types reflect specific phonological properties, which in turn are signaled by the acoustic/phonetic properties of speech". Dellwo (2006) presented a method called VarcoΔC to account for between-language fluctuations in speech tempo, due, in part, to the different syllable structure and phonotactic patterns typical across languages. The measures and acoustic correlates introduced by Ramus et al. (1999) or by Dellwo (2006) aimed to capture ways in which durational features might have a bearing on the perception of rhythm patterns. The formula for a Pairwise Variability Index, normalised to account for differences in speech rate across speakers, the nPVI described above and adopted in Grabe & Low (2002), and Low et al. (2000), also gave the added dimension of capturing localised variability between pairs of vocalic or intervocalic intervals. Durational characteristics of segments are often considered a strong indicator of some form of prominence, and the ordering of such prominent elements in relation to non-prominent ones may lead to a perception of different rhythm as Nokes & Hay (2012: 4) note: "Other factors held equal, a longer vowel length will give rise to a percept of syllable stress, and thus rhythmic prominence, in English".

2.2 Durational features in Maltese English

The relevance of taking note of durational factors as a 'marked' characteristic of MaltE has often been foregrounded in the literature, as well as anecdotally, and here we return to the idea that essentially, our mental image of what rhythm captures, can be described as the ordering of prominent and non-prominent elements in the flow of a person's speech. In the case of MaltE, the issue of the duration of segments may be seen as one type of realisation of prominence, though clearly not the only one. But certainly, it can be considered a good angle from which to begin examining the concept of rhythm in this variety of English. It is of course quite likely that prominence is variously realised by a range of elements and that these together combine to create certain effects in speech. In other words, the study of rhythm in a given variety may well only begin to come together once different phonetic/phonological features have been analysed, and then eventually examined in relation to each other.

Although research on MaltE to date has not often focused overtly on rhythm, there are repeated, even if only oblique references to features which have durational characteristics embedded in them. Descriptions relating to the phonemic inventory of MaltE are relevant to this research (for example, (Vella 1995; Debrincat 1999; Bonnici 2010). Vella (1995: 74) concludes that: "The M[alt]E vowels differ from their R[eceived]P[ronunciation] equivalents in terms of their quality since they tend to approximate to the quality of corresponding vowels in the Maltese system.". Azzopardi (1981) presents a comprehensive description of the vowel inventory of Maltese. Amongst other conclusions, she notes patterns of vowel duration that may have a bearing on similar patterns in MaltE. Although the issue of possible transfer of Maltese as L1 onto MaltE is not considered further here it is still worth bearing in mind Azzopardi's conclusion that in Maltese, "Vowels in unstressed syllables are as long and sometimes longer than vowels in stressed syllables" (Azzopardi 1981: 120).

Particular attention is given to schwa, both in its own right as a vowel not readily found in MaltE, but also, with regards to its pivotal role in the rhythm patterns of SSBE and other major and widely codified varieties (see e.g. Deterding 2001). Giegerich (1992) suggests that the vowel schwa does not constitute part of the phonemic inventory of English (variety unspecified), as it is not in contrast with any other vowel, but rather, is a popular option for reduction in weak-stressed syllables. Roach (2009: 102) also comments that "ə is not a phoneme of English, but is an allophone of several different vowel phonemes when those phonemes occur in an unstressed syllable". Schwa is also not part of the phonemic inventory of Maltese (Azzopardi 1981; Borg & Azzopardi-Alexander 1997). Calleja (1987: 90) notes that her MaltE speakers "make minimal use of vowel reduction and of weak forms".

Not enough research has as yet been carried out on natural speech data in Maltese for it to be possible to assert that schwa is never present in the language. This is in fact even more so for MaltE. However, given its potentially questionable status as a phoneme both in English as an idealised or prototypical unspecified variety, and more definitely, in Maltese, it may be expected that spoken MaltE is likely to show a preference for full vowels and less evidence of schwa. As Vella (1995: 75) notes: "The fact that /ə/ is rarely realised in M[alt]E) can therefore be hypothesized to be an important factor in the different rhythmic quality of M[alt]E as compared to that of R[eceived]P[ronunciation]". Debrincat (1999: 70) further describes how 48.5% of her samples of MaltE speech did not contain evidence of schwa, which she took as "a clear indication of the fact that [the relative infrequency of] /ə/ is probably a contributing factor to the accent of M[alt]E speakers".

There is a healthy body of previous research both on MaltE and on other varieties of English that encourages a closer look at aspects of the durational characteristics of MaltE which may combine to generate a perception of variation in the rhythmic characteristics of this variety. §3 below describes the study carried out. Data from six speakers of MaltE were analysed. An earlier perception study (Grech 2015) had served to locate the six speakers on a continuum ranging from highly identifiable as Maltese people speaking in English, through to not at all identifiably Maltese.

3 Methodology

3.1 Speaker data

Both Vella (1995), and Bonnici (2010) point towards a distribution of phonetic variation as a function of specific registers or contexts and this could only be adequately analysed in more natural speech. At the same time, a durational analysis of vowels across different speakers using the formula described in §2.1 above requires directly comparable data. It was considered useful, therefore, to record speakers performing a series of tasks ranging from reading scripted text aloud (these data were labelled as "TextAloud" in the study), to speaking more spontaneously. Only the data from the scripted text is considered for the nPVI analysis here given the requirement of speech involving directly comparable data which would allow comparison of the realisation of aspects of duration by different MaltE speakers. Variability in the reduction or non-reduction of full vowels to schwa nevertheless also draws on and is informed by the analysis of the data involving samples of more spontaneous speech. It has been noted that the context and register of natural speech in MaltE may well trigger slightly different speech styles, which may in turn affect aspects of duration and rhythm Vella (1995). Thus while the study of both inter-and intra-speaker variability in vowel durations is necessarily restricted to directly comparable scripted texts, the study of schwa adds another dimension to the question of vowel duration in MaltE across different registers. The directly comparable scripted text (TextAloud) gave participants the opportunity to do a careful reading, and may also have triggered an echo of drilled pronunciation practice from earlier schooldays. On the other hand, the more spontaneous speech data elicited as participants were focused on a range of tasks was expected to yield more naturalistic – and therefore, presumably, less carefully monitored – speech.

Six speakers, three male and three female, were recorded in settings familiar to them, using a Tascam DR-100DKII 24bit palm-held digital recorder. The speakers were identified as Maltese, having been brought up and schooled in Malta, and were aged between 38 and 65 years old. One of the speakers, Sp6, had the same background and linguistic profile as the others, but had also lived in England for 4 years. It was expected that she would present some features more closely associated with the SSBE variety, having been directly exposed to this while in England, but it was considered important to include her contribution, in order to evaluate listener responses, as well as corresponding nPVI indices. In particular, greater variability across vowel durations was expected for this speaker.

3.2 Data collection and analysis

The same theme, subject matter, and therefore lexis, were retained across all speaking tasks, and centred around an Information Gap type of activity commonly used in communicative language teaching classes. Information Gap speaking tasks are typically devised in order to simulate the need to communicate, but at the same time, they also serve to distract participants (or learners, in a class) from worrying about being observed. The HCRC Map Task (Anderson et al. 1991) is one such activity which was devised specifically for this purpose. The tasks tend to be engaging so that participants become more focused on successfully managing and completing the task at hand, rather than worrying about the fact that they are being recorded (or observed in a class).

The key Information Gap activity around which all other tasks were centred here took the shape of the familiar childhood game 'Spot the Difference', with the information gap generated by a task where two speakers worked as a pair. Each speaker was given a different version of a picture and instructed to identify six differences between the two pictures. The other related tasks involved using the same lexis provided by the activity to describe each picture in full, to frame in sentences, and finally, to read out loud in a descriptive story format. The latter task was coded as 'TextAloud' in the analysis, and was used to carry out an nPVI analysis. All the other data were coded according to their task format as 'Difference' for the Spot the Difference activity, 'Sentences', in which speakers were recorded saying sentences using the same target words generated in the Spot the Difference activity, and finally 'Description', where speakers were asked to simply describe the picture in front of them. Across the text types, all vowels including instances of 'schwa' where this could be expected in a weak stressed position were measured and analysed.

The nPVI analysis was based on the formula established originally in Grabe & Low (2002). The present study also incorporated Nokes & Hay (2012)'s modification to measure individual segments rather than vocalic or intervocalic intervals. In the current study, vowel duration was used to capture the aspect of timing in rhythm. Therefore the nPVI formula was applied to measure the duration of each vowel, together with the difference in duration between each successive vowel pair. The final index of durational variability across all vowels was then calculated from an average of all the differences between the successive vowel durations in each speaker's TextAloud data. A high index indicates more variability across pairs of vowels, while a low index indicates less variability. TextAloud transcriptions for the six speakers were extracted, tabulated in Excel and sorted into vowel segments as shown below in Table 1. The table illustrates an example of the itemisation of each word recorded, as in this case, Speaker 2 read the scripted text out loud. Table 1 shows the vowel segment of each word (or segments if the word is multisyllabic, as in *cartoon*) together with its duration measured in milliseconds. The final column presents a normalised PVI, computed as the absolute value of the difference in duration between each pair of vowels, divided by the mean duration of each pair.

The final index (shown in Table 2) is then calculated as the average of all the differences measured for each speaker, resulting finally, in an index for each of the six speakers. This entire calculation is referred to as nPVI. Note here that Grabe and Low's vocalic intervals are replaced by individual vowel segments. In the original Grabe & Low (2002) study, a vocalic interval is measured from the onset of the first vowel to the offset of the last one, thus in *the arched handlebars*, /ɪ/ or /ə/ in *the* together with the following /ɑː/ in *arched* would be measured as one interval together. Since we are interested in vowel durations as a possible indicator of rhythm, we have followed Nokes & Hay (2012), in measuring vowels as segments, rather than as vocalic intervals. The results therefore describe the durations of vowels in the six different MaltE speakers, whilst also giving an indication of any variability in vowel length that may or may not be immediately evident.

Table 1: Sample, extract from Sp(eaker) 2 vowel segment analysis using nPVI

Speaker/Location	Word	Segment	Segment Duration (ms)	nPVI (normalised)
Sp2_TextAloudpvi_textgrid	This	i	59	
Sp2_TextAloudpvi_textgrid	is	i	45	0.27
Sp2_TextAloudpvi_textgrid	a	a	58	0.25
Sp2_TextAloudpvi_textgrid	cartoon	a	49	0.17
Sp2_TextAloudpvi_textgrid	cartoon	oo	157	1.05
Sp2_TextAloudpvi_textgrid	of	0	55	0.96

4 Results: Variability in vowel segments in Maltese English

The results of the nPVI analysis measuring variation in the duration of successive vowel segments are given in Table 2. The results indicate a high degree of variability in vowel duration patterns in Sp6, expressed as the highest index, while Sp1, Sp2 and Sp3 have a comparatively much lower index, indicating much less variability in duration across successive pairs of vowels.

Table 2: Normalised Pairwise Variability Index (nPVI) for 6 MaltE speakers ranked in order of increasing nPVI value

Speaker	nPVI
Sp3 – male	49.5
Sp1 – male	55.1
Sp2 – female	56.8
Sp4 – male	57.9
Sp5 – female	69.7
Sp6 – female	81.1

The index range across the six speakers is particularly remarkable considering they can all, to different extents, be considered to be speakers of the same variety of English (although see comment on Sp6, below). The resulting indices give a clear picture of the extent to which vowel duration patterns vary across the six speakers. There is a particularly large difference between Sp3 with an index of 49.5 compared with Sp6, with an index of 81.1. For comparison, Nokes & Hay (2012) obtained roughly the same range of index, from 51.5 to 82.5 (Nokes & Hay 2012: 11), with the higher indices corresponding to earlier recordings, and the lower indices corresponding to more recent recordings over 120 years, during which time, New Zealand English was coming to be perceived as more syllable-timed[1]. Although it is to be noted that nPVI results across different participant cohorts producing different texts cannot be directly compared, the pattern of results is still nevertheless informative. This present study, together with the first comprehensive study in Grabe & Low (2002), followed later by Nokes and Hay's (2012) reinterpretation all yield a picture of a clear continuum of variation in the realisation of vowel durations. In all cases, the higher the index, the closer the association with the traditional perception of "stress-timed" rhythm. Conversely, a lower index is associated with a perception of "syllable-timed" rhythm. On Grabe & Low (2002)'s scale, for example, Spanish, an example of a purportedly syllable-timed language, obtained an index of 29.7, compared with a much higher index of 57.2 for English, an example of a stress-timed language. In the present study, variation in the extent to which vowel durations differ within speakers is evident in the six speakers chosen as examples of different points on the continuum of variation in MaltE (see Figure 1). In Figure 2, Speakers 1 to 6 have been ordered according to the perception ratings they received when judged in the listening task by the 28 native MaltE speaker-listeners in the earlier study (Grech 2015). Accordingly, Sp1 was perceived as highly identifiably Maltese by 89% of native MaltE listeners while Sp6 was perceived as identifiably Maltese by only 4% of the participants, and thus was considered the least identifiable amongst the MaltE speakers studied. Notably, Sp6 is the speaker marked as the potential outlier, having lived for some time in England, and for whom features of vowel duration were expected to pattern differently as compared to those of the rest of the participant cohort. Sp2 and Sp3 were also highly identifiable as Maltese, while Sp4 and Sp5 were judged to be moderately identifiable.

Confirming the visible correspondence evident in Figure 2, Pearson's correlation indicates a significant negative correlation -0.883, (p value = 0.02) for identifiability and nPVI. Those speakers rated as highly identifiable have a correspond-

---

[1]Grabe & Low (2002) also obtained similar ranges of indices, this time in a synchronic study of normalised PVI of vocalic intervals in 18 different languages. The languages examined included English, German and Dutch, perceived as stress-timed languages, as well as Spanish, considered syllable-timed, and Polish, considered rhythmically mixed (Grabe & Low 2002).

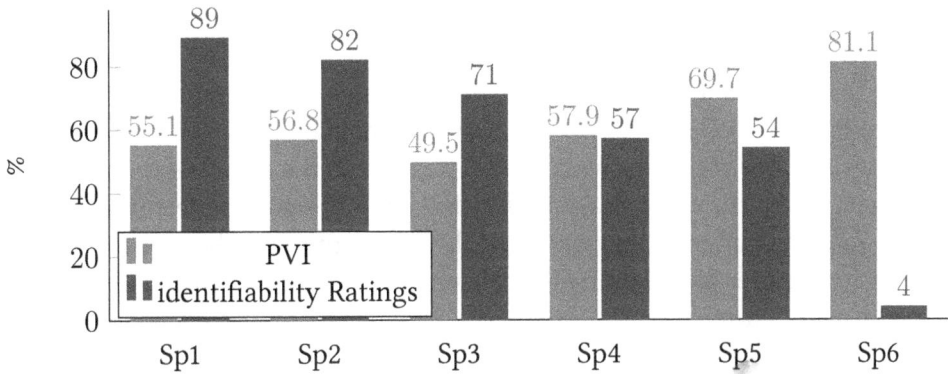

Figure 2: Vowel duration patterns and identifiability judgments for 6 MaltE speakers

ingly relatively low variability index. Sp6, rated as not identifiably Maltese, had the highest variability index, whilst the two moderately identifiable MaltE speakers also presented a relatively low variability index, though not as low as that for the most identifiable speakers.

Further investigation of the vowel durational patterns of each of the six MaltE speakers' extent of the use of the schwa vowel yields a correspondingly predictable pattern. Figure 3 presents the proportion of full vowels preferred over schwa, across all instances where schwa was possible, for each speaker.

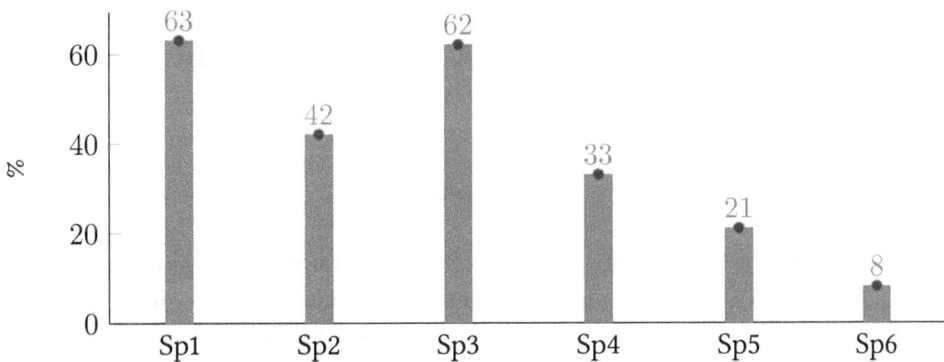

Figure 3: Percentage (%) of full vowels in words where schwa could be expected in 6 MaltE speakers

As the figure illustrates, the most highly identifiable MaltE speakers show a strong preference for using full vowels where schwa could have been used. Conversely, Sp6, rated the least identifiably MaltE speaker, had very few instances of full vowels, showing, instead, a preference for schwa. Pearson's correlation indicated a significant correlation between highly identifiable MaltE and a preference for full vowels over weakened ones. Analysis returned a positive correlation 0.857157 (p value = 0.03) for highly identifiable MaltE and preference for full vowels. These results provide further support to the idea that the variability index yielded by the nPVI analysis, which is itself designed to test variability in vowel duration patterns, may be a useful way to approach the matter of trying to identify features and characteristics more likely to trigger the perception of a MaltE accent in a speaker.

Further analysis of the preference for full vowels over schwa across different speech styles (spontaneous and more natural speech *vs.* scripted and more careful speech) also yields a potential indication of endonormative variation in MaltE (see more on this below). Figure 4 illustrates the proportion of vowels realised as full vowels rather than as schwa in the scripted TextAloud, compared with those in spontaneous speech, by speaker.

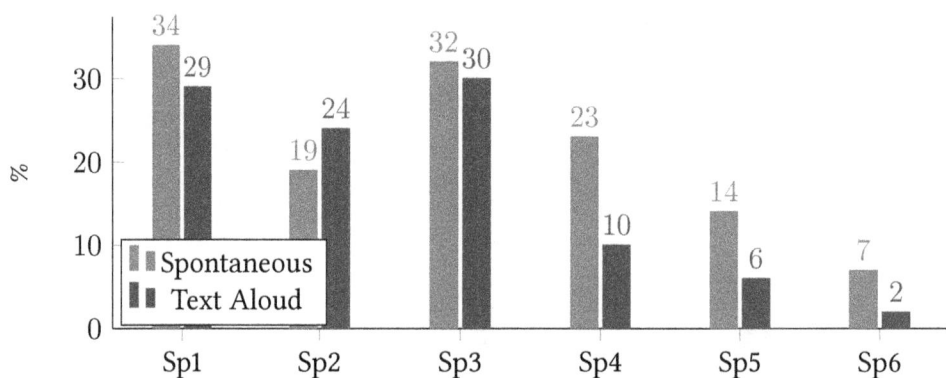

Figure 4: Percentage (%) of full vowels in words where schwa could be expected in two different speech styles

The data shown in this figure confirm that the first three speakers, also rated most identifiably MaltE, have a preference for full vowels over schwa, although the proportion of full vowels is sometimes higher in the spontaneous speech styles. The consistent distinction between the greater preference for full vowels over reduced ones in spontaneous speech could be seen as an indicator of trends of change in the variety of MaltE. While this needs further investigation, it is reasonable to suggest that scripted text triggers learnt patterns typical of those encouraged in a school environment, where undoubtedly standardised versions of SSBE may have been the ones modelled, or at least, aspired to. Conversely, spontaneous speech might be seen to capture speech patterns which undergo less self-monitoring, and therefore, potentially, are a more robust indicator of how this dialect is likely to change over time.

Interestingly, the same pattern is also observed in the remaining speakers, who are all rated as less identifiably MaltE. Again, the least identifiably MaltE speaker, Sp6 shows a clear preference for schwa over full vowels, while the moderately identifiable MaltE speakers, Sp4 and Sp5, show moderate preference for full vowels, but much less so than Sp1, Sp2 and Sp3. However, all 3 less identifiably MaltE speakers still show a greater preference for full vowels over reduced ones in spontaneous, compared with scripted speech. This is interpreted here as an indicator of MaltE starting to shape its own norms, rather than looking to other more established dialects for doing this.

5 Conclusion

There is considerably less variability in the duration of successive vowels as measured by the nPVI amongst speakers more readily identified as being Maltese based on their MaltE accent. A corresponding pattern of slightly greater variability in the duration of successive vowels, again as measured by the nPVI, is seen in those speakers still identified as being Maltese, but who are considered more moderately typical of a Maltese person speaking in English. Conversely, Sp6, the speaker expected to have some features of SSBE, having lived in the UK for some time, and only considered minimally identifiable by 4% of the 28 native MaltE speaker-listeners, showed a marked preference for vowel reduction and vowel weakening and consequently a higher nPVI reflecting the highly variable nature of durations in the successive vowels for this speaker.

The combined effect of more or less variability in the duration of successive vowel segments over longer stretches of speech may in turn lead to a perception of different rhythm patterns. This may be especially noticeable at the extreme ends of the index range, where one speaker presents a high index of variability and another speaker presents a much lower one. However it is also noticeable that the 3 most identifiably Maltese speakers cluster within the lower end of the index, while the moderately identifiable speakers display higher indices, but still not approaching the highest index obtained by the speaker who is least identifiable as a MaltE speaker. On the one hand, therefore, the nPVI can be interpreted in relation to how the indices cluster around 3 main points, ranging from little variability to high variability. On the other hand, the nPVI may also serve to refine the broad categories to capture more subtle distinctions between one speaker and the other, including among those who might be described as using a more-or-less "syllable-timed" as compared to a "stress-timed" rhythm. Therefore within these broad categorisations, it can be suggested that the nPVI could be used as a means to identify further variation. This interplay between broad categorisation and within-category variation may be a useful feature to capture in the exploration of emergent varieties of languages.

A key observation which emerges from these results is that they can be seen to provide evidence of variation within the variety, suggesting a shift towards endonormative stabilisation. Native listeners can establish when somebody is or is not using MaltE, but they can also distinguish variation within MaltE. The high degree of negative correlation between different listener ratings for MaltE identifiability, and indices of variability in the duration of successive vowels suggests that this feature is a strong indicator of MaltE as a distinct variety, as well as of variation within MaltE. Results show that a low index representing less variability in vowel duration as measured by the nPVI correlates with a highly identifiable MaltE speaker, a midway index correlates with a moderately identifiable MaltE speaker, while a high index indicating a strong degree of variability is linked with a speaker not readily identifiable as MaltE. Predictably, the schwa feature across these same speakers also yielded evidence of variation to echo the nPVI findings, in that the highly identifiable MaltE speakers (Sp1, Sp2, Sp3) made significantly less use of schwa across all speech styles, while the least identifiable MaltE had more widespread use of schwa. Further indications that variability in the use of schwa and vowel duration more generally may also be a function of different speech styles also emerge from the analysis. It is worth noting that this is not a case of categorical presence or absence. Rather, there is evidence of both intra-speaker variation, as well as inter-speaker variation. All speakers exhibited a degree of variability across vowel durations, and all speakers also presented some instances of vowel reduction, including use of a schwa at times.

This paper therefore presents evidence of a fair degree of variation within MaltE with respect to vowel duration, which in turn has a bearing on the perception of rhythm. Variation in vowel duration, both in itself (preferred use of full vowels rather than schwa), and in so far as variation in successive vowel durations contributes to differences in rhythm, can also be seen to be a trigger in the perception of MaltE.

The findings from this study set the stage for further work on variation in MaltE at the phonetic/phonological levels, particularly in relation to those elements which may affect the duration of both vowels and consonants at the local level, and consequently rhythm more globally. Among the characteristics and features already under preliminary investigation in Grech (2015), rhoticity is noteworthy, also because greater use of a postvocalic 'r' may trigger compensatory shortening in the preceding vowel, while an absence of this feature may also in part account for differences in vowel durations as compared to contexts where an 'r' would not be expected. The features discussed here, and others where durational properties can be captured and analysed at the phonetic level, may combine to generate a perception of variability in rhythm in MaltE at the phonological level. This dual focus of analysis at both the phonetic and the phonological levels of certain features may therefore be a useful approach to developing a more refined understanding of variation in this emerging variety of English.

References

Abercrombie, David. 1967. *Elements of general phonetics.* Edinburgh: Edinburgh University Press.

Anderson, Anne H., Miles Bader, Ellen Gurman Bard, Elizabeth Boyle, Gwyneth Docherty, Simon Garrod, Stephen Isard, Jacqueline Kowtko, Jan McAllister, Jim Miller, Catherine Sotillo, Henry S. Thomson & Regina Weinert. 1991. The HCRC Map Task Corpus. *Language and Speech* 34(4). 351–366. DOI:10.1177/002383099103400404

Arvaniti, Amalia. 2009. Rhythm, timing, and the timing of rhythm. *Phonetica* 66. 46–63. DOI:10.1159/000208930

Arvaniti, Amalia. 2012. The usefulness of metrics in the quantification of speech rhythm. *Journal of Phonetics* 40(3). 351–373. DOI:http://dx.doi.org/10.1016/j.wocn.2012.02.003

Azzopardi, Marie. 1981. *The phonetics of Maltese: Some areas relevant to the deaf.* University of Edinburgh dissertation.

Beckman, Mary E. 1992. Evidence of speech rhythms across languages. In Yoh'ichi Tohkura, Eric Vatikiotis-Bateson & Yoshinori Sagisaka (eds.), *Speech perception, production and linguistic structure*, 457–463. Tokyo: OHM Publishing Co.

Bonnici, Lisa. 2010. *Variation in Maltese English: The interplay of the local and the global in an emerging postcolonial variety.* Davis, CA: University of California dissertation. http://linguistics.ucdavis.edu/pics-and-pdfs/DissertationBonnici.pdf, accessed 2016-11-30.

Borg, Albert. 1980. Language and socialization in developing Malta. *Work in Progress, Department of Linguistics, University of Edinburgh* 13. 60–71.

Borg, Albert & Marie Azzopardi-Alexander. 1997. *Maltese*. London, New York: Routledge.

Braj, B. Kachru (ed.). 1992. *The other tongue: English across cultures*. Champaign, Ill: University of Illinois Press.

Brincat, Joseph. 2011. *Maltese and other languages: A linguistic history of Malta*. Malta: Midsea Books.

Calleja, Marisa. 1987. *A study of stress and rhythm as used by Maltese speakers of English*. University of Malta MA thesis.

Camilleri-Grima, Antoinette. 2013. A select review of bilingualism in education in Malta. *International Journal of Bilingual Education and Bilingualism* 16(5). 553–569. DOI:10.1080/13670050.2012.716811

Couper-Kuhlen, Elizabeth. 1986. *An introduction to English prosody*. London: Edward Arnold.

Debrincat, Romina. 1999. *Accent characteristics and variation in Maltese English*. University of Malta MA thesis.

Dellwo, Volker. 2006. Rhythm and speech rate: A variation coefficient for deltaC. In *Language and language-processing: Proceedings of the 28th linguistic colloquium*, 231–241.

Deterding, David. 2001. The measurement of rhythm: A comparison of Singapore and British English. *Journal of Phonetics* 29(2). 217–230.

Giegerich, Heinz J. 1992. *English phonology: An introduction*. Cambridge: Cambridge University Press.

Grabe, Esther & Ee-Ling Low. 2002. Durational variability in speech and the rhythm class hypothesis. *Papers in Laboratory Phonology* 7. 515–546.

Grech, Sarah. 2015. *Variation in English: Perception and patterns in the identification of Maltese English*. Msida: University of Malta. https://www.um.edu.mt/library/oar/bitstream/handle/123456789/5439/15PHDLIN001.pdf?sequence=1&isAllowed=y, accessed 2016-11-30.

Grech, Sarah & Alexandra Vella. 2015. Rhythm as a cue to identifiability in Maltese English. In The Scottish Consortium for ICPhS 2015 (Ed.) (ed.), *Proceedings of the 18th International Congress of Phonetic Sciences*. Glasgow, UK: the University of Glasgow.

Ladd, D. Robert. 2011. In John A. Goldsmith, Jason Riggle & Alan C. L. Yu (eds.), *Handbook of Phonological Theory*, 2nd edn. Oxford: Blackwell.

Low, Ee-Ling, Esther Grabe & Francis Nolan. 2000. Quantitative characterizations of speech rhythm: Syllable-timing in Singapore English. *Language and Speech* 43(4). 377–341.

Milroy, James & Lesley Milroy. 2012. *Authority in language: Investigating standard English*. London: Routledge.

Nespor, Marina, Mohinish Shukla & Jacques Mehler. 2011. Stress-timed vs. Syllable-timed languages. In Marc van Oostendorp, Colin J. Ewen, Elizabeth Hume & Keren Rice (eds.), *The Blackwell companion to phonology II*, 1147. Oxford: Blackwell.

Nokes, Jacqui & Jennifer Hay. 2012. Acoustic correlates of rhythm in New Zealand English: A diachronic study. *Language Variation and Change* 24(1). 1–31. DOI:http://dx.doi.org/10.1017/S0954394512000051

Pike, Kenneth L. 1945. *The intonation of American English*. Ann Arbor, Michigan: University of Michigan Press.

Ramus, Franck, Marina Nespor & Jacques Mehler. 1999. Correlates of linguistic rhythm in the speech signal. *Cognition* 73. 265–292.

Roach, Peter. 1982. On the distinction between 'stress-timed' and 'syllable-timed' languages. In D. Crystal (ed.), *Linguistic Controversies*. London: Edward Arnold. http://www.personal.reading.ac.uk/~llsroach/phon2/frp.pdf.

Roach, Peter. 2009. *English phonetics and phonology: A practical course*. 4th edn. Cambridge: Cambridge University Press.

Schneider, Edgar W. 2003. The dynamics of new Englishes: From identity construction to dialect birth. *Language* 79(2). 233–281.

Thusat, Joshua, Emily Anderson, Shante Davis, Mike Ferris, Amber Javed, Angela Laughlin, Christopher McFarland, Raknakwan Sangsiri, Judith Sinclair, Victoria Vastalo, Win Whelan & Jessica Wrubel. 2009. Maltese English and the nativization phase of the dynamic model. *English Today* 25(2). 25–32. DOI:10.1017/S0266078409000157

Vella, Alexandra. 1995. *Prosodic structure and intonation in Maltese and its influence on Maltese English*. University of Edinburgh dissertation.

Vella, Alexandra. 2013. Languages and language varieties in Malta. *International Journal of Bilingual Education and Bilingualism* 16. 532–552. DOI:0.1080/13670050.2012.716812

Chapter 9

On the characterisation of Maltese English: An error-analysis perspective based on nominal structures in Maltese university student texts

Natalie Schembri

University of Malta

The characterisation of varieties of English is an ongoing process that has focused on speech communities around the world for whom English is the mother tongue or is one of two main languages competing for dominance in a bilingual setting, as is the case for Maltese English. This paper aims to contribute to the growing body of research on Maltese English as a variety in its own right (e.g. Vella 1995; Schembri 2005; Hilbert & Krug 2012; Krug & Rosen 2012). It reflects on the theoretical assumptions that underpin its characterisation as a dialect in a bilingual setting distinct from Standard English and therefore identifiable on grammatical and lexical as well as phonological levels (see Trudgill 2002, for example, for a characterisation of Standard English along these lines). It analyses nominal phrase structure data from university student texts produced by 30 undergraduate Commerce students at the University of Malta. The study focuses on affixation, compounding and prepositional usage and examines the contention that not all deviations from Standard English can be given the status of characteristics of Maltese English. Applying an error analysis approach to the analysis of the data, it distinguishes between developmental errors that are untraceable to Maltese as the background language, and transfer errors that have this origin by definition. It further contends that only those transfer errors that fossilize over time are capable of achieving the status of core characteristics of Maltese English. Following studies such as Hyltenstam (1988), the analysis works on the assumption that fossilized transfer errors are identifiable in the current data by virtue of the fact that they are still present in the output of participants who have achieved advanced learner status. From a varieties-of-language point of view, once fossilized transfer errors

Natalie Schembri. On the characterisation of Maltese English: An error-analysis perspective based on nominal structures in Maltese university student texts. In Patrizia Paggio & Albert Gatt (eds.), *The languages of Malta*, 225–246. Berlin: Language Science Press. DOI:10.5281/zenodo.1181799

have been identified, their status ceases to be considered as erroneous and is construable instead as characteristic of the variety (Selinker 1974). The study concludes that the overuse of the preposition *of* was the most likely error type to fossilize and gain status as a stable nominal feature of Maltese English. As a Maltese bilingual, I use my first-hand understanding of the Maltese English linguistic scenario to provide some insights into what is by linguistic standards still a young and developing linguistic variety.

1 Introduction

The characterisation of varieties of language centres around the identification and description of linguistic features that make specific varieties distinct from others of the same language. From a language description perspective, the central theoretical issue is the distinction between common core features and stylistically significant features (Crystal & Davy 1969), with the descriptive emphasis falling on the latter. Common core features occur across varieties and fulfil the fundamental cohesive function of basic building blocks of the language that allow it to operate as a unified system. In contrast, stylistically significant features are distinctive by virtue of their lack of common occurrence, as is the case with specialised terminology, or by virtue of some aspect of their use that makes them variationally distinct, such as the relatively high frequency of passive forms in academic writing (Swales 1990). A comprehensive description of a regional variety would therefore comprise a description of significant features at all linguistic levels that are regionally distinct in both the variety's spoken and written forms.

This ongoing process is in its initial stages in the case of Maltese English, a variety of English spoken on the Maltese islands where Maltese is the national language and English has official status (as stated in the Constitution of Malta, Articles 5(1) and 5(2)). This paper aims to contribute to the growing body of research describing regional features of Maltese English in its written form (e.g. Schembri 2005; Hilbert & Krug 2012; Krug & Rosen 2012). It will employ an error-analysis approach in an initial attempt to identify and characterise regional nominal features of Maltese English in a corpus of academic commerce texts, with a focus on distinguishing these from other nominal features that are present in the variety but do not necessarily identify it as Maltese English. The study will start by exploring the theoretical assumptions that underpin the role error analysis can play in identifying regional characteristics. These will be followed by the methodological procedures undertaken to collect and analyse the noun phrase data in §3; §4 will then provide the error analysis and some conclusions as to possible candidates that characterise the variety are drawn in the last section.

2 Theoretical background

This section will outline the theoretical framework underlying the identification of features of Maltese English in this study. It will explain how an error-analysis approach and its characteristic distinction between developmental and transfer errors can be employed to advantage in the identification of regional features. The pivotal argument will be the role fossilization of transfer errors plays in the development of a set of features that become common across speakers of a variety to the extent that they configure as its identifying characteristics.

2.1 Deviation from standard varieties: The role of developmental errors and transfer errors

Error analysis has provided a basic distinction in the identification and classification of errors, or output that varies from standard usage (Corder 1974). Although the distinction is normally applied in the analysis of learner output, it will be argued here that it can also be used to advantage in the identification of regional features as specified below. The distinction is based on the application of a systematic comparison of deviant structures in learner varieties to corresponding target-language structures in the standard variety, a principle first introduced by Lado (1957) as the contrastive analysis hypothesis. Systematic deviant structures are first defined as erroneous and characterised as developmental or transfer errors after comparative analysis (see, for example, Dulay & Burt 1974 for an application in the analysis of bilingual children's speech). Developmental errors are target-language generated (Richards 1974: 173) and are generally understood to be the result of simplification of target-language structures, for example, when target-language rules are overapplied (Jain 1974). Developmental errors are therefore intralingual in nature, and are in fact also evident in native-speaker output in children (Jain 1974).

In contrast, transfer errors are interlingual in nature and are seen to be present when intralingual explanations are ruled out and an examination of corresponding background language structures indicates that negative transfer of linguistic knowledge has taken place (Lado 1957; Wardaugh 1975). By virtue of their provenance therefore, transfer errors establish a contextual link with the speaker's background language that developmental errors do not, an important point to bear in mind for the purposes of this study.

As a first premise on the application of this distinction in variational contexts, it is important to foreground the fact that it is a distinction endemic to linguistic output in bilingual situations. Transfer only comes into play when a background language provides pre-existing linguistic knowledge the speaker perceives as transferable to the target language. Furthermore, a speaker's perception of what is and is not transferable changes and becomes more accurate as knowledge of target-language structures improves (Taylor 1975). This to the extent that the majority of errors in advanced learner output are expected to be developmental (McLaughlin 1987). Data from Thewissen (2013) in fact shows a trend towards plateauing in various errors occurring across learners from three different language backgrounds from upper intermediate level[1] onwards. This is identified as one of the three main error developmental profiles in her data taken from the International Corpus of Learner English. The phenomenon that is of interest to this study, however, is the fact that in spite of a general trend to the contrary, some systematic transfer errors will remain in advanced learner output, providing traces of the background language that eventually establish themselves as stable features in the target language (Selinker 1974).

2.2 Regional varieties and fossilization

In the context of regional variation, the notion that some deviant linguistic phenomena are resistant to the kind of change that results in the achievement of target-language norms and consequent native-like competence has particular significance. It can in fact be argued that a widespread systematic failure by speakers of a specific speech community to adapt to target-language norms is crucial to the development of regional varieties. Selinker (1974) has described the tendency of certain deviant structures to remain in the output of speakers over time and stabilize themselves in the output of learners even in advanced learner competences as fossilization. He defines fossilized linguistic material as "linguistic items, rules, and subsystems which speakers of a particular NL will tend to keep in their IL relative to a particular TL, no matter what the age of the learner or amount of explanation and instruction he receives in the TL" (Selinker 1974: 36). There is currently some sense of dissatisfaction with lack of clarity relating in particular as to whether fossilisation is a product- or a process-oriented concept and whether it is global (relating to general linguistic competence) or local (relating to specific areas of language use; see Fidler 2006 for a review of relevant literature). However, this basic definition has prevailed and will be used in this study, which is a product-oriented analysis focusing on specific areas of language use and therefore has a clear orientation in terms of these two issues. To foreground issues more central to this study, the focus on contrast in the defi-

---

[1] As defined by the Common European Framework of Reference

nition of Selinker (1974) makes it clear that fossilization has particular relevance in bilingual contexts. Furthermore, fossilized competences are competences that have reached a mature stage of development at which a depletion of errors has taken place to leave a reduced set of errors characterised by resistance to target-language norms. As pointed out in §2.1, an indication that a speaker has reached this level of competence is the presence of a high proportion of developmental errors in relation to transfer errors.

To put this into a variationist perspective, an important point that needs to be considered is the perception of Selinker (1974) that "not only can entire IL competences be fossilized in individual learners performing in their own interlingual situation, but also in whole groups of individuals, resulting in the emergence of a new dialect [...] where fossilized IL competences may be the normal situation" (p. 38). Selinker's argument indicates that fossilized competences include both developmental and transfer errors. However, it is the contention of this paper that only those fossilized errors in advanced learner competences that are capable of contextualising the linguistic output, that is fossilized *transfer* errors, are capable of gaining the status of core characteristics of a regional variety. Any co-existing fossilized developmental errors will serve to identify the variety as deviant from the standard variety, but will not have the ability to mark it as regional. Previous work in the characterisation of Maltese English has tended to ignore this distinction. It is therefore the purpose of this study to examine the linguistic output of Maltese university students in its capacity as advanced learner output, with a view to identifying initial possible candidates characterising Maltese English as a regional variant. Initial work in this direction was carried out in an earlier study (Schembri, under review) that focused on article usage, singular and plural forms and noncount nouns and identified overuse of the definite article as a likely nominal feature of Maltese English. The current study will consider affixation, compounding and prepositional errors to provide a more comprehensive picture of nominal characteristics of the variety. It will apply an error-analysis approach to identify both developmental and transfer errors in so doing and will also provide some insight into fossilized developmental errors that play a role in characterising the variety but have secondary status as non-context bound features.

3   Methodology

This section will outline the details of the methodological procedures undertaken for the purposes of data collection. Apart from the noun phrases that constituted the primary data, secondary data was collected through a questionnaire as a source of information about the subjects' language background. The Faculty of Economics, Management and Accountancy provided scripts from the May/June 1997 session and noun phrases were collected from them as specified below. All potential participants were sent a consent form and sampling was carried out on the pool of consenting candidates.

3.1 Participants

All participants had satisfied the University of Malta entry requirements and had a pass at Grade 5 or better in English in the Secondary Education Certificate (SEC) (*General Entry Requirements* 2010). It should be noted that this allows for a fairly broad spectrum of linguistic competence levels. Participants were following one of the four degree courses run by the Faculty of Economics, Management and Accountancy. These were the Bachelor of Commerce, the Bachelor of Commerce (Honours), the Bachelor of Arts (Honours) in Accountancy and the Bachelor of Arts (Honours) in Tourism. Examinations were held at the end of the first year, which is common to the first three courses, and subsequently during the third year and the fourth or fifth year depending on the length of the course. Three sets of examination scripts from three different student cohorts were therefore available at the point of data collection.

In order for sampling to take place, potential participants were asked to fill in a questionnaire with their demographic details and details relating to their language background. This information was used to filter out participants whose native language was not Maltese and whose language competence might have been influenced by atypical language exposure. Two hundred and thirty seven candidates from the May/June 1997 session answered the questionnaire, 30 of whom were considered atypical because they were foreign, had dual nationality, had a foreign parent or had lived in an English-speaking country for a significant period of time. A random sample of 10 candidates from each year group was chosen after this filtering had taken place and noun phrases were collected from the scripts produced by the 30 candidates chosen. The subjects were sixteen males and fourteen females who had been educated in Malta. They had received formal instruction in English between the ages of 5 and 16, at least. Twenty-seven of them were between eighteen and twenty-four years old when they sat for the examinations in question, and the remaining three were in their early thirties. As Hyltenstam (1988) has pointed out, adult learners have been considered the "natural population" (p. 69) for studies of fossilisation, on the basis that higher levels of mastery act as an automomatic filter for deviances that are not likely to be fossilizable (p.70).

3.2 Collection and analysis of noun phrase data

Two hundred and fifty noun phrases were collected manually from the scripts of each of the thirty subjects to make up a corpus of 7,500 noun phrases. The definition of a noun phrase used was that given by Quirk et al. (1985) and considers phrases functioning "as subject, object, and complement of clauses and as complement of prepositional phrases" (p. 245) to be nominal. Pronouns were not included.

Once the corpus was complete, each noun phrase was judged erroneous or error-free by the researcher and doubts as to errors in specialised terminology and border-line cases were double checked by a specialist in the field and a second rater respectively. The researcher satisfied the criteria of Etherton (1977: 72) regarding the qualities needed for satisfactory error judgement. Apart from being a linguist by profession and therefore in possession of "an understanding of how the English language works or genuine curiosity on this point", she had the required level of competence in the language,[2] was a native speaker of Maltese and had taught for a number of years at the level concerned.

Data was collected as evenly as possible from the first, middle and last parts of essay-type questions answered by the subjects. First-year students had answered 12 essay-type questions on average and third-year and honours students 25-26 questions. The ratio of erroneous to error-free structures was then computed for each subject. Noun phrases classified as erroneous were given target forms as close to the original structures as possible. Care was taken to disregard infelicities of style and concentrate on instances of incorrect usage. All structures were listed as output from a specific subject (i.e. candidate) and numbered for ease of identification. In the error analysis that follows, these details are given in a bracket at the end of each example. For example, Subject 2: 184 indicates the error in the example preceding it occurred in the 184th noun phrase collected from the output of the second candidate. Errors are given in enough context to identify them as such and italicised for ease of identification. Corresponding target forms are given immediately below. Erroneous structures were subsequently categorised on the basis of structure and error-type to facilitate the identification of any existing patterns and enable errors of a similar type to be discussed in tandem. In the discussion, an attempt was made to distinguish between devel-

---

[2]Etherton (1977: 72)'s criteria specify a "high standard of English". The researcher's standard of English was considered high enough to warrant her inclusion as a member of the Academic English Team at the Institute of Linguistics of the University of Malta whose role was to ensure and maintain standards of English at the university. At the time the study was undertaken she had been fulfilling this role for five years.

opmental and transfer errors on the basis of comparative analysis carried out in line with the theoretical assumptions underlying the study.

4 Error analysis

This section will provide a systematic error analysis of affixation, compounding and prepositional errors in that order. It will characterise the errors in the data falling under these three categories as developmental or transfer errors and will subsequently consider their possible status as fossilized features and potential candidates as nominal characteristics of Maltese English. A general picture of erroneous versus error-free noun phrases broken down by student group is given in Table 1.

Table 1: Average of erroneous versus error-free noun phrases across year groups

Student group	Average of erroneous noun phrases	Average of error-free noun phrases
First-year students	45 (18%)	205 (82%)
Third-year students	35 (14%)	215 (86%)
Honours students	32 (13%)	218 (87%)
Total	112 (15%)	638 (85%)

The results in Table 1 indicate an overall 15% error rate average located in noun phrases in the data. These include the three types of error examined in this paper, as well as other error types such as faulty article usage, proform errors and the misuse of singular and plural forms. The subset of errors falling under the three categories examined in this paper are given as raw scores in Table 2.

Table 2: Frequency of propositional affixation and compounding errors

Error type	Frequency (n)
Prepositional errors	29
Affixation errors	21
Compounding errors	7

4.1 Affixation errors

The errors discussed in this section concern faulty nominal word-formation processes involving affixation located in the head of the NP. These are of two types: the first type involves word class changes that result in lack of correspondence between form and function. One example is "insurance *brokering*" (Subject 11: 34), where the verb form is being incorrectly used as a noun instead of *brokerage*. The second type involves affixation processes resulting in the formation of non-words, as in the use of the *un-* prefix in "*unadmissible* assets" (Subject 22: 227). The next two sections will consider the two different types of error in turn.

4.1.1 Lack of correspondence between form and function

Different factors were seen to come into play in errors of affixation that resulted in lack of correspondence between form and function. "The reduction of the target language to a simpler system" (Jain 1974: 191), or simplification, was a likely motivator in cases of non-suffixed forms that were in need of a suffix, as in the three errors in (1) and (2) below:

(1) Subject 3: 154, 155
     *Physiological needs include the very basic ones for survival – **drink** and **eat** here come to mind.*
     'Physiological needs include the very basic ones for survival – drinking and eating here come to mind.'

(2) Subject 2: 184
     *or dies for force reasons, that is during arrest or to the **safeguard** of others or during state emergencies*
     'or dies for force reasons, that is during arrest or the safeguarding of others or during state emergencies'

The base forms *drink, eat* and *safeguard* all require the suffix -*ing* to change their word class into the nouns appropriate for use in their current contexts. All three are base forms of verbs, and *drink* and *safeguard* can also function as nouns, albeit with different meanings to the ones intended here. Although *eat* cannot function as a noun, the tendency to use base forms as opposed to more complex affixed forms requiring a choice of suffix is present in all three.

The opposite is however the case in (3), where the suffix -*ing* has erroneously been added to the base form *search*, which is the noun needed in this context:

(3) Subject 9: 139
   *needs such as exploration and the **searching** for meaning and knowledge*
   'needs such as exploration and the search for meaning and knowledge'

The unnecessary addition of the suffix could be indicative of a more advanced type of error occurring at a stage in the learning process when affixation is being used rather than avoided, but is overapplied in some cases.

The data also provided a case of affixation involving an incorrect choice of suffix:

(4) Subject 11: 34
   *insurance **brokering***
   'insurance brokerage'

This error may be conditioned by the fact that *-ing* is much more productive than *-age* and might therefore be functioning as a default suffix until a more detailed understanding of affixation is in place. It should also be noted that, as opposed to *eat*, *drink*, *search* and to some extent also *safeguard*, *brokerage* has a more specialised usage and the subject who made the error may still have been developing some familiarity with the lexeme and its different forms in the process of acquiring new vocabulary in this field.

The above analysis suggests these types of problems are developmental in nature insofar as they deal with simplification of target-language structures or the use of intralingual processes that are valid in themselves but incorrectly applied.

4.1.2 Non-words

Affixation processes sometimes resulted in the formation of non-words. The following three examples show non-existent words resulting from an incorrect choice of the negative prefix:

(5) Subject 22: 226
   *loans that are **unadequately** secured*
   'loans that are inadequately secured'

(6) Subject 22: 227
   ***unadmissible** assets*
   'inadmissible assets'

(7) Subject 17, 146
   *the disorders created when rule of law is weak or **inexistent***
   'the disorders created when rule of law is weak or nonexistent'

The first two errors were made by the same subject and, as in the case of *-ing* earlier, it is possible that *un-* is being used as a kind of default negative suffix, particularly since it is more productive than *in-*. The use of *inexistent* in the third example is not likely to be such a case, however, since *in-* is not as productive as *un-*.

Other cases of non-words resulting from NP affixation were the following:

(8) Subject 1: 191
     illegitimation
     'illegitimacy'

(9) Subject 7: 180
     incapacitance
     'incapacitation'

(10) Subject 5: 200
     enbreechment
     'breech'

The first two examples, taken from the output of different subjects, show the suffix *-ation* being overapplied in (8) and replaced by *-ance* in (9). More evidence would be needed to deduce whether the use of a default suffix is in operation. It is possible that the Maltese cognate *illeġittimazzjoni*, where *-azzjoni* corresponds formally to *-ation*, influenced the choice in the first case. In the second case, the Maltese cognate *kapacità* is not suffixed; however, my intuition as a Maltese speaker would indicate that the final accented *à* is more in harmony with *-ance* than with *-ation*. These two examples indicate some possible traces of transfer in the use of affixation and suggest that not all word-formation processing errors are necessarily developmental in nature, particularly where cognates are concerned. The third example, on the other hand, cannot be attributed to transfer, and the unnecessary addition of a suffix to *breech* is probably a result of lack of familiarity with its double function, which would make the error intralingual and therefore developmental.

Although there is clearly different patterning at work, what is interesting in the above three examples is the fact that they are all specialised terms from Law, which is a subject area Commerce students are tested on, but not one they are particularly familiar with. On the basis that studies such as Nation (1993) show that specialised vocabulary increases in tandem with one's understanding of the subject matter, these errors can be taken as an indication that learners need some time to familiarise themselves with the different forms of new lexemes and, particularly in the case of cognates, may fall back on their knowledge of the L1 to fill in any existing gaps.

4.2 Compounding errors

Other types of non-forms in the data concerned the use of non-existent phrases, most of which were unacceptable noun compounds. Compound nouns have been found to be problematic in Alamin & Ahmed (2012) who explained that students studying Science at Taif University in Saudi Arabia who had previously studied English as a foreign language for five to ten years failed to use compound nouns correctly in spite of having been taught their use in scientific English.

Since compounding is not possible in Maltese, direct transfer cannot be considered as possible motivation for errors of compounding. Contrastive analysis suggests it is more likely that the motivation is avoidance. As is evident from the following examples, the correct target form for most unacceptable noun compounds in the data is a postmodifying prepositional phrase:

(11) Subject 3: 192
      Ombudsman decisions
      'decisions taken by the ombudsman'

(12) Subject 13: 127
      *a new **management line of though*** [sic]
      'a new line of thought in management'

(13) Subject 21: 142
      the Dividend Article of the Treaties number 10
      'point Number 10 of the Dividend Article of the Treaties'

(14) Subject 4: 171
      *the **human personality** and his behaviour*
      'the personality and behaviour of human beings'

It is possible that the construction of erroneous compound nouns in the above cases is an attempt to avoid prepositional phrases, which involve the notoriously difficult area of prepositional usage (Jain 1974) and it is interesting to consider to what extent such strategies may be influenced by the background language.

In a contrastive study, Schachter (1974) considered avoidance in the light of the acquisition of English relative clauses by native speakers of Persian, Arabic,

Chinese, and Japanese. She found that the Persian and Arabic learners produced significantly more, albeit at times erroneous relative clauses in English than the Chinese and Japanese learners. One of the insights that came out of the study was the fact that avoidance possibly occurred as a result of the perception of language distance resulting from the postnominal position of relative clauses in English, as contrasted with their prenominal position in Chinese and Japanese.

In cases such as those in Schachter's (1974) study, knowledge of corresponding background language structures can be seen to influence target-language output, and some element of transfer therefore understood to be present, if indirectly. With respect to prepositional usage in English, however, avoidance can much more readily be interpreted as a result of the degree of arbitrariness in prepositional usage present in the target language itself (Jain 1974), and less so as a background language related issue. It is however interesting to note that in the current data, the prepositions in all the examples would have been correct had they been directly translated from Maltese, and that with the possible exception of 11, which has a relatively simple structure, it is not unlikely that avoidance was significantly conditioned by the level of complexity of the corresponding target-language structures.

With respect to whether or not any specific erroneous noun compounds are likely to fossilize as stable developmental features of the variety, it is difficult to come to any definitive conclusion. As in the case of the production of errors occurring as a result of valid affixation processes, it is doubtful whether the production of erroneous noun compounds is productive and widespread enough to be fossilizable, and a large-scale study would need to be conducted to determine whether this is the case.

4.3 Prepositional errors

Errors in prepositional usage were found in twenty-seven out of the thirty subjects. This is in line with what one would expect since prepositions are considered one of the areas of the surface structure of English that are "more facilitative of indeterminacy than others" (Jain 1974: 205) and are therefore highly problematic for learners, including those at an advanced stage of their language learning. A number of recent studies on adult learners with semitic background languages show correspondingly high frequencies of errors involving prepostions. Gholami & Zeinolabedini (2015), for example, found prepositions to be one of the four grammatical areas with the most frequent errors in a corpus of sixty Iranian medical research articles published in international English journals (p. 64). In this study, the published versions of the articles were compared to their first drafts to identify which areas had required grammatical improvement in the process of publication. Although the data is largely comparable, it included instances such as the replacement of 'to' instead of a dash in phrases such as '8-10', which would not be considered error types in the current study. In another recent study on the written production of sixty Iranian adult students' performance in a mock IELTS test, prepositions accounted for 10.9% of grammatical errors (Nosrati & Nafisi 2015). Similarly, an earlier study involving 50 male and 50 female advanced Iranian EFL learners found misuse of prepositions accounted for 13.5% of syntactic errors in female writers and 15.5% of syntactic errors in males (Boroomand & Rostami Abusaeedi 2013); and Al-Harafsheh & Pandian (2012) listed adjectives with prepositions as the second most frequent type of adjectival error in a test on the use of adjectives administered on 150 twenty-two-year-old Jordanian students at Al-Albeyt University. Similar indications of the problematic nature of prepositions were present in an error analysis carried out on forty-nine third-year university students majoring in English in Northeast Normal University Changchun with Chinese as their first language. In this study, prepositional errors accounted for 11.6% of errors produced in a narrative essay.

In the current study, errors involving prepositional usage were in most cases located in phrases that involved an incorrect choice of preposition whose target form needed a simple substitution of preposition, or else more complex modification of the prepositional phrase or its substitution with some form of premodification. What shall be considered here is whether any specific prepositional error type is a likely candidate for fossilization and if that is the case, if it can be considered a possible characteristic of Maltese English on the basis that it is the result of negative transfer from Maltese.

The most common errors needing a simple substitution of preposition were cases of *for* being replaced incorrectly by *of*, as in the following:

(15)   Subject 9: 148
       the need of beauty, order and symmetry
       'the need for beauty, order and symmetry'

(16)   Subject 7: 166
       the need of esteem
       'the need for esteem'

(17)   Subject 6: 200
       reason of arrest
       'reason for arrest'

(18)   Subject 27: 181
       the best price **of** assets
       'the best price for assets'

These errors can be considered transfer errors since the phrases are directly translated from Maltese, with the preposition *of* translating *ta'*. *Of* is also seen to incorrectly replace other prepositions, such as *to* and *about* respectively in the following:

(19)   Subject 10: 198
       *the right **of** life*
       'the right to life'

(20)   Subject 9: 180
       *the film **of** Nature and Nurture*
       'the film about Nature and Nurture'

In both examples, *ta'* again gives a valid version in Maltese, although *għal* is also possible in (19). Direct transfer where *of* translates *ta'* is again therefore likely.

As in (19), *ta'* is also seen to replace *to* in the following examples, however with a different target form that requires the base form of the verb to follow it:

(21)   Subject 2: 225
       *his need **of** feeling loved*
       'the need to be loved'

(22)   Subject 9: 146
       *the need **of** being seen at his best*
       'the need to be seen at his best'

(23)   Subject 18: 56
       *the failure **of** paying attention*
       'the failure to pay attention'

In (23), direct transfer is likely since the Maltese translation would be *in-nuqqas ta' attenzjoni*. Example (21) could follow the same structure translated as *il-bżonn ta' l-imħabba*; however, *li* is also possible if a verb follows the preposition instead of a noun to produce *il-bżonn li tkun maħbub*. The latter structure would also be needed for a translation of (22) in *il-bżonn li jidher fl-aħjar tiegħu*. In the latter two cases transfer through direct translation of the preposition can be ruled out since *li* does not translate *of.*

Examples (21), (22) and (23) introduce a set of examples where V*ing* follows *of* to produce NP + *of* + V*ing*. This structure is perfectly acceptable in English in certain cases but is used erroneously as indicated above and in the following examples:

(24) Subject 16: 97
      *the prevention **of letting** hardware get damaged by humidity or mishandling*
      'the prevention of harware damage caused by humidity or mishandling'

(25) Subject 16: 94
      *The prevention **of losing** information*
      'The prevention of information loss'

(26) Subject 27: 226
      *the pursuit **of making** higher profits*
      'the pursuit of higher profits'

In these three cases, *of* needs to be followed by NP to produce the NP + *of* + NP structure that was used erroneously in (15–20) above. Maltese would tend to have an NP following *of* so that direct transfer would have favoured the correct choice of structure. However, it would also have favoured *damage of hardware* and *loss of information* respectively in the first two examples since compounding is not possible. It is difficult to determine whether the resulting double use of *of* may have created some perception of awkwardness the writers wanted to avoid, but this still rules out direct transfer. It is more likely that the NP + *of* + V*ing* structure is being overapplied until further familiarization limits its usage to acceptable environments.

The last set of errors concerned postmodifying prepositional phrases whose target structures required some form of premodification. Occasionally, as in (27), an adjective was needed instead:

(27) Subject 1: 216
      *various roles **of managers***
      'various managerial roles'

It is likely that the Maltese equivalent would favour a stucture with *ta'* which would indicate direct transfer.

Postmodifying prepositional phrases more commonly needed to be replaced by an *'s* genitive:

(28)   Subject 22: 169
*the consent **of** the partners*
'the partners' consent'

(29)   Subject 24: 85
*an opinion **of** the auditor on the truth and fairness of the financial statements*
'the auditor's opinion on the the truth and fairness of the financial statements'

(30)   Subject 27: 54
*the advantages associated with the use **by** the company **of** debt capital*
'the advantages associated with the company's use of debt capital'

It is possible to interpret the above errors as the result of negative transfer
since in all three cases Maltese would have a postmodifying prepositional phrase
with *ta'*. It is, however, also possible to use the same structure in English in other
cases, and therefore the errors can also be interpreted as the overapplication of a
TL rule. However, the *of* construction to indicate possession is less common in
English, and it is usually the more common structure that is overapplied when
more than one realisation is possible. A crosslinguistic motivation is therefore
more likely.

Lastly, postmodifying prepositional phrases with *of* also replaced compound
nouns, as can be seen in the following:

(31)   Subject 7: 50
*a fixed rate **of** tax*
'a fixed tax rate'

(32)   Subject 28: 50
*the confidence **of** investors*
'investor confidence'

(33)   Subject 7: 84
*an accountant **for** the government*
'a government accountant'

(34)   Subject 16: 136
*the Brandt Commission **of** the 1990*
'the 1990 Brandt Commission'

These errors are clearly crosslinguistic in nature, since in Maltese a postmodifying prepositional phrase would be used in such cases and its substitution with some form of premodification would not be possible. It is interesting to note that the subjects who had erroneous compound nouns in their production (see §4.2) did not make these kinds of errors. This suggests the two error types are indicative of different stages of development, with erroneous postmodification of the type shown in Examples (31–34) above preceding the production of erroneous compound nouns. The fact that different stages of development are characterised by the quality of the errors and not simply by error rates has recently been shown in a study on error rates and error types in three different IELTS bands by Müller (2015). Nezami & Najafi (2012) also found significant differences across low, mid and high proficiency groups on error types made in a TOEFL-based written English test taken by 103 Iranian students of English at two universities in Iran.

As is clear from the above, the majority of prepositional errors concern *of*, which shows a wider application of its use than its target-language usage would allow, and suggests a tendency for its application as a preferred option when in doubt. The above analysis indicates it is likely to replace *for* in NP + *of* + NP structures, but may also replace other prepositions such as *to* and *about*. As the analysis of previous errors related to the overuse of affixes suggests, it is not unusual for learners to overuse the most common realisation of a grammatical form, particularly if there is overlap in meaning and some degree of arbitrariness in their application, as is the case here. More importantly in relation to issues of characterisation of the variety, the data suggest that the preference for *of* is triggered by the usage of *ta'* in Maltese in such cases.

Other relatively frequent errors related to *of* are postmodifying prepositional phrases replacing *'s* genitives or compound nouns, which add to the frequency of problematic structures starting with NP + *of* likely to be the result of transfer and strengthen the possibility that a preference for such structures is a possible feature of Maltese English. Less clear cases of transfer with initial NP + *of* structures that contribute to this general picture are NP + *of* + V*ing* structures. The possibility of prepositional usage being affected by the L1 follows findings by Koosha & Jafarpour (2006) indicating that errors in the collocation of prepositions in a test administered on 200 Iranian university English majors were more than twice as likely to be interlingual in nature (68.4% as opposed to 31.6% intralingual errors).

5 Conclusion

This study applied an error-analysis approach to errors of affixation, compounding and prepositional usage in Maltese university students' commerce texts in an attempt to identify nominal characteristics of Maltese English. With respect to affixation, it concluded that with the exception of some evidence of transfer in cognates, affixation errors were mostly developmental in nature and unlikely candidates for fossilization. Transfer was even less evident in noun compounds, where avoidance of complex prepositional phrases was seen to be the most probable cause of error. Prepositional errors were mostly *of*-related, and were the errors that showed the clearest evidence of transfer. There was some indication that *of* might be functioning as a preferred preposition in cases of doubt as to the correct choice of preposition. It was concluded that the overuse of *of* was the most likely type of error to fossilize and gain status as a stable nominal feature of Maltese English.

More evidence is needed to determine whether any of the developmental error types found in the data are likely candidates for fossilization. One of the issues that needs to be addressed with respect to affixation and compounding and other errors of this type is to what extent fossilization is likely in such cases. The point is that it is not the affixation process in itself that is erroneous, but its overapplication in specific cases. What needs to be determined is therefore whether any specific usage of an incorrect form has fossilized, and this is difficult to do unless the noun happens to be commonly used. Unlike highly productive linguistic forms, such as the definite or indefinite article, fossilization of linguistic items that are not highly productive would need substantial amounts of data for enough instances of their usage to give clear indications as to whether fossilization is taking place. Furthermore, such usage would need to be found across subjects to determine whether fossilization is ideolectal or else more widespread and therefore possibly variational. A further question is whether actual lack of productiveness of linguistic items may deter fossilization in any case, particularly if repeated usage is found to be a determining factor.

This study has extended the examination of nominal features of Maltese English initially examined in Schembri (under review). Further evidence is however necessary to consolidate the findings from both these studies and to create a more comprehensive picture of regional features characterising the variety, particularly since the dataset is not extensive. It is also important at this point to consider more recent data to see whether current linguistic trends match those evident in the data collected in 1997 for this study. Although variational change takes time to establish itself, the timespan at this point is probably large enough for any significant linguistic development to become evident.

On a more general note, the discussion of the theoretical underpinnings of the identification of such features, in particular the role of fossilization and the distinction between the status of developmental and transfer features in such a context needs to be further developed. A clearer understanding is also needed of what determines which features in a given variety are likely to fossilize and which are more likely to develop to native speaker competence levels. A detailed examination of such issues will shed light on the development of regional varieties in bilingual contexts.

References

Alamin, Abdulamir & Sawsan Ahmed. 2012. Syntactical and punctuation errors: An analysis of technical writing of university students Science College. *English Language Teaching* 5. 2–8. Taif University, KSA.

Al-Harafsheh, Abdallah Nahar & Ambigapathy Pandian. 2012. The use of English adjectives among Jordanian EFL students in Al-Albeyt University: An error analysis. *Language in India* 12. 675–695.

Boroomand, Faezeh & Ali Asghar Rostami Abusaeedi. 2013. A gender-based analysis of Iranian EFL learners' types of written errors. *International Journal of Research Studies in Language Learning* 2. 79–92.

Corder, Stephen Pit. 1974. The significance of learners' errors. In Jack C. Richards (ed.), *Error analysis: Perspectives on second language acquisition*, 19–27. London: Longman.

Crystal, David & Derek Davy. 1969. *Investigating English style.* New York: Longman.

Dulay, Heidi C. & Marina K. Burt. 1974. You can't learn without goofing. In Jack C. Richards (ed.), *Error analysis: Perspectives on second language acquisition*, 95–123. London: Longman.

Etherton, Alan R. B. 1977. Error analysis: Problems and procedures. *English Language Teaching Journal* 32. 67–78.

Fidler, Ashley. 2006. Reconceptualizing fossilization in second language acquisition: A review. *Second Language Research* 22. 398–411.

General Entry Requirements. 2010. http://www.um.edu.mt/registrar/students/general_entry_requirements. Accessed 2010.

Gholami, Javad & Maryam Zeinolabedini. 2015. A diagnostic analyis of erroneous language in Iranian medical specialists' research papers. *Journal of Tehran University Heart Center* 10. 58–67.

Hilbert, Michaela & Manfred Krug. 2012. Progressives in Maltese English: A comparison with spoken and written text types of British and American English. In Marianne Hundt & Ulrike Gut (eds.), *Mapping unity and diversity world-wide: Corpus-based studies of New Englishes*, 103–136. Amsterdam: John Benjamins.

Hyltenstam, Kenneth. 1988. Lexical characteristics of near-native second-language learners of Swedish. *Journal of Multilingual and Multicultural Development* 9. 67–84.

Jain, Mahawir P. 1974. Error analysis: Source, cause and significance. In Jack C. Richards (ed.), *Error analysis: Perspectives on second language acquisition*, 189–215. London: Longman.

Koosha, Mansour & Ali Akbar Jafarpour. 2006. Data-driven learning and teaching collocation of prepositions: The case of Iranian EFL adult learners. *Asian EFL Journal* 8. 192–209.

Krug, Manfred & Anna Rosen. 2012. Standards of English in Malta and the Channel Islands. In Raymond Hickey (ed.), *Standards of English: Codified varieties around the world*, 117–138. Cambridge: Cambridge University Press.

Lado, Robert. 1957. *Linguistics across cultures: Applied linguistics for language teachers*. Ann Arbor: The University of Michigan Press.

McLaughlin, Barry. 1987. *Theories of second-language learning*. London: Edward Arnold.

Müller, Amanda. 2015. The differences in error rate and type between IELTS writing bands and their impact on academic workload. *Higher Education Research & Development* 34. 1207–1219.

Nation, Paul. 1993. Vocabulary size, growth, and use. In Robert Schreuder & Bert Weltens (eds.), *The bilingual lexicon*, 115–134. Amsterdam: John Benjamins.

Nezami, Ali & Mousa Sadraie Najafi. 2012. Common error types of Iranian learners of English. *English Language Teaching* 5. 160–170.

Nosrati, Vahede & Mahdieh Nafisi. 2015. Contrastive analysis of male and female candidates' errors in writing and speaking modules of IELTS. *International Journal of Language Learning and Applied Linguistics World* 9. 77–91.

Quirk, Randolph, Jan Svartvik, Geoffrey Leech & Sidney Greenbaum. 1985. *A comprehensive grammar of the English language*. Essex: Longman.

Richards, Jack C. 1974. A non-contrastive approach to error analysis. In Jack C. Richards (ed.), *Error analysis: Perspectives on second language acquisition*, 172–188. London: Longman.

Natalie Schembri

Schachter, Jacquelyn. 1974. An error in error analysis. *Language Learning* 24. 205–214.

Schembri, Natalie. 2005. *Noun phrase structures in Maltese university students' commerce texts: A study in academic Maltese English.* Munich: Lincom Europa.

Selinker, Larry. 1974. Interlanguage. In Jack C. Richards (ed.), *Error analysis: Perspectives on second language acquisition*, 31–54. London: Longman.

Swales, John. 1990. *Genre analysis: English in academic and research settings.* Cambridge: Cambridge University Press.

Taylor, Barry P. 1975. The use of overgeneralization and transfer learning strategies by elementary and intermediate students of ESL. *Language Learning* 25. 73–107.

The Constitution of Malta Act, Chapter 1 of the Laws of Malta. 1964.

Thewissen, Jennifer. 2013. Capturing L2 accuracy developmenta patterns: Insights from an error-tagged EFL learner corpus. *The Modern Language Journal* 97. 77–101.

Trudgill, Peter. 2002. *Sociolinguistic variation and change.* Edinburgh: Edinburgh University Press.

Vella, Alexandra. 1995. *Prosodic structure and intonation in Maltese and its influence on Maltese English.* University of Edinburgh dissertation.

Wardaugh, Ronald. 1975. The contrastive analysis hypothesis. In John H. Schumann & Nancy Stenson (eds.), *New frontiers in second language learning*, 11–19. Massachusetts: Newbury House.

Chapter 10

Language change in Maltese English: The influence of age and parental languages

Manfred Krug

Lukas Sönning
University of Bamberg

In this study, which is based on questionnaire data collected in 2013 from 430 Maltese informants, we investigate ongoing language change in Maltese English. We concentrate on 63 pairs of lexical variants that are known to differ in usage between British English and American English (e.g. *vacation* vs. *holiday*). Overall, informants clearly tend towards BrE usage. Regardless of the statistical approach we adopt, our studies show consistently apparent-time trends towards a less exclusively British English usage in Malta, converging on a more globalized usage of lexical items, in particular among the youngest cohorts. This confirms trends reported for older Maltese English data (collected in 2008; see Krug 2015). While Age emerges as the most important factor in our data, lexical choices are also sensitive to the native languages of the informants' parents. When the mother's native language(s) includes English, the informants' lexical choices are biased in the expected direction, figuring in an increase in Britishness of the informants. Informants whose parents' L1 is neither English nor Maltese show the highest degree of linguistic globalization. Overall, the native language(s) of the mother appeared to be more influential than that of the father.

1 Introduction

Maltese and English are the two official languages in the Republic of Malta. Not surprisingly, therefore, bilingualism is widespread: In the *Census of Population*

/||| Manfred Krug & Lukas Sönning. Language change in Maltese English: The influence of age and parental languages. In Patrizia Paggio & Albert Gatt (eds.), *The languages of Malta*, 247–270. Berlin: Language Science Press.
DOI:10.5281/zenodo.1181801

and Housing 2005 (2012) (the latest census which collected such information), 88% of the population aged 10 and older, i.e. some 300,000 people living on the archipelago, reported to speak at least some English. With 93% of the population speaking Maltese as a first language (*ibid.*), English is a second language for the vast majority of speakers. Frequency of use and exposure to the English language vary considerably, however. About 9% of the population use English as the – or a – main language at home. As is often the case in places with a colonial history involving British rule, the varieties of English that are spoken in Malta represent in actual fact a continuum between an acrolectal variety (a near-RP pronunciation with a grammar and lexicon that is very similar to standard British English) on the one hand, and basilectal varieties on the other. The latter are characterized by typical EFL learner features and more structural parallels with Maltese, i.e. contact features, plus extensive code-switching.[1] In this contribution on lexical items usage, we will use the term "Maltese English" (or "MaltE", for short) to cover the entire continuum of varieties of English spoken and written in Malta.

In this study, which is based on questionnaire data from 430 Maltese informants collected in 2013, we investigate ongoing change in English language usage in Malta. In 2007 and 2008, pilot web-based studies and first questionnaire-based studies were carried out to empirically investigate the varieties of English in Malta and their relation to the major reference varieties of standard British and American English. In the present study, we will concentrate on data from 2013, which have not been subjected to statistical analysis to date. After an outline of the methodologies employed, §2 will present descriptive statistics, §3 inferential statistics. The first focus of our analysis will be apparent-time studies, i.e. the factor Informant Age. We shall also investigate closely the influence of participants' gender, the native language(s) of the mothers and fathers of the informants as well as interactions between these factors.

2 Methodology

For the statistical analyses presented in this paper, informants with more than one third missing answers in the questionnaire were excluded ($n = 6$), leaving a total of 424 informants for analysis. We concentrate on 68 pairs of lexical vari-

---

[1]Compare the continuum described in Vella (1994), Bonnici (2010) and such notions as *mixed Maltese English*. Compare also the discussion of Maltese English and its relation to Schneider's (2007) model of postcolonial Englishes in Thusat et al. (2009), Bonnici et al. (2012) and Grech (2015).

ants using the *Bamberg questionnaire for lexical and morphosyntactic variation in English* (see Appendix for exemplification; Krug & Sell 2013 for methodological detail; Krug et al. forthcoming for the full questionnaire). Given a choice between two referentially synonymous items that are known to have differed in usage between British English (BrE) and American English (AmE) in the late 20th century (cf., e.g. Algeo 2006), informants select whether they always use one of the two variants, prefer one over the other, have no preference, or do not use any of them (see Figure 7 in the Appendix). For expository clarity, we will use expressions such as *pairs, binaries* and *British* vs. *American English usage,* although these are clearly simplifications. Some items have more than two alternatives, e.g. *dummy – pacifier – soother* (or compare *X with/to/and Y*).[2] Similarly, we simplistically use *BrE* (or *AmE,* as the case may be) when we refer to 'more British' (e.g. *backwards* vs. *backward*), 'exclusively British' (e.g. *-isation* spellings) or 'traditionally British' items (e.g. *lorry* vs. *truck*).

Items exceeding 20% missing cases (i.e. informants ticking that they use neither of the two variants offered) were excluded from the analysis ($n = 5$). These were *bicentenary/bicentennial, glocalis/zation, storm in a teacup/tempest in a teapot, laund(e)rette/laundromat,* and *a drop in the ocean/bucket.* Consequently, 63 items remain in the ensuing analysis.

The questionnaire data were converted from ordinal ratings into numerical values (cf. Rohrmann 2007; Agresti & Finlay 2009: 40 for translating ordinal into interval scales), with usage preferences ranging from −2 for exclusively AmE usage to +2 for exclusively BrE usage. For the statistical analysis of the questionnaire, the following values are assigned to the five possible answers:

- +2 if the informant reports consistent use of the (more) British variant;

- +1 if the informant reports more frequent use of the (more) British variant;

- 0 if the informant has no preference;

- −1 if the informant reports more frequent use of the (more) American variant;

- −2 if the informant reports consistent use of the (more) American variant;

- no entry if the informant claims to use neither of the two variants.

---

[2]In the questionnaire, raters can add comments regarding their own preference and alternative terms in each case (see Figure 7 in the Appendix).

Automatic digitization was combined with extensive manual post-editing. The following analyses are based on the overall mean questionnaire score for each of our 424 informants, which may range from −2 to +2. To safeguard against distorted averages, we imputed missing item values based on the full set of informants' ratings. More specifically, we applied mean imputation adjusted by subject and item effects. That is, the imputed value for each cell reflected the overall tendency for the informant (with subjects showing an overall trend towards British usage receiving higher fill-in values) and item (with items showing bias towards the British variant receiving higher fill-ins). To this end, we ran a mixed-effects model (using the lme4 package in R, Bates et al. 2015) with subject and item as random factors and then derived fill-in values by adding to the intercept the random effects for the particular cells. This procedure takes into account differences between items and informants. A reanalysis of the data shows that our conclusions are not affected by this imputation (compared to an analysis simply excluding missing cases).

3 Results

3.1 Descriptive statistics

3.1.1 Methodological caveats and major trends

As for the reliability of the findings presented here, the lower the proportion of respondents opting for "I never use either expression" in our questionnaire, the more confident we can be about the results. Figure 8 in the Appendix gives the proportion of respondents reporting to use none of the two binaries. Out of our 68 lexical binaries, 63 have over 85% of informants responding that they use one or both of the variants. The remaining five binaries have been excluded from the analysis, since they have between 20% and 35% missing cases. We would have to exert greater caution in interpreting the results because of a significant gap (greater than 10%) between them and the remaining items (see Figure 1). The set of excluded items is interesting, nevertheless: Two learned words known primarily from formal and academic discourse (*bicentenary/bicentennial* and *glocalis/zation*) score lowest of all 68 items. In addition, there are two phraseological units (*a drop in the ocean/bucket* and *a storm in a teacup/a tempest in a teapot*), which seem infrequent in MaltE. Notice that another phraseological unit – with only 10% missing cases, however – ranks sixth lowest in terms of usage rate: *touch wood/knock on wood*. This suggests that idioms may be relatively rare in current, mainstream MaltE. The fifth binary with many missing cases is *laun-*

derette vs. *laundromat*, which appears to be an uncommon concept in the 21st century when most members of Western societies have access to washing machines in their homes (or dorms, condominiums etc).

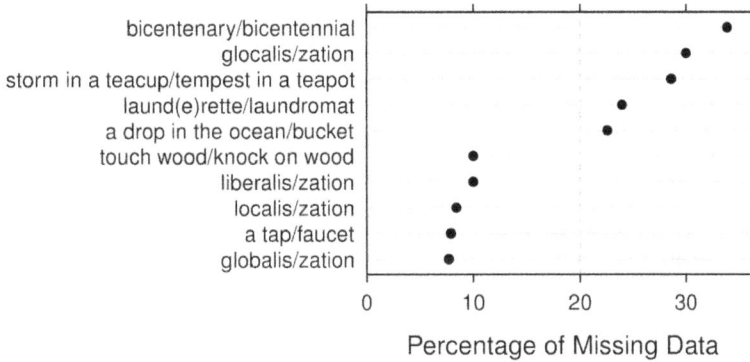

Figure 1: Proportion of respondents reporting to use none of the two given lexical alternatives: The 10 least frequently used lexical items (traditionally BrE/AmE terms)

Let us turn to the overall results. Unsurprisingly, given the history of English in Malta, half a century after independence, the Maltese informants still clearly tend towards BrE usage. The overall mean in 2013 is +0.85 (the standard deviation being 0.35; the overall median +0.87). This compares with an arithmetic mean of +1.0 in 2008 (see Krug & Rosen 2012 for detail). On average, therefore, Maltese informants reported more frequent use of the British English terms, but the preference appears to have somewhat weakened over the five years between 2008 and 2013.

Figure 2 shows a dot plot (cf. Sönning 2016) of the mean rating and standard deviation for each individual pair. Clearly, the preference for (more) British terms comes in degrees:

- British usage dominates for the vast majority of our lexical items (52 of the 63 binaries have values greater than 0).

- About half of the binaries display strong BrE preferences and have means greater than 1, with some items being used almost exclusively in the BrE variant (e.g. *postman, roundabout, pushchair, petrol, football*).

- Hovering around an arithmetic mean of about 0, eight items display a fairly neutral usage. This is to say that they are used – on average – interchangeably by individual informants or that their BrE and AmE variants

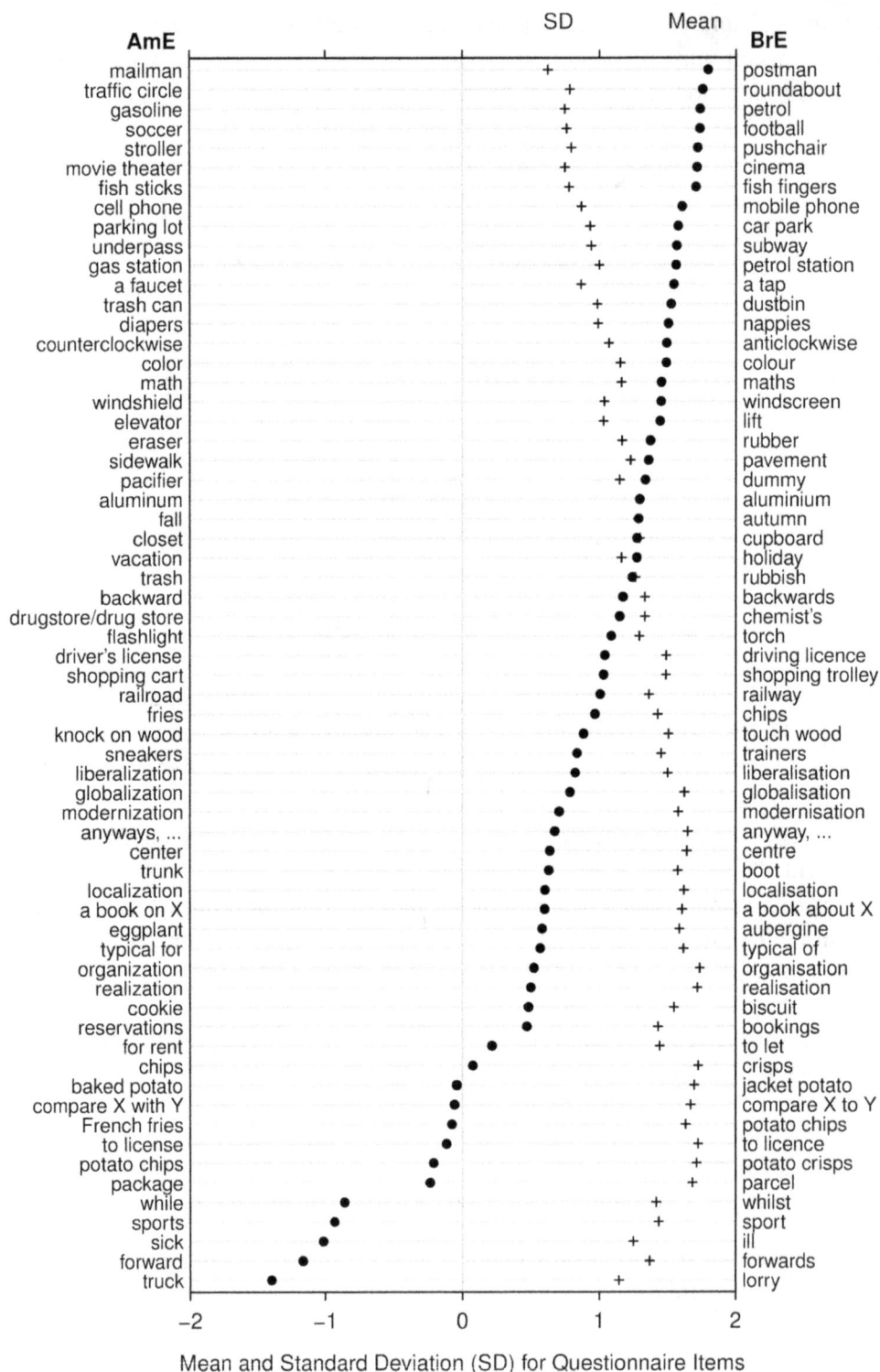

Figure 2: Distribution of the 63 lexical binaries

are preferred by comparable numbers of informants (or strongly preferred by some and slightly dispreferred by twice as many). In descending order from slightly more British to slightly more American usage, these are: *to let* vs. AmE *for rent; (potato) crisps* vs. AmE *(potato) chips; jacket potato* vs. AmE *baked potato; compare X to/with Y; package*, which is slightly preferred over BrE *parcel*. A special case is the verb *to license* vs. *to licence*. Here we may assume that people freely choose, possibly due to a potentially unknown minimal and non-systematic spelling difference between an allegedly BrE and AmE variant. Interestingly, this item has the highest standard deviation in our data set (of nearly 2). Most informants therefore reported using only one of the two options rather than having genuinely free variation as individuals. It would be interesting to compare actual corpus citations in Malta and also intuition- as well as corpus-based data from other varieties worldwide, including the reference varieties of British and American English.

- Few items are preferred in their (traditionally) more American form, the most striking one being *truck*[3], which is strongly favoured over (erstwhile) BrE *lorry* with a mean value of about −1.5. *Sick*, too, is preferred to *ill*. A special case is *while*, which is clearly also the unmarked choice in modern British usage when compared to *whilst*. *Forward*, too, is special because the noun (known from football) may have played a role in the informants' ratings. This is suggested by a strong preference for *backwards* (to AmE

---

[3]Cf. *OED Online* 2016 *Online s.v. truck* n.2 (meaning 3g), whose earliest citations for 'a motor vehicle for carrying goods and troops etc.' are Canadian (from 1916) and U.S. American (1930), the latter actually pointing to British-American differences: "American English has universally chosen *motor truck* and *truck* rather than *auto-truck* or the British *lorry*" (*AmericanSpeech 5, 274*). Despite a first British attestation from 1932, even a quotation from 1950 points to transatlantic differences: "Many soldiers in the last war will remember that 'gas' might or might not be petrol and a 'truck' might or might not be a lorry" (*Times*, 27 Apr. 1950, 6/7). We are grateful to an anonymous reviewer for pointing out that *truck* is a relatively old English loanword in Maltese, as is indicated by a Semitic plural form (*trakk-ijiet*), which differs from the -*s* plurals of more recent loanwords like *film-s, printer-s, kompjuter-s*. In the absence of phonological factors in the plural formation of Maltese loanwords (like sonority of the stem-final phoneme), we can only reconcile such observations with the textual evidence presented from the *OED* by assuming that, while there was early variation (from at least 1932 onwards) in British English between *truck* and *lorry*, the predominant BrE lexical choice remained *lorry* until at least the 1950s. Further factors may be meaning specification (for instance in military domains) and the co-existence of different meanings of *truck* (especially 'large motor vehicle for carrying goods' and 'smaller motor vehicle with an open, load-carrying surface'), although in our questionnaire we refer explicitly to a 'large motor vehicle for carrying goods by road' (see Appendix, Figure 7).

backward) among the Maltese informants, which is not commonly used nominally. The preference for *sports* (over traditionally BrE *sport*) seems to be an analogy to other school subjects and disciplines like *physics* or *linguistics.*

Prior to conducting the questionnaire study on a large scale and in different regions of the world, internet-based data were collected on the Maltese domain .mt for the lexical binaries, first in order to test feasibility and hypotheses, e.g. relating to colonial lag (by comparing the British and US-American domains .uk and .us) and later to check the reliability and external validity of intuition-based data. The internet data for items that eventually figured in the questionnaires are provided in Table 6 in the Appendix. Three items from the questionnaire were excluded from the internet ranking:

- the American alternative to *biscuit*, i.e. *cookie* (when used generically for something sweet and crispy, not necessarily containing chocolate chunks) occurs commonly as a digital cookie ('authentication method', 'trace of visited websites') on the internet;

- a digital *shopping trolley* is virtually always a *shopping cart*;

- an internet *chemist's* is virtually always a *drugstore* or figures under a certain brand name; also the online occurrences of *chemist's* would have to be disambiguated because the term routinely refers to a profession not targeted in the questionnaire proper.

Rank-based correlations for the remaining items show a highly significant association between web frequencies and pilot questionnaire data from 2008, with Spearman's rank correlation at $r = 0.63$, $p < .0001$, 95% CI [0.44; 0.76] (for comparison: Kendall's tau = 0.43, $p < .0001$; 95% CI [0.30; 0.58]). Needless to say, such strongly correlated ranks enhance considerably the reliability of both independently collected data sets (and conclusions drawn therefrom) as the likelihood that two rankings consisting of 65 items spuriously produce highly significant correlations approximates zero.

3.1.2 Apparent-time distributions and diachronic trends

Informant Age is the single-most influential factor in our data, explaining the largest share of the variation found (cf. §3.2 below for inferential statistics). Figure 3 displays a clear trend: The younger the informants become, the more likely

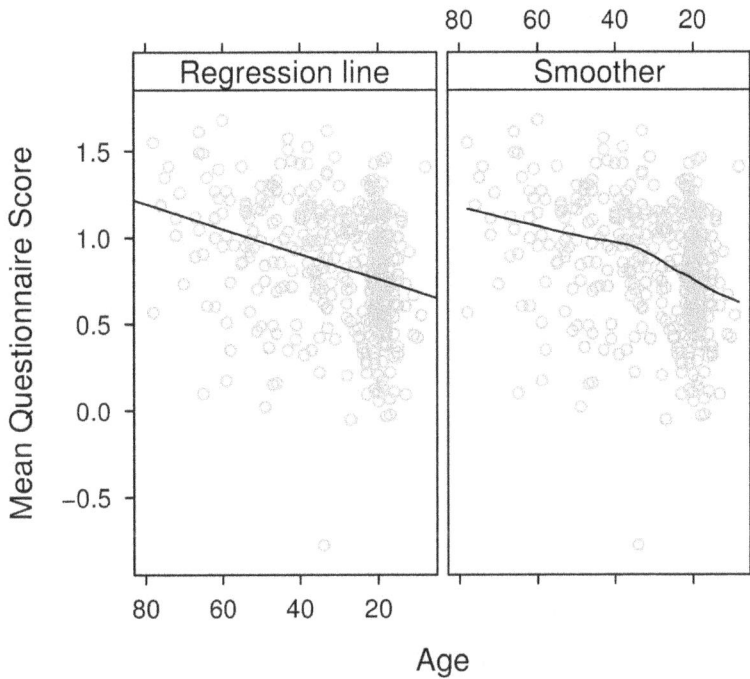

Figure 3: Mean score by Age (all informants): Least-squares regression line and lowess smoother

they become to use American forms. Whichever method we apply, the mean difference between our oldest and youngest informants is about 0.5. The right panel in Figure 3 overlays a lowess smoother (Cleveland 1979), an exploratory tool that detects non-linearity in the data. The latter throws into relief that roughly between the ages 40 and 15, there is a pronounced increase in Americanization. In fact, *globalization* (on which see Krug et al. 2016) would be the more adequate label here because almost all Maltese informants still have positive, i.e. British, arithmetic means; they are merely becoming more neutral, as it were, as they approach a mean value of 0. Owing to the high number of respondents in the relevant age cohorts of the present study, we are quite confident that this is not a spurious finding and would attribute this strengthening of an already existing trend to increased language contact with non-British English for speakers under 40. Conceivable is also the weakening of prescriptive BrE pressures in education. It seems noteworthy, therefore, that our data suggest a rough temporal correlation between speeded-up globalization for informants under 40 and a change in teacher education: Until the 1970s, teachers were mostly trained by British personnel, but more recently teachers have been trained by bilingual Maltese native-speaker scholars at the University of Malta (Calleja 1994: 192, Martinelli & Raykov 2014: 2).

3.1.3 Influence of parental languages

For the analysis of the effect of parental native languages, three groups were compared: (i) Maltese as L1, (ii) English or both English and Maltese as L1, and (iii) other L1s. Table 1 shows the cross-tabulated distribution of Mother's and Father's native language for the 424 respondents in the analysis. Rather unexpectedly, overall the parents' native languages are very similarly distributed: around 85% of both fathers (n = 342) and mothers (n = 348) speak exclusively Maltese as a native language; around 10% have fathers (n = 43) or mothers (n = 42) who speak English (plus possibly Maltese) as a native language. And around 6% to 7% have mothers (n = 24) or fathers (n = 29) whose L1 is neither English nor Maltese. Furthermore, there seems to be an association between Mother's and Father's L1. This is especially noticeable for the groups "E(+M)" and "Other". Thus, informants with one parent who speaks English as native language have a disproportionate likelihood of the second parent also speaking English as an L1 (that share is about 50%; compared to an overall share of 10% in the sample). The same is true for parents with an L1 different from English and Maltese.

Table 1: Distribution of parents' native language(s)

		Father			Total of mothers
		M	E(+M)	Other	
	M	320	21	7	348
Mother	E(+M)	15	20	7	42
	Other	7	2	15	24
Total of fathers		342	43	29	414

Figure 4 shows the distribution of questionnaire scores by Mother's and Father's native language, respectively. As is evident from the left panel, informants with a mother whose L1 background includes English are more likely to tend towards British lexical choices than informants whose mother's L1 is exclusively Maltese or a language other than Maltese or English. If the mother's native language is neither English nor Maltese, then both mean and median values are lower, i.e. more American or globalized. The right panel shows that in our data

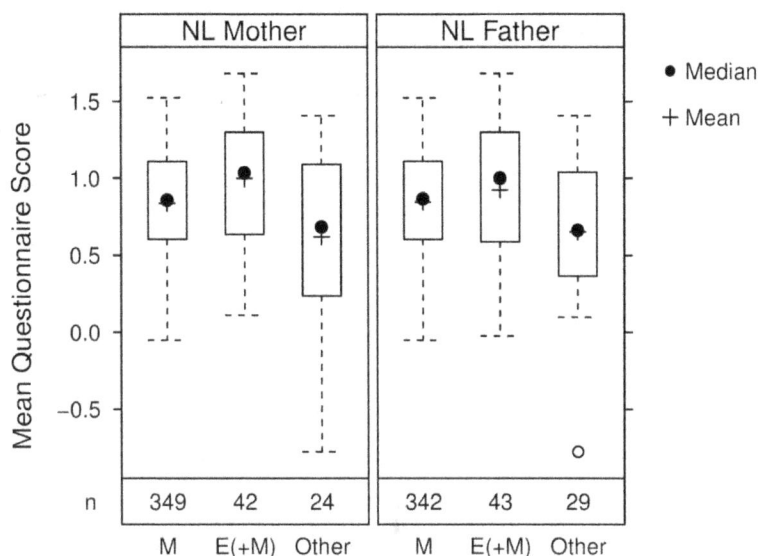

Figure 4: Mean questionnaire score by Mother's and Father's native language(s)

exactly the same tendencies obtain for the influence of the native language(s) of the informants' fathers as for their mothers. Such results are not counterintuitive: For one, native speakers of English in Malta (especially of the older, parental generations) tend to be British or oriented towards BrE usage. For another, those speakers in Malta whose native language is neither English nor Maltese are statistically more likely to have been in contact with or exposed to (more) American English or to non-native (and thus potentially more globalized) varieties than native English speakers in Malta.

Table 2 shows that both means and medians are strikingly similar in each row. The closest value for every mean and median of the Father's native language is that in the respective cell of the Mother's native language. In other words:

- When an informant's mother's L1 is (only) Maltese, he/she has almost the same mean and median as an informant whose father's L1 is (only) Maltese.

- When an informant's mother's L1 is English (plus possibly Maltese), he/she has almost the same mean and median as an informant whose father's L1 is English (plus possibly Maltese).

- When an informant's mother's L1 is neither English nor Maltese, he/she has almost the same mean and median as an informant whose father's L1 is neither English nor Maltese.

Table 2: Father's and Mother's native language: Frequency (n) and mean (M) and median (Mdn) questionnaire score

Native language	Father			Mother		
	n	M	Mdn	n	M	Mdn
Maltese	342	0.85	0.87	349	0.84	0.86
English (or English and Maltese)	43	0.92	1.00	42	1.00	1.04
Other	29	0.65	0.66	24	0.62	0.68

It appears reasonable to assume that the relative influence of mother's and father's language use may differ between male and female informants. Specifically, boys may be more likely to identify with their fathers and thus more likely to adopt the linguistic behaviour of the father (see Hurd et al. 2009 on role models). While the same may hold for girls and mothers, we may also speculate that, on average, language contact between mothers and children is generally higher, which would suggest that boys and girls are influenced by their mother in similar ways. To explore possible role model effects of fathers (on sons) as well as language contact-induced levelling of influence of mothers on children in general, we carried out subgroup analyses. Figure 5 shows the influence of Mother's and Father's L1 separately for male and female informants. Indeed, there appears to be an interaction between Gender and parental L1. For Mother's L1, male and female informants show the same pattern of influence. The effect is more pronounced for male informants, however. The effect of Father's native language, on the other hand, in fact appears to differ for male and female informants. The rightmost panel in Figure 5 suggests that for female informants, there is no effect of their father's native language on the use of lexical binaries; however, there emerges an interesting pattern for men: If male informants have a father whose native language is (or includes) English, these informants' use of lexical items receives a boost towards traditionally British terms. The mean values closest to the neutral zero, and thus the highest degrees of linguistic globalization, are found for male informants whose fathers' native language is neither English nor Maltese. Our data therefore suggest that male Maltese are more strongly influenced by their father's L1 than female language users of English in Malta, at least as far as lexical usage is concerned.

The descriptive analyses in the present section have identified various potential factors for the choice between British and American lexical binaries in our data set. The following section will elaborate on these aspects with the help of inferential statistical analyses. The descriptive trends will be subject to statistical

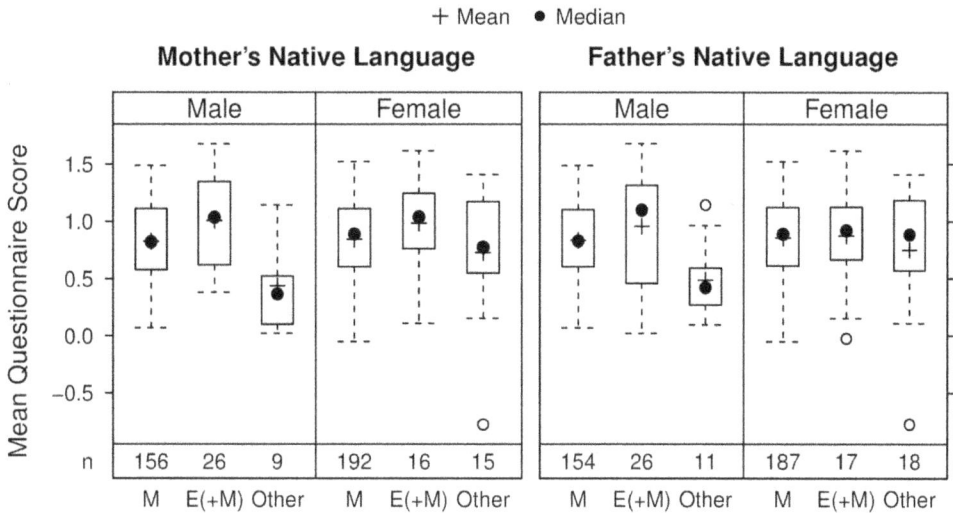

Figure 5: Interaction of Mother's and Father's native language with Gender

significance tests in order to determine whether the patterns in our sample can be generalized to the population of speakers of Maltese English.

3.2   Inferential analysis: The interaction of informants' age and their parents' native languages

In essence, the aim of the inferential analysis is to determine the degree of (un-)-certainty associated with each of the potential factors and trends outlined above. The pool of explanatory factors is reduced to a set of predictors whose effect is generalizable to the population, i.e. whose pattern of influence is relatively robust in the sense that it can be relied on with a sufficient degree of confidence. We use multiple linear regression to model questionnaire score as a function of potential explanatory factors. The selection of variables for the final model was based on the criterion of statistical significance. As can be seen in 3, the distribution of Age in our sample is skewed, with an overrepresentation of younger informants. The variable was therefore log-transformed before modelling.

In the process of model selection, informant Gender was removed since – in the presence of the other factors – this variable did not contribute significantly to the explanation of lexical choices, i.e. the usage of more or less British and American variants. Nor did the interactions between either one of the parental native languages and informant Gender pass the critical threshold. On the basis of the present data, therefore, the different patterns identified in Figure 5 for male and female participants cannot be generalized to the entire population of MaltE speakers. The final model includes Age (log-transformed), Mother's native language and Father's native language. Tables 3 and 4 provide a technical summary of the model, listing the coefficients and the type II analysis of variance with F-tests for each term in the model, respectively. While Age and Mother's native language both reached the p-value criterion of 0.05, Father's native language may be described as trending towards the established benchmark. We decided to retain it in the model for two reasons: First, a chi-squared test showed a statistically significant association between Father's and Mother's native language, χ^2 (4) = 209.16, p < 0.0001 (Cramer's V = 0.50). As Table 1 shows, parents were likely to have the same native language(s). Knowing the mother's L1 thus allows us to guess the father's L1 at above-chance level. From a statistical perspective, these variables thus contribute very similar information to the model. This introduces collinearity and reduces the precision of (and confidence in) model parameters. As a result, the p-values for both Father's and Mother's native language are inflated. Second, and more importantly, including both parental L1s as predictors in the model allows us to judge their relative importance, i.e. to determine whether (the native language of) the mother or father is more influential in shaping informants' lexical preferences.

The relative importance of Age and parental native language on the preference for BrE vs. AmE variants will be illustrated and discussed using (i) the proportion of variance explained by each variable and (ii) effect displays (see Figure 6 below). Overall, the model accounts for 15% of the variation in questionnaire scores. Table 5 shows the proportion of variance explained by each factor, a useful measure of the relative importance of the three variables in the model. The metrics were calculated with the package relaimpo (Grömping 2013) in R, using the lmg metric (Lindeman et al. 1980: 119 ff). Age clearly emerges as the most important factor, explaining more than 10% of the variance. This corresponds to a correlational effect size measure of around 0.32, which, according to the benchmarks suggested by Cohen (1988), may be considered a medium-sized effect. Parental native languages contribute less to the overall model, with Mother's native language at 3.5% (r = 0.19) and that of the father just below 2% (r = 0.13). The fact that Age outranks parents' native languages is partly due to the uneven distribution of parental native languages: With more than 80% of mothers and fathers having Maltese as a native language, there is not much variation between informants (cf. Table 1). Importantly, however, Mother's native language accounts for more variation than that of the father.

Table 3: Type II analysis-of-variance table for the terms in the model

Source	SS	df	F	p	
Age (log-transformed)	5.52	1	49.59	$8.1\,e^{-12}$	***
Mother's native language	1.55	2	6.98	.001	**
Father's native language	.53	2	2.36	.096	

Table 4: Coefficients for the model

Coefficient	Estimate	SE
Intercept	.02	.12
Age (log-transformed)	.25	.04
Mother's native language (reference: Maltese)		
English (and Maltese)	.18	.06
Other	−.14	.09
Father's native language (reference: Maltese)		
English (and Maltese)	.00	.06
Other	−.17	.08

Note. N = 414, k = 6, residual SD = .33, adjusted R^2 = .15

Table 5: Comparison of the predictors: Proportion of the variance explained

Predictor	Variance explained
Age (log-transformed)	10.2 %
Mother's native language	3.5 %
Father's native language	1.8 %

Figure 6 shows effect displays (Fox 1987) for the three factors in the model. These were constructed with the effects package (Fox 2016b) in R. Such displays allow for closer inspection of each factor in a similar fashion to the descriptive charts above. Importantly, the patterns in these displays are usually more trust-worthy, since they take into account (i.e. control for) the influence of the other factors in the model. In other words, they show the effect of a specific predictor while holding constant the effect of the remaining factors. The effect displays show fitted mean values and 95% confidence intervals, which indicate the preci-sion of the estimates (for more information see Fox & Weisberg 2011: 172-177, Fox 2016a). Such displays greatly facilitate the interpretation of multivariate models and make it possible to directly compare effect magnitudes and patterns across different factors.

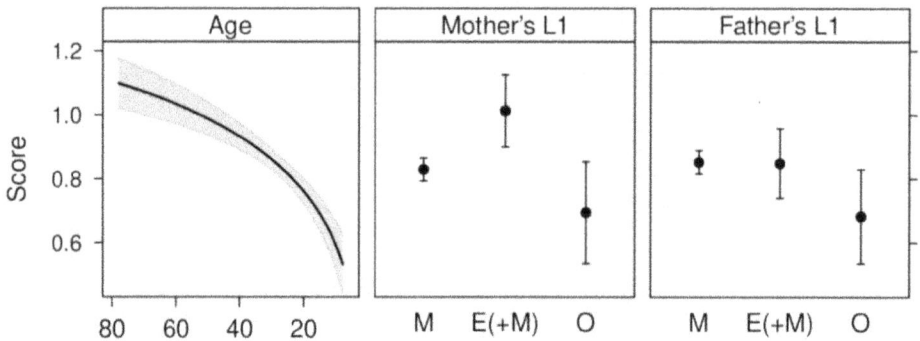

Figure 6: Effect display for the model: Estimates with 95% confidence intervals

The first panel in Figure 6 shows the main effect of Age, which was discussed above. The non-linearity of the trendline that was apparent in Figure 4 also emerges here, with younger cohorts showing an increasingly stronger trend to-wards more AmE or globalized language use. While informants aged 60 and older score above 1.0, informants younger than 20 typically score below 0.7. The con-fidence interval for the linear trend indicates some uncertainty for the older co-horts due to the (relatively) small number of older informants (see Figure 3). The second panel in Figure 6 exhibits the same pattern as Figure 4, with English or bilingual (English and Maltese) mothers triggering a stronger tendency towards British variants. While Maltese is intermediate, the group of informants whose parents have native languages other than Maltese or English appears to be more globalized in terms of their lexical preferences. The rightmost panel shows simi-lar trends for Father's native language as regards "Maltese" and "Other". In contrast, however, fathers with English (and Maltese) as their native language do not bias their offspring towards a preference for British items. A comparison of the factors in Figure 6 further underlines the role of Age as the most important factor: the fitted values range from 0.6 to around 1, thus covering a range of 0.4 in respondents' overall mean values. The levels of Mother's native language, on the other hand, cover a range of 0.3, while Father's native language only accounts for differential effects in the range of around 0.15.

4   Discussion

On the basis of a hitherto unanalysed data set from 2013, we essentially confirm, but also significantly qualify, properties and trends reported for older Maltese English data and their relation to aspects of globalization (cf. Krug & Rosen 2012; Krug 2015). In the descriptive part of this paper, we showed that while the vast majority of items in MaltE are preferred in their BrE form, there are exceptions indicating that (erstwhile) AmE items such as *truck, sports, package* are preferred over their (traditional) British counterparts *lorry, sport, parcel*, respectively.[4]

In apparent-time studies, we visualized and isolated as statistically significant the influence of informants' age, thus establishing for Maltese English novel patterns of ongoing language change (cf. Labov 1990). Regardless of the statistical approach and regression model we adopted, all our studies yielded strong apparent-time trends towards a less exclusively British English usage in Malta, converging on a more globalized usage of lexical items. This trend was seen to be nonlinear and gained pace among the younger cohorts (cf. Figure 3 and the curvilinear shape of the leftmost panel in Figure 6).

Since the comparison of apparent-time and real-time studies of the same phenomena in a clear majority of cases reflects actual diachronic change (cf. Cukor-Avila & Bailey 2013), we conclude that we are witnessing ongoing language change in Malta with regard to the choice of the lexical binaries under investigation. Previous apparent-time studies in linguistics have focused on phonetic, inflectional and syntactic features, whereas we tested lexical binaries. We see, however, no fundamental differences that would forbid applying the same principles to our data. Since we did not elicit information on stigmatized lexical items, there is, we believe, no reason to assume age-graded behaviour for our data (cf.

---

[4]Notice that the standard deviation for *parcel* vs. *package* is among the highest in our data set (similarly to the verb *to licence* and spellings ending in *-is/zation*; see § 3.1 and Figure 2 above). The apparent-time trend suggests that, rather than having free variation, informants over 35 prefer *parcel*, whereas younger cohorts show a pronounced shift towards *package*. (cf.

Labov 1994: 98-112). Abrupt reversal to older usage preferences seems unlikely as long as no major changes in language and education policies occur.

While Informant Age is the single most important factor for explaining the variation found in our dataset, the native languages of the informants' parents also play a role. More specifically, the native language(s) of the mother appeared to be more influential than that of the father, at least as far as their offspring's lexical choices are concerned. It was evident (and statistically significant) that when the mother's native language(s) included – in Malta, a typically British-oriented form of – English, the informants' lexical choices were biased in the expected direction, figuring in higher mean values, i.e. increased Britishness of both male and female informants' choices (cf. Figure 4). The influence of fathers was less obvious, and this is, prima facie at least, an intuitively plausible result: Children in Malta in all likelihood still have, on average, more language contact with their mothers than fathers and thus are more likely to be influenced by their mother's than their father's lexical choices.

Furthermore, our data suggest tentatively (cf. Figure 5) that male informants are more strongly influenced than female informants by their fathers' native language(s). While this trend needs to be confirmed by additional research, it is in line with non-linguistic studies (the transferability of which needs to be treated with even greater caution); such studies, at least, have occasionally shown gender-matched role models to be more influential than non-matched role models (cf. Hurd et al. 2009). One question emerging from this contribution therefore seems to offer particularly interesting avenues for future research: Does the linguistic behaviour of fathers have a greater impact on their son(s) than on their daughter(s) language beyond the narrow confines of lexical choices and in regions other than Malta? If the answer to both parts of the question is yes (or probably yes), it would be fascinating to investigate whether similar tendencies can be found for other cognitive-behavioural domains in studies of human psychology or evolutionary anthropology.

Acknowledgements

We are grateful to two anonymous reviewers for their valuable comments. The usual disclaimers apply.

Appendix

Table 6: Web data from 2007 (percentage of BrE variants among hits) and questionnaire data from 2008 (average across all subjects)

Item	Web 2007	Malta 2008	Item	Web 2007	Malta 2008
a drop in the ocean	100.0	1.44	torch	88.0	1.52
laundrette	100.0	1.08	pushchair	87.8	1.86
roundabout	99.9	1.93	fish fingers	86.7	1.85
rubber	99.5	1.51	chips	84.4	.91
driving licence	99.2	1.35	bicentenary	83.3	.46
cinema	99.1	1.77	rubbish	82.9	1.57
mobile phone	98.6	1.74	subway	79.2	1.91
petrol	98.2	1.91	jacket potato	77.8	.02
colour	98.0	1.81	liberalisation	75.6	.98
aluminium	97.8	1.62	crisps	72.5	.72
petrol station	97.4	1.80	modernisation	71.3	1.01
holiday	97.4	1.35	boot	68.3	.80
trainers	97.3	1.14	lorry	66.8	-1.71
a tap	97.1	1.84	licence	64.0	.18
dummy	95.3	1.55	globalisation	62.7	.83
bookings	94.7	.13	to let	58.8	.37
postman	94.3	1.93	backwards	55.8	1.06
football	94.2	1.67	cupboard	53.1	1.59
maths	93.9	1.80	nappies	50.9	1.70
railway	93.6	1.41	glocalisation	50.0	.81
car park	93.5	1.73	ill	48.8	-1.02
dustbin	93.1	1.69	sport	45.8	-1.33
centre	92.8	1.17	aubergine	41.7	.45
in autumn	92.1	1.59	realisation	40.4	.78
pavement	92.0	1.64	whilst	28.3	-1.02
storm in a teacup	90.9	1.64	potato chips	22.3	.02
localisation	90.1	.94	organisation	21.9	.70
touch wood	90.0	1.10	potato crisps	21.4	.57
anticlockwise	89.5	1.79	parcel	1.7	.01
windscreen	88.8	1.69	forwards	0.6	-1.09

	I always use this expression	I use this expression more often	I have no preference	I use this expression more often	I always use this expression		I never use either expression	Explanation / Comment
to licence	○	○	○	○	○	to license	○	
elevator	○	○	○	○	○	lift	○	
localisation	○	○	○	○	○	localization	○	
truck	○	○	○	○	○	lorry	○	*(large motor vehicle for carrying goods by road)*
maths	○	○	○	○	○	math	○	
cell phone	○	○	○	○	○	mobile phone	○	
modernisation	○	○	○	○	○	modernization	○	
diapers	○	○	○	○	○	nappies	○	*(for babies)*
organisation	○	○	○	○	○	organization	○	
package	○	○	○	○	○	parcel	○	*(something you send by mail)*
pavement	○	○	○	○	○	sidewalk	○	*(for pedestrians, next to street)*
gasoline	○	○	○	○	○	petrol	○	
petrol station	○	○	○	○	○	gas station	○	
mailman	○	○	○	○	○	postman	○	
pushchair	○	○	○	○	○	stroller	○	*(for toddlers)*
railroad	○	○	○	○	○	railway	○	
realisation	○	○	○	○	○	realization	○	
traffic circle	○	○	○	○	○	roundabout	○	*(for cars)*
rubber	○	○	○	○	○	eraser	○	
trash	○	○	○	○	○	rubbish	○	
shopping trolley	○	○	○	○	○	shopping cart	○	
sports	○	○	○	○	○	sport	○	
storm in a teacup	○	○	○	○	○	tempest in a teapot	○	
underpass	○	○	○	○	○	subway	○	*(path for pedestrians under a road)*
to let	○	○	○	○	○	for rent	○	
flashlight	○	○	○	○	○	torch	○	*(electric lamp)*
touch wood	○	○	○	○	○	knock on wood	○	
sneakers	○	○	○	○	○	trainers	○	
whilst	○	○	○	○	○	while	○	
windshield	○	○	○	○	○	windscreen	○	
a book about chemistry	○	○	○	○	○	a book on chemistry	○	
compare X to Y	○	○	○	○	○	compare X with Y	○	
typical of	○	○	○	○	○	typical for	○	
Anyways, ...	○	○	○	○	○	Anyway, ...	○	

Figure 7: Questionnaire excerpt

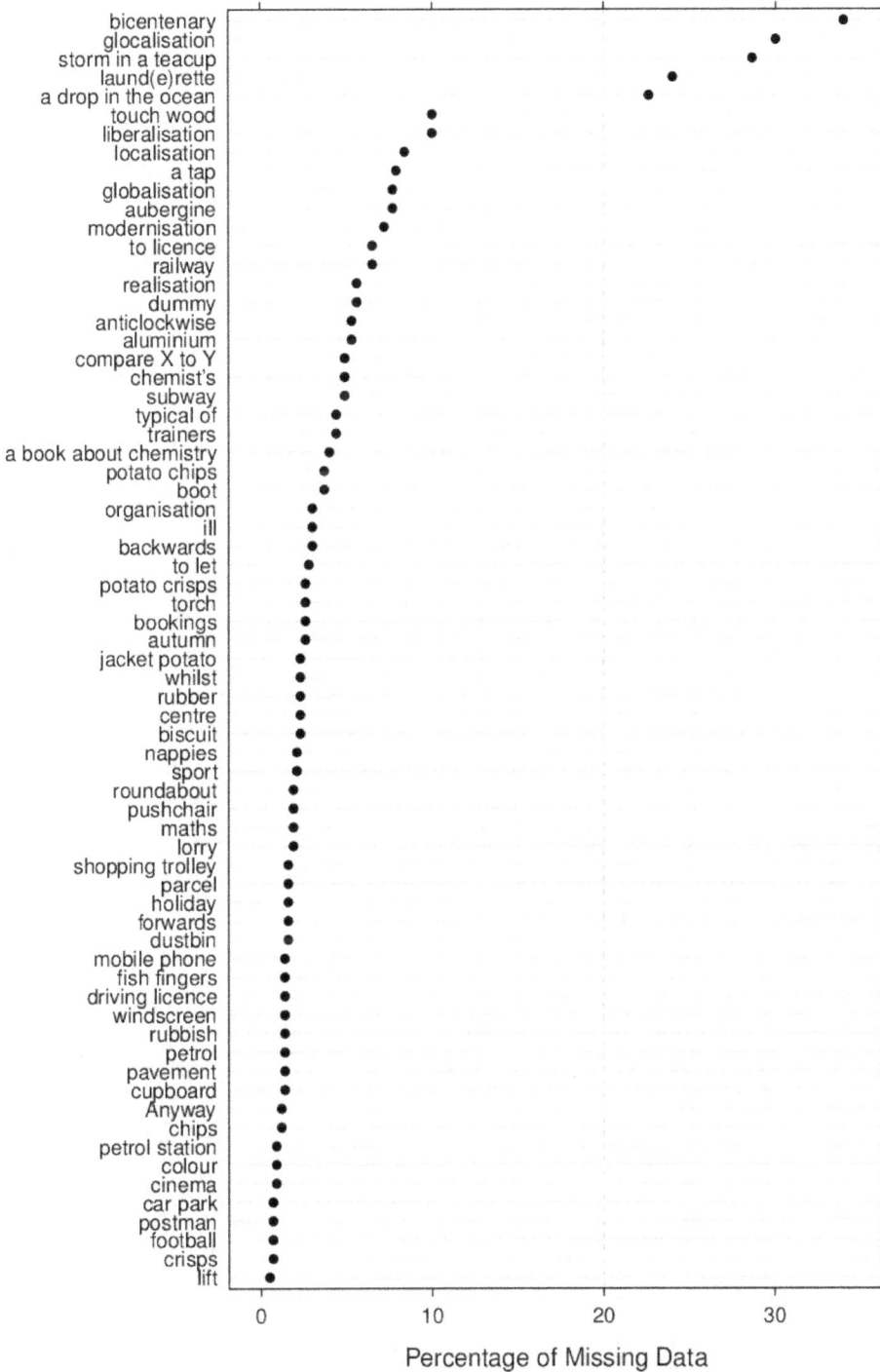

Figure 8: Percentage of respondents choosing "I never use either expression" (more/traditionally BrE terms given)

References

Agresti, Alan & Barbara Finlay. 2009. *Statistical methods for the social sciences.* 4th edn. London: Pearson.

Algeo, John. 2006. *British or American English: A handbook of word and grammar patterns.* Cambridge: Cambridge University Press.

Bates, Douglas, Martin Maechler & Ben Bolker. 2015. Fitting linear mixed-effects model using lme4. *Journal of Statistical Software* 67(1). 1–48.

Bonnici, Lisa. 2010. *Variation in Maltese English: The interplay of the local and the global in an emerging postcolonial variety.* Davis, CA: University of California dissertation. http://linguistics.ucdavis.edu/pics-and-pdfs/DissertationBonnici. pdf, accessed 2016-11-30.

Bonnici, Lisa, Michaela Hilbert & Manfred Krug. 2012. Maltese English. In Bernd Kortmann & Kerstin Lunkenheimer (eds.), *The Mouton World Atlas of Variation in English,* 653–668. Berlin: Mouton de Gruyter.

Calleja, James. 1994. The evolution of education in Malta: A philosophy in the making. *Revue du monde musulman et de la Méditerranée* 71. 185–197.

Census of Population and Housing 2005. 2012. Valletta. http://www.nso.gov.mt, accessed 2012-12-12.

Cleveland, William S. 1979. Robust locally weighted regression and smoothing scatterplots. *Journal of the American Statistical Association* 74(368). 829–836.

Cohen, Jacob. 1988. *Statistical power analysis for the behavioral sciences.* Hillsdale: Erlbaum.

Cukor-Avila, Patricia & Guy Bailey. 2013. Real time and apparent time. In Jack K. Chambers & Natalie Schilling (eds.), *The handbook of language variation and change,* 2nd edn., 239–262. Oxford: Blackwell.

Fox, John. 1987. Effect displays for generalized linear models. *Sociological Methodology* 17. 347–361.

Fox, John. 2016a. *Applied regression analysis and generalized linear models.* Thousand Oaks: Sage.

Fox, John. 2016b. R package 'effects'. *R package version* 3. 1. https://cran.r-project. org/web/packages/effects/effects.pdf, accessed 2016-12-08.

Fox, John & Sanford Weisberg. 2011. *An R companion to applied regression.* Thousand Oaks: Sage.

Grech, Sarah. 2015. *Variation in English: Perception and patterns in the identification of Maltese English.* Msida: University of Malta. https://www.um.edu.mt/ library/oar/bitstream/handle/123456789/5439/15PHDLIN001.pdf?sequence= 1&isAllowed=y, accessed 2016-11-30.

Grömping, Ulrike. 2013. R package 'relaimpo'. *R package version* 2. 2. https://cran.
r-project.org/web/packages/relaimpo/relaimpo.pdf, accessed 2016-11-30.

Hurd, Noelle M., Marc A. Zimmerman & Yange Xue. 2009. Negative adult influences and the protective effects of role models: A study with urban adolescents.
Journal of Youth Adolescence 38(6). 777–789.

Krug, Manfred. 2015. Maltese English. In Jeffrey P. Williams, Edgar Schneider,
Peter Trudgill & Daniel Schreier (eds.), *Further studies in the lesser-known varieties of English,* 8–50. Cambridge: Cambridge University Press.

Krug, Manfred, Michaela Hilbert & Ray Fabri. Forthcoming. Maltese English mor-
phosyntax: Corpus-based and questionnaire-based studies. In Alexandra Vella
& Ray Fabri (eds.), *Towards a description of Maltese English.* Bochum: Brockmeyer. Special issue of Il-Lingwa Taghna.

Krug, Manfred & Anna Rosen. 2012. Standards of English in Malta and the Channel Islands. In Raymond Hickey (ed.), *Standards of English: Codified varieties
around the world,* 117–138. Cambridge: Cambridge University Press.

Krug, Manfred, Ole Schützler & Valentin Werner. 2016. Patterns of linguistic
globalization: Integrating typological profiles and questionnaire data. In Olga
Timofeeva, Sarah Chevalier, Anne Gardner & Alpo Honkapohja (eds.), *New approaches to English linguistics: Building bridges,* 35–66. Amsterdam: Benjamins.

Krug, Manfred & Katrin Sell. 2013. Designing and conducting interviews and
questionnaires. In Manfred Krug & Julia Schlüter (eds.), *Research methods
in language variation and change,* 69–98. Cambridge: Cambridge University
Press.

Labov, William. 1990. The intersection of sex and social class in the course of
linguistic change. *Language Variation and Change* 2. 205–254.

Labov, William. 1994. *Principles of language change: Internal factors.* Oxford:
Blackwell.

Lindeman, Richard H., Peter F. Merenda & Ruth Z. Gold. 1980. *Introduction to
bivariate and multivariate analysis.* Glenview: Scott Foresman.

Martinelli, Victor & Milosh Raykov. 2014. An overview of teacher education in
Malta. *Journal of International Forum of Educational Research* 1(2). 1–12. http:
//ejournal.ifore.in, accessed 2016-12-08.

OED Online. 2016. Oxford: Oxford University Press.

Rohrmann, Bernd. 2007. *Verbal qualifiers for rating scales: Sociolinguistic considerations and psychometric data.* Melbourne: University of Melbourne. http://
www.rohrmannresearch.net/pdfs/rohrmann-vqs-report.pdf, accessed 2016-
12-08. Project report.

Schneider, Edgar W. 2007. *Postcolonial English: Varieties around the world.* Cambridge: Cambridge University Press.

Sönning, Lukas. 2016. The dot plot: A graphical tool for data analysis and presentation. In Hanna Christ, Daniel Klenovšak, Lukas Sönning & Valentin Werner (eds.), *A blend of MaLT: Selected contributions from the Methods and Linguistic Theories Symposium,* 101–129. Bamberg: University of Bamberg Press.

Thusat, Joshua, Emily Anderson, Shante Davis, Mike Ferris, Amber Javed, Angela Laughlin, Christopher McFarland, Raknakwan Sangsiri, Judith Sinclair, Victoria Vastalo, Win Whelan & Jessica Wrubel. 2009. Maltese English and the nativization phase of the dynamic model. *English Today* 25(2). 25–32. DOI:10.1017/S0266078409000157

Vella, Alexandra. 1994. *Prosodic structure and intonation in Maltese and its influence on Maltese English.* Edinburgh dissertation.

Chapter 11

Maltese Sign Language: Parallel interwoven journeys of the Deaf community and the researchers

Marie Azzopardi-Alexander

Institute of Linguistics, University of Malta

This article traces the rapid development of Maltese Sign Language (LSM) from a language that was reportedly restricted to informal day-to-day communication by the Deaf community, to one that is now widely used in both informal and formal settings, including in the context of academic subjects such as the sciences, and in the context of professional activities. The article gives an account of LSM from a historical perspective, paying particular attention to its roots within the Deaf community, culminating in its recent recognition as an official language of Malta.

1 Introduction

This article traces the rapid development of Maltese Sign Language (LSM) from a language that is reported to have been used only for informal day-to-day communication by the Deaf[1] community (Llewellyn-Jones 1986: 7) to one that is used in both informal and formal settings and for a variety of academic subjects such as science as well as in applications such as professional hairdressing and automotive civil engineering (Azzopardi-Alexander 2015: 55 ff). A noteworthy vocabulary explosion occurred rapidly to meet the demands of signers, particularly since access to secondary and post-secondary education was enabled through sign language interpreters since 2001.

---

[1]The use of lowercase *deaf* will refer to any or all hearing-impaired persons whereas uppercase *Deaf* will be restricted to those who use sign language and consider themselves members of the Deaf community.

Marie Azzopardi-Alexander. Maltese Sign Language: Parallel interwoven journeys of the Deaf community and the researchers. In Patrizia Paggio & Albert Gatt (eds.), *The languages of Malta*, 271–292. Berlin: Language Science Press. DOI:10.5281/zenodo.1181803

This development parallels the research interest in LSM originating in the 1980s (see Section 3) and culminating around ten years later with the setting up of the Maltese Sign Language Research Project at the University of Malta's Institute of Linguistics.[2] This led to the start of courses in Maltese Sign Language taught by young Deaf adults and the compilation of the Maltese Sign Language Dictionary (see Azzopardi-Alexander 2003 and Azzopardi-Alexander 2004), work that is now continuing on the online version. Nevertheless, LSM is a minority language in a tiny island and the Deaf community faces the enormous challenge of surviving within the already bilingual setting of Maltese and English (Azzopardi-Alexander 2015: 52).

2 Looking back

2.1 Undocumented beginnings

Very little is known about the hearing-impaired population in Malta (henceforth the deaf) beyond that recorded in its educational history. Looking around one can still see those, now elderly, deaf persons who did not benefit from the educational system and who still managed to survive. It is impossible to gauge their quality of life. No attempt has been made to ask for their stories probably because research has so far been limited to the more easy-to-access younger members of the Deaf community. The older Deaf who did not access education at all must have been limited in their communication to matters of every day life with those who have lived with them or who are in their close vicinity (e.g. local shopkeepers). The only source of information on this is hearsay – people who remember "il-mutu" or "il-muta" (the dumb man or woman) who stuck out in the locality. Their vocal communication amounted to unintelligible vocalisations to the outsider but was sufficient to get by with family and other acquaintances who understood and presumably used home-made signs. They were sheltered by strong family structures. A few are still identifiable in various towns and villages. They did not usually work beyond occasional odd jobs given by family members or friends and their social interactions were limited. It would be desirable to enable them to record their own perspectives before their world disappears. Similar stories are known elsewhere because hearing family members have told them (e.g. various migrants to the US reported by Torres 2009 and many others) or because others who were themselves Deaf could present the Deaf perspective more reliably (e.g. Corker 1996).

---

[2]http://www.um.edu.mt/linguistics/research/maltesesignlang

2.2 Seedlings of the Deaf community

Deaf children in Malta were given the opportunity to attend school for the first time in 1956 though some whose hearing loss was not too severe were sent to their local school prior to that, in spite of the school's inability to cater specifically for them in any way. They were expected to fit in. Nevertheless, unlike in other places such as the UK, the USA and mainland Europe, there were never any boarding schools for the Deaf in Malta – probably because the size of the island combined with the small number of deaf children does not warrant residential education. Hence the Deaf community did not flourish beyond what interaction could be fitted into the school day.

Although deaf and Deaf children were educated together in the one school, the educational system was intensively oral-aural, "with auditory training, lip-reading and speech lessons taking a good slice off the time-table." (A. Galea 1991: 36) The time for the rest of the curriculum was significantly reduced. Signing was not presented as a means of full access at the school for the deaf since few teachers could use more than a few signs though they gradually moved towards a more total-communicative approach in the 1980s. This meant that access to the ordinary curriculum was very limited. "Besides the three Rs[3] these children were trained in carpentry, printing, lace making, needlework and home economics, thus preparing them for a better future." (A. Galea 1991: 38) English was not taught in the special unit apart from "a few common words and phrases" if they were going to the Trade School. This was not challenged by the educators although, as the Head of the Deaf Unit of the time admitted, "We have always found that by teaching only Maltese in our schools we are condemning our deaf children to be second class citizens in a country where Secondary Education, public examinations etc. have a predominant English background." (A. Galea 1991: 39)

Parents started to consider mainstreaming[4] their deaf children motivated by the knowledge that their children would not be missing much in the mainstream that they would have accomplished at the Deaf Unit where basic literacy and numeracy formed the bulk of the curriculum. "The method of aural-oral teaching ... at times has been enforced even with children who could not follow it, with the result that the latter could neither communicate orally or in an officially recognised sign language.... and have had to resort to a primitive environmental sign language understood only amongst themselves." (A. Borg 1991: 50-51)

---

[3]The three Rs are reading, writing, and arithmetic.

[4]Mainstreaming refers to education within regular schools. Mainstreaming deaf children in Malta preceded the Inclusive Education movement in the 1990s where all children with disability were welcomed into regular schools and usually granted the help of a Learning Support Assistant.

Thus, at the request of one or two of the parents, deaf children started to be mainstreamed in the 1970s over the next few years as a result of the parents' growing awareness that special education for deaf children was far from being academically at par with what they would be exposed to in the mainstream. Where intensive parental/family support could be given, some children did very well in the mainstream. We are told that a deaf child "absorbed and is absorbing a lot of our attention and time ... interpreting for her most of the time" (Bezzina 1991: 45). Others did not thrive within the mainstream school system (A. Galea 1991: 38). This is no surprise particularly because at the time mainstream primary school classes tended to be much larger, often 30% larger than the current average of 17.6 in State schools, 25.4 in Church schools and 20.2 in Independent schools (National Statistics Office 2016). Moreover, deaf children had to have extensive parental academic support at home to enable them to cope with the learning of their hearing peers.

2.3 Mainstreaming – dissolution of the deaf-deaf contact

Professionals such as psychologists, social workers and even priests were unable to communicate with deaf youngsters or adults and this was felt throughout. Teachers often took on the role of interpreters where ex-students turned to them for help of all kinds. Families – usually one particular hearing member of the family – often acted as interpreter but in some situations this did not happen. Even those who completed their secondary education successfully and continued into post-secondary level did not feel completely at ease in the hearing world. One of the most academically successful youngsters states publicly at the 1991 conference *Partnership between Deaf People and Professionals* that using signs with deaf people made communication quicker and easier but he would always speak to hearing people. Unfortunately he felt left out when his work-mates "do not always tell me what has happened, because deafness is a hidden handicap, so they forget to explain to me. This also happens to other people like my swimming coach and also my teachers." He also anticipated problems were he to have a hearing girlfriend because "hearing people do not know enough about the deaf."

> I think I am different from hearing people. They can communicate quickly. I communicate slowly. Hearing people can communicate easily. Sometimes I communicate with difficulty.

> Like myself, deaf people in Malta have difficulties at home, at work, and at other places. I am very lucky that I have little or no problems with my

family at home but I know that many deaf people have a lot of problems with their family (K. Borg 1991: 41).

He concludes with a "wish that in the future, deaf people in Malta would have more opportunities to improve the quality of their life" (K. Borg 1991: 43). Sign language made life much easier but with the size of the Deaf Maltese community, there are inevitable disadvantages if Deaf youngsters and adults are to work and socialise within the dominantly hearing community, greater disadvantages than those of larger populations with larger Deaf communities.

Mainstreaming separates the deaf from each other completely. Often, there is only one deaf child in a school. I have occasionally been present when a deaf child is introduced to other deaf persons and s/he is surprised and then exhilerated to realise that s/he is not alone, not the only deaf one any more.

The small group of girls and the small group of boys who were educated together in mainstream schools continued to form a miniature community. These two groups were separate from the Deaf Unit and were even freer to foster sign language. By that time, in the early 1990s, a qualified teacher of the deaf who was a fluent signer[5] facilitated their access to some of the secondary school curriculum. The teacher challenged the children to develop signs they required for the subjects they followed in the mainstream and to discuss the different signs they came up with in order to agree on usable signs. The children's friendship blossomed, particularly because they shared more than they could share with hearing peers with whom they often felt left out since communicating was an effort. Retelling jokes and stories to deaf peers can become frustrating for hearing youngsters, slowing down spontaneous conversation. Summaries of everyday conversations filters out jokes and other important titbits that are technically not really informative, even at home within the family. The fact that the children in these groups managed to continue into post-secondary education may point to the fact that this kind of semi-mainstreaming may reap benefits and should be considered as a way forward.

3 The emergence of Maltese Sign Language

It is commonly acknowledged that "Very little is known about the history of sign languages; most evidence is anecdotal. It is likely that in the past, as in the present, there has been some contact between signers from different countries ..." (Woll

---

[5]She had qualified as a teacher of the deaf in the UK in 1991 and her ability to use British Sign Language led her to progress quickly to becoming fluent in Maltese Sign Language.

1984: 81) It could be said that many of the deaf children at the hearing-impaired unit in Pietà formed the first Maltese community of Deaf people along with the two small groups of children taught together in the mainstream (see §2.2). Of course, they were very young and did not include Deaf adults so they did not have the advantages of exposure to adult sign language except in the case of one particular child whose parents were also Deaf. This reaped some benefits to the others as well who were exposed to the adult Deaf community more extensively in their late teens through the Deaf club. However, on the whole they were deprived of the continuity of sign language users which is important to all Deaf communities and they were left to their own devices in constructing signs. Later, teachers used signs from British Sign Language (BSL) and from Gestuno[6] (Llewellyn-Jones 1986), though most of these were not retained in the long term.

Deaf communities emerge naturally when profoundly deaf people meet on a regular basis. This has been known to happen in schools for the deaf across continents (Reilly & Reilly 2005). In spite of the lack of adult to child sign language exposure, and in spite of the mainly oral educational setting, Maltese Deaf youngsters are captured signing by Peter Llewellyn-Jones during visits to the Deaf Unit. One of the teachers of the deaf who taught the children at the Pietà Deaf Unit at the time observes five years later: "It is fascinating ... to see how resourceful the hearing impaired can be, even in the most difficult situations. Also fascinating is their ability to find or, better still, invent signs adapted from their local environment" (A. Borg 1991: 50). Alex Borg also observes how the deaf turn to "natural gestures in a kind of basic sign language" at the Deaf Unit.

The Deaf youngsters had started to develop signs distinct from those of BSL and Gestuno imported by teachers of the deaf since the vocabulary was published in 1975. Some of the signs developed as all the deaf children started to come together at the Deaf Club and reflected more of the Maltese reality and culture as time went by. The sign for DAR (HOUSE) reflects the flat roofs although most Maltese children would still draw the typical sloping roofed house; the sign for RAĠEL (MAN) reflects the cap worn by mainly elderly Maltese men. The term Maltese Sign Language was used first by Llewellyn-Jones (1986: 7) and subsequently by researchers in their discussions with members of the Deaf community in the mid-1990s and in the first publication of the Maltese Sign Language Project, the first volume of the Dictionary (Azzopardi-Alexander 2003) as well as

---

[6]Gestuno was the name given to the first pulication of internationally-agreed on sign vocabulary useful at international meetings. However, this soon developed into International Sign to enable more Deaf people to understand each other in international settings (e.g. The World Federation of the Deaf congresses).

in subsequent publications (Azzopardi-Alexander 2009; Azzopardi-Axiaq 2005). The acronym for Maltese Sign Language was established internationally as LSM in accordance with the Maltese name *Lingwa tas-Sinjali Maltija.*

4 The emergence of the Deaf community

A number of people and events led to the Deaf moving beyond the 'control' of the hearing teachers and parents who led the Association. Nevertheless some hearing individuals recognised the need for the deaf to be masters of their own destiny, to move away from what can be considered kind-hearted but nevertheless paternalistic attitudes of the hearing. This was important for them to develop their own identity and belong as first-class citizens to a decidedly Deaf community which was Deaf-led.

A. Borg (1991) mentions the setting up of a Maltese Sign Language Project. However, attempts to follow up the reference pointed to the Bristol University Deaf Studies-led research project, which involved collecting data of Maltese Sign Language along with data of other European and Middle Eastern sign languages and was not a Malta-initiated project – at least the author could not trace any references to it. It seems to point, instead, to the intention of the Special Education Department to look into the use of sign language in deaf education with the help of the UK agencies mentioned in the Llewellyn-Jones (1986) report. Nothing appears to have come out of the project in terms of deaf education, sign language interpreting or even other professionals specialised with the deaf which were listed in the 'General Comments and Suggestions' section of the report.

Bezzina (1991) reports that he established and coordinated a self-help group of parents of deaf children who met regularly and organised educational and social events for their children that included the whole family, enabling them and eventually deaf adults to meet on a regular basis (Bezzina 1991: 45). Moreover, Bezzina was very concerned about the lack of use of Maltese Sign Language in education and wanted to expose deaf children and their families to sign language since many deaf children "are leaving school unable to speak, read, write or communicate manually except with close relatives and/or friends" (Bezzina 1991: 46). Out of context this reflects that in the past most decisions concerning the Deaf were made in hearing-led settings. However, more recent events indicate the Deaf are now in a position to determine what happens to their community. In fact many Deaf activists were involved in discussions during the phase where the Maltese Sign Language Law was being discussed (see §10.1).

Bezzina was the mind (and spirit) behind the opening of the Deaf Club in 1981 at Lascaris Wharf in Valletta. This enabled the Deaf to come together with the expected results that Maltese Sign Language was used much more extensively, it was passed on to the younger deaf who became primary users and hence they contributed to its development by extending its vocabulary to meet their needs, and Deaf adults started marrying and continuing to visit the Deaf Club with their mainly hearing children. Bezzina expressed two important thoughts publicly:

> ... we have to give the deaf adults more space. We have to believe in their capabilities. The Maltese deaf adults should gradually lead their own community ... Maybe this conference will be the start of a Deaf Pride movement based on the Maltese Deaf Culture with the Maltese Sign Language as the Unifying force between the members of this community (Bezzina 1991: 48-49).

5 Deaf culture and identity

One important milestone was reached when classes of Maltese Sign Language started to be taught at the University of Malta Institute of Linguistics and were later offered also as evening classes by the Education Department and the Malta College of Arts, Science and Technology (MCAST) where they are still a popular addition to the evening course programmes offered by the two institutions.

Recently, changes were made to the Maltese Sign Language courses in order to make deaf culture part of the course design rather than in answer to incidental questions asked by interested hearing adults. This reflects the greater confidence of the Deaf tutors in presenting themselves as members of a minority group identifiable by their language but fitting into the hearing world.

The 'voice' of the Deaf can be seen in their language pride and their conscious ownership reflected in the active and conscious formation of new signs whenever the need arises. They are aware that they cannot work independently of each other because consensus is required for signs to thrive. It is hoped that more research will focus on the process of sign formation from the initial makeshift iconic sign to the more subtle signs (Azzopardi-Alexander 2009), from the first use instigated by an immediate need to the time when it becomes accepted by the larger group of signers.

6 Deaf education

Although over the years deaf children have been supported, they still share the dilemma of American (and probably many other) deaf children receiving a little service from a lot of professionals and still "falling through the cracks." (Oliva & Lytle 2014: 198). Oliva & Lytle (2014) recommend, on the basis of the research done particularly in the VL2 Labs[7] by Petitto and her team, "ongoing support from an individual who has been schooled in all the issues they face" to enable their Individual Educational Plan[8] to be fulfilled (Oliva & Lytle 2014: 198), in particular the development of bimodal bilingual skills. The advantages of being bimodal bilingual can be attested both in the cognitive as well as in linguistic, educational and socio-emotional domains, particularly in identity formation. Previous concerns about the learning of sign language having a negative impact on the deaf child, especially educationally and specifically on learning spoken language, can now be shelved as archaic. Indeed, early learning of sign language provides the Deaf child with support in learning the spoken and written language:

> Does the knowledge of a natural sign language facilitate Deaf children's learning to read and write? The data collected in this study seem to lead to a positive answer to this question, by showing a strong relationship between LSF (French Sign Language) and written French skills developed by bilingual Deaf children (Niederberger 2008: 45).

Although a great deal of work still needs to be done in this area, Niederberger asserts the strong positive relationship between early exposure to a sign language, particularly to abundant narrative exposure and literacy in the language spoken around the Deaf child. Moreover, the research points to the use of metalinguistic skills in sign language that positively impacts the child's development of the written language.

Pace (2007: 43) considers the lack of a language policy for deaf children as an 'area of concern' which "continues to hamper a clear understanding of the linguistic, socio-emotional and cultural needs of deaf children" and which reflects on "the contribution of deaf adults in the education of deaf children...(and) the development of suitable assessment protocols for LSM, Maltese and Maltese English....". The role of Deaf adults in supporting sign language within the home

---

[7]The Brain and Language Lab for Neuroimaging developed by Laura-Ann Petitto in 2012.

[8]Every deaf child has an Individual Educational Plan (IEP) in Malta. However, there is lack of monitoring how and by whom the plan is to be realised beyond what is said at the IEP biannual meetings.

was a recommendation made in 1998 along with several others by the Kummis-sjoni Ministerjali dwar l-Edukazzjoni tal-Persuni Neqsin mis-Smigħ (Ministerial Commission on the Education of the Hearing-Impaired). This would enable Maltese Sign Language to develop with continuity. So far, the Deaf themselves have no way of working for this continuity and research cannot contribute to more than establishing what the different varieties consist of and how they differ from each other.

7 Maltese Sign Language – From basic to refined

It must be assumed that Maltese deaf individuals probably made use of signs at home that were iconic or which extended from local non-deaf signs used by others in the community. If deaf persons did not actually meet anywhere except by coincidence, then one can assume that they used signs we now call 'home signs' that shared the usual features of any basic sign language used for day to day activities with family and close friends: iconicity, the mirroring to different degrees of the physical or other identifiable features of referents. More abstract concepts were most likely expressed through association with more iconic signs with which the abstract concepts are associated. Thus, for example, the signs for days of the week were expressed through the signs for the major activity of the day such as the sign for doing the laundry. Thus, as soon as Maltese deaf children started to meet on a more regular basis at school they communicated using these signs, each adjusting to signs of other members of the group where these seemed to them to be 'better' signs i.e. ones that were faster to produce, or which shared more elements of the group's different signs for the same object or concept.

Since Maltese deaf adults did not usually get married (A. Galea 1991) until around the late 1970s, probably because they did not usually meet except by coincidence, there did not seem to be any generation-to-generation transfer of signs. It is the first community of signers who attended the school for the deaf who must have formed the first Maltese Sign Language, however basic. From then on, it is likely that every other group who came together at the school would have learnt and possibly contributed to the then relatively slow development of the language since their lives were still very restricted in educational terms. The first recording of signs was carried out for the comparative study of signs across around 20 sign languages in Europe and the Middle East led by the Bristol University European Centre for Sign Language Research. A. Borg (1991) refers to the local part of the study as "a feasibility study on Maltese signs currently used at that time" (A. Borg 1991: 52)[9] As mainstreaming replaced the deaf unit, youngsters were again separated off in their district schools. However, once the Deaf Club was opened they had recourse to the other Deaf members and hence to sign language. Nevertheless, because their education went well beyond that of the older deaf, their need for signs beyond the every-day signs enabled sign language to flourish. The result was also a discontinuity such that the older Deaf currently use different signs from those of the younger Deaf. Contacts with Deaf communities overseas, facilitated by the social media, and sometimes leading to lasting relationships involving commitment, is now visible through signs borrowed from such contacts. Some of the adult Deaf are able to point to different members to indicate "heavy borrowers". Whether the borrowed signs replace the local ones in the long term needs to be seen. Many Deaf youngsters resist using the borrowed signs possibly because of their language pride.

The more recent rapid increase in sign vocabulary (see Section 3) is a response to the very rapid changes in the lives of the Deaf. The most noteworthy vocabulary explosion occurred rapidly to meet the demands of signers who had a sign language interpreter at school[10] and followed classes in science and in various other subjects. Signs had to be created to cover the vocabulary for the subjects for which sign language interpreting service was made available, starting with Mathematics, Home Economics and proceeding to Physics, Biology and much more. Since these signs are still being inputted for the forthcoming online Maltese Sign Language dictionary we are still unable to specify the size of the vocabulary. The creation of new signs led to their discussion with peers and a growing consciousness of what they were involved in when they needed to create new signs. They discussed how they signed different concepts and whether they liked or disliked what they had come up with. They analysed what aspects they liked and what they did not like and this growing consciousness and refined metalinguistic skills constitute a much-used resource though some would insist on keeping the more iconic signs.

Deaf signers have been interpreting daily news bulletins on TV since 2012, and the school curriculum has been made more accessible to Deaf children first at secondary school especially since the first sign language interpreter was appointed by the Deaf Association in 2001. Access across educational levels, including University, through sign language interpreting is currently provided on request, sub-

---

[9]However, no information about this is available in the public domain and information from the Education Department is currently unavailable.

[10]Sign Language interpreters have, to date, only had informal training with substantial input by the Deaf community prior to their acceptance as competent for the task. Formal training is currently being planned.

ject to availability. Adolescents and young adults have started to follow part-time evening courses after full-time work. Growing confidence in their abilities once they are ensured of access is changing the Deaf lifestyle even though they still lag behind their hearing peers academically.

8 The contribution of the research community

This development of Maltese Sign Language parallels the research interest in LSM originating around 1994 and leading to the setting up of the Maltese Sign Language Research Project at the University of Malta Institute of Linguistics. The project to some extent triggered the Deaf community's heightened pride and interest in their sign language.

The first main aim of the project was the compilation of the Maltese Sign Language Dictionary which resulted in two published volumes (Azzopardi-Alexander 2003 and Azzopardi-Alexander 2004), and two completed but unpublished volumes. It was not financially viable to publish the hard copies and, since then, work progressed in view of having an online version. Work on this met with some difficulties which slowed down progress, but it is currently hoped that the online dictionary will be available in a relatively short time. It is also hoped that arrangements can be made to enable its regular update. The work on the dictionary brought together small groups of Deaf youngsters and adults for periods of time discussing among themselves the signs they used. They were all volunteers. The hearing researchers soon recognised the fact that signing changed in their presence and so the initial data collection was not used. Furthermore, there was no other study – linguistic or otherwise - on which to base the data collection apart from what was reported by Llewellyn-Jones (1986).

Very soon it was possible to engage two Deaf researchers to work on a part-time basis as sponsorship of the project by their employers.[11] This enabled the signing for the data collection to be more natural since no hearing researchers were involved. A fresh start was made by asking the Deaf participants to take full charge of the data collection. One of the participants was in a position to present signs used by the older generation and this enriched the project unexpectedly. Occasional meetings took place to point out gaps and ask questions about usage but it was considered unnecessary to interfere beyond this.

The Deaf did not adjust their signing but simply worked together. They often disagreed of course, a healthy step towards more representative data. This meant

---

[11]The Bank of Valletta and the Works Department sponsored the project by allowing one of their employees to join the research team for the equivalent of a 1 day a week basis for several years.

that they were becoming more sophisticated meta-linguistically. They were intrigued by the fact that their language was of interest to University academics. This helped them sign more openly in most settings and they became conscious of many things they had not previously thought about in terms of themselves as communicators using sign language.

Entries in the Maltese Sign Language dictionaries (Azzopardi-Alexander 2003 and Azzopardi-Alexander 2004) include a description of the signs in Maltese and English, frames from video clips showing from one to three components of each sign as well as the signwritten form of the sign following the Valerie Sutton SignWriting system (Sutton 1995). Figure 1 shows a page from the first volume of the dictionary, *Animals*, which is the only volume that includes illustrations. Figure 2 shows a page from the second volume of the dictionary, *Places*. The image on the top right of each entry is the signwritten form. This is being updated for the online dictionary on the basis of M. Galea (2014).

The first volume, Animals, has just over 100 entries. The second volume, Places, has over 360 entries. The online dictionary that should be launched in March 2018 will contain all volumes including those that have not been published each of which contains around 350 entries. There are around 3,000 entries in total so far.

The online dictionary will have the advantage of video recordings for the full sign and hence provide a better teaching and learning resource than static video clips. Eventually signs will need to be placed in proper contexts as illustrations of the various entries. More financial input is required to enable the maintenance and the development of the dictionary. The Deaf community can be engaged directly to ensure that this is activated.

9 Academic research on Maltese Sign Language

Work on the dictionary entries generated a great deal of linguistic information most of which still needs to be investigated in depth. However, one can see the strands within the language tapestry within which Maltese Sign Language flourishes. It is possible to trace some interesting contact phenomena (see Azzopardi-Alexander 2015, especially pp. 57 ff) in studying the dictionary entries.

In the short history of the study of Maltese Sign Language there are only a few pieces of work that derive from academic study. However, some of the works completed so far on LSM are significant and should constitute a bridge to more extensive studies.

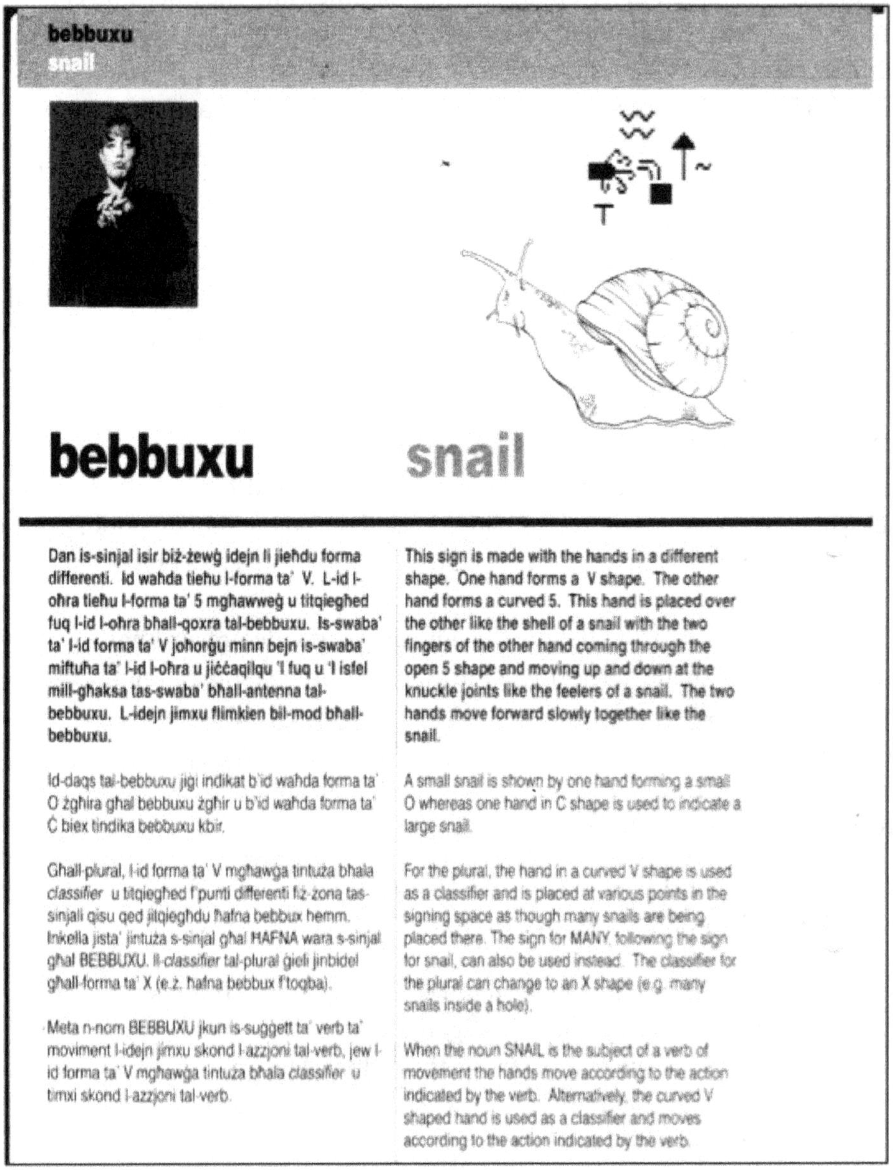

bebbuxu
snail

bebbuxu   **snail**

Dan is-sinjal isir biż-żewġ idejn li jieħdu forma differenti. Id waħda tieħu l-forma ta' V. L-id l-oħra tieħu l-forma ta' 5 mgħawweġ u titqiegħed fuq l-id l-oħra bħall-qoxra tal-bebbuxu. Is-swaba' ta' l-id forma ta' V joħorġu minn bejn is-swaba' miftuħa ta' l-id l-oħra u jiċċaqilqu 'l fuq u 'l isfel mill-għaksa tas-swaba' bħall-antenna tal-bebbuxu. L-idejn jimxu flimkien bil-mod bħall-bebbuxu.

This sign is made with the hands in a different shape. One hand forms a V shape. The other hand forms a curved 5. This hand is placed over the other like the shell of a snail with the two fingers of the other hand coming through the open 5 shape and moving up and down at the knuckle joints like the feelers of a snail. The two hands move forward slowly together like the snail.

Id-daqs tal-bebbuxu jiġi indikat b'id waħda forma ta' O żgħira għal bebbuxu żgħir u b'id waħda forma ta' Ċ biex tindika bebbuxu kbir.

A small snail is shown by one hand forming a small O whereas one hand in C shape is used to indicate a large snail.

Għall-plural, l-id forma ta' V mgħawġa tintuża bħala classifier u titqiegħed f'punti differenti fiż-żona tas-sinjali qisu qed jitqiegħdu ħafna bebbux hemm. Inkella jista' jintuża s-sinjal għal ĦAFNA wara s-sinjal għal BEBBUXU. Il-classifier tal-plural jieħi jinbidel għall-forma ta' X (e.ż. ħafna bebbux f'toqba).

For the plural, the hand in a curved V shape is used as a classifier and is placed at various points in the signing space as though many snails are being placed there. The sign for MANY following the sign for snail, can also be used instead. The classifier for the plural can change to an X shape (e.g. many snails inside a hole).

Meta n-nom BEBBUXU jkun is-suġġett ta' verb ta' moviment l-idejn jimxu skond l-azzjoni tal-verb, jew l-id forma ta' V mgħawġa tintuża bħala classifier u timxi skond l-azzjoni tal-verb.

When the noun SNAIL is the subject of a verb of movement the hands move according to the action indicated by the verb. Alternatively, the curved V shaped hand is used as a classifier and moves according to the action indicated by the verb.

Figure 1: Extracts from the Maltese Sign Language Dictionary Volume 1 (Azzopardi-Alexander 2003) for the entry BEBBUXU / SNAIL

Amerika (L-)
America

Amerika ta' fuq (L-)
North America

Amerka (L-) (ta' fuq)

America (north)

Dan is-sinjal isir biż-żewġ idejn forma ta' 5 miftuħ u bil-pala thares 'il ġewwa. Is-swaba' ta' id jidhlu bejn is-swaba' ta' l-id l-ohra u jimxu f'ċirku orizzontali 'l barra minn ġenb ghan-nofs u ghall-ġenib l-iehor. Ghalkemm dan huwa s-sinjal ghal L-AMERIKA TA' FUQ, ġieli jitkompla bis-sinjal ghal FUQ biex issir enfażi fuq il-kuntrast ma' l-Amerika ta' Isfel. Dan isir b'id wahda li tiehu l-forma ta' 1 bil-pala ta' l-id thares 'il barra u bil-wernej thares 'il fuq. Is-sinjal użat mill-ġenerazzjoni ta' qabel isir biż-żewġ idejn forma ta' 5 miftuħ u bil-pala thares 'il ġewwa. Is-swaba' jmissu imbaghad jitbieghdu u jimxu f'ċirku orizzontali 'l barra sakemm jerġghu jiltaqghu.

This sign is made with two hands in the shape of open 5 with palms facing inwards. The fingers of both hands fit into each other and the hands rotate in a horizontal circle from side to centre and to the other side without letting go.
Although this is the sign for NORTH AMERICA, it is often followed by the sign for UP to emphasize the contrast with South America. This is made with one hand in the shape of 1 with the palm facing outwards and with the index finger pointing upwards. The sign is made differently by the older generation. The two hands take the shape of open 5 with palms facing inwards. The fingers touch and then move away in a circle in a horizontal direction and then meet again.

Amerika t'Isfel (L-)
South America

Amerika t'Isfel (L-)

South America

Dan is-sinjal isir biż-żewġ idejn forma ta' 5 miftuħ u bis-swaba' stirati. Id wahda titqieghed bil-pala thares 'il ġewwa fuq il-livell tas-sider. L-id l-ohra titqieghed bil-pala thares 'il barra u bis-saba' l-kbir jistrieh fuq is-saba' l-kbir ta' l-id l-ohra. Ġieli jintużaw is-sinjali ghal L-AMERIKA u ghal ISFEL wara xulxin flok dan is-sinjal differenti ghal kollox.

This sign is made with two hands in the shape of open 5 with stretched-out fingers. One hand is placed at chest level with the palm facing inwards. The other hand is placed with palm facing outwards and with the thumb leaning on the thumb of the other hand. Sometimes the sign for AMERICA is immediately followed by the sign for DOWN instead of using this totally different sign.

Figure 2: Extract from the Maltese Sign Language Dictionary Volume 2 (Azzopardi-Alexander 2004) for the entries AMERICA and SOUTH AMERICA

Early interest resulted in two undergraduate theses. These include a study of the communicative competence of a young Deaf boy who used very little speech and who signed to his family. The thesis includes a compilation of signs used by the child (D'Amato 1988). At the time there was no contact between the child and other Deaf persons, old or young. So it would be interesting to compare the lexicon compiled with that of current LSM. Another study seven years later focussed on two Deaf adults who used extensive signing in their communication. They were educated at the Deaf Unit (Porter 1995). Another 6 years later we find a study of the sign language used by two children one of whom had used sign language all his life with his signing Deaf parents (Azzopardi 2001) whereas another study focussed on the narrative skills of Maltese youngsters (Fenech 2002).

The first Master's thesis is a comparative study of the communication skills of 3 deaf children, a cochlear-implanted child with post-lingual hearing loss, one Deaf child who used both speech and sign as she had been exposed to sign soon after diagnosis and was brought up by a signing speaking family and a Deaf child who signed but spoke very little (Azzopardi-Axiaq 2005).

A huge milestone was reached with the Master's thesis that focussed on LSM classifier constructions (M. Galea 2006), as well as with the study of how the Maltese Deaf construct signs at different levels of abstraction in different lexical fields (Mifsud 2010). These works could be considered as initiating sign linguistics research on LSM. M. Galea (2006) is a detailed study of the way classifiers are constructed in the LSM and how they behave. Galea analyses the internal structure of LSM classifier handshapes as well as their orientation and movement. She considers the 3-way notional classification of classifier handshapes in the literature – that of Whole Entity, Size and Shape Specifier and Handle Handshapes classifiers and discusses its limitations. Different movements of classifiers are discussed in detail as is the function of holds (stationary classifier handshape) in combination with the other elements such as the articulating (moving) hand in creating prepositional meaning, maintaining reference and differing contact resulting in different lexical meaning. Galea also discusses how movement can be meaningful within the signed construction but can also form part of the lexical meaning of the sign itself. She concludes that the distinction between these constructions is signalled by non-manuals such as eye-gaze rather than by hand movement and hence that the verbal versus nominal distinction in LSM involves these non-manuals. She thus opens up a whole new area of research that calls for immediate attention. In the course of the study, she questions whether sign linguists, internationally, were unduly concerned about establishing parallels with spoken language research and thus moved their attention away from important considerations stemming exclusively from the manual modality.

Mifsud (2010) showed how LSM enables its users to distinguish between different levels of abstraction through structural means. She found the use of simultaneous morpheme compositions, reduced morphemes resulting from extensive assimilation of handshape, location, orientation and movement to form a unitary whole as well as compounding with reduced movements. She identifies the different features involved in the compression of superordinate signs as including loss of movement within constituent parts, loss of morphemes, faster transitions of handshapes, handshape differences and durational compression (Mifsud 2010: 150). These structural characteristics resemble the sign formations reported in other sign langauges such as ASL (Klima & Bellugi 1979: 225 ff).

Different linguistic aspects are tackled by M. Galea (2014) within the context of adapting the Valerie Sutton SignWriting System as a standardised way of writing Maltese Sign Language. In this work Galea investigates the way pronominals work in LSM in great detail. She then looks into how agreement verbs are used in relation to these pronominals. The study presents a very interesting linguistic analysis and is the start, it is hoped, of further in-depth linguistic research into this relatively new sign language. Naturally, there is a very long way to go. Some of that mileage will hopefully be covered by Deaf researchers themselves in the not too distant future. M. Galea (2014) in fact involves the Deaf perspective to reach the decisions expounded in the work.

10   Maltese Sign Language officially recognised in Malta

10.1   Recognition

When this article was started, the Maltese Parliament was expected to put the Maltese Sign Language Bill through its third reading in November 2015. The Bill was put through Parliament on March 16th 2016 and became an Act[12] signed by the President of Malta, Marie Louise Coleiro Preca, on March 24th 2016. The Sign Language Law ACT No. XVII of 2016 (ATT Nru XVII tal-2016) provides for the setting up a Sign Language Council similar to that set up within the Danish Sign Language Law.[13] The Deaf community currently has 3 representatives on the newly appointed Sign Language Council. The law could make a great change to their lives and, particularly, to the future of the Deaf through fuller access all

---

[12]http://www.justiceservices.gov.mt/DownloadDocument.aspx?app=lp&itemid=26704&l=1
[13]http://dsn.dk/tegnsprog/about-the-danish-sign-language-council

round. Since LSM has become an official language, resources should be created to benefit the Deaf community, particularly within education. In a few years, it is hoped that Deaf children will access all of the primary and secondary school curriculum as well as higher education through sign language interpreters. The interpreting service goes hand in hand with the recognition of LSM in Malta both because the interpreting service is being requested more extensively by the Deaf community and because more full-time interpreters will be employed particularly once sign language interpreter training is offered.

A great deal of work needs to be done in order to build the resources necessary for all this. Official recognition is just the gate being opened. The community is tiny and human resources in the field are limited. It is hoped that the motivation and hard work of the Council members will enable the Deaf to achieve better and lead fuller lives.

The law will only be as strong as the Council, empowered by the human resources who constitute it and by the financial resources it will have to enable them to recommend the appropriate measures and monitor their delivery.

10.2 Great expectations

The current number of full-time sign language interpreters, five, means that in practice the present number of interpreters can cope with only a very limited part of Deaf children's school day. The expected growth of the service goes hand in hand with the recognition of LSM in Malta. Once the importance of the early exposure to sign language is recognised and the number of sign language interpreters increases to give full educational access to each Deaf child, the achievements of Deaf children will improve and there will be a good number who would be able to access higher education. This will parallel the development in other countries. So far no profoundly prelingual deaf or Deaf Maltese youngster has followed a degree course at university. It is partly because very often profoundly deaf children do not achieve the same academic results as their hearing peers and partly because, even when they do, they have not, so far, been able to access the lectures delivered in spoken language and available to them by very limited auditory means alone and corresponding lip-reading which equates to visual guesswork.

Naturally, it also depends on how demanding parents are. Parents have always been a major force to contend with. It is hoped they will continue to be. Unfortunately, there is limited understanding resulting from lack of readily available information.

Little is known about bimodal bilingual education for the Deaf locally. Bi-modal bilingual education is known to facilitate Deaf children's development of "positive self-esteem and a strong sense of identity" and to show "evidence of improved pupil attainment" (Swanwick & Gregory 2007: 19). In both the mainstream and schools for the Deaf settings "good practice exists where deaf adults have a specific responsibility as role models and also potentially as mentors for the deaf pupils as they develop their identities, esteem and confidence. The papers presented at the Multimodal Multilingual Outcomes workshop in Stockholm[14] in June 2016 pointed to the advantages of sign bilingualism for all children with hearing loss, even those with cochlear implants.

A review of local deaf education must take place with the involvement of all stakeholders, including those who are intent on excluding sign language from their deaf children's lives. Evidence-based information must be available to help parents and young people make the right choices for the right reasons.

11 Conclusion

This attempt to work out the history of Maltese Sign Language and of the community that uses it is still not as complete as one would like. What is needed is to engage the older Deaf to narrate their own perspective of what happened. They report that they have only recently started to use LSM with pride instead of restricting it to settings with Deaf participants with no hearing onlookers. There are still some who would say that they are stared at but this does not stop them using it because they recognise it as a worthy means of communication and of interest to academics. They act as participants for data that forms the basis of academic research. Gradually they will themselves be the researchers. M. Galea (2014) has shown that they are able to contribute to metalinguistic thought and discussion and so there is an urgent need to enable some of them to work on academic research. As the Maltese Deaf continue to use and develop their language and contribute to academic research through their collaboration with hearing researchers, their meta-linguistic skills are likely to become more sophisticated than those of language users in only the spoken modality. This is an inevitable result as the research becomes meaningful to them and so they could be given opportunities to become protagonists in academic research.

---

[14]http://www.ling.su.se/om-oss/evenemang/workshops-och-konferenser/multimodal-multilingual-outcomes-in-deaf-and-hard-of-hearing-children-1.285132

References

Azzopardi, Marie. 2001. *The Maltese Sign Language (LSM) variety of two Deaf Maltese children: An analysis.* Institute of Linguistics University of Malta BA Hons thesis.

Azzopardi-Alexander, Marie. 2003. *Dizzjunarju – il-Lingwa tas-Sinjali Maltija vol.1 Annimali.* Malta: Fondazzjoni Zvilupp Lingwa tas-Sinjali Maltija.

Azzopardi-Alexander, Marie. 2004. *Dizzjunarju – il-Lingwa tas-Sinjali Maltija vol.2 Postijiet.* Malta: Fondazzjoni Zvilupp Lingwa tas-Sinjali Maltija.

Azzopardi-Alexander, Marie. 2009. Iconicity and the development of Maltese Sign Language. In Ray Fabri (ed.), *Maltese linguistics: A snapshot in memory of Joseph A. Cremona (1922-2003)*, 93–116. Bochum: Brockmeyer.

Azzopardi-Alexander, Marie. 2015. Accommodation of Maltese Sign Language – the forging of an identity. In Jacek Mianowski, Katarzyna Buczek & Aleksandra R. Knapik (eds.), *Languages in contact 2014*, 47–80. Wroclaw, Poland: Philological School of Higher Education & Committee for Philology, Polish Academy of Sciences Wroclaw Branch, in cooperation with International Communicology Institute, Washington, D.C.

Azzopardi-Axiaq, Sonia. 2005. *A study of the communication skills of a small group of deaf children.* University of Malta MA thesis.

Bezzina, Alfred. 1991. Parents of deaf children. In *Partnership between deaf people and professionals*, 44–49. Proceedings of the Conference held 27/7 to 2/8/1991 at the Grand Hotel Verdala, Rabat, Malta.

Borg, Alexander. 1991. How the Maltese deaf communicate. In *Partnership between deaf people and professionals*, 50–54. Proceedings of the Conference held 27/7 to 2/8/1991 at the Grand Hotel Verdala, Rabat, Malta.

Borg, Karl. 1991. A deaf person's view of life for deaf people in Malta. In *Partnership between deaf people and professionals*, 41–43. Proceedings of the Conference held 27/7 to 2/8/1991 at the Grand Hotel Verdala, Rabat, Malta.

Corker, Mairian. 1996. *Deaf transitions: Images and origins of Deaf families, Deaf communities and Deaf identities.* London: Jessica Kingsley Publ.

D'Amato, Tania. 1988. *Some aspects of the communicative competence of a Maltese deaf boy.* University of Malta B. Ed. Hons thesis.

Fenech, Damaris. 2002. *Narrative skills in Maltese sign-oriented Deaf 13 – 14 year olds.* University of Malta B.Sc. Hons thesis.

Galea, Antoinette. 1991. An outline of the growth and the present state of education of the deaf in Malta. In *Partnership between deaf people and professionals*,

35–40. Proceedings of the Conference held 27/7 to 2/8/1991 at the Grand Hotel Verdala, Rabat, Malta.

Galea, Maria. 2006. *Classifier constructions in LSM: An analysis.* University of Malta. Institute of Linguistics. MA thesis.

Galea, Maria. 2014. *SignWriting (SW) of Maltese Sign Language (LSM) and its development into an orthography: Linguistic considerations.* Dissertation. University of Malta.

Klima, Edward & Ursula. Bellugi. 1979. *The signs of language.* Cambridge, Massachusetts: Harvard University Press.

Llewellyn-Jones, Peter. 1986. *Report on phase III of the project A Visit to Malta 30th november to 11th december 1986.* Tech. rep.

Mifsud, Maria. 2010. *A study of superordinates and hyponyms in Maltese Sign Language.* University of Malta MA thesis.

National Statistics Office. 2016. *New release – student enrollments in 2014-2015.* Valletta. https://nso.gov.mt/en/News_Releases/View_by_Unit/Unit_C4/ Education_and_Information_Society_Statistics/Documents/2016/News2016_ 202.pdf, accessed 2017-10-24.

Niederberger, Nathalie. 2008. Does the knowledge of a natural sign language facilitate deaf children's learning to read and write? In Carolina & Morales-López (eds.), *Sign bilingualism*, 29–50. Amsterdam: John Benjamins Publ. Co.

Oliva, Gina A. & Linda Risser Lytle. 2014. *Turning the tide – making life better for Deaf and hard of hearing schoolchildren.* Washington D.C.: Gallaudet University Press.

Pace, Terry. 2007. *Early intervention for hearing impaired children 0 - 3 and their families. A policy proposal.* University of Manchester PG Dipl. thesis.

Porter, Denise. 1995. *Aspects of the communication system of two Maltese adults with a hearing impairment.* University of Malta B.Sc. Hons thesis.

Reilly, Charles B. & Nipapon Reilly. 2005. *The rising of lotus flowers. Self-education by Deaf children in Thai boarding schools.* Washington, D.C.: Gallaudet University Press.

Sutton, Valerie. 1995. *Lessons in sign writing: Textbook.* La Jolla, CA: Deaf Action Committee for Sign Writing.

Swanwick, Ruth & Susan Gregory. 2007. *Sign bilingual education - policy and practice.* Gloucestershire, UK: Douglas McLean Publ.

Torres, Andrés. 2009. *Signing in Puerto Rican.* Washington D.C.: Gallaudet University Press.

Woll, Bencie. 1984. The comparative study of different sign languages: Preliminary analyses. In Filip Loncke, Penny Boyes-Braem & Yvan Lebrun (eds.), *Recent research on European sign languages*, 79–91. Lisse: Swets & Zeitlinger.

Name index

Name index

Language index

Subject index

www.ingramcontent.com/pod-product-compliance
Lightning Source LLC
Chambersburg PA
CBHW082147150426
42812CB00076B/2297